Thi

(

# FOUNDATIONS OF FUTURES MARKETS

# FINANCIAL ECONOMISTS OF THE TWENTIETH CENTURY

This series includes specially invited selections of articles by economists whose work has made an important and distinct contribution to financial economics in the late twentieth century.

Wherever possible, the articles in these volumes have been reproduced as originally published using facsimile reproduction, inclusive of footnotes and pagination to facilitate ease of reference.

Titles in the series include:

Financial Markets and Corporate Finance
Selected Papers of Michael J. Brennan
*Michael J. Brennan*

Foundations of Futures Markets
Selected Essays of A.G. Malliaris
*A.G. Malliaris*

# Foundations of Futures Markets

Selected Essays of A.G. Malliaris

A.G. Malliaris

*Walter F. Mullady, Sr Professor of Business Administration, Department of Economics and Department of Finance, Loyola University Chicago, USA*

FINANCIAL ECONOMISTS OF THE TWENTIETH CENTURY

**Edward Elgar**

Cheltenham, UK • Northampton, MA, USA

Published by
Edward Elgar Publishing Limited
Glensanda House
Montpellier Parade
Cheltenham
Glos GL50 1UA
UK

Edward Elgar Publishing, Inc.
136 West Street
Suite 202
Northampton
Massachusetts 01060
USA

A catalogue record for this book
is available from the British Library

**Library of Congress Cataloguing in Publication Data**

Malliaris, A.G.
    Foundations of futures markets : selected essays of A.G. Malliaris
/ A.G. Malliaris.
    (Financial economists of the twentieth century)
    Includes index.
    1. Futures I. Title. II. Series.
HG6024.A3M335   2000
332.64′5—dc21

99–41671
CIP

ISBN 1 85898 836 5 ✓

Printed and bound in Great Britain by Biddles Ltd, Guildford and King's Lynn

# Contents

## PART IV   FINANCIAL FUTURES

## PART V   CONCLUSIONS

# Acknowledgements

The publishers wish to thank the following who have kindly given permission for the use of copyright material.

Elsevier Science Ltd for excerpt: 'Portfolio Theory', with G.M. Constantinides in R. Jarrow et al. (eds), *Finance*, North-Holland, 1995, pp. 1–30.

John Wiley and Sons, Inc. for the following articles from the *Journal of Futures Markets*: 'Linkages between Agricultural Commodity Futures Contracts', with Jorge L. Urrutia, **16**(5), August 1996, 595–609; 'Searching for Fractal Structure in Agricultural Futures Markets', with Marco Corazza and Carla Nardelli, **17**(4), 1997, 433–73; 'Volume and Price Relationships: Hypotheses and Testing for Agricultural Futures', with Jorge L. Urrutia, **18**(1), 1998, 53–72; 'Tests of Random Walk of Hedge Ratios and Measures of Hedging Effectiveness for Stock Indexes and Foreign Currencies', with Jorge L. Urrutia, **11**(1), 1991, 55–68; 'The Impact of the Lengths of Estimation Periods and Hedging Horizons on the Effectiveness of a Hedge: Evidence from Foreign Currency Futures', with Jorge L. Urrutia, **11**(3), 1991, 271–89.

Kluwer Academic Publishers for article: 'Volume and Volatility in Foreign Currency Futures Markets', with Ramaprasad Bhar, *Review of Quantitative Finance and Accounting*, **10**, 1998, 285–302.

Routledge Ltd for excerpt: 'Equity and Oil Markets Under External Shocks', with Jorge L. Urrutia in Dilip K. Ghosh and Edgar Ortiz (eds), *The Global Structure of Financial Markets*, 1997, pp. 103–16.

Society for Industrial and Applied Mathematics for articles: 'Martingale Methods in Financial Decision-Making', *Society for Industrial and Applied Mathematics Review*, **23**(4), October 1981, 434–43; 'Itô's Calculus in Financial Decision Making', *Society for Industrial and Applied Mathematics Review*, **25**(4), October 1983, 481–96.

Springer-Verlag for excerpts: 'Random Walk vs. Chaotic Dynamics in Financial Economics', with G. Philippatos in F. Gori et al. (eds), *Nonlinear Dynamics in Economics and Social Sciences*, 1991, pp. 99–122; 'Financial Modelling: From Stochastics to Chaotics and Back to Stochastics', with Jerome L. Stein in M. Bertocchi et al. (eds), *Modelling Techniques for Financial Markets and Bank Management*, 1996, pp. 1–16.

The *International Journal of Finance* for article: 'Time Series Properties of Foreign Currency Hedge Radios', with Jorge L. Urrutia, **5**(2), 1993, 542–63.

# Foreword
## Jerome L. Stein

Ironically, the economics of futures markets is one of the least understood and yet one of the most fruitful and intellectually stimulating areas of economics. The theory has great implications for macroeconomics and risk management by intermediaries. The rationale of the price system is that it facilitates the optimal allocation of goods and services between producers and consumers over space during a relatively short period of time. The rationale of futures markets is that they facilitate the intertemporal allocation of storable goods between the present and the future. They help to establish the value to consumers of a commodity or financial instrument today relative to an informed opinion of its likely value in the future. The futures markets not only establish the relative prices of commodities used today and their expected value in the future, but also facilitate risk management. Without futures markets, either too little or too much of commodities, or command over commodities, would be stored.

Some of the recent major topics in macroeconomics and international finance – intertemporal optimization, rational or asymptotically rational expectations – have been integral parts of the economics of futures markets for at least half a century. Very few economists, with the notable exceptions of J.M. Keynes, Paul Samuelson and Milton Friedman, among others, have been familiar with both macroeconomics and futures markets. Samuelson's work, 'Proof that Properly Anticipated Prices Fluctuate Randomly' (1965), was a major theoretical development that was the foundation of what has been called 'the efficient market hypothesis'. This hypothesis led to the intellectual revolution in finance and, along with the risk management aspects of the economics of futures markets, has had profound implications for the financial markets, including that for the industry producing and marketing MBAs.

Tassos Malliaris is an extremely thoughtful and objective economist. His survey papers show his panoramic comprehension, and his contributions both acknowledge generously the work of others and demonstrate his creativity. His book offers instruction and produces joy for those who read it and reflect upon his analysis. The eighteen chapters in this collection give both a comprehensive and balanced perspective of the field of futures markets.

There are several parts to this volume. The chapters in the Overview survey the major contributions of the field and evaluate the individual contributions of the various authors. This way, the reader is given an expert and comprehensive tour through some sixty important papers. The methods used in futures markets are presented in four papers in the second section. A.G. Malliaris is known to the profession for his two very successful advanced monographs: 'Stochastic Methods in Economics and Finance' and 'Differential Equations, Stability and Chaos in Dynamic Economics' both co-authored with W.A. Brock. His skillful expertise in both stochastic and deterministic methods is evident in the papers of this section, and the reader who does not wish to study these methods in depth is offered a valuable introduction in the papers reprinted here.

The articles in the sections on Agricultural Futures and Financial Futures are the specific contributions to the field by Professor Malliaris and his co-authors. Several of these papers have stimulated much research, such as the behaviour of hedge ratios and the fractal nature of futures prices. His contribution to the relationships between prices and volume is also noteworthy. Both PhD students and researchers in the field of futures markets will find the articles in these two sections highly motivational for further research.

I highly recommend this extremely well written and thoughtful book to the profession of microeconomists, macroeconomists who are concerned with intertemporal optimization and rational expectations, and those concerned with risk management and the role of financial derivatives.

Division of Applied Mathematics, Brown University
December, 1998

# Preface

> That is a good book which opened
> with expectation and closed with profit.
>
> *Amos B. Alcott*

Albert Einstein once said that 'all our science, measured against reality, is primitive and childlike, and yet it is the most precious thing we have'. In this book I offer to you, the reader, a selection of my best research papers in futures markets that address important questions about the complex economic reality of these markets. These papers are contained in chapters 5 to 17 and were written over a period of several years. All have been previously published, primarily in economics journals.

To make the book self-contained, I have included chapters 2, 3 and 4, which give an overview of the field of futures markets. These three chapters present the unified theory of futures markets which has been developed over the years in the outstanding papers of the profession. I wrote these three chapters for the Elgar Reference Collection on *Futures Markets*. Numerous students have received instruction from these three chapters and the reader who wishes to be introduced into the field will find them very informative.

To add further value to the book, I have written two new chapters. Chapter 1 gives a detailed introduction to the contents of the book while chapter 18 presents topics for future research. In particular, chapter 18 describes five areas of current and future research. Both PhD graduate students and professional researchers will find useful suggestions for topics to be investigated.

Euripides proclaimed that 'courage is worth nothing if the gods withhold their aid'. The courage I needed to do the work contained in this book is minor compared with my great fortune to work with truly remarkable co-authors. They gave me instruction, inspiration and creative joy. They made me a better economist and often a better person. I happily acknowledge my gratitude to my co-authors who helped me produce some of my work in this book and elsewhere.

I wish to recognize the following persons: Ramaprasad Bhar (University of Technology, Sydney), William A. Brock (University of Wisconsin, Madison), Fwu-Ranq Chang (Indiana University), George Constantinides (University of Chicago), Marco Corazza (University of Venice), Alex Kondonassis (University of Oklahoma), Mary Malliaris (Loyola University, Chicago), Carla Nardelli (University of Venice), George Philippatos (University of Tennessee), Jerome Stein (Brown University) and Jorge Urrutia (Loyola University, Chicago). It is with joy that I dedicate this book to all my co-authors.

My wife Mary Malliaris, my son Steven Malliaris, my colleague George Kaufman and my two assistants, Vasiliki Blesseos and Antonio La Rocca, have given me valuable help during the preparation of this book with copyright permissions, bibliographical searches, editorial assistance and proofreading. Dymphna Evans, the commissioning editor at Edward Elgar Publishing, has offered me great encouragement and expert advice. I am deeply thankful to all.

Finally, I thank you, my readers, for your interest in this book. I hope that you find an unexpected idea that will inspire your minds and delight your hearts.

A.G. (Tassos) Malliaris
Chicago
30 March 1999

# PART I

# OVERVIEW

# [1]

## Introduction

This introduction offers a synopsis of the sixteen papers selected for this book whose broad theme is the economics of futures markets. These markets have received a great deal of attention during the last twenty years because of the proliferation of derivative instruments. Such financial innovation has, in turn, stimulated new research. Most of the papers in this volume are the outcome of this increased interest in derivative markets.

Futures markets are distinct economic institutions and before the reader is invited to study them, it will be beneficial to elucidate what markets do in general, and what futures markets do in particular.

Not every primitive society has had markets: anthropologists teach us that societies existed in which reciprocal gift giving was the norm rather than trading. In such societies, prices did not exist and their members did not exchange their goods and services in an impersonal market. In contrast to such non-market societies, others invented the social institutions of specialization and trading and thus created the primitive concept of market. Market economies have evolved rather slowly over many centuries.

The Industrial Revolution, along with global trade, contributed to specialization and exchange. Legal and financial organizations were created to make exchange efficient and thus the social institution called 'market' was perfected.

The recent collapse of the former Soviet Union along with the rejection of anti-market rhetoric by Communist China have served to elevate the ideology of free markets to a new apotheosis. This ideology claims that markets give sellers the opportunity to offer goods and services that maximize their profits or provide other, more general entrepreneurial goals. Simultaneously, consumers achieve the largest benefits by being free to choose the purchase of the goods and services they want most. Since both buyers and sellers are better off because of the exchange of goods and services provided by markets, the logical conclusion is reached that markets enable a society to achieve its highest economic well-being.

Markets are divided into two broad groups: cash markets and futures markets. Consider for example the spot market for automobiles. On any given day and time, car manufacturers produce a variety of vehicles which are sold through dealers to interested consumers. The primary characteristic of the spot market is the exchange of the product or service for payment. The typical car buyer receives the car and agrees to pay the appropriate price either in cash or with a credit arrangement.

Futures markets differ from spot markets because, often, there is no delivery of the commodity or service purchased or sold and, furthermore, there is no full payment. Futures markets exist to trade contracts. They are highly organized institutions with well-defined functions. They demonstrate a strong symbiotic relationship to the cash markets of the underlying product and thus have themselves evolved as the cash markets have progressed.

The organization of futures markets stems from the fact that they were established as commodity exchanges in the mid-nineteenth century. In these exchanges, both in the past and now, well-designed contracts are traded by market participants, who do not necessarily wish to deliver or receive the physical commodity. Rather, these traders wish either to protect their inventory of the physical commodity or to specu-late about its price evolution. When the twin institutions of a margin account and the daily resettlement were perfected, futures markets experienced sufficient liquidity to enable them to generate price discovery for a standard commodity. This price dis-covery has emerged as the primary function of a futures market.

Commodity futures markets have existed for a long time. In contrast, financial futures are a recent development. Currency futures markets appeared in the early 1970s, as a result of the abandonment of the Bretton Woods International Monetary System on 15 August 1971. Interest Rate and Stock Index Futures contracts followed in the 1980s. The growth of these financial futures has been explosive as has been the academic research output. A sample of this research is presented in the essays collected in this volume.

**Content of this book**
The chapters are organized into four topics. The first topic offers an overview of futures markets. In addition to this introduction, the overview covers three important questions: why are futures markets different from cash markets? How do prices behave in these markets and, finally, what are the recent developments in financial futures markets? Each of these three questions is answered in a comprehensive manner in Chapters 2, 3 and 4, respectively.

The second topic addresses issues of methodology. In futures markets, as in other areas of economics, researchers have used several methods. Chapters 5, 6, 7 and 8 review martingale methods, Itô's calculus, chaotic dynamics and the theory of port-folio selection, respectively.

Martingale methods have found fertile ground for applications in financial markets in general and futures markets in particular, because they use the language of conditional probability to make precise the notion of market efficiency. The premier tool of con-tingent claims pricing has been Itô's calculus which generalizes the concept of random walk from the discrete case to the continuous one and allows the financial theorist to derive price expressions for the derivative asset by making certain assumptions about the price behaviour of the underlying asset.

Chaotic dynamics, as a methodology of financial modelling, argues that asset prices in general, and futures prices in particular, can be expressed as highly complex, nonlinear relations which, although deterministic, may appear random due to the un-certainty of the initial conditions of such price dynamics. Finally, Chapter 8 presents both the static and the continuous-time dynamic portfolio selection theory which answers the question: how should an investor allocate his or her wealth among several assets so that for a given desired level of returns, the risk of the portfolio is minimized?

**Agricultural futures**
Agricultural futures trading began in Osaka, Japan, during the seventeenth century and has flourished in Chicago during the past several decades. Research related to

these markets has been extensive. Chapters 9 through 12, in this section, address both old and new topics. The question as to whether there are any price linkages between agricultural commodity futures contracts is considered in Chapter 9.

Microeconomic theory teaches us that there are two economic relationships between any two commodities, that is, substitutability and complementarity. For example, if the price of corn increases, cattle feeders may use soybean meal as a substitute, and vice versa. Thus, corn and soybean meal are substitutes. Alternatively, if the price of soybean oil increases dramatically and soybeans are crushed to supply such oil, this process also produces more soybean meal and may result in a drop in the price of soybean meal. This shows that soybean oil and meal are complementary.

In addition to microeconomic theory, there are other reasons to expect interdependence between agricultural commodity futures contracts such as crop production costs, weather and other climatological factors and exogenous supply or demand shocks. These factors are discussed in detail in Chapter 9, the null hypothesis is formulated and empirical tests are performed to identify existing relationships.

Chapter 10 offers a comprehensive study of two fundamental hypotheses about the statistical properties of futures prices. The actual distribution of spot or futures price changes or returns is an issue of fundamental importance to financial economists. In the much-celebrated theory of market efficiency, current prices reflect fully all publically available information and thus, price changes or returns are random because they are driven by new information. These random returns are postulated to be normally distributed and are obtained from assets that follow lognormal price distributions. This chapter investigates the notion of randomness and the hypothesis of lognormal distribution of futures prices. Evidence is presented that supports the fractal structure of futures returns. To show that asset prices follow fractal processes is to show more than random walk. Fractal processes generalize random walks because, in addition to their irregularity, they are also self-similar and the dimension of the set can be computed. These ideas are explained in detail in Chapter 10.

The relationship between volume and price volatility has been studied in detail in the futures markets literature. The topic is of interest because the price and volume relationship can provide insight about the market structure. Furthermore, technical analysts often use volume data to confirm bullish or bearish sentiments among traders. Assuming that futures prices follow an Itô process, and that volume and prices are related through the microeconomic model of supply and demand, Chapter 11 derives certain relationships between volume and price volatility. These are then tested empirically using data for the six agricultural futures contracts: corn, wheat, oats, soybean, soybean meal and soybean oil. It is found that price and volume are cointegrated and that this longrun relationship is stronger in the direction of price to volume.

The section on agricultural futures concludes with Chapter 12, which is both methodological and empirical. Methodologically, this chapter asks the essential question: do futures prices follow stochastic processes or are they driven by chaotic dynamics? Obviously, the current literature overwhelmingly supports the stochastic paradigm articulated by the efficient market hypothesis. In contrast to this hypothesis, chaotic dynamics has not proposed any models that describe asset price behaviour. In this chapter, we modify the well-known Lorenz chaotic dynamics system by offering an economic interpretation for it and then we test whether or not data support this model. We do not find strong evidence that chaotic dynamics describe futures prices.

**Financial futures**
The introduction of financial futures occurred in the early 1970s when foreign currency contracts started trading at the Chicago Mercantile Exchange. The fixed exchange regime of the Bretton Woods International Monetary System collapsed in August 1971 when the United States Government realized that its gold reserves were not sufficient to allow full convertibility of dollar reserves held by foreign banks. On 15 August 1971, President Nixon announced that the United States would no longer sell gold to foreign central banks for dollars.

This decision eliminated the link between the dollar and gold and introduced the world to a system of flexible exchange rates. Various international agreements took place aiming to reduce the foreign exchange fluctuations that ushered in the era of the managed float. The elimination of fixed exchange rates introduced risks associated with exchange rate fluctuations that in turn led to foreign currency hedging and speculation.

Chapter 13 reviews the portfolio approach to hedging and asks the crucial question: how stable are the hedge ratios? Earlier studies had found empirical evidence that hedge ratios are not stable. Using larger sets of empirical data, Chapter 13 confirms that hedge ratios are indeed unstable and their behaviour follows a random walk.

The random walk behaviour of hedge ratios has implications for the real world hedging policies. Any hedging strategy involves the estimation of a hedge ratio and a hedging horizon. Traditionally, the estimation of a hedge ratio includes the selection of an appropriate sample size of cash and futures data and also an estimation technique. The simplest estimation technique, suggested by the Ederington methodology of the optimal hedge ratio, is ordinary least squares. Other methods have also been proposed. Suppose the researcher chooses to estimate the hedge ratio using ordinary least squares. Should a small, medium or large sample size be used? Often a large sample allows a better estimate of the hedge ratio when the coefficient of determination is used as a criterion of how good the relationship is between the independent and dependent variables. Chapter 14 performs different experiments using various criteria for the effectiveness of the hedging strategy and concludes that a small sample and a short hedging horizon are, in general, better than other alternatives.

The issue of the behaviour of hedge ratios is revisited in Chapter 15 using the same hypothesis as in Chapter 13, namely that hedge ratios follow random walks but employ a different methodology. Using the Lo and MacKinlay variance-ratio test, it is found that the random walk hypothesis cannot be rejected. This finding is consistent with the results of Chapter 13 and both indicate that the traditional methods of hedging must be reviewed because such unstable hedge ratios cannot provide perfect hedges.

Chapter 14 investigates two hypotheses: first, it is claimed that the Persian Gulf crisis had a stronger impact on the oil market than in the equity market; and second, that the causal relationship between stock and oil prices increased during this crisis. Using two separate methodologies, evidence is found to support both hypotheses.

Chapter 15 is a companion to Chapter 11; both study relationships between price and volume using different sets of data and different methodologies. In this chapter, we find supportive evidence, for all foreign currencies, that price volatility is a determinant of trading volume changes. We also find evidence that price volatility is a determinant of the unexpected component of the changes in trading volume.

The contributions of this book conclude with a selection of research problems. The dynamism and importance of any field is influenced by the collection of open problems. This chapter offers several problems to stimulate further research.

## Scope

From the preceding discussion, one may conclude that the chapters in this volume suggest a broader rather than a narrower scope of the field of futures markets. The reader will find, first, three introductory chapters that offer an inclusive analysis of all the important aspects of futures markets. Then, the reader will find four chapters on methodological issues. Furthermore, both the traditional agricultural futures markets are discussed in four chapters, as well as the modern financial markets in five chapters. In addition to a broader scope, this book also offers a balanced coverage among the standard topics.

The book is addressed to both graduate students and researchers in the field of futures markets and financial economics. Students can learn much from the three introductory chapters that review the field. They can also benefit from the methodological chapters. Researchers can find useful ideas in topics such as market efficiency, the fractal or chaotic behaviour of asset prices, asset volatility and volume, hedge ratio behaviour and hedging strategies, risk management and the impact of global shocks on financial markets.

The purpose of this book is to give instruction which, if done properly, produces joy upon reflection and contemplation. Aristotelians will remind us that the utilitarian approach to science challenges us to find some usefulness and practicality in ideas. In a topic such as futures markets, very little can be said that is not useful or applied and thus there is no fear that this book is utopian. What is hoped, however, is that readers with a Platonic disposition will also like this book as its ideas guide them to the world of intellectual wonder.

# [2]

# Futures markets: why are they different?

## Introduction

A typical market for a commodity, a service or a financial instrument can be divided into the *cash market* and the *futures market*. The cash market, in turn, is divided into the *spot market* and the *forward market*.

Consider for example the spot market for crude oil. On any given day and time, crude oil producers, dispersed all over the globe, sell to interested crude oil merchants certain quantities for certain prices. The primary characteristic of the spot market is cash payment or appropriate credit arrangements upon delivery of the commodity or service, with such delivery taking place now. Numerous specific factors such as demand schedules of buying merchants, supply schedules of producers, industrial organization of the market (monopolistically competitive, oligopolistic or other), inventory accumulation or depletion, possible government regulations, various grades of crude oil, credit arrangements for payments and possibly several other economic variables, all play an important role in characterizing a *spot market*. Nevertheless, when we refer to a spot market we abstract from all such conditions and concentrate on the current delivery and current payment.

In contrast to a spot market, a *forward market* is simply a cash market for deferred delivery and payment. When a refinery enters into a forward contract with an oil producer, it agrees to buy a certain quantity of crude oil of a certain grade at a prespecified price on a certain future date, perhaps in thirty or ninety days. Such a forward contract is a custom-made agreement between the buyer and the seller with particular specifications for future delivery and payment. In other words, a forward contract is tailored to the needs of the parties in terms of quality, quantity, time and place of delivery and also in terms of financial arrangements.

Let us now examine the *futures market* for crude oil and ask why it is different from cash markets, both spot and forward. Like any other market, there are buyers and sellers; however, what these people trade is a highly standardized futures contract. For example, at the New York Mercantile Exchange buyers and sellers trade a crude oil futures contract of a fixed size of 1000 barrels of a specific quality (light sweet crude) to be delivered on a prespecified date and place. Furthermore, the trading of this futures contract takes place at the New York Mercantile Exchange in a certain pit using the format of an open outcry auction. Immediately after the buyer and the seller establish a position, the execution is guaranteed by the clearing house which acts as a seller to all buyers and as a buyer to all sellers. Thus, futures markets are different because they are characterized by the standardization of the futures contracts and their trading in highly organized exchanges.

The ideas presented above in the context of cash and futures markets for crude oil are readily generalized to other markets such as agricultural, precious metals, foreign currencies, interest rates, stock indexes and various others. What is, however, a more challenging task is to explain why there are a myriad of cash markets and only a few dozens of futures markets. Put differently, the economic system of all nations consists primarily of cash markets. In these markets, particularly when they function competitively, that is without government intervention and monopolistic forces, cash prices are formed by supply and demand conditions. Competitive prices in turn, lead to an efficient allocation of the economy's resources. Microeconomics, general equilibrium analysis and welfare economics all study the mechanics and properties of an economy's price system with a primary emphasis on cash markets. In contrast to such markets and in a small number of organized exchanges certain futures contracts are traded. Why do these futures markets exist and what is their economic role?

## Historical evidence

To motivate an answer to the questions asked, we examine two relevant developments from the history of commodity trading presented in LaPlante (1984): the early Japanese rice market during the Tokugawa era, 1603–1868, and the futures markets in Chicago from 1830 to 1870.

During the seventeenth century, Japanese agriculture was organized under the feudal system with absentee landlords collecting rice crops from their workers. A typical landlord would haul and sell his rice shortly after harvest in the Osaka spot market and use such cash to finance his expenses until next harvest time. History reveals that most nobles often had to raise cash between harvests to meet some unforeseen financial emergency. They did so by selling forward contracts, that is by agreeing to deliver during the next harvest season a preagreed quantity of rice for a preagreed price, provided the merchant who bought such a forward contract was willing to offer the landlord a cash down payment.

Over the decades, these forward contracts, called *rice tickets*, became standardized in terms of rice grade (there were four grades available) and contract term (the year was divided into three four-month periods). Furthermore, and of much more significance, these rice tickets became negotiable and thus the object of trading. For example, if a merchant had purchased a rice ticket entitling him to buy 10,000 bushels of rice at a certain price and if a few weeks later and prior to harvest and delivery the price of rice had increased (say due to expectations of a poor harvest), such a merchant could sell the rice ticket for a profit to another merchant.

These negotiable rice tickets became the object of intense trading and led to the formation of the first commodity exchange in the city of Osaka in 1650. The centre piece of the Osaka Rice Exchange was its clearing house that cleared and guaranteed all trades.

Next, let us consider, briefly, futures markets developments in the USA with particular emphasis on Chicago from 1830 to 1870. It is easy to imagine that just after periods of harvest and when various crops such as corn, wheat and soybeans were hauled to Chicago for sale in large quantities, supplies far exceeded the immediate demands. Such supply gluts would cause prices to drop often to extremely low levels. The lack of sufficient storage and the limited means of transportation during this period contributed to even greater price variability. The Chicago Board of Trade was incorporated in 1859 partly in response to such significant swings in the spot prices of agricultural products. Farmers, commercial grain elevator firms, food processing companies and grain speculators, among others, traded agricultural futures contracts at the Chicago Board of Trade to protect future crops and inventories from price uncertainty and to profit from successful speculation.

## Futures market characteristics

What are the key characteristics of futures markets as illustrated by these brief historical descriptions? First, futures markets are *derivative markets*. They exist because a cash market exists. While a given asset is traded in the cash market, the object of the futures market is the trading of a certain contract based on this asset. Recall the cash rice market and the Osaka futures market where rice tickets were the object of trading. Also, consider the cash corn market and the corn futures contracts traded at the Chicago Board of Trade. Currently several very active cash markets, such as the US long-term debt market, the New York Stock Exchange equity market and the Eurodollar market all have motivated the creation of derivative futures markets. The corresponding derivative markets are the US 30-year Treasury Bond futures contract traded at the Chicago Board of Trade, the S&P 500 Index futures contract traded at the Chicago Mercantile Exchange and the Eurodollar futures contract also traded at the Chicago Mercantile Exchange. Obviously, many more futures markets exist.

One needs to be careful not to interpret the notion of derivative markets as meaning that they are in the shadow of the real cash markets and thus less important. Actually, because derivative markets trade a standardized contract with low transaction costs and a high degree of liquidity, such derivative markets are the immediate entry port for price information. Thus futures markets often lead cash markets in price discovery.

Second, it is not true that futures markets exist for every cash market. For example there are no futures markets for cars, housing or health care. Usually, futures markets develop when there are large competitive cash markets with *volatile prices*. In other words, price uncertainty in a cash market contributes to the creation of a futures market. As an illustration recall that under the Bretton Woods international monetary system, a fixed exchange rate regime prevailed with national currencies pegged to the US dollar at prespecified parities. In turn the US dollar was anchored to the gold reserves of the US government at the rate of $35 per ounce of gold. Such a system eliminated exchange rate uncertainty from the early 1950s to the late 1960s. Then on 15 August 1971 the US suspended its obligation to exchange gold reserves for US dollars accumulated by foreign national banks. This occurred because of inadequate US gold reserves in contrast to a world US dollar glut. As exchange rates began to float in the early 1970s, a futures market developed at the Chicago Mercantile Exchange, called the International Monetary Market, to facilitate the distribution of risks associated with the increased exchange rate volatility.

Third, futures markets are highly *organized* and very *liquid*. Both the contracts traded and the rules of trading are quite specific. Furthermore, futures trading usually involves a large number of competitive traders who meet in a pit of an organized exchange with every trade being guaranteed by the exchange's clearing house. Cash markets, both spot and forward, are usually less organized and less liquid. As an extreme illustration of the liquidity issue, during the October 1987 stock market crash, the otherwise highly liquid specialists of the New York Stock Exchange interrupted their trading because of huge imbalances between sell and buy orders in most stocks.

This illiquidity in the cash market did not spill over into the futures market. The Major Market Index futures contract, traded at the Chicago Board of Trade, remained actively traded during the crash.

While more characteristics can be cited, enough has been exposited to allow us to answer the questions asked earlier: why do futures markets exist and what is their economic role? Simply put, futures markets exist for *risk management* purposes. Cash markets allow prices to be established among buyers and sellers which in turn act as signals for the efficient allocation of the economy's resources. In contrast, futures markets allocate risks. The most important risk is the price variability of an asset.

Consider, for example, a multinational computer company with production facilities in several countries and with substantial sales coming from abroad. Such a multinational is exposed to both costs of production and sales uncertainty because of exchange rate fluctuations. One way to manage such an exchange rate risk is for this multinational to engage in foreign currency hedging. *Hedging* is defined as the use of futures contracts to minimize the risk of a current or future cash position. For hedging to materialize, some traders must be willing to assume the hedger's risk for an appropriate risk premium. Such traders are called speculators.

As hedgers and speculators trade, and as these traders interchange their role by speculators protecting their positions (acting as hedgers) and hedgers induced by extreme price movements taking speculative positions, futures markets generate prices. This competitive price formation process, called *price discovery*, is the second most important role of futures markets. Furthermore such price discovery facilitates production and consumption decisions and, therefore, contributes to the optimal allocation of resources over time. For example, suppose that futures prices for distant contracts are significantly higher than those of early delivery. Such information would encourage consumption in the short run and increased production in the longer run. Grossman (1977) offers a detailed analysis of the informational role of futures markets.

Having described some of the futures markets key characteristics – derivative markets for large and very active cash markets with volatile prices, carefully designed contracts, trading in a liquid and well-organized futures exchange, and trades guaranteed by a clearing house – we can answer easily the question asked earlier: why do futures markets exist? Futures markets exist to manage risks associated with volatile price changes of certain assets and to offer speculative opportunities.

Economic deregulation during the past two to three decades has caused increased volatility in foreign currencies, debt instruments and stock indexes. Some of the most actively traded contracts now are derivatives of such financial assets. These contracts were mostly developed in the USA during the 1980s. As world financial markets have grown, financial futures have been developed by foreign exchanges. If one, however, pays attention only to recent developments in these financial futures, one would miss the rich ideas developed in the early classics dealing primarily with agricultural futures. We review these ideas in the next section.

**The early classics**

Working (1962) presents a detailed record of the results produced by the research on futures markets during the period 1920–60. In this classic paper and in its numerous references one can easily identify the formation of several ideas that are currently part of our received doctrine. Here we consider four such foundational concepts.

First, an idea that has underscored the distinction between cash and futures markets is the concept of *open-contract* introduced in 1922. Open interest as it is called today, or open-contract in Working's terminology, denotes the total number of outstanding contracts at the end of the day. No such concept exists for cash markets, whose primary function is to facilitate buying and selling of goods and services. Put differently, cash markets make possible the transfer of ownership in return for payment. As was exposited earlier, futures markets exist to facilitate the trading of standardized contracts as means of risk management and speculation. Open interest measures the total number of such outstanding contracts held by traders. Because for every trader who buys a contract there exists one who sells it, open interest may be viewed as the total number of contracts bought but not yet sold back, or sold but not yet bought back. Open interest increases in the early life of a contract, peaks a few weeks prior to expiration and then decreases. At contract expiration, open interest reaches zero because futures traders do not intend to take or make physical delivery and therefore each trader clears his/her outstanding position.

Second, the concept of *hedging*, developed in the mid-1930s, has fundamentally changed the view of futures markets, whose existence, prior to this time, was attributed primarily to speculation. Recall that hedging usually means the matching of a risk from holding an asset, whose price fluctuates, with an opposing risk from a futures contract on the same or similar asset. During the mid-1930s, this notion of hedging was extended in several dimensions: carrying-charge hedging, operational hedging, selective hedging and anticipatory hedging.

*Carrying-charge hedging* designates the combined operation of storage and hedging for profit. Producers of a commodity, or those who use it as a raw material, may choose storage of the commodity and sale of futures contracts if the basis, that is the difference between spot and futures prices, is high. Such a transaction is currently called arbitrage and it attempts to capture profits from the narrowing of the basis.

*Operational hedging* entails the placing and lifting of hedges in quick succession to facilitate asset operations. Because such operations occur over very short intervals – a few hours to a few days – this kind of hedging assumes no or very little change in the basis.

*Selective hedging* occurs when the holder of an asset chooses to hedge (fully or partially) or not to hedge according to price expectations. The motivation of such hedging is not strictly risk avoidance but also the desire to speculate on price expectations.

Finally, *anticipatory hedging* takes place when the appropriate futures position serves as a temporary substitute for the future purchase of an asset or the future payment of an obligation. This hedging is also guided by price expectations.

The above brief exposition of the multipurpose concept of hedging illustrates that hedging when defined narrowly as insurance, that is sole avoidance of risk, is very limited. Once hedging is recognized as a business activity motivated by different purposes, it enriches the role of futures markets and refocuses the reason of their existence. It is not claimed that speculation, that is the holding of a net long or a net short position for profit, is not important in futures markets; rather Working

(1962) clarifies that futures markets are driven primarily by forces other than speculation.

Third, the simplistic view that hedgers participate in futures markets to transfer their risks to speculators naturally led to the notion of *risk premium*, that is the necessary reward demanded by speculators to assume the risks of hedgers. If the hedgers are net short in futures, it follows that speculators must be net long. Under such conditions, Keynes proposed his theory of *normal backwardation*, which argues that speculators will only be net long if they expect, on average, futures prices to increase. The average gains from such an increase may be viewed as the risk premia earned by speculators, or equivalently the risk premia paid by hedgers.

Working argues that the empirical evidence for normal backwardation is inconclusive. Furthermore, if the existence of risk premia produces the tendency for futures prices to rise, then such a concept cannot always be supported by the evidence. Obviously, not all futures prices tend to increase on average. Therefore, the risk premium concept must be replaced by a broader notion. Gray (1961) proposes the *market-balance* concept to describe the relationship between the amount of hedging and speculation. If, as argued by normal backwardation, significant futures price increases occur, which confirm the presence of risk premia, such evidence can be attributed to lack of balance in the market.

Put differently, heavy net selling by hedgers could generate high returns for speculators, but this must be viewed as a special case. Once the concept of hedging is extended to include the various activities described earlier, imbalances between multipurpose hedging and speculation may decrease. When futures markets are in balance, futures prices do not follow clear trends but rather they fluctuate randomly. Such random behaviour does not support the theory of normal backwardation nor the presence of a risk premium.

Fourth, Working offers several insights on the *random behaviour* of futures prices. Research on the behaviour of futures prices during 1920–60 played an important role in the development of the efficient market hypothesis during the 1960s. In the 1920s, it was believed that futures prices were highly unreliable and did not reflect correctly existing information, with such prices following random fluctuations with some cyclicality impressed upon them. Two decades later these ideas were replaced by newer concepts which became the precursors of *market efficiency*. These newer concepts included the idea that futures prices follow a random walk and the idea that these prices were reliably anticipatory. The latter concept meant that prices reflected the best possible current appraisals of future prospects.

Working's collection of new concepts produced by the futures market research during 1920–60 was formalized in several papers such as Johnson (1959–60), Stein (1961), Samuelson (1965) and others. Johnson uses a mean variance portfolio approach to analyse a mixture of hedging and speculative activity. The model explains how price expectations can affect various market positions. Stein also uses a risk return portfolio approach to show graphically the simultaneous determination of spot and futures prices and the allocation between hedged and unhedged inventory. Samuelson establishes that futures prices follow a martingale under the assumption that such futures prices at time $t$ are the best estimates of the expected spot price at expiration of the contract conditioned to information available at time $t$.

The next two sections illustrate some of the ideas just presented in a more formal way.

### Hedging and the competitive firm

Consider a competitive firm which faces price uncertainty, that is, the price of its product $p$ is a random variable with subjective density function $f(p)$ and mean $E(p) = \mu$. Such a firm produces only one output. Denote the quantity of the output $x$ and its cost $c(x)$, assuming $c(0) \geq 0$ and $dc(x)/dx = c'(x) > 0$. The firm is assumed to have a von Neumann–Morgenstern utility function $u$ defined on profit $\pi$, and the firm's objective is to maximize its profit by producing the optimum quantity $x$. We write

$$\underset{x}{\text{Max}} \; E[u(\pi)] = \underset{x}{\text{Max}} \int_0^\infty u[px - c(x)] \; f(p) \; dp. \tag{2.1}$$

The first-order condition is

$$E[u'(\pi)(p - c'(x))] = 0 \tag{2.2}$$

and the second order condition satisfies

$$E[u''(\pi)(p - c'(x))^2 - u'(\pi) c''(x)] < 0. \tag{2.3}$$

Make the appropriate assumptions that $u'(\pi) > 0$, $u''(\pi) < 0$ and $c''(x) > 0$ to conclude that a unique, positive and finite quantity $x$ exists that satisfies the necessary and sufficient conditions (2.2) and (2.3). Rewrite (2.2) as

$$E[u'(\pi) p] = E[u'(\pi) c'(x)]$$

and subtract from both sides $E[u'(\pi) \mu]$ to get

$$E[u'(\pi)(p - \mu)] = E[u'(\pi)(c'(x) - \mu)]. \tag{2.4}$$

We claim that

$$E[u'(\pi)(p - \mu)] \leq 0. \tag{2.5}$$

To show that (2.5) holds begin with expression

$$\pi(x) - E(\pi) = [px - c(x)] - [\mu x - c(x)] = (p - \mu) x. \tag{2.6}$$

From (2.6) we need to consider two cases when $p \geq \mu$ and when $p < \mu$. Suppose that $p \geq \mu$. Then $\pi(x) \geq E(\pi)$ from (2.6) and

$$u'(\pi) \leq u'(E(\pi)) \tag{2.7}$$

because $u'(\pi) > 0$ and $u''(\pi) < 0$. In the second case when $p < \mu$, similar reasoning yields $\pi(x) < E(\pi)$ and

$$u'\left(\pi\right) > u'\left(E\left(\pi\right)\right). \tag{2.8}$$

Using (2.7) and (2.8) conclude that

$$u'\left(\pi\right)\left(p - \mu\right) \leqslant u'\left(E\left(\pi\right)\right)\left(p - \mu\right).$$

Take the expectation of this last expression to conclude that (2.5) holds

$$E\left[u'\left(\pi\right)\left(p - \mu\right)\right] \leqslant E\left[u'\left(E\left(\pi\right)\right)\left(p - \mu\right)\right] \leqslant u'\left(E\left(\pi\right)\right)E\left(p - \mu\right) = 0. \tag{2.9}$$

Now that (2.5) is established we can use the fact that $u'\left(\pi\right) > 0$ to get from (2.4) that

$$E\left[u'\left(\pi\right)\left(c'\left(x - \mu\right)\right)\right] \leqslant 0 \tag{2.10}$$

implies that

$$c'\left(x\right) \leqslant \mu. \tag{2.11}$$

This result is very important. It says that a risk averse competitive firm that faces price uncertainty will select a lower level of output than (or at most equal to) the amount chosen by a similar firm with no price uncertainty. In other words, uncertainty reduces output.

Next, we want to illustrate how the existence of a futures market may change the behaviour of a competitive firm under price uncertainty. Suppose that a futures market exists for the single commodity that the firm produces. Thus the firm has the choice to hedge at a certain price $b$ a certain quantity $h$ of its output $x$. The firm's objective now is

$$\underset{x,\,h}{\text{Max }} E\left[u\left(\pi\right)\right] = \underset{x,\,h}{\text{Max }} \int_0^\infty u\left[p\left(x - h\right) + bh - c\left(x\right)\right] f\left(p\right) dp. \tag{2.12}$$

The first order conditions are

$$\frac{\partial E\left[u\left(\pi\right)\right]}{\partial x} = \int_0^\infty u'\left(\pi\right)\left[p - c'\left(x\right)\right] f\left(p\right) dp = 0 \tag{2.13}$$

$$\frac{\partial E\left[u\left(\pi\right)\right]}{\partial h} = \int_0^\infty u'\left(\pi\right)\left[b - p\right] f\left(p\right) dp = 0 \tag{2.14}$$

Obviously (2.13) is the same as (2.2). However, the presence of a futures market changes the results by providing (2.14). Add (2.13) and (2.14) to obtain

$$E\left[u'\left(\pi\right)\left(b - c'\left(x\right)\right)\right] = \left[b - c'\left(x\right)\right] E\left[u'\left(\pi\right)\right] = 0. \tag{2.15}$$

Recall that $u'\left(\pi\right) > 0$. Then (2.15) holds when $b = c'\left(x\right)$ which says that the competitive firm will produce that level of output $x$ for which marginal cost equals the certain futures price $b$.

The relation between the futures price $b$ today and the expected spot price in the future $E(p)$ determines the firm's hedging decisions. Rewrite (2.14) as

$$E[u'(\pi)(b-p)] = E[u'(\pi)] E(b-p) + \text{Cov}[u'(\pi), -p] = 0. \qquad (2.16)$$

This says that if the futures price equals the expected price, that is $b = E(p)$, then the firm will hedge its entire output. If the futures price is less than the expected price, that is $b < E(p)$, then the firm will either hedge less than its entire output, or if the futures price is very low in comparison to $E(p)$, the firm may speculate by buying in the futures markets, that is $h < 0$. If the futures price is greater than the expected price, that is $b > E(p)$, the firm will speculate by selling an amount greater than its output, that is $h > x$. Several additional results may be found in Holthausen (1979), but enough has been exposited to illustrate analytically that the existence of futures markets influences the production decision of the firm and also that hedging is a multipurpose activity.

## Behaviour of futures price

To explain Samuelson's (1965) argument we need to introduce some notation. Let $p(t)$ denote the spot price of an asset at time $t$ and $p(t + T)$ the spot price at $T$ periods from $t$. The futures price quoted at time $t$ is $y(t, T)$ where $T$ denotes the periods between $t$ and the expiration of the contract. As $t$ approaches $t + T$, the sequence of futures prices becomes

$$y(t, T), \; y(t + 1, T - 1), \; y(t + 2, T - 2), \; \dots \dots \; y(t + T, 0). \qquad (2.17)$$

The question is: under what conditions is the sequence in (2.17) a martingale? Recall that a *martingale* generalizes the simple idea of a random walk given by $x(t + 1) = x(t) + \varepsilon(t + 1)$ where $\varepsilon(t + 1)$ is a random variable with mean zero and a given variance. We say that a pair of random variables denoting prices and information $\{p(t), I(t); t = 0,1,2\dots\}$ follows a martingale if

$$E[p(t + 1) \mid I(t)] = p(t) \qquad (2.18)$$

with $I(t) \subset I(t+1)$. In (2.18) we claim that the best estimate of tomorrow's expected price conditioned on today's information, denoted by $I(t)$, is today's actual price.

Assume now what Samuelson calls the *Axiom of Mathematically Expected Price Formation* expressed as

$$y(t, T) = E[p(t + T) \mid I(t)]. \qquad (2.19)$$

This axiom says that today's futures price $y(t, T)$ reliably anticipates the spot price $p(t + T)$ at the expiration of the contract subject to all publicly available information today. Using (2.19) we need to show

$$E[y(t + 1, T - 1) \mid I(t)] = y(t, T). \qquad (2.20)$$

Observe that (2.20) follows from (2.19) and the law of iterated expectation from probability theory

$$E[y(t+1, T-1) \mid I(t)]$$
$$= E[E[p(t+1+T-1) \mid I(t+1)] \mid I(t)]$$
$$= E[p(t+T) \mid I(t)] = Y(t, T). \tag{2.21}$$

The intuitive meaning of this last expression is this: tomorrow's expected price constrained by today's information equals today's actual futures price because tomorrow's futures price is assumed to be the best estimate of the spot price at expiration. Put differently, Samuelson has shown that if at any given time prior to contract expiration traders efficiently use all available information to anticipate correctly the settlement price at expiration, then futures prices are a martingale. Observe that futures prices converge at expiration to the cash price; otherwise there would be opportunities for riskless arbitrage between cash and futures markets.

**Institutions**

The preceding analysis has emphasized the role of *organized exchanges* in the futures markets. Telser (1981) explains the three reasons why such organized markets exist.

According to the first view organized futures markets exist to facilitate hedging, that is, they exist because they offer insurance against price risk. The second view places the emphasis on speculation: they exist to offer speculative opportunities.

From our exposition of Working's analysis we can conclude that these two explanations are both limited and competitive. They are limited because both interpret the concepts of hedging and speculation narrowly. They are competitive because the insurance function of an exchange is viewed positively while that of speculation is viewed negatively, likening futures exchanges to gambling casinos.

The third and broader view supported by Telser is that futures exchanges facilitate trading among buyers and sellers. Obviously, modern organized futures exchanges are institutions that evolved over a long period by adapting to the needs of futures markets. Actually, these institutions still continue to evolve today as they incorporate the numerous technological, computer and software advances.

What are the important characteristics of an organized exchange? As was discussed earlier, it is critical to have a well-designed standardized contract that describes all the relevant conditions clearly. The goal in designing a futures contract is to make it a highly liquid instrument of trade with each unit of the contract being a perfect substitute for another unit. Since money is the most liquid commodity, ideally a futures contract should offer the two liquidity characteristics of money: low transactions costs and highly elastic excess demand.

Successful exchanges keep transactions costs very low by charging small fees and requiring low margin requirements. A typical fee or commission for a contract valued at, say $100,000 ranges most often between $1 to $50 while the margin requirement averages at about 10 per cent of the nominal value of the contract. The high elasticity of excess demand is achieved by selecting futures instruments for large cash markets and by encouraging a large number of traders to participate.

A highly elastic excess demand means that even significant amounts of contracts sold need not cause major changes in prices. Therefore, if the distribution of the market clearing prices has low standard deviation during a given period, we can conclude that this market is liquid. Conversely, if the market is not very liquid and trades are executed at equilibrium prices that differ significantly, one would expect the standard deviation of such a price distribution to be high.

Beyond having a standardized contract, a futures exchange is characterized by confining trading to its members. Obviously, members who execute orders as agents on behalf of their clients are regulated by the exchange. Limiting trading to members only enables the exchange to operate efficiently. Naturally, trading among fellow members can be faster and cheaper than trading with unknown persons as often happens in cash markets with no membership requirements. Furthermore, all members share the common goal of making their futures exchange financially successful and increasing the value of their membership.

The third characteristic of any futures exchange is the *clearing house*. Edwards (1983) describes in detail many significant aspects of this remarkable institution whose major role is to maintain the financial integrity of the exchange. Recall from our earlier discussion that the financial integrity of an exchange is accomplished by having the clearing house acting as a buyer to every seller and as a seller to every buyer. If trader A buys an S&P 500 futures contract from trader B, both traders record their trade and submit their trade tickets to their respective clearing agents. The clearing agents submit the trades to the exchange's clearing house. If the index increases and trader A makes a profit, such a profit is received from the clearing house which collects from trader B his or her loss.

The clearing house acts as a guarantor of all transactions without incurring losses because its members, who function as clearing agents for traders, deposit substantial sums as margins. Such a policy guarantees the financial integrity of the exchange. Clearing agents may extend credit to traders and require low margins to encourage trading and liquidity. A daily accounting is provided for trading losses and gains. If losing traders do not have in their accounts sufficient sums of money to cover such losses, they will be asked to provide the necessary funds before they are allowed further trading. Thus by *marking to market* all positions daily, or more frequently during turbulent times – as during the crash of 19 October 1987 – the clearing house prevents the accumulation of large losses and reduces its own exposure to risk without sacrificing liquidity.

Government regulation of these exchanges is a subject of great interest and of long history. Pashigian (1986) identifies three possible explanations for government regulation of the futures industry. First, one can argue that government regulation is needed to protect the unsophisticated or inexperienced investor. Second, one can explain government regulation in the broader context of equating speculation with gambling. Finally, there is regulation because it is demanded by politically powerful special interest groups such as the farmers. Obviously, not all farmers at all times have opposed futures trading. However, some farmers have opposed futures trading, often claiming without convincing documentation that futures trading lowers farm prices.

Miller (1990) carefully reviews the US futures industry from a world-wide perspective and evaluates the impact of government regulation from an international perspective. The key idea here is that regulation affects the industry's competitiveness negatively by increasing costs of production. Current regulatory initiatives must take carefully into account the balancing of all gains and losses from such government intervention in the futures exchanges activities. Otherwise foreign competition from organized exchanges overseas and off-floor trading will intensify and the US futures exchanges may lose.

Broadly speaking, the 1933 and 1934 US securities acts have established the Securities Exchange Commission (SEC) as the regulatory agency over US securities exchanges. In 1974 the Commodity Futures Trading Commission (CFTC) was created to regulate futures exchanges. The SEC, an older agency, has an extensive set of rulings and procedures while the CFTC as a much younger agency has much less government support and influence. The presence of two regulatory agencies with different histories, resources and political influence has created past problems and is an issue often revisited by regulators.

## Market characteristics

The importance of a standardized contract traded at an organized futures exchange with a clearing house has already been emphasized. As we continue to explain the various differences between cash and futures markets we now turn to a description of futures markets characteristics. Such characteristics include, among others, the continuous auction in the trading pit of a futures exchange, commodity exchange seats, the notion of margin levels and the role of price limits on price volatility.

Consider a given standardized futures contract such as the soybean, Treasury Bond or the S&P 500 contract. Unlike the corresponding cash markets which have different forms of organization, all three of these contracts, and in general all futures contracts, are traded in a pit or ring of an exchange floor with bids and offers announced by open outcry. Trades are executed continuously throughout a trading session (around six hours during the day and for a few hours for some contracts during evenings) whenever a bid is hit or an offer lifted by another trader.

The *open outcry* of buy and sell orders is designed to expose all orders to competitive pricing. To promote such competition the highest bid price and the lowest offer receive strict priority in the pit and lower bidders must remain silent when a higher bid can be heard. Similarly, higher offerers must be quiet when a lower offer is announced. As traders observe the market action they can choose to raise bids or lower offers at any time to increase their probability of executing trades.

There is no time priority for the execution of trades. If a bond trader has been trying to buy at 95 while another decided to do the same one minute later, there is nothing to guarantee that the first trader will buy before the second. In addition to no time priority there is no 'all-or-nothing' order in futures trading. If a trader wishes to buy ten contracts at a price of 95 he or she cannot refuse to buy only five from another trader at the price of 95. Finally, in an open outcry environment, bids and offers live only as long as they can be heard.

These few important rules along with several others demonstrate how well organized futures markets are in comparison to most cash markets. In addition to such detailed rules, market participants include various subcategories of hedgers and speculators.

Recall the several types of hedging activities identified by Working (1962) such as carrying-charge, operational, selective and anticipatory hedging.

Similarly, speculators can be categorized into position speculators, short-term speculators (day traders) and scalpers. Position speculators buy or sell futures contracts because they anticipate certain price changes will unfold during the next few days to few weeks. Such position speculators most often are trend followers. Day traders or short-term speculators are the ones who choose to trade for themselves rather than execute orders through a floor broker. They are active market participants who speculate on intra-day price movements but who usually clear their positions at the end of the trading day. Scalpers are market makers who quote bids and offers expecting to earn a return by providing market liquidity. Silber (1984) gives a detailed account of the behaviour of scalpers.

Independent of the various categories of traders, futures exchanges are organizations owned by their member traders. There are different types of memberships. For example the oldest membership is known as full membership which grants trading rights in all markets of the futures exchange. There is also an associate membership which offers trading rights in all but some markets. Even more specialized memberships exist allowing trading in some specific market. These and other types of membership, often described as seats, are themselves the object of trading and their prices at any point in time reflect the present value of future commissions. These future commissions depend on expected future trading volume. Pashigian (1986) and Chiang, Gay and Kolb (1987) offer an economic analysis of commodity exchange seat prices which as an institution offers a further illustration of the numerous differences between cash and futures markets.

The reader may recall that in discussing the institutions of futures markets in the preceding section we noted that low margin requirements accompanied by marking to market daily both encourage liquidity. Low margin requirements, however, have been related by some to destabilizing price fluctuations caused by excessive speculation. This view has been advanced in various studies by the Board of Governors of the Federal Reserve System.

Hartzmark (1986) develops a model of trader behaviour to analyse the impact of margins on contract demand, price level and volatility. His analysis traces the effects of changes in margin requirements across different trader groups such as commercial, noncommercial, large, small, informed or uninformed. He shows that changes in margin requirements ultimately affect the composition of traders in the market. Since liquidity costs and risk preferences among traders vary, one cannot a priori determine the impact of an across-the-board margin increase on the composition of traders. Hartzmark demonstrates both theoretically and empirically that regulation of margin requirements to reduce excessive speculation is difficult to justify and concludes by recommending that such regulation is unnecessary.

If one eliminates the use of margin requirements as a means to limit excessive volatility, and if we assume that such excessive volatility is an undesirable feature of futures markets, we can ask the question: how can excess volatility be reduced? Ma, Rao and Sears (1989) review the role of price limits on volatility. A *price limit* is the maximum amount of price change a contract is allowed on a single trading day. When a futures contract price moves to the maximum amount of its price limit, trading is halted. Following the market crash of 19 October 1987, such price limits have been imposed upon stock indexes as means to reduce excessive volatility. However, price limits have been an important element of the characteristics of futures markets for a long time. For example the Treasury Bond futures contract has had a 2-point daily price limit, and other appropriate price limits have existed for agricultural and metallurgical contracts. Furthermore, these price limits have been initiated by futures exchanges rather than regulatory agencies. Brennan (1986) develops a theory of price limits in futures markets by arguing that price limits may act as a partial substitute for margin requirements.

Ma, Rao and Sears (1989) show that price limits appear to give the market breathing room to re-evaluate the developments leading to the trading halt. On the day after the price limit is activated and also on the following days, data show that trading volume does not decrease which suggests that liquidity is maintained and the price discovery process is not impacted upon negatively. The limits also appear to be accompanied by substantial reductions in volatility.

Having presented several market characteristics of futures markets, we next address the issue of volatility in more detail.

## Volatility

The reader may recall that price volatility in the cash market contributes to the success of the futures contract. Volatile cash markets such as equity, foreign currencies, precious metals, energy, government bonds and agricultural, among others, have generated the need for risk management and thus have supported futures trading. The issue of volatility studied here is not the cash markets as a causal factor of volatility. Instead the question is: do futures markets increase or decrease the price volatility of cash markets?

The same question can be asked differently: do futures markets destabilize or stabilize cash markets? Theoretically, economists have offered two answers. Kaldor (1939) has argued that futures markets could under certain conditions destabilize cash markets. One possible way that this behaviour may materialize is when we distinguish between skilled and unskilled speculators trading in the futures markets. If skilled speculators try to anticipate correctly the behaviour of the unskilled speculators rather than anticipating fundamental developments, Kaldor claims that such behaviour may increase volatility. Note that in Kaldor's argument, increased volatility is associated with speculation and provides theoretical support for government intervention in futures markets. For example, in 1958 the US Congress enacted a law prohibiting futures trading in onions because of large price fluctuations in the cash market attributed to destabilizing futures trading.

Several studies have attempted to resolve this issue. Powers (1970) reviews several such studies and also describes the second answer given by Working (1962) and others. According to the second answer, cash volatility is reduced under futures markets because futures trading increases market information and thus improves cash market efficiency.

Following Powers, decompose the time series of cash prices, denoted by $p(t)$, into a systematic component associated with fundamentals, denoted by $s(t)$, and a random error, $\varepsilon(t)$, with mean zero and a given variance. Write

$$p(t) = s(t) + \varepsilon(t) \tag{2.22}$$

The variance of the series $p(t)$ can be written as

$$\text{Var } p(t) = \text{Var } s(t) + \text{Var } \varepsilon(t) \tag{2.23}$$

assuming that the covariance, $\text{Cov }(s(t), \varepsilon(t)) = 0$.

Suppose now that a successful futures market is introduced. The simple decomposition of the price volatility in the last equation into two components, that is, fundamental volatility and noise volatility, allows us to be more specific about the impact of futures markets. When it is argued that futures markets increase volatility, does this refer to increasing Var $s(t)$ or Var $\varepsilon(t)$? Similarly, if it is claimed that futures markets reduce cash volatility, does this mean that Var $s(t)$ or Var $\varepsilon(t)$ goes down? Powers hypothesizes that futures markets with their price discovery characteristic and the continuous incorporation of new information contribute to the reduction of fundamental volatility, Var $s(t)$, and focuses on noise volatility, Var $\varepsilon(t)$. Using the variate difference model, Powers concludes that for cash markets of pork bellies and live beef, noise volatility was reduced after the introduction of futures markets.

Independent of the question about the impact of the futures market on the cash price volatility is the behaviour of the futures price volatility. Anderson (1985) addresses this important question by discussing some determinants of the futures price volatility. One theory proposes that the volatility of futures prices increases as the time of contract maturity decreases. This hypothesis is known as the *maturity effect* and is supported by the fact that progressively more information becomes available as the delivery date approaches.

The second hypothesis is proposed by multiperiod analysis of the simultaneous determination of equilibrium prices in cash and futures markets and associates high futures volatility with significant uncertainty in fundamentals. Anderson also conducts empirical tests and finds support for the maturity effect hypothesis. Milonas (1986) derives the theoretical basis for the maturity effect hypothesis and tests it on eleven futures markets. The results show that in ten out of the eleven futures markets, the maturity effect is a significant determinant of price volatility. Finally, while Anderson and Milonas study the determinants of futures price volatility, Cornell (1981) hypothesizes and finds empirical support that futures price volatility increases trading volume.

## Speculation

From the emergence of the Osaka Rice Exchange in 1650 to the stock market crash of 19 October 1987, the concept of speculation has challenged both economists and government regulators. Yet we do not have a precise definition for this remarkable concept. One explanation for the lack of a definition is the fact that speculation has several meanings. Among these meanings we review the following four which are not totally distinct from each other.

First, in the static partial equilibrium analysis supply and demand fundamentals determine price; speculation is not mentioned. More generally, in an Arrow–Debreu general equilibrium economy with complete markets, the Walrasian auctioneer establishes prices at which trades occur and again speculation has no purpose. In contrast to static, both partial and general equilibrium analysis, allowing for dynamic shocks and recalculation of prices over time, introduces the elemental role of speculation which is associated with forecasting. Futures traders who establish certain positions from a few hours to several days, known as position traders, offer an illustration of the first meaning of speculation as a forecasting activity.

Second, rational traders participate in trading because they expect gains. The concept of normal backwardation introduced above illustrates how certain traders are willing to share the producers' risk for an expected gain. Thus speculation is related to insurance offered as a way to obtain gains. Although speculation as a form of insurance is a long-term notion extending from a few days to a few months, scalpers may also be viewed as an illustration of rational traders who engage in very short run trading for gain. As Silber (1984) describes these speculators, their horizon is between one and three minutes and their expected gains are earned for the liquidity that they provide.

Third, suppose that all traders receive the same piece of information. Can we claim that all traders will interpret this information exactly the same way? If different traders interpret differently the same information, one may view speculators as traders who bet on opposite sides of the market because of their divergent views of existing information.

Finally, speculation is often associated with arbitrage activity. Such arbitrage may occur between cash and futures or as a spread between a nearby and a distant futures contract.

Gray (1961) reviews the early controversial literature on the *risk premium* and argues that it is difficult to confirm its existence in futures markets. Dusak (1973) revisits the risk premium hypothesis using the capital asset pricing model for wheat, corn and soybean futures contracts. She finds the systematic risk for these futures contracts to be close to zero. Bessembinder (1992) and Kolb (1992) offer recent empirical studies of the same issue. These studies and their numerous references illustrate how diffiicult it is to develop theoretically and show empirically what the expected gains of speculation really are.

Consider next the role of speculation as forecasting or perhaps taking positions by a superior interpretation of available information. Irwin, Krukemyer and Zulauf (1993) investigate the investment performance of public commodity pools. Since advisors to such commodity pools are carefully selected as traders with vast experience and superior records, it is reasonable to hypothesize that such speculators outperform the market. The authors find that returns of public commodity pools are consistent with market efficiency. This means that these pools earn a gross return just sufficient to offset the costs and risks of collecting and interpreting existing information.

## Corporate hedging

Nance, Smith and Smithson (1993) revisit the topic of hedging from the perspective of a corporate firm. They mailed a questionnaire to Chief Executive Officers of 535 firms, the union of the Fortune 500 and the S&P 400. Completed questionnaires were received from 194 firms, with usable responses from 169. From these 169 firms in the usable sample, 104 had used hedging instruments during the fiscal year 1986. Hedging instruments included in addition to futures also swaps and options.

Earlier, several types of hedging were discussed. Nance, Smith and Smithson extend these early ideas by identifying the important determinants of corporate hedging. They hypothesize that such determinants may include (i) reduction in expected taxes, (ii) reduction in expected transactions costs of firms in financial distress and (iii) reduction in agency costs. The data suggest that firms which hedge face more progressivity in tax schedules, have less coverage of fixed claims, are larger, have more growth options in their investment opportunities and, finally, employ fewer hedging substitutes. In other words, unlike the typical agricultural firm of the period reviewed by Working (1962), whose hedging behaviour was primarily motivated by price risks associated with its inventory, the determinants of hedging, some 30 years later, are more complex. This complexity is directly related to the fact that the large corporate firms today are much more complex than the earlier ones. Furthermore, what corporate firms hedge today is not just their output and inventory but rather their entire firm value.

## Conclusion

Futures markets have had a long history and a remarkable growth. Their evolution has been driven by the fact that prices are volatile in several large cash markets that are competitive and free of negative government regulations. Typical such markets include the agricultural, metal, energy, foreign currencies, equity and interest rate related debt instruments.

Demand and supply fundamentals in such markets change almost continuously, often quite dramatically, causing large price fluctuations and generating corresponding risks. Risk management considerations have given the impetus in the creation of futures markets. These futures markets have succeeded because of their detailed organization which includes the trading of a well-defined contract by members and customers of members, with each trade being guaranteed by the exchange's clearing house.

This chapter has contrasted cash and futures markets. The central theme has been that both the institutional and market characteristics of futures markets are distinct and different from cash markets. Once futures markets are viewed as highly organized with characteristics often superior to those of cash markets, then their importance is clearly comprehended. Furthermore, the notion that futures markets are derivative markets is not understood to mean they are of secondary importance but of equal or perhaps superior significance. Actually, numerous futures markets, such as in stock indexes, government bonds, Eurodollars and oil among others, are the first to be impacted upon by the release of new information. The high liquidity and extensive organization of these futures markets allows the assimilation of new inforrnation to take place more efficiently than in the corresponding cash markets.

The theme of how futures markets are different from cash markets has also been supported by the evolution of academic research. This chapter has emphasized the notions of hedging, speculation and volatility in a unifying way rather than simply summarizing the results of key academic contributions. In summary, futures markets are remarkable institutions which demonstrate the creativity of free enterprise and scholarly research at its very best.

# References

Anderson, R.W. (1985), 'Some determinants of the volatility of futures prices', *The Journal of Futures Markets*, **5**, 331–48.

Bessembinder, Hendrik (1992), 'Systematic risk, hedging pressure, and risk premiums in futures markets', *The Review of Financial Studies*, **5**, 637–67.

Brennan, Michael J. (1986), 'A theory of price limits in futures markets', *Journal of Financial Economics*, **16**, 213–33.

Chiang, R.C., G.D. Gay and R.W. Kolb (1987), 'Commodity exchange seat prices', *The Review of Futures Markets*, **6**, 1–10.

Cornell, B. (1981), 'The relationship between volume and price variability in futures markets', *The Journal of Futures Markets*, **1**, 303–16.

Dusak, Katherine (1973), 'Futures trading and investor returns: an investigation of commodity market risk premiums', *Journal of Political Economy*, **81**, 1387–406.

Edwards, F.R. (1983), 'The clearing association in futures markets: guarantor and regulator', *The Journal of Futures Markets*, **3**, 369–92.

Gray, Roger W. (1961), 'The search for a risk premium', *Journal of Political Economy*, June, 250–60.

Grossman, S.J. (1977), 'The existence of futures markets, noisy rational expectations, and informational externalities', *Review of Economic Studies*, **44**, 431–49.

Hartzmark, M.L. (1986), 'The effects of changing margin levels on futures market activity, the composition of traders in the market, and price performance', *Journal of Business*, **59**, S147–S180.

Holthausen, Duncan M. (1979), 'Hedging and the competitive firm under price uncertainty', *American Economic Review*, **69**, 989–95.

Irwin, Scott H., Terry R. Krukemyer and Carl R. Zulauf (1993), 'Investment performance of public commodity pools: 1979–1990', *The Journal of Futures Markets*, **13**, 799–820.

Johnson, L.L. (1959–60), 'The theory of hedging and speculation in commodity futures', *Review of Economic Studies*, **27**, 139–51.

Kaldor, N. (1939), 'Speculation and economic stability', *Review of Economic Studies*, **7**, 1–27.

Kolb, Robert W. (1992), 'Is normal backwardation normal?', *The Journal of Futures Markets*, **12**, 75–91.

LaPlante, Duncan J. (1984), 'Growth and Organization of Commodity Markets', in P.J. Kaufman (ed.), *Handbook of Futures Markets*, John Wiley & Sons, pp. 3–54.

Ma, Christopher K., Ramesh P. Rao and R. Stephen Sears (1989), 'Volatility, price resolution and the effectiveness of price limits', *Journal of Financial Services Research*, **3**, 165–99.

Miller, M.H. (1990), 'International competitiveness of U.S. futures exchanges', *Journal of Financial Services Research*, **4**, 387–408.

Milonas, Nikolaos T. (1986), 'Price variability and the maturity effect in futures markets', *The Journal of Futures Markets*, **6**, 443–60.

Nance, D.R., D.W. Smith, Jr and C.W. Smithson (1993), 'On the determinants of corporate hedging', *The Journal of Finance*, **48**, 267–84.

Pashigian, B. Peter (1986), 'The political economy of futures market regulation', *Journal of Business*, **59**, S55–S84.

Powers, M.J. (1970), 'Does futures trading reduce price fluctuations in the cash markets?', *The American Economic Review*, **60**, 460–4.

Samuelson, P.A. (1965), 'Proof that properly anticipated prices fluctuate randomly', *Industrial Management Review*, **6**, 41–9.

Silber, W.L. (1984), 'Marketmaker behavior in an auction market: an analysis of scalpers in futures markets', *The Journal of Finance*, **39**, 937–53.

Stein, J.L. (1961), 'The simultaneous determination of spot and futures prices', *American Economic Review*, **51**, 1012–25.

Telser, L.G. (1981), 'Why there are organized futures markets?', *Journal of Law and Economics*, **24**, 1–22.

Working, H. (1962), 'New concepts concerning futures markets and prices', *American Economic Review*, **43**, 432–59.

# Futures markets: how do prices behave?

## Introduction

The fundamental role of every market is the formation of prices. In futures markets, such price formation receives even greater importance because risk transference and price discovery, as the two major contributions of these markets, both depend on the process of price formation.

It is the purpose of this chapter to analyse the behaviour of prices in futures markets. More specifically we offer a discussion on three interrelated questions:

1. How are futures prices formed?
2. Do futures prices follow a random walk?
3. What is the distribution of future prices?

## Pricing

Consider a representative futures market such as the futures market for gold. At the most elementary level, the answer to the question of how futures prices are formed is by supply and demand. But what are supply and demand in the context of a futures market?

Recall that trading in a futures market involves the buying and selling of well-designed contracts. Therefore, supply and demand refer to schedules of prices and corresponding quantities supplied and demanded for a specific contract of 100 ounces of gold of certain purity for delivery on a specific date. Buyers of this contract express their demand as a schedule of futures prices with corresponding quantities demanded for this contract while sellers express their supply, again as a schedule of futures prices with corresponding quantities offered for the same contract.

Given the special nature of futures markets with hedgers, speculators and market makers being the main participants, we can aggregate among all hedgers and speculators, some of whom may be sellers while others are buyers, and assume that hedgers are in the aggregate net sellers while speculators are net buyers. This is not an unrealistic assumption because hedging usually involves insuring an asset with a short futures position. Large commercial hedgers are usually short futures. To account for the possibility that hedgers may also be long futures, we aggregate all hedging positions and simply assume that the overall net position of hedgers is short, that is, volume of short positions by hedgers is larger than the volume of long positions. For a proper functioning of a futures market and formation of prices, this net short position must be met at equilibrium with a net long position initiated by speculators and market makers.

### An illustration

Suppose that the daily demand by speculators for the December gold futures contract is given by

$$P_s = 410 - 0.003\, Q_s \qquad\qquad (3.1)$$

where $P_s$ and $Q_s$ denote futures price and quantity of futures contracts traded by speculators.

Unlike the ordinary demand schedule of microeconomics where the intercept does not have any particular meaning other than describing the price at which no quantity is demanded, the number 410 in equation (3.1) reflects an expectation of speculators. Note that equation (3.1) describes the buying behaviour of speculators when the expected future spot price is below $410. If speculators have homogeneous expectations that the expected future spot price at the expiration of the December futures contract will be $410, then they will be buyers at lower December futures prices because buying low and selling at a higher expected price offers an expected gain. If, on the other hand, speculators have the same expectation about $410 but the December futures contract trades at higher prices, these speculators will become net sellers of the December futures. This is why equation (3.1) is graphed to illustrate that speculators can be either long or short depending on their expectations.

Consider next the supply offered by hedgers given by

$$P_h = 260 + 0.002\, Q_h \qquad\qquad (3.2)$$

where $P_h$ and $Q_h$ denote price and quantity of the supply schedule of hedgers. Notice that hedgers are net sellers only when the futures price is above $260. Below $260, hedgers reserve their position by becoming net buyers. For example, hedgers may believe that at expected future spot price below $260, commercial producers will not cover their marginal cost and thus gold futures contracts selling below $260 must be a buying opportunity.

Combining equations (3.1) and (3.2) we can solve for the equilibrium December futures price of $320 and equilibrium quantity of December futures contracts of 30,000. Graph 3.1 describes the analysis presented.

Next, suppose that speculators receive new information and revise their homogeneous expectations of the expected future spot price to $415. Their increased demand now is

$$P_s = 415 - 0.003\, Q_s \qquad\qquad (3.3)$$

which with the unchanged supply of equation (3.2) yields a new December futures price of $322, and a new equilibrium quantity of December futures contracts of 31,000. Thus, the increased expectations of speculators are incorporated into the December futures price.

This simple analysis has identified the critical factors in the formation of futures prices, that is the behaviour of hedgers and speculators and their expectations. As information flows into the market and as this information is used to revise the demand and supply schedules, futures prices incorporate the arrival of such information. Unlike non-futures markets where buyers and sellers seldom reverse their roles, in futures markets participants reverse their positions continuously.

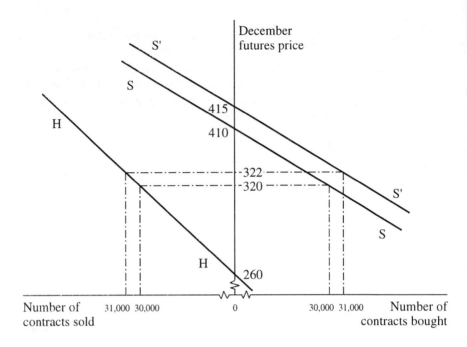

*Graph 3.1*

## Pricing models

The introductory analysis and numerical example of the last two sections incorporate two important elements of most pricing models, the risk transference and price discovery functions of futures markets.

The risk transference function refers to hedgers using futures contracts to minimize their risk exposure from price fluctuations of their production output or inventory. This behaviour is expressed as a supply function assuming that hedgers are in the aggregate net short sellers. The *risk transference* function is accomplished when speculators and market makers, at appropriate futures prices, buy futures contracts from hedgers. Such a transaction shifts the price risk from hedgers to speculators and establishes the risk transference role of futures markets.

The price discovery function of futures markets means that the formation of futures prices impacts the pricing in cash markets. Of course, cash prices also influence futures prices with such simultaneous price dynamics being determined by an arbitrage process. However, the influence of cash prices on futures prices is not surprising because futures are derivative markets whose existence depends on cash markets. What economists wish to emphasize by the price discovery property is that futures markets are certainly influenced by cash markets but more importantly they also influence cash markets. Furthermore these price dynamics involve not only cash and futures prices, that is the basis, but also current futures prices and expected future spot prices at the expiration of a given contract.

The interdependence between cash and futures markets is captured in the numerical illustration by the intercepts of equations (3.1) and (3.2) because such numbers denote the aggregate homogeneous expectations of speculators and hedgers about the expected future spot price. The expectations about cash prices at a future date when the futures contract will expire influence currently formed futures prices.

What needs to be emphasized is that the December futures price of $320 also offers valuable information to the cash market traders who, by using it in their trading, will cause the cash price to be impacted by the futures one. Futures traders' expectations about future spot prices corresponding to the expiration data of the futures contract will, along with other variables such as the elasticity of the demand and supply schedules in equations (3.1) and (3.2), determine futures prices. Expectations about future spot prices via futures trading translate into actual futures prices.

The ideas presented above have been formalized in numerous pricing models. Conceptually there are two broad categories of pricing models. The first group has its origin in the theory of storage of Kaldor (1939), Working (1948), Brennan (1958), Telser (1958) and others. According to the theory of storage, the difference between the contemporaneous spot and futures prices, that is the basis, for storable commodities can be explained in terms of interest and warehousing costs and a convenience yield on inventory. Let $F(t, T)$ and $S(t)$ denote futures price at time $t$ with settlement or expiration at $T$ and the spot price at time $t$, respectively. The theory of storage proposes the relationship

$$F(t, T) = S(t) [1 + R(t, T)] + W(t, T) - C(t, T) \qquad (3.4)$$

where $S(t) R(t, T)$ is the interest foregone, $W(t, T)$ is storage and insurance cost and $C(t, T)$ is the marginal convenience yield from an additional unit of inventory. Observe that the convenience yield arises because holding physical inventory could offer value when such inventory is needed to meet unexpected demand.

In contrast to the theory of storage, Cootner (1960), Dusak (1973) and others have proposed that the futures price can be expressed as

$$F(t, T) = S(t) + E_t[P(t, T)] + E_t[S(T) - S(t)]. \qquad (3.5)$$

In equation (3.5), the futures price is the sum of the spot price plus two additional terms. The term $E_t[P(t, T)]$ denotes an expected risk premium and $E_t[S(T) - S(t)]$ denotes an expectation or forecast of the spot price change between $t$ and the expiration $T$.

Fama and French (1987) discuss these two models in some detail and empirically test them for twenty-one agricultural, wood and animal products and metals. Their sample data range from early 1966 to mid-1984. Detailed statistical testing offers evidence in support of equation (3.4). For the second model in equation (3.5), the authors find evidence of forecast power for ten out of twenty-one commodities and time-varying expected risk premiums for only five commodities.

Garbade and Silber (1983) develop a model that describes the interrelationship between futures and spot prices. Under certain assumptions such as no taxes or transaction costs, no limitations on borrowing, no warehouse fees and no spoilage, no limitations on short sales and a term structure of interest rates that is flat, they derive an equation similar to (3.5) with the futures price being equal to the spot prices plus a premium. They then argue that such an equation would hold provided that the supply of arbitrage services was infinitely elastic. This means that if the equality between the futures price and cash price plus the premium, or more generally the equalities in equations (3.4) or (3.5), are violated, then a market participant can earn a riskless profit by following an appropriate strategy. The very large response by market participants to benefit from such a riskless arbitrage when the equality in the pricing model is violated is defined as an infinitely elastic supply of arbitrage.

For reasons such as transaction costs, taxes and possible non-availability of large credit, the response of traders to pricing violations is not infinitely elastic. Put differently, it is possible to observe significant deviations from pricing relationship of the type in equations (3.4) or (3.5). Garbade and Silber (1983) show that at one extreme, when there is no arbitrage, the spot and futures prices will follow uncoupled random walks which means that there will be no tendency for prices in the futures and cash markets to converge. In this extreme case, the risk transfer and price discovery functions of futures markets are eliminated.

At the other extreme, when arbitrage activities are highly elastic so that even the most minor price violation is immediately restored, the prices in futures and cash markets will follow identical random walks and there will be no meaningful economic distinction between them. For the intermediate cases, prices will follow an intertwined random walk. Empirical analysis by Garbade and Silber for seven commodities shows that all of the markets are well integrated over a period of one or two months but that there is considerable slippage between cash and futures markets over shorter periods, especially for grains. The gold and silver markets, however, are highly integrated even over one day.

At a more advanced level, Peck (1976) and more recently Stein (1992) offer pricing models for futures markets which extend the supply and demand relationships for hedgers and speculators by incorporating rational expectations. As a consequence of these models, the stabilizing role of the futures markets on cash markets can be clearly demonstrated. One way to show the stabilizing role of the futures market is first to develop supply and demand dynamics for the cash market that generate cobweb cycles. In the absence of a futures market, cobweb cycles occur because market participants have no alternative but to form their expectations from past price behaviour. However, in the presence of an active futures market, producers use the futures prices rather than lagged spot prices to make their decisions, thus creating convergent fluctuations that stabilize the cash market. A detailed proof is presented in Peck (1976) and Stein (1992).

**Futures and forwards prices**
The analysis presented and models discussed have exclusively emphasized the formation of futures prices. Contrary to popular opinion, forward prices are not always equal to futures prices. Often differences exist. French (1983) gives a comprehensive comparison of both the theoretical reasons and empirical evidence on this issue.

To motivate the pricing of a forward contract, which almost always involves physical delivery, consider the simple two-period case. Let $t$ denote today and $t + 1$, $t + 2$ denote the subsequent two periods. The contract will be executed on period $t + 2$. Denote by $V_{ij}$ the price of the asset when the economy is at state $i$ at $t + 1$ and at state $j$ at $t + 2$. Assume that both $i = 1,2$ and $j = 1,2$. In other words, we assume that the economy experiences two states in each period. Allowing more states is straightforward.

There are two relevant economic variables: $V_{ij}$, the price of the asset, and $r_{ij}$, interest rates. Schematically, use the following decision diagram:

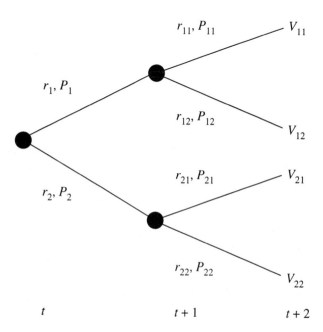

*Figure 3.1*

Figure 3.1 illustrates that moving from period $t$, now, to period $t + 1$, tomorrow, the economy's interest rates will go either to $r_1$, with probability $P_1$ or to $r_2$, with probability $P_2 = 1 - P_1$. From period $t + 1$ to $t + 2$, interest rates will go to $r_{11}$ or $r_{12}$, provided they were at $r_1$ at $t + 1$ (with probabilities $P_{11}$ and $P_{12}$ respectively) or to $r_{21}$ or $r_{22}$ (with probabilities $P_{21}$ and $P_{22}$ respectively), provided they were at $r_2$ at $t + 1$. The $V_{ij}$ denote expectations about the price of the asset at time $j$ provided that state $i$ of the economy materialized at time $t + 1$.

Since no money changes hands at time $t$, both the buyer and the seller of a forward contract are willing to transact if the present values of the expected price $V_{ij}$ and the forward price, denoted $G(t)$, are equal. Note that although $G(t)$, the forward price, is agreed upon today (at time $t$), it is paid at time $t + 2$; this explains why we consider present values. Such present values are given by

$$G(t) \left[ \frac{P_1 P_{11}}{(1+r_1)(1+r_{11})} + \frac{P_1 P_{12}}{(1+r_1)(1+r_{12})} + \frac{P_2 P_{21}}{(1+r_2)(1+r_{21})} + \frac{P_2 P_{22}}{(1+r_2)(1+r_{22})} \right]$$

$$= \frac{V_{11} P_1 P_{11}}{(1+r_1)(1+r_{11})} + \frac{V_{12} P_1 P_{12}}{(1+r_1)(1+r_{12})} + \frac{V_{21} P_2 P_{21}}{(1+r_2)(1+r_{21})} + \frac{V_{22} P_2 P_{22}}{(1+r_2)(1+r_{22})}. \tag{3.6}$$

From (3.6) we can immediately solve for the forward price $G(t)$ given below

$$G(t) = \frac{\dfrac{V_{11} P_1 P_{11}}{(1+r_1)(1+r_{11})} + \dfrac{V_{12} P_1 P_{12}}{(1+r_1)(1+r_{12})} + \dfrac{V_{21} P_2 P_{21}}{(1+r_2)(1+r_{21})} + \dfrac{V_{22} P_2 P_{22}}{(1+r_2)(1+r_{22})}}{\dfrac{P_1 P_{11}}{(1+r_1)(1+r_{11})} + \dfrac{P_1 P_{12}}{(1+r_1)(1+r_{12})} + \dfrac{P_2 P_{21}}{(1+r_2)(1+r_{21})} + \dfrac{P_2 P_{22}}{(1+r_2)(1+r_{22})}} \tag{3.7}$$

Having obtained the forward price for the simplified two-state, two-period case we next present the futures price.

Let $F(t)$ denote the futures price agreed upon today to be executed at period $t + 2$. What makes the computation of the futures price interesting is the *daily settlement* procedure. According to this procedure, administered by the Clearing House of futures exchanges, the futures contract, both for the buyer and the seller, is priced to market daily. Thus, if the futures price at $t + 1$ is $F_i$ with $i = 1,2$ denoting the state of the economy, then unless $F_i = F(t)$, the party in whose favour the price moved by $F_i - F(t)$ must immediately be paid this amount by the losing party. Recall that such a settlement does not occur in a forward market. The economic justification of daily settlement is explained by the desire of organized exchanges to reduce risk by allocating potential price changes across the life of the futures contract in lieu of a one time settlement at the maturity of the contract.

Using the same decision theoretic diagram as Figure 3.1, note that daily settlement means that the $F_i$, $i = 1,2$ must be adjusted by the amount

$$F_i - F(t) \tag{3.8}$$

which, if appropriately discounted should be a fair game with zero present value. In symbols,

$$\sum_i \frac{[F_i - F(t)] P_i}{1+r_i} = 0 \tag{3.9}$$

which yields that

$$F(t) = \frac{\dfrac{F_1 P_1}{(1+r_1)} + \dfrac{F_2 P_2}{(1+r_2)}}{\dfrac{P_1}{(1+r_1)} + \dfrac{P_2}{(1+r_2)}}. \tag{3.10}$$

So far, it appears that $F(t)$ in equation (3.10) resembles (3.7). However, note that $F_1$ and $F_2$ in (3.10) are each discounted values of asset prices expected to prevail at $t + 2$. For $i = 1,2$, observe that

$$F_i = \frac{\dfrac{V_{i1}P_{i1}}{1+r_{i1}} + \dfrac{V_{i2}P_{i2}}{1+r_{i2}}}{\dfrac{P_{i1}}{1+r_{i1}} + \dfrac{P_{i2}}{1+r_{i2}}}. \tag{3.11}$$

Put $F_i$, $i = 1,2$ of equation (3.11) in equation (3.10) and perform the necessary algebra to conclude that

$$F(t) = \frac{\dfrac{V_{11}P_1P_{11}}{(1+r_1)(1+r_{11})} + \dfrac{V_{12}P_1P_{12}}{(1+r_1)(1+r_{12})} + \dfrac{V_{21}P_2P_{21}}{(1+r_2)(1+r_{21})} + \dfrac{V_{22}P_2P_{22}}{(1+r_2)(1+r_{22})}}{\left[\dfrac{P_1}{1+r_1} + \dfrac{P_2}{1+r_2}\right]\left[\dfrac{P_1P_{11}}{1+r_{11}} + \dfrac{P_1P_{12}}{1+r_{12}} + \dfrac{P_2P_{21}}{1+r_{21}} + \dfrac{P_2P_{22}}{1+r_{22}}\right]}. \tag{3.12}$$

A simple comparison of equations (3.7) and (3.12) shows that both expressions have the same numerator. Therefore differences or similarities between $G(t)$ and $F(t)$ depend on the denominator. Fisher Black (1976) showed that when interest rates are nonstochastic, that is constant, then $G(t) = F(t)$. This is trivial to see from the explicit expression in equations (3.7) and (3.12). In general however, forward prices $G(t)$ need not be equal to futures prices $F(t)$.

**Efficiency**
The random walk behaviour of futures prices was initially suggested by Working (1934), who also developed a theory of anticipatory prices in Working (1958). The exhaustive literature on the random walk behaviour of asset prices is known as *market efficiency*. Despite the existence of several puzzling and conflicting results, in general, and in futures markets in particular, the theory of efficient markets remains a central pillar of modern financial economics.

Paul Samuelson (1965) developed the efficient market hypothesis to rationalize the random walk behaviour, whereby the current price fully reflects all relevant information. Since the flow of such information between now and the next period cannot be anticipated, efficient market price changes are serially uncorrelated. In other words, the randomness in price changes is caused by the random flow of unanticipated information.

During the past twenty years, the theory of market efficiency has been refined analytically, mathematically and statistically. The concept of information has been made more precise. The notion of random walk was generalized to martingales and Itô processes and numerous sophisticated statistical tests were employed to test the theory. Grossman and Stiglitz (1980) have addressed several important analytical issues of the theory of efficient markets. They argue that the notion of market efficiency is inconsistent with the reality of costly arbitrage. They develop a simple model with a constant absolute risk-aversion utility function and show that costless information is both necessary and sufficient for prices to fully reflect all available information. Efficient markets theorists realize that costless information is a sufficient condition for market efficiency. However, they are not always clear that it is also a necessary condition.

It is not surprising to find that along with numerous studies confirming market efficiency, there are many studies rejecting it. Two important surveys by Fama (1970) and (1991) review several aspects of the market efficiency debate. These apply to asset prices in general rather than to futures prices more specifically.

Among the numerous papers that studied the appropriateness of random walk or the martingale model on futures markets, we mention selectively the following: first, the Treasury-Bill, Treasury-Bond and gold futures markets were investigated by Chance (1985), Klemkosky and Lasser (1985), Cole, Impson and Reichenstein (1991), and MacDonald and Hein (1993); second, the Agricultural Commodities and Live Cattle markets were investigated by Leuthold (1972), Bigman, Goldfarb and Schechtman (1983), Canarella and Pollard (1985), Maberly (1985), Bird (1985), Elam and Dixon (1988) and Johnson, Zulauf, Irwin and Gerlow (1991); third, the metal futures market was investigated by Gross (1988) and Chowdhury (1991); fourth, the foreign currency markets were investigated by Glassman (1987), Ogden and Tucker (1987), Harpaz, Krull and Yagil (1990), and Lai and Lai (1991).

Evaluating the above studies one observes that many writers hold positive opinions on market efficiency. Chance (1985) believes that the Treasury-Bond futures market correctly anticipates the information contained in the announcement of the rate of change of the Consumer Price Index. MacDonald and Hein (1993) comment that the Treasury-Bill futures market may not be as inefficient as once presumed in terms of weak form efficiency, though this market does not provide optimal forecasts. Maberly (1985) demonstrates that in the grain futures markets, the inference that the market is inefficient for more distant futures contracts is due to the bias that results from using inappropriate statistical estimation methods. Elam and Dixon (1988) attack the inefficiency grain market argument using several Monte-Carlo experiments to demonstrate that very often the F-test tends to wrongly reject the true model. The research of Canarella and Pollard (1985) suggests that the efficient market hypothesis cannot be rejected for corn, wheat, soybeans and soybean oil. Gross (1988) claims that the hypothesis of efficient copper and aluminium markets cannot be rejected on the evidence of semi-strong efficiency tests. Saunders and Mahajan (1988) show that stock index futures pricing is efficient.

However, numerous investigators have identified evidence of market inefficiency. Leuthold (1972) concludes that his results cast serious doubt that cattle futures prices behave randomly. Bird (1985) discovers that for coffee and sugar the efficient market hypothesis is invalid and for cocoa there is also some evidence of inefficiency but of limited economic significance. Harpaz, Krull and Yagil (1990) perform tests for efficiency of the US Dollar Index futures contracts during the period 1985–8 which result in their rejection of the null hypothesis that this futures market is efficient during the period. By using methods of cointegration for the five major forward currency markets, Lai and Lai (1991) offer evidence not favourable to the joint hypothesis of market efficiency and no-risk premium. Goldenberg (1989) argues that the theory of market efficiency implies that futures prices have no memory. Yet his results show that intraday transaction prices of the S&P 500 Index futures contracts have memory. The empirical results presented in Chowdhury (1991) indicate the rejection of the efficient market hypothesis for four nonferrous metals – copper, lead, tin and zinc – not traded on the London Metal Exchange. Ma, Dare and Donaldson (1990) challenge the market efficiency hypothesis by confirming the presence of overreaction in several futures markets. They find that agricultural futures tend to overreact to significant events, whereas financial futures prices tend to underreact to significant events.

Finally, many authors have considered the appropriateness of the efficient market hypothesis for specific futures contracts in specific time periods. Bigman, Goldfarb and Schechtman (1983) believe that the market can be generally characterized as efficient for the futures contracts on wheat, soybeans and corn, six weeks before delivery or less. For longer-term futures contracts, their tests reject the market efficiency hypothesis. Johnson, Zulauf, Irwin and Gerlow (1991) use a combination of profit margin trading rules to test the market efficiency of the soybean complex. Their findings suggest that while nearby soybean complex futures price spreads are efficient, distant soybean complex futures price spreads are not efficient. The results of Klemkosky and Lasser's (1985) Treasury-Bond market efficiency tests do not agree totally with the conclusions drawn from earlier studies. Glassman (1987) reports evidence of joint multimarket inefficiency in foreign currency futures markets during some of the thirty-eight contract periods studied. Much of the inefficiency appeared to be short term in duration (one week or less). Cole, Impson and Reichenstein (1991) conclude that the Treasury-Bill futures rates provide rational one- and two-quarters-ahead forecasts of futures spot rate which are the forecast horizons that seem to be of most interest to the public. However, they believe the rationality of four-quarters-ahead futures forecasts should be rejected. Neftci and Policano (1984) investigate the effectiveness of technical analysis by examining the performance of two strategies: trendline and moving averages. Using daily observations for gold and Treasury Bills for about five years, they conclude that the moving average method has some predictive power while the results are mixed for the trendline approach.

Although the papers cited thus far investigate the market efficiency of futures trading, Cox (1976) investigates the effect of organized futures trading on the efficiency in spot markets. Cox develops a theoretical model and tests it for six different commodities. He shows that futures trading increases market information and contributes to market efficiency of the spot market. Cox confirms the value of the price discovery function of futures markets by demonstrating that a spot market becomes more efficient when there is futures trading.

**Price distributions**
The actual distribution of spot or futures price changes or returns is an issue of great importance. In an efficient market such returns are often postulated to be normally distributed. The theoretical foundations underlying such assumptions are not always clear. Most often, these assumptions are motivated by the methodology of statistical inference.

It was Bachelier (1900) who first constructed a random walk model for security and commodity prices. Bachelier assumed that successive price differences $P(t + dt) - P(t)$ are independent and normally distributed random variables with mean $\mu dt$ and variance $\sigma^2 dt$, that is

$$P(t + dt) - P(t) \sim N(\mu dt, \sigma^2 dt). \tag{3.13}$$

Later on, as a result of the empirical work of Osborne (1959), such normal distributions were replaced by the notion that asset returns are independent and log-normally distributed that is

$$\ln [P(t + dt) / P(t)] \sim N(\mu dt, \sigma dt). \tag{3.14}$$

This idea had a phenomenal impact on financial theory by introducing processes to describe the behaviour of security and futures prices. The Black–Scholes option pricing model is one of the most celebrated results of this tradition.

In a seminal paper, Mandelbrot (1963) proposed a radically new approach to the modelling of price variation. He replaced the normal distribution by another family of probability laws, referred to as *stable-Paretian*.

From the papers by Osborne (1959) and Mandlebrot (1963), followed Fama and Roll (1968, 1971) and numerous others. These are carefully reviewed in Akgiray and Booth (1988) with emphasis on stock returns. Although most papers reject the normal distribution hypothesis in favour of the stable-Paretian, studies exist that further reject the stable-Paretian, but not in favour of normality.

Earlier, Stevenson and Bear (1970) and Dusak (1973) offered evidence in support of the stable-Paretian distribution. More recently, Helms and Martell (1985), using data for commodities traded on the Chicago Board of Trade, conclude that returns of futures prices, although they are not normally distributed, are closer to normal than to other members of the family of Pareto distributions. Contrary to their results, Cornew, Town and Crowson (1984) claim that the stable-Paretian distribution offers a better fit for futures returns of several contracts than the normal distribution. Similarly, So (1987) confirms that currency futures and spot returns are stable-Paretian, while Hall, Brorsen and Irwin (1989) and Hudson, Leuthold and Sarassoro (1987) claim that futures returns are not stable-Paretian. Finally, Gribbin, Harris and Lau (1992) use a newly developed statistical methodology to conclude that futures prices are not stable-Paretian distributed.

## Chaos

The various empirical studies that have rejected the theory of market efficiency have also encouraged financial economists to seek alternative explanations for the time series behaviour of asset returns. This literature is known as the *chaotic dynamics* approach to asset returns. Several studies, such as Blank (1991) and DeCoster, Labys and Mitchell (1992), have offered evidence that futures prices appear to follow low dimensional chaotic dynamics. Below, some essential aspects of this new methodology are described.

The logical way to proceed in the analysis of chaotic dynamics is to give a precise definition. The definition given is purely mathematical and can be found in several books such as Devaney (1986). First, it is necessary to explain a few terms.

Consider a real-valued function $f : R \rightarrow R$. We are interested in the time series generated by this function starting from some arbitrary $x_0 \in R$. Denote by $f^2 \equiv f[f(x)] \equiv f o f(x)$ where $o$ means composition and in general let $f^n = f o f o \dots o f(x)$ mean $n$ compositions. The time series takes the values

$$x_0, f(x_0), f^2(x_0), \dots, f^n(x_0), \dots, \quad (3.15)$$

for $t = 0, 1, 2, \dots, n$. For equation (3.15) to describe a chaotic function it must satisfy three requirements.

First it must sample infinitely many values. To make this idea precise we say that $f : R \rightarrow R$ is *topologically transitive* if for any pair of open sets $U$ and $V$ in the real line $R$ there is an integer $k > 0$ such that $f^k(U) \cap V \neq \phi$.

The second requirement is sensitive dependence on initial conditions. We say that the function $f : R \rightarrow R$ has *sensitive dependence* on initial conditions if there exists a $\delta > 0$ such that for any $x \in R$ and any neighbourhood $N$ of $x$, there is a $y \in N$ and an integer $n > 0$ such that

$$|f^n(x) - f^n(y)| > \delta. \quad (3.16)$$

This condition says that there are time series that start very close to each other but diverge exponentially fast from each other.

The third requirement involves a property of the periodic points of the function $f$, namely that these periodic points are dense in $R$. We say that a point $x \in R$ is *periodic* if for $n > 0$, $f^n(x) = x$. The least positive integer $n$ for which $f^n(x) = x$ is called the *prime period* of $v$.

We can summarize our analysis by giving the definition of a chaotic function. We say that a function $f : R \rightarrow R$ is *chaotic* if it satisfies three conditions:

1. $f$ is topologically transitive.
2. $f$ has sensitive dependence on initial conditions.
3. $f$ has periodic points that are dense in the real numbers.

Observe that this is a precise mathematical definition which is not motivated by stock market price behaviour. Yet, each condition can be given a financial interpretation. The first condition requires the time series dynamics to be rich in the sense that it takes infinitely many different values. This condition makes a chaotic map similar to random walk because each value is different from all the previous ones. Of course, in random walk this happens because we are sampling from an infinite population. On the other hand, in chaotic dynamics we do not have sampling; instead we have a nonlinear equation that generates many different values. Note that for both the random walk and for the chaotic dynamics, it is possible for certain values to occur more than once in the time series. What we are emphasizing is that such a repetition is very unlikely. The first condition of topological transitivity requires the time series to be rich in the sense that it takes infinitely many different values. Intuitively, such a map can move under iteration, that is through time, from one arbitrarily small neigh-bourhood to any other. Since the space cannot be decomposed into two disjoint open sets which are invariant under the map (by definition), the points not only can wander anywhere (since they cannot be blocked) but actually will wander everywhere.

The second condition casts serious difficulties on forecasting. Although a chaotic map is deterministic and knowing today's value immediately allows one to compute tomorrow's price, the same exact equation can generate very dissimilar time series if we are uncertain about when the series got started and at what initial value $x_o$. To contrast with a random walk, recall that the past and future values are independent because we are sampling from an infinite population of values. The inability to forecast is due precisely to this statistical independence. In a chaotic function, however, we know exactly the relationship between the past and the future but we are unable to predict because we cannot be sure as to when we started and with what value.

The third condition gives a chaotic function structure. It essentially requires that the chaotic function exhibits important regularities. However, these regularities are hidden in the sense that no researcher could explore the infinite number of patterns of the periodic points and their limits. In an analogous manner, the random walk can be said to have some structure given to it by the properties of the distribution that characterizes the population. Again, no researcher could explore the infinite sample paths that a random walk process can generate. This analogy between the structure of a chaotic function and a random walk should not be understood as meaning that both have exactly the same structure. Although we do not know how to compare correctly the structure of a chaotic function to that of a random walk, a chaotic map involves infinite nonlinear iteration functions and, therefore, its structure could be viewed as being more complex compared to the structure of a random walk. More technically, one can argue that in chaotic dynamics because the set of periodic points is dense in $R$, for any point in $R$, there exists a sequence of periodic points which converges to this point. Thus, it appears intuitively that a structure exists because of the mere existence of the periodic points which cluster around each point in the domain. Therefore, due to the fact that periodic points are dense, each point in the domain can be identified by a sequence of periodic points, which converges to it. However, in the random walk case, each point is identified by its probability of occurrence which is described by the normal density function.

The mathematical result that makes chaotic dynamics very interesting is the existence of *strange attractors*. In studying various chaotic maps, mathematicians discovered that as time increases, despite the turbulent behaviour of such maps that appears random, the time series values indeed converge to a set. Furthermore, the set which, of course, depends on the specific map is not one of the standard sets of stability theory such as a point, a circle, or a torus. Because the attractors of chaotic maps are not as the regular attractors of ordinary differential equations, they were named *strange*.

A precise mathematical definition of a strange attractor is given in Guckenheimer and Holmes (1983) along with several beautiful illustrations. A simple definition of a *strange attractor* of a chaotic dynamical system is a compact set, denoted $S$, such that almost all initial conditions in the neighbourhood of $S$ converge to $S$. The neighbour-hood of $S$ from where almost all initial conditions yield time series that converge to $S$ is called the *basin of the strange attractor*.

The existence of a strange attractor implies that the randomness of chaotic dynamics has significant hidden structure. In contrast, the random walk behaviour of a time series describes uncertainty in a more extreme way than chaotic dynamics because a random walk series does not converge to a strange attractor but instead wanders forever. Naturally, the important empirical question is: Given a time series of futures prices, how can we distinguish whether it is generated by a random walk or a chaotic process?

There are several techniques that can be used. Brock and Malliaris (1989) give a brief description of these methods while Brock, Hsieh and LeBaron (1991) discuss them in detail. Here we plan to describe only one of the most fundamental techniques, called the correlation dimension, because it is used widely in the futures literature. This method was developed by Grassberger and Procaccia (1983).

Suppose that we are given a time series of price changes $\{dP(t) : t = 0, 1, 2, \ldots T\}$. Suppose that $T$ is large enough so that a strange attractor has begun to take shape. Use this time series to create pairs, that is $dP^2(t) \equiv \{ [dP(t), dP(t+1)] : t = 0, 1, 2, \ldots T\}$ and then triplets and finally M-histories, that is $dP^M(t) \equiv \{ [dP(t), \ldots dP(t+M-1)] : t = 0, 1, 2, \ldots T\}$. In other words we convert the original time series of singletons into vectors of dimension 2, 3, ... M. In generating these vectors we allow for overlapping entries. For example if $M = 3$, we have a set of the form $\{ [dP(0), dP(1), dP(2)], [dP(1), dP(2), dP(3)], \ldots [dP(T-2), dP(T-1), dP(T)] \}$. Such a set will have $(T+1) - (M-1)$ vectors. Mathematically, the process of creating vectors of various dimension from the original series is called an *embedding*.

Suppose that for a given embedding dimension, say $M$, we wish to measure whether these $M$-vectors fill the entire $M$-space or only a fraction. For a given $\varepsilon > 0$ define the *correlation integral*, denoted by

$$C^M(\varepsilon) = \frac{\textit{the number of pairs } (s, t) \textit{ whose distance } \| dP^M(s) - dP^M(t) \| < \varepsilon}{T^2_M} \tag{3.17}$$

$$= \frac{\textit{the number of } (s, t), \, 1 \leqslant t, \, S \leqslant T, \, \| dP^M(s) - dP^M(t) \| < \varepsilon,}{T^2_M}$$

where $T_M = (T+1) - (M-1)$, and as before

$$dP^M(t) = [dP(t), dP(t+1), \ldots, dP(t+M-1)].$$

Observe that $\| \cdot \|$ in (3.17) denotes vector norm. Using the correlation integral we can define the *correlation dimension* for an embedding dimension $M$ as

$$D^M = \lim_{\substack{\varepsilon \to 0 \\ T \to \infty}} \frac{\ln C^M(\varepsilon)}{\ln \varepsilon}. \tag{3.18}$$

In (3.18) ln denotes natural logarithm. Finally, the correlation dimension $D$ is given by

$$D = \lim_{M \to \infty} D^M. \tag{3.19}$$

Technical accuracy requires that $D^M$ in equation (3.18) is a double limit, first in terms of $T \to \infty$ and then in terms of $\varepsilon \to 0$. However, in practice $T$ is usually given and it is impossible to increase it to infinity. Thus the limit $T \to \infty$ is meaningless in practice and moreover $M$ is practically bounded by $T$. Therefore, we only consider the limit $\varepsilon \to 0$ in (3.18).

Blank (1991) discusses in detail the empirical aspects of the methodology of chaos and offers several calculations for soybeans and the S&P 500 futures contracts. His correlation dimension estimates are low and interpreted along with other techniques offer evidence that soybeans and the S&P 500 futures contracts have a chaotic non-linear generating process.

### Hedging

Suppose that a gold mining firm has a weekly output of 10,000 ounces of gold. Because the recent trend of spot gold pricing has been a gradually declining one, the gold producer decides to hedge his total weekly production in the futures market by selling 100 December futures contracts at $386.20. Table 3.1 summarizes the cash and futures position today and a week later.

*Table 3.1*

| Cash position | Futures position |
|---|---|
| *Today:* Anticipate output of 10,000 ounces in one week which if available today could be sold for $383.10 an ounce. | *Today:* Sell 100 December futures contracts of 100 ounces each for $386.20 |
| *A Week Later:* Output is produced and 10,000 ounces in the cash market for $378.00 an ounce. | *A Week Later:* Buy 100 December futures contracts of 100 ounces each for $381.10 |
| *Foregone cash receipts =*<br>10,000*5.10 = **$51,000** | *Profits from futures =*<br>100*100*5.10 = **$51,000** |

Notice that in the illustration of Table 3.1 the reduced cash receipts due to the drop in price from $383.10 today to $378.00 a week later are recovered exactly by the profits from the futures transactions. The two amounts of $51,000 are exactly equal because the difference between futures and cash prices today, called *basis*, is equal to $(386.20 - 383.10 = 3.10)$ and is the same a week later, that is $(381.10 - 378 = 3.10)$.

Motivated by this illustration we can now discuss two theories of hedging: the traditional and portfolio approaches. Let $P_s^1, P_f^1$ denote spot and futures prices today and $P_s^2, P_f^2$ be the corresponding prices next period. The units of the asset to be hedged are written as $X_s$.

First consider the unhedged position given by

$$U = X_s [P_s^2 - P_s^1] \tag{3.20}$$

which simply describes the profit or loss from the spot price change between two periods. Assuming that prices, both cash and futures, follow random walks or more generally martingales with mean zero and variances $\sigma_s^2$ and $\sigma_f^2$ respectively, the expectation and the risk of the unhedged position are

$$E(U) = E\{X_s[P_s^2 - P_s^1]\} = X_s\, E[P_s^2 - P_s^1] = X_s[E(P_s^2) - P_s^1] = 0 \qquad (3.21)$$

$$\mathrm{Var}(U) = X_s^2\, \sigma_s^2 > 0. \qquad (3.22)$$

Equation (3.21) says that because prices from one period to the next are as likely to increase as they are to decrease, the average gain or loss of an unhedged position is zero. However, the unhedged position remains risky because the variance of price changes is positive.

Next, consider the hedged position, $H$, assuming that the basis does not change as in the illustration of Table 3.1

$$H = X_s\,[P_s^2 - P_s^1] - X_f[P_f^2 - P_f^1]. \qquad (3.23)$$

In (3.23), let $X_s = X_f$ with futures position being the opposite of the cash. Taking the expectation and computing the risk of (3.23) write

$$E(H) = X_s[E(P_s^2) - P_s^1] - X_f[E(P_f^2) - P_f^1] = 0 \qquad (3.24)$$

$$\mathrm{Var}(H) = X_s^2\, \sigma_b^2 = 0. \qquad (3.25)$$

Note again that the expectation of the hedged position described in (3.24) is equal to zero, as in (3.21), for the same reason, namely, the martingale behaviour of cash and futures prices. But unlike (3.22), which expresses the positive risk of the unhedged position, (3.25) shows that the risk of the hedged position is nonexistent because $\sigma_b^2 = 0$. This means that the variance of the basis is zero which follows from the assumption that the basis is constant. Thus the traditional hedging approach described in (3.24) and (3.25) is preferred to the unhedged position in (3.21) and (3.22) because it eliminates risk. What causes risk to be totally eliminated is the assumption that the basis remains constant.

In an influential paper, Ederington (1979) analyses the general case of hedging when the basis does not remain constant. Using the general methodology of portfolio theory, Ederington formulates the hedging decision as follows: let $R$ denote the return on a portfolio that includes both a spot asset of a quantity $X_s$ and a futures asset of a quantity $X_f$. The quantities $X_s$ and $X_f$ need not be equal. Let

$$R = X_s\,[P_s^2 - P_s^1] - X_f[P_f^2 - P_f^1] \qquad (3.26)$$

denote the return from the cash and futures position. Usually the futures position is the opposite in sign to that of the cash, but in (3.26) there is no such restriction. Taking the expectation of (3.26) and using the martingale property of price behaviour, we obtain

$$E(R) = X_s E[P_s^2 - P_s^1] - X_f E[P_f^2 - P_f^1] = 0. \qquad (3.27)$$

The risk associated with (3.26) is given by

$$\text{Var}(R) = X_s^2 \sigma_s^2 + X_f^2 \sigma_f^2 + 2X_s X_f \sigma_{sf} \qquad (3.28)$$

where $\sigma_s^2$, $\sigma_f^2$ and $\sigma_{sf}$ denote the variance of differences in the spot price, futures price and covariance between spot and futures prices, respectively.

Let $b = [-X_f/X_s]$ denote the proportion of the spot quantity that is hedged. Using $b$, equation (3.28) can be rewritten as

$$\text{Var}(R) = X_s^2[\sigma_s^2 + b^2\sigma_f^2 - 2b\sigma_{sf}]. \qquad (3.29)$$

The objective is to minimize the risk in (3.29) by optimally choosing the hedge ratio $b$, that is

$$\partial \text{Var}(R)/\partial b = X_s^2[2 \, b\sigma_f^2 - 2\sigma_{sf}] = 0, \qquad (3.30)$$

which yields

$$b = \sigma_{sf}/\sigma_f^2. \qquad (3.31)$$

The result in (3.31) says that if the investor wishes to reduce the risk due to price fluctuations, she may choose the optimal hedge ratio in (3.31) computed as the covariance of spot and futures price differences over the variance of futures price differences. In practice (3.31) is also computed using ordinary least squares with spot price differences being the dependent variable and futures price differences being the independent variable. For more sophisticated methodologies of hedge ratio estimation see Myers (1991) and Adler and Detemple (1988). Marshall and Herbst (1992) also generalize the hedging decision in the context of portfolio selection. We conclude this section with an illustration.

Consider the following weekly spot and settlement futures prices of crude oil.

| Spot price in dollars per barrel | December *futures price* in dollars per barrel Traded at NYM; contract size 1000 barrels |
|---|---|
| 17.00 | 18.00 |
| 19.80 | 20.00 |
| 17.70 | 18.50 |
| 16.30 | 17.50 |
| 20.50 | 20.50 |
| 22.95 | 22.25 |
| 25.96 | 24.40 |
| 24.49 | 23.35 |
| 30.09 | 27.35 |
| 25.89 | 24.35 |

Suppose that an oil refinery buys 50,000 barrels of crude oil at $25.89 and to cover itself from the risk of a price drop in crude oil it immediately places a short hedge by selling futures contracts at $24.35 each. One week later the oil refinery sells the 50,000 barrels of crude oil at a spot price of $20.99 and closes its hedge by buying futures contracts at a price of $20.85.

There are two ways to compute the optimal hedge ratio $b$:

(a)  by using $\sigma_{sf}/\sigma_f^2$.
(b)  by using the regression analysis:

$$b = \frac{N \cdot \sum_{i=1}^{n} (F_i S_i) - (\sum_{i=1}^{n} F_i)(\sum_{i=1}^{n} S_i)}{N \cdot \sum_{i=1}^{n} F_i^2 - (\sum_{i=1}^{n} F_i)^2}.$$

| $i$ | Spot | Futures | $S_i$ | $F_i$ | $S_i {*} F_i$ | $F_i^2$ | $(S_i - \mu_s)$ | $(F_i - \mu_f)$ | $(F_i - \mu_f)^2$ | $(S_i - \mu_s)(F_i - \mu_f)$ |
|---|---|---|---|---|---|---|---|---|---|---|
| 0 | 17 | 18 | | | | | | | | |
| 1 | 19.8 | 20 | 2.8 | 2 | 5.6 | 4 | 1.812222 | 1.294444 | 1.675586 | 2.345821 |
| 2 | 17.7 | 18.5 | −2.1 | −1.5 | 3.15 | 2.25 | −3.08778 | −2.20556 | 4.864475 | 6.810265 |
| 3 | 16.3 | 17.5 | −1.4 | −1 | 1.4 | 1 | −2.38778 | −1.70556 | 2.90892 | 4.072488 |
| 4 | 20.5 | 20.5 | 4.2 | 3 | 12.6 | 9 | 3.212222 | 2.294444 | 5.264475 | 7.370265 |
| 5 | 22.95 | 22.25 | 2.45 | 1.75 | 4.2875 | 3.0625 | 1.462222 | 1.044444 | 1.090864 | 1.52721 |
| 6 | 25.96 | 24.4 | 3.01 | 2.15 | 6.4715 | 4.6225 | 2.022222 | 1.444444 | 2.08642 | 2.920988 |
| 7 | 24.49 | 23.35 | −1.47 | −1.05 | 1.5435 | 1.1025 | −2.45778 | −1.75556 | 3.081975 | 4.314765 |
| 8 | 30.09 | 27.35 | 5.6 | 4 | 22.4 | 16 | 4.612222 | 3.294444 | 10.85336 | 15.19471 |
| 9 | 25.89 | 24.35 | −4.2 | −3 | 12.6 | 9 | −5.18778 | −3.70556 | 13.73114 | 19.2236 |
| | Sum | | 8.89 | 6.35 | 70.0525 | 50.0375 | | | 45.55722 | 63.78011 |
| | Average | | 0.987778 | 0.705556 | | | | | | |

Using the data in the above worksheet, the first method yields:

$$\sigma_f^2 = \frac{\sum_{i=1}^{n} (F_i - \mu_f)^2}{N}, \quad \sigma_{sf} = \frac{\sum_{i=1}^{n} [(F_i - \mu_f)(S_i - \mu_s)]}{N}, \quad b = \frac{\sigma_{sf}}{\sigma_f^2} = \frac{63.78011}{45.55722} = 1.4$$

The second method yields:

$$b = \frac{N {*} \sum_{i=1}^{n} (F_i S_i) - (\sum_{i=1}^{n} F_i)(\sum_{i=1}^{n} S_i)}{N {*} \sum_{i=1}^{n} F_i^2 - (\sum_{i=1}^{n} F_i)^2} = \frac{9{*}70.0525 - 6.35{*}8.89}{9{*}50.0375 \, (-6.35)^2} = 1.4$$

The results of the traditional and optimal hedge are summarized in Tables 3.2 and 3.3.

*Table 3.2    Using the traditional hedge*

| Cash position | Futures position |
| --- | --- |
| *Today:*<br>Buy 50,000 barrels of crude oil at $25.89 | *Today:*<br>Sell 50 December futures contracts of 1000 barrels each at $24.35 |
| *A Week Later:*<br>The 50,000 barrels of crude oil are sold at $20.99. | *A Week Later:*<br>Buy 50 December futures contracts of 1000 barrels each at $20.85. |
| *Loss* = 50,000*4.90 = **$245,000** | *Profits from futures* =<br>50*1000*3.50 = **$175,000** |

*Table 3.3    Using the optimal hedge*

| Cash position | Futures position |
| --- | --- |
| *Today:*<br>Buy 50,000 barrels of crude oil at $25.89. | *Today:*<br>Sell 1.4*50 = 70 December futures contracts of 1000 barrels each at $24.35. |
| *A Week Later:*<br>The 50,000 barrels of crude oil are sold at $20.99. | *A Week Later:*<br>Buy 70 December futures contracts of 1000 barrels each at $20.85. |
| *Loss* = 50,000*4.90 = **$245,000** | *Profits from futures* =<br>70*1000*3.50 = **$245,000** |

## Conclusions

This chapter has asked the key question of how futures prices behave and has provided an extensive analysis. The behaviour of futures prices is determined in highly liquid futures markets where speculators, hedgers, arbitrageurs, market makers and other traders buy and sell well designed contracts via an open outcry continuous auction. This price formation is both affected by and also influences the underlying cash market and offers the valuable functions of price discovery and risk transference.

The behaviour of futures prices and their interrelationship with the underlying spot market have been conceptually presented in two broad categories of pricing models. The first category emphasizes the theory of storage which explains the difference between the contemporaneous spot and futures prices for storable commodities in terms of interest and warehousing costs and convenience yield on inventory. The second category expresses the futures price as the sum of the spot price plus two additional terms: an expected risk premium and a forecast of the spot price between now and the expiration of the futures contract.

Related to price behaviour is the central question of whether futures prices follow random walks. Actually some of the early work by Working (1934) described the random walk behaviour of futures prices long before such behaviour was considered for cash assets. The statistical behaviour of random walk and the financial theory of market efficiency are discussed. Several studies which investigate the appropriate applications of these theories are examined. The recent methodology of chaos is also presented.

Because futures prices vary in relation to cash prices and natural variations in cash prices create risk, the hedging activity emerges. Hedging occurs whenever an asset may decrease in value or an obligation may increase. This chapter offers a detailed analysis of hedging both for the simple case when the basis is constant and the more general case when the basis fluctuates.

Thus far, the price behaviour, market efficiency and hedging involved all futures markets. However, each of the existing numerous futures markets offers remarkable insights into the functioning and special characteristics of such specific markets. A valuable selection of individual markets is found in Roll (1984), Fama and French (1988), Stevens (1991) and Antoniou and Foster (1992).

## References

Adler, M. and J. Detemple (1988), 'Hedging with futures in an intertemporal portfolio context', *Journal of Futures Markets*, **8**, 249–69.

Akgiray, V. and G. Booth (1988), 'The stable law model of stock returns', *Journal of Business & Economic Statistics*, **6**, 51–7.

Antoniou, A. and A.J. Foster (1992), 'The effect of futures trading on spot price volatility: evidence for Brent Crude oil using garch', *Journal of Business Finance & Accounting*, **19**, 473–84.

Bachelier, L. (1900), 'Téorie de la spéculation', *Annales de l'Ecole Normale Supérieure*, 21–86.

Bigman, D., D. Goldfarb and E. Schechtman (1983), 'Futures market efficiency and the time content of the information sets', *Journal of Futures Markets*, **3**, 321–34.

Bird, P.J.W.N. (1985), 'Dependency and efficiency in the London terminal markets', *Journal of Futures Markets*, **5**, 433–46.

Black, F. (1976), 'The pricing of commodity contracts', *Journal of Financial Economics*, **3**, 167–79.

Blank, S. (1991), 'Chaos in futures markets? A nonlinear dynamical analysis', *Journal of Futures Markets*, **11**, 711–28.

Brennan, L. (1958), 'The supply of storage', *The American Economic Review*, **48**, 50–72.

Brock, W., D. Hsieh and B. LeBaron (1991), *Nonlinear Dynamics, Chaos and Instability: Statistical Theory and Economic Evidence*, Cambridge, MA: MIT Press.

Brock, W. and A.G. Malliaris (1989), *Differential Equations, Stability and Chaos in Dynamic Economics*, Advanced Textbooks in Economics, Amsterdam: North-Holland.

Canarella, G. and S.K Pollard (1985), 'Efficiency of commodity futures: a vector autoregression analysis', *Journal of Futures Markets*, **5**, 57–76.

Chance, D.M. (1985), 'A semi-strong form test of the efficiency of treasury bond futures market', *The Journal of Futures Markets*, **5**, 385–405.

Chowdhury, A.R. (1991), 'Futures market efficiency: evidence from cointegration tests', *The Journal of Futures Markets*, **11**, 577–89.

Cole, C.S., M. Impson and W. Reichenstein (1991), 'Do treasury bill futures rates satisfy rational expectation properties?', *The Journal of Futures Markets*, **11**, 591–601.

Cootner, P.H. (1960), 'Returns to speculators: Telser vs. Keynes', *Journal of Political Economy*, **68**, 396–404.

Cornew, R., D. Town and L. Crowson (1984), 'Stable distribution, futures prices, and the measurement of trading performance', *The Journal of Futures Markets*, **4**, 531–57.

Cox, Charles C. (1976), 'Futures trading and market information', *Journal of Political Economy*, **84**, 1215–37.

DeCoster, G.P., W.C. Labys and D.W. Mitchell (1992), 'Evidence of chaos in commodity futures prices', *The Journal of Futures Markets*, **12**, 291–305.

Devaney, R. (1986), *An Introduction to Chaotic Dynamical Systems*, Menlo Park, CA: Benjamin/Cummings Publishing.

Dusak, K. (1973), 'Futures trading and investor returns: an investigation of commodity market risk premiums', *Journal of Political Economy*, **81**, 1387–405.

Ederington, L.H. (1979), 'The hedging performance of the new futures markets', *Journal of Finance*, **34**, 157–70.

Elam, E. and B.L. Dixon (1988), 'Examining the validity of a test of futures market efficiency', *The Journal of Futures Markets*, **8**, 365–72.

Fama, E.F. (1970), 'Efficient capital markets: review of theory and empirical work', *Journal of Finance*, **25**, 383–417.

Fama, E.F. (1991), 'Efficient capital markets: II', *Journal of Finance*, **70**, 1575–617.

Fama, E.F. and R. Roll (1968), 'Some properties of symmetric stable distributions', *Journal of the American Statistical Association*, **63**, 817–36.

Fama, E.F. and R. Roll (1971), 'Parameter estimates for symmetric stable distributions', *Journal of the American Statistical Association*, **66**, 331–8.

Fama, E.F. and K.R. French (1987), 'Commodity futures prices: some evidence on forecast power, premiums, and the theory of storage', *Journal of Business*, **60**, 55–73.

Fama, E.F. and K.R. French (1988), 'Business cycles and the behavior of metals prices', *Journal of Finance*, **43**, 1075–93.

French, K.R. (1983), 'A comparison of futures and forwards prices', *Journal of Financial Economics*, **12**, 311–42.

Garbade, K.D. and W.L. Silber (1983), 'Price movements and cash discovery in futures and cash markets', *Review of Economics and Statistics*, **65**, 289–97.

Glassman, D. (1987), 'The efficiency of foreign exchange futures markets in turbulent and non-turbulent periods', *The Journal of Futures Markets*, **7**, 245–67.

Goldenberg, David H. (1989), 'Memory and equilibrium futures prices', *The Journal of Futures Markets*, **9**, 199–213.

Grassberger, P. and I. Procaccia (1983), 'Measuring the strangeness of strange attractors', *Physics*, vol. 9-D, 189–208.

Gribbin, D.W., R.W. Harris and H.S. Lau (1992), 'Futures prices are not stable-Paretian distributed', *The Journal of Futures Markets*, **12**, 475–87.

Gross, M. (1988), 'A semi-strong test of the efficiency of the aluminium and copper markets at the LME', *The Journal of Futures Markets*, **8**, 67–77.

Grossman, S.J. and J.E. Stiglitz (1980), 'On the impossibility of informationally efficient markets', *The American Economic Review*, **70**, 393–408.

Guckenheimer, J. and P. Holmes (1983), *Non Linear Oscillations, Dynamical Systems and Bifurcations of Vector Fields*, New York: Springer-Verlag.

Hall, J., B. Brorsen and S. Irwin (1989), 'The distribution of futures prices: a test of the stable Paretian and mixture of normals hypothesis', *Journal of Financial and Quantitative Analysis*, **24**, 105–16.

Harpaz, G., S. Krull and J. Yagil (1990), 'The efficiency of the U.S. dollar index futures market', *The Journal of Futures Markets*, **10**, 469–79.

Helms, B.P. and T.F. Martell (1985), 'An examination of the distribution of futures price changes', *The Journal of Futures Markets*, **5**, 259–72.

Hudson, M., R. Leuthold and G. Sarassoro (1987), 'Commodity futures prices changes: recent evidence for wheat, soybeans, and live cattle', *The Journal of Futures Markets*, **7**, 287–301.

Johnson, R.L., C.R. Zulauf, S.H. Irwin and M.E. Gerlow (1991), 'The soybean complex spread: an examination of market efficiency from the viewpoint of a production process', *The Journal of Futures Markets*, **11**, 25–37.

Kaldor, N. (1939), 'Speculation and economic stability', *Review of Economic Studies*, **7**, 1–27.

Klemkosky, R.C. and D.J. Lasser (1985), 'An efficiency analysis of the T-bond futures market', *The Journal of Futures Markets*, **5**, 607–20.

Lai, K.S. and M. Lai (1991), 'A cointegration test for market efficiency', *The Journal of Futures Markets*, **11**, 567–75.

Leuthold, Raymond M. (1972), 'Random walk and price trends: the live cattle futures market', *Journal of Finance*, **27**, 879–89.

Ma, C.K., W.H. Dare and D.R. Donaldson (1990), 'Testing rationality in futures markets', *The Journal of Futures Markets*, **10**, 137–52.

Maberly, E.D. (1985), 'Testing futures market efficiency. A restatement', *The Journal of Futures Markets*, **5**, 425–32.

MacDonald, S.S. and S. E. Hein (1993), 'An empirical evaluation of treasury bill futures market efficiency: evidence from forecast efficiency tests', *The Journal of Futures Markets*, **13**, 199–211.

Mandelbrot, B. (1963), 'The variation of certain speculative prices', *Journal of Business*, **36**, 394–419.

Marshall, J.F. and A.F. Herbst (1992), 'A multiperiod model for selection of a futures portfolio', *The Journal of Futures Markets*, **12**, 411–28.

Myers, Robert (1991), 'Estimating time-varying optimal hedge ratios on futures markets', *The Journal of Futures Markets*, **11**, 39–53.

Neftci, S.N. and A.J. Policano (1984), 'Can chartists outperform the market? Market efficiency tests for "technical analysis"', *The Journal of Futures Markets*, **4**, 465–78.

Ogden, J.P. and A. Tucker (1987), 'Empirical tests of the efficiency of the currency futures options market', *The Journal of Futures Markets*, **7**, 695–703.

Osborne, M.F.M. (1959), 'Brownian motion in the stock market', *Operations Research*, **7**, 145–73.

Peck, Anne E. (1976), 'Futures markets, supply response, and price stability', *Quarterly Journal of Economics*, **90**, 407–23.

Roll, R. (1984), 'Orange juice and weather', *The American Review*, **74**, 861–80.

Samuelson, P. (1965), 'Proof that properly anticipated prices fluctuate randomly', *Industrial Management Review*, **6**, 41–9.

Saunders, E.M. and A. Mahajan (1988), 'An empirical examination of composite stock index futures pricing', *The Journal of Futures Markets*, **8**, 210–28.

So, J. (1987), 'The sub-Gaussian distribution of currency futures: stable Paretian or non-stationary?', *Review of Economics and Statistics*, **69**, 100–07.

Stein, J.L. (1992), 'Cobwebs, rational expectations and futures markets', *Review of Economics and Statistics*, **74**, 127–34.

Stevens, S.C. (1991), 'Evidence for a weather persistence effect on the corn, wheat, and soybean growing season price dynamics', *The Journal of Futures Markets*, **11**, 81–8.

Stevenson, R.A. and R.M. Bear (1970), 'Commodity futures: trends or random walks?', *Journal of Finance*, **25**, 65–81.

Telser, L.G. (1958), 'Futures trading and the storage of cotton and wheat', *Journal of Political Economy*, **66**, 233–55.

Working, H. (1934), 'A random-difference series for use in the analysis for time series', *Journal of the American Statistical Association*, **29**, 11–24.

Working, H. (1948), 'Theory of the inverse carrying charge in futures markets', *Journal of Farm Economics*, **30**, 1–28.

Working, H. (1958), 'A theory of anticipatory prices', *American Economic Review*, **48**, 188–99.

# [4]

# Financial futures: a global innovation

## Introduction

*Financial futures* is a term that describes contracts in interest rate sensitive instruments such as Treasury Bills, Eurodollars, Treasury Notes or Treasury Bonds, or stock indexes such as the S&P 500 Index, the Value Line Index or the Nikkei 225 Stock Index, or foreign currencies such as the Japanese Yen, the German Mark or the British Pound.

The long evolution of futures markets dates back to the establishment of the Osaka Rice Exchange during the seventeenth century. However, financial futures are a relatively new innovation that began in 1972, with the inauguration of the International Monetary Market at the Chicago Mercantile Exchange.

The success of these financial futures has been remarkable as witnessed by the phenomenal growth of the volume of contracts traded which has significantly surpassed the volume of contracts traded in traditional futures markets such as agricultural, metallurgical and energy futures markets. Furthermore, the rapid volume growth of financial futures is not a phenomenon experienced only in US futures exchanges. Several non-US futures exchanges, such as the London International Financial Futures Exchange (LIFFE), the Paris Marche à Terme International de France (MATIF) and the Tokyo International Financial Futures Exchange (TIFFE), have actively traded financial futures contracts. Thus, the impressive success of these new instruments is indeed a global innovation.

How can all these developments be explained? Miller (1986) argues that the major impulses have come from deregulation and taxation. It is known that in the USA the collapse of the Bretton Woods International Monetary System in 1971 eliminated fixed exchange rates. The old system of fixed exchange rates was replaced by the managed float – a system allowing exchange rates to be flexible within certain target bands. These bands were frequently reviewed by the appropriate monetary and treasury authorities of several advanced industrialized countries. The collapse of fixed exchange rates and the introduction of flexible ones essentially deregulated foreign currencies by allowing foreign currency markets to determine rates instead of holding governments responsible for maintaining fixed exchange rates.

Flexible exchange rates and speculation about the frequent realignment of key world currencies created exchange rate uncertainty which in turn generated the need for hedging and the opportunity to speculate.

A few years after the introduction of flexible exchange rates came the removal of certain interest rate ceilings and the deregulation of the US Savings and Loan industry as well as the Banking industry. These changes were partially the result of increasing interest rates caused by the restrictive monetary policy of the Federal Reserve Bank under Paul Volcker during the late 1970s and early 1980s. During these few years, the USA and several other major industrial countries experienced high inflation and great interest rate volatility for both the short and long ends of the yield curve. Again such interest rate volatility encouraged hedging and speculation in interest sensitive financial instruments.

Further deregulation of US markets, along with substantial tax cuts during the first term of the Reagan Administration, generated rapid economic growth and substantial increases in the prices of US stock equities. This volatility in the various US stock indexes naturally led to portfolio hedging and speculation. The 19 October 1987 stock market crash further intensified the demand for stock index derivative instruments.

The US deregulation and tax reform during the last twenty years has also been spread to Europe and, to a lesser degree, to Japan. For example, the Single European Act of 1992 may be viewed as a bold step towards integration of the goods, services and labour markets of the fifteen members of the European Union but also towards deregulation of their capital markets.

All these briefly described remarkable changes in the US and elsewhere, along with rapid improvements in computer technology, have contributed to the free price movement of financial assets driven by market forces rather than being constrained by regulatory restrictions. Such free price movements, in turn, have fuelled the global growth of financial futures.

It is the purpose of this chapter to offer an overview of the fundamental concepts related to stock indexes, interest rate sensitive financial instruments and foreign currencies. Related to stock indexes are the important topics of portfolio hedging and index arbitrage. The October 1987 crash is also reviewed.

## Stock indexes

There are several futures contracts based on popular stock indexes. Four well-known indexes are the S&P 500 Index, the New York Stock Exchange Composite Index, the Nikkei 225 Index and the Major Market Index.

The *S&P 500 Index* is a value weighted index with each of the 500 stocks being weighted in proportion to the market value of all outstanding shares. For example

$$\text{S\&P 500 Index at time } t = \frac{\sum_{i=1}^{500} N_{i,t} P_{i,t}}{\text{O.V.}} * 10$$

where $N_{i,t}$ is the number of outstanding shares of firm $i$ at time $t$; $P_{i,t}$ is the price per share of firm $i$ at time $t$ and O.V. denotes the base original valuation in 1941–3.

The *New York Stock Exchange Index* is broader than the S&P 500 Index and includes all the stocks listed on the New York Stock Exchange. This is also a value weighted index similar to the S&P 500 Index.

The *Nikkei 225 Index* is a price weighted index that gives a weight to each stock that is proportional to its price. It includes the largest 225 Japanese firms. Another popular index which is also price weighted is the *Major Market Index*. It consists of twenty stocks chosen from the list of thirty stocks included in the Dow Jones Industrial Average. The formula for a typical price weighted index is

$$\text{Index at time } t = \frac{\sum_{i=1}^{N} P_{i,t}}{\text{Divisor}}$$

where $P_{i,t}$ denotes the price of a given stock $i$ and time $t$ with a total of $N$ stocks. The divisor is used to adjust for stock splits, stock dividends and other changes.

Consider the S&P 500 Stock Index futures contract traded at the Chicago Mercantile Exchange. It is currently the most active stock index futures contract. The first important concept to discuss is the pricing of stock index futures.

Following Cornell and French (1983), first assume that capital markets are perfect, that is that there are no taxes or transaction costs, there are no restrictions on short sales and assets are perfectly divisible. Let $r$ denote the risk free borrowing and lending rate, both assumed to be equal and constant. Furthermore assume that there are no dividends.

Under these simplifying assumptions, the *price of a stock index futures* contract at time $t$ with maturity at time $T$, denoted by $F(t, T)$ is given by

$$F(t, T) = S(t)\, e^{r(T-t)} \tag{4.1}$$

where $S(t)$ is the cash stock index at time $t$. This equation holds because the cost of carry for a non-dividend paying stock index is the risk free interest rate.

Introducing dividends to equation (4.1) is straightforward. Let $d$ denote the annualized dividend yield. Then (4.1) becomes

$$F(t, T) = S(t)\, e^{(r-d)(T-t)} \tag{4.2}$$

which says that dividends partially offset the interest cost of carry. In other words an investor who purchases the cash stock index and carries it until the stock index futures contract expires at $T$ foregoes the interest on her funds but she receives the dividends during the holding period $(T - t)$.

Cornell and French extend equation (4.2) to include taxes and then examine empirically the validity of their pricing model. They conclude that their theoretical model consistently overpredicts the observed futures prices. They explain this overprediction by acknowledging that their pricing model fails to consider the timing option. This refers to the option the stockholders have to reduce their taxes by realizing capital losses and deferring capital gains. Investors who hold futures contracts do not have this timing option because all capital gains and losses must be realized either by the maturity of the futures contract or at the end of the year, whichever comes first. Once this tax option is included in the model, the predicted futures prices are reduced.

Stoll and Whaley (1990) develop a relationship like (4.2) and then convert it into returns by using (4.2) and

$$F(t-1, T) = S(t-1)\, e^{(r-d)[T-(t-1)]}, \tag{4.3}$$

which expresses (4.2) at time $t - 1$. Divide (4.2) by (4.3) to obtain

$$\frac{F(t, T)}{F(t-1, T)} = \frac{S(t)}{S(t-1)} e^{(r-d)[(T-t)-(T-t+1)]}. \tag{4.4}$$

Simplify (4.4) and let $R_{F,t} = \ln[F(t, T) - F(t-1, T)]$ and $R_{S,t} = \ln[S(t) - S(t-1)]$ to conclude

$$R_{F,t} = R_{S,t} - (r-d). \tag{4.5}$$

Note that equation (4.5) implies that the rate of return on the futures contract equals the rate of return on the cash stock index less the net cost of carry.

Equation (4.5) offers additional theoretical implications. For example, the standard deviation of the rate of return on futures equals the standard deviation of the rate of return on the cash index. Also the contemporaneous rates of return $R_{F,t}$ and $R_{S,t}$ are perfectly positively correlated. These and possibly more implications are based on the validity of (4.5) for all periods $t$.

Extensive empirical research by Stoll and Whaley (1990), Kawaller, Koch and Koch (1987) and others offers evidence that index futures returns tend to lead the cash index by about a few minutes. This evidence supports the notion that futures markets, in general, and index futures, in particular, are impacted on first by the flow of new information, primarily because of the depth of their liquidity.

Subrahmanyam (1991) offers a detailed theoretical model to explain the immense liquidity of the S&P 500 Index futures and its informational role. The central idea of the model is that stock index futures trading offers a preferred trading medium to uninformed liquidity traders because their losses due to adverse trades with informed traders will usually be lower in this stock index futures market than the cash market for individual stocks.

**Arbitrage**

Can violations of equation (4.5) occur? Transactions costs and taxes can cause violations. Institutional factors such as the infrequent trading of certain stocks in the index can cause the stock price index to lag actual developments which could possibly be incorporated faster into the futures index. Furthermore, any cash stock index, such as the S&P 500 Stock Index, involves time delays in the continuous computation and reporting of the index as it represents all the actual individual stock transactions.

When discrepancies occur in equations (4.3) or (4.5), or similar models between cash and futures indexes or their returns, then arbitrage opportunities arise. For example if the actual futures index price exceeds its theoretical value calculated from a model such as (4.3), traders may consider buying the cash (a basket of 500 stocks) and selling the expensive futures index. Alternatively, if the actual futures index price is lower than its theoretical value, traders may buy futures index contracts and sell the cash index.

These arbitrage strategies in stock index futures and cash index are known as *index arbitrage*. Because this form of arbitrage is often executed by using computer programs it is called *program trading*. Approximately 10 per cent of the daily volume of stock shares traded at the New York Stock Exchange is attributed to program trading.

Obviously, computer trading relies on pricing models that are significantly more complicated than the ones developed in the previous section. Such models take into account tax considerations and transaction costs for cash equities and futures. They also address the uncertain behaviour of dividends and interest rates. Some of these aspects are presented in a theoretical paper by Brennan and Schwartz (1990) who develop an optimal strategy for index arbitrage and illustrate it using simulations.

MacKinlay and Ramaswamy (1988) offer evidence of substantial and sustained discrepancies between cash and futures indexes in the USA, while Yadav and Pope (1990) confirm similar results for London's FTSE-100 contract traded at LIFFE.

**Portfolio insurance**
Portfolio insurance in its simplest form involves a securities position comprised of an underlying portfolio plus an insurance policy designed to limit portfolio loss through a specified expiration date. For example the stop-loss strategy is an elementary form of portfolio insurance. In this case, the portfolio is liquidated if it drops below a certain value over some time interval, thus avoiding further losses. Such a portfolio insurance strategy can protect the portfolio against losses but has several disadvantages, such as execution difficulties, transaction costs, tax considerations, timing of re-entry and others.

More generally, *portfolio insurance* refers to a collection of techniques applied to ensure that the value of a portfolio does not drop below a specific level. Among these techniques the concept of short hedging is quite relevant.

To illustrate the concept of portfolio insurance in its short hedging form consider a portfolio manager who wishes to protect her $100 million portfolio from a possible market correction during the next two weeks. Suppose that this portfolio is passively managed by being indexed to the S&P 500 Index. Thus the beta of the portfolio is equal to one.

As in the case of protecting agricultural, metallurgical or energy assets, the portfolio manager can sell short the S&P 500 Index Futures. Such a short hedge is summarized in Table 4.1.

*Table 4.1   Portfolio short hedge*

| Stock market | Futures market |
| --- | --- |
| *Today:*<br>Hold $100 Million portfolio indexed to S&P 500.<br>Cash S&P 500 Index is 501.20. | *Today:*<br>Sell 399 S&P December futures contracts @ 502.75. |
| *Two weeks later:*<br>Portfolio has declined by 7.25 per cent cent to $92,750,000<br>Cash Index is 464.86. | *Two weeks later:*<br>Buy 399 S&P December futures contracts @ 466.40. |
| *Portfolio loss* = **–$7,250,000** | *Profit* = 399*500* [502.75 – 466.40]<br>= **$7,251,825** |
| *Net profit*: **$1,825** ||

To explain Table 4.1 first note that the S&P 500 futures contract traded at the Chicago Mercantile Exchange is priced by multiplying the value of the index by $500. Also recall that the value of the futures contract is usually higher than the cash S&P 500 Index. Let the S&P 500 Index be 501.20 and let the S&P 500 December futures Index be 502.75. This means the basis is equal to 1.55.

The manager uses the formula

$$\text{Number of contracts} = \frac{V_P}{V_C} = \frac{\$100,000,000}{501.20*500} = 399.04 \qquad (4.6)$$

Observe that equation (4.6) converts the $100 million portfolio to a certain number of contracts where $V_P$ denotes value of the portfolio and $V_C$ denotes value of the cash index. Because $V_C$ cannot be traded as an index, often (4.6) is used with a denominator $V_F$ denoting the value of the futures contract. Thus instead of (4.6) one can also use

$$\frac{V_P}{V_F} = \frac{\$100,000,000}{502.75*500} = 397.81. \qquad (4.7)$$

Obviously, the difference between equations (4.6) and (4.7) is insignificant.

Once the appropriate number of futures contracts is determined using equations (4.6) or (4.7), the remainder of Table 4.1 is simple. The manager enters a short hedge to protect her portfolio from a potential loss. The period of portfolio insurance can vary from a few days to the expiration of the futures contract. If further insurance is needed, the manager may roll into futures contracts having later expiration dates.

Suppose that a correction of −7.25 per cent materializes over two weeks after the short hedge is placed and at that point the manager no longer worries about further declines. Thus, she closes the short position by purchasing index futures contracts. Note that the cash loss of $7,250,000 has been offset by the futures gain of $7,251,825. Is this always possible?

A short hedge such as the one in Table 4.1 works well provided the basis remains constant (see Chapter 3). Recall that the basis today is 1.55 and two weeks later it is also 1.55 (ie 466.40 − 464.85 = 1.55). If the basis is variable then an optimal hedge ratio must be computed using the portfolio approach. Then equations (4.6) or (4.7) must be adjusted by this optimal hedge ratio, denoted as $\beta_F$, to become

$$\text{Number of contracts} = \frac{V_P}{V_C} * \beta_F. \qquad (4.8)$$

A final adjustment is required when the particular portfolio hedged has a beta that is different from the index used as a proxy for the market. Letting $\beta_P$ denote the beta of the specific portfolio relative to the S&P 500 Index, then (4.8) becomes

$$\text{Number of contracts} = \frac{V_P}{V_C} * \beta_F * \beta_P \qquad (4.9)$$

Table 4.2 illustrates (4.8) and (4.9).

*Table 4.2    Portfolio short hedge with $\beta_F$ and $\beta_p$*

| Stock market | Futures market |
| --- | --- |
| *Today:* <br> Hold $100 Million on Technology portfolio. <br> Cash S&P 500 Index is 501.20. | *Today:* <br> Sell 546 S&P December futures contracts @ 503.75. |
| *Two weeks later:* <br> Portfolio has declined by 9.36% to $90,640,000 <br> Cash S&P 500 Index is 468.60. | *Two weeks later:* <br> Buy 546 S&P December futures contracts @ 469.45. |
| *Portfolio loss = –$9,360,000* | *Profit* = 546*500* [503.75 – 469.45] <br> = **$9,363,900** |
| | *Net profit* = **$3,900** |

Consider a portfolio manager whose $100 million Technology portfolio has a beta of $\beta_p = 1.44$. Let the optimal hedge ratio be $\beta_F = 0.95$ and suppose that today's S&P 500 cash Index and December futures are 501.20 and 503.75 respectively with a basis of 2.55. Two weeks later the S&P 500 Index has declined by 6.5 per cent to 468.60 and the S&P 500 December futures Index is at 469.45, that is, the basis has decreased to 0.85. The portfolio has experienced a greater decline because of its higher beta. Suppose that the portfolio loss is $9,360,000, that is 9.36 per cent. Note that given $\beta_F = 0.95$ and $\beta_p = 1.44$, equation (4.9) yields

$$\text{Number of contracts} = \frac{\$100,000,000}{501.20*500} * (0.95) * (1.44) = 546. \qquad (4.10)$$

If instead of using equation (4.10) with its adjustments for $\beta_F$ and $\beta_p$, equation (4.6) was used and the portfolio manager had sold 399 contracts instead of 546, observe that such a short hedge would not have provided sufficient insurance for this Technology portfolio. A simple calculation yields 399* [503.75 – 469.45] *500 = 6,842,850 as the profit from the futures position which is significantly lower than the profit in Table 4.2.

Table 4.2 underscores the importance of changes in the basis and the role of the portfolio's beta when hedging with stock index futures. These issues are further discussed by Figlewski (1984) who also analyses the impact of hedging horizons. For example, Figlewski reports that one day hedges were subject to much higher basis risk than one week hedges.

Having illustrated the concept of a short hedge as a simple way to manage the risk of portfolio losses, we can now evaluate its effectiveness. Obviously, if a manager correctly anticipates a portfolio decline, an appropriate short hedge using equation (4.9) can be quite effective. But what if an anticipated loss does not materialize and instead the portfolio increases in value while a short hedge is also in place? In such a case, cash profits are offset by losses from the short hedge. To avoid such cases, *dynamic hedging* is often used by portfolio managers who, at each period, choose to increase or decrease the fraction of their portfolio that is insured by a futures position.

A different approach that allows portfolio protection from a decline without eliminating profits from a rise is the use of put options on an index. These puts are costly however. Merrick (1988) reviews several important issues related to portfolio insurance for both stock index futures and also puts. Finally Brennan and Schwartz (1988) address the issue of time-invariant portfolio insurance strategies. These are portfolio insurance strategies that do not depend on a fixed time horizon. An overall evaluation of portfolio insurance methods is given in Bookstaber and Langsam (1988).

## Volatility and the October 1987 crash

On Black Monday, 19 October 1987, in less than four hours the US stock market lost about 1.5 trillion dollars, five times the amount of the US annual budget deficit at that time. This dramatic and surprising 23 per cent decline, as measured by the S&P 500 Index, renewed several old claims that cash market volatility increases because of the derivatives markets.

The impact of a futures market on the price volatility of the cash market is, of course, an old topic studied by numerous economists. Kaldor (1939) has argued that under certain conditions a futures market could destabilize the cash market. More specifically, Kaldor claims that if we distinguish between skilled and unskilled speculators and assume that the skilled speculators try to anticipate the behaviour of the unskilled speculators, instead of assessing market fundamentals, such a behaviour may increase market volatility.

Actually even before Kaldor (1939), Taussig (1921) introduced the concept of *feedback trading*. Taussig states that speculators tend to buy as prices are rising and tend to sell as prices are falling. The additional buying when prices are rising generates positive feedback and causes prices to go even higher. Similarly, the additional selling when prices are falling produces negative feedback and increases further pressure for lower prices. These large swings in prices increase volatility in futures markets which is then transmitted to cash markets.

In his numerous writings, Working has defended the many useful economic functions of futures markets. In particular, Working (1953) explains that in an ideal futures market, the futures price reflects the best estimate of what the spot price will be at the expiration of the futures contract. If futures prices move out of line with expectations about the fundamentals, arbitrage activity will continue until equilibrium conditions are restored in both the futures and the cash markets. Such arbitrage between cash and futures markets helps to reduce price movements and thus decreases cash price volatility.

These early and opposing views about the impact of futures markets on the volatility of the cash markets have focused primarily on agricultural commodities. However, independent of the ideas of these and many other economists who have empirically studied this important topic, the October 1987 Stock Market Crash has renewed the interest on the interplay between cash and futures markets. The October 1987 Crash has raised two questions: why was the initial downward pressure on prices transformed into the dramatic 23 per cent decline? Why was the volatility increased from an average of about 20 per cent to over 100 per cent as measured by the annualized standard deviation of daily returns for the S&P 500 Index?

Harris (1989) studies the 1987 Crash by focusing on various aspects of the relationship between the cash and futures stock index markets. Harris offers evidence suggesting that during the Crash there was a breakdown between the cash and the futures stock index markets. In other words, during the Crash the cash and futures stock index markets effectively functioned as two separate entities. The economic link between the cash and futures markets broke down, apparently because arbitrage became very risky as prices were rapidly collapsing. When the two markets stopped being linked together it was difficult for the futures market to perform its risk management function. For example, when rapid declines in the cash index market triggered short hedging for portfolio insurance purposes in the futures market, such strategies caused futures prices to decline further and often such declines were larger than the declines in the cash markets.

Antoniou and Garrett (1993) study the minute by minute FTSE 100 futures and index prices on 19 and 20 October 1987 and confirm that a similar breakdown between cash and futures stock index markets also occurred in London. Their evidence suggests that while the futures market exacerbated the decline, the cause of the breakdown lies with the cash stock market.

Although Harris and Antoniou and Garrett study in detail the October 1987 Crash in New York and London, they do not give answers to the questions raised earlier about the possible causes of the Crash and of the increased volatility. Numerous theories have been proposed to explain the causes of the Crash, but none to this day appears to be fully satisfactory. Santoni (1988) presents an overview of some explanations of the Crash.

The second question about the causes of increased volatility is partially addressed by Grossman (1988). He claims that the volatility of a stock index can rise because of current lack of information about the extent to which dynamic hedging strategies are in place. To substantiate his claim, Grossman distinguishes between portfolio insurance strategies that use a real security such as a put option and ones that use a synthetic security such as cash and index futures.

If a put is traded on an index, then its price would reveal important information about the desire of portfolio managers to sell their stocks consequent to a correction. If the demand for such puts is very high, the put's price will also be high and its implied volatility will also increase. By showing market participants the true high cost of their plans, some might be discouraged from purchasing such puts, thus reducing further market pressures to increase volatility.

Although much more research is needed to understand how markets become destabilized and to what extent, if any, futures markets contribute to such destabilization, policy makers have used three mechanisms to control stock price volatility. First, as with most futures markets, margin levels can be used to discourage destabilizing speculation in stock index futures. Obviously, the situation is not so simple and there exists an enormous literature that addresses the effectiveness of margin requirements on both stocks and stock index futures.

Hardouvelis (1988) finds that margins on stocks have an important impact on volatility. He shows that an increase in margin requirements decreases stock market volatility. Hsieh and Miller (1990) criticize Hardouvelis's results by arguing that he was picking up a spurious relationship. Since margins change only infrequently, the time series has a great deal of persistence. Observe also that stock market volatility is also persistent. Thus, Hsieh and Miller argue, given two persistent series, regressing one variable on the other can falsely show a significant relationship when there is in fact none.

In futures markets, the relationship between margins and volatility is usually referred to as the prudential exchange hypothesis. This hypothesis claims that futures exchanges usually increase margin requirements when price volatility increases. This is done to reduce trading risks and to preserve the financial integrity of the market. Thus, in futures markets, the causal link between margins and volatility runs from volatility to margins and not vice versa.

The second mechanism used to control volatility is to set price limits. Price limits for stock and futures indexes are also known as circuit breakers. Traditionally, futures markets have used price limits as a policy tool to reduce the probability of an overreaction to news. Price limits determine the maximum amount of price change in a given trading day from the previous settlement price. If bids and offers fall within the bounds of price limits, then trading continues; otherwise trading stops and can resume if both buyers and sellers agree to a price within these limits. Unlike this mechanism of price limits in the futures markets, the circuit breakers introduced after the October 1987 Crash require that trading stops for a certain period of time after a circuit breaker is triggered. Proponents of circuit breakers claim that they offer market participants the opportunity to cool off.

Finally, the third proposed mechanism to reduce stock market volatility is to impose a tax for each transaction of a futures contract. The purpose of a transactions tax is to reduce noise trading without disrupting price discovery. The logic of this argument is based on a distinction between informed traders and uninformed ones. The uninformed traders are often called noise traders and may cause price volatility to increase more than is justified by changes in economic fundamentals. A transactions tax will increase costs to noise traders and may discourage their feedback trading. On the other hand, the cost to informed traders will also increase but, because they believe in the value of their information, they continue to trade and thus contribute to the formation of prices reflecting fundamentals. This topic is discussed in detail in Kupiec (1991).

### Interest rates and insurance

Interest rate futures constitute one of the most successful financial futures innovations. Actually, in several US and foreign futures exchanges, interest rate futures contracts are among their most, and quite often the most, heavily traded contracts. For example, the long-term US Treasury Bond futures contract traded at the Chicago Board of Trade and the three-month Eurodollar futures contract traded at the International Monetary Market of the Chicago Mercantile Exchange are the most successful contracts of these exchanges. Similarly, for MATIF in Paris, LIFFE and the Tokyo International Financial Futures Exchange, their most successful futures contracts are also interest rate futures.

The general reasons for the great success of interest rates futures have already been analysed in the introduction and include financial deregulation and taxation. Beyond these, however, we must also include the enormous cash market for corporate, consumer and government debt. As interest rates fluctuate, the value of this debt changes creating hedging needs and speculative opportunities. Recent advances in academic research have made it possible to hedge an enormous variety of cash debt by using a small number of interest rate futures contracts such as the Thirty-year US Treasury Bond, or the Ten-year US Treasury Note or the Ninety-day US Treasury Bill or the Eurodollar among others. In this section we illustrate the *price sensitive method* of hedging presented in Kolb and Chiang (1981).

Let $P$ denote today's price of a bond with coupon $C(t)$ and yield $r$. Recall that $P$ is defined as

$$P = \sum_{t=1}^{M} \frac{C(t)}{(1+r)^t} \tag{4.11}$$

with $M$ denoting years to maturity. As yields change continuously, the price of a bond also changes. To compute price fluctuations due to interest rate changes one needs to take the derivative of $P(0)$ in (4.11) with respect to $r$ as follows.

$$\frac{dP}{dr} = \sum_{t=1}^{M} \left[ \frac{C'(t)(1+r)^t - (t(1+r)^{t-1} C(t)}{(1+r)^{2t}} \right]$$

$$= \sum_{t=1}^{M} \left[ -\frac{t(1+r)^{t-1} C(t)}{(1+r)^{2t}} \right] \tag{4.12}$$

$$= \sum_{t=11}^{M} \left[ -\frac{tC(t)}{(1+r)^{t+1}} \frac{P}{P} \right]$$

$$= -D \frac{P}{1+r}.$$

To explain this derivation first observe that the numerator inside the summation consists of the derivative of the numerator of (4.11), denoted $C'$, times the denominator minus the derivative of the denominator of (4.11) times its numerator, all divided by the denominator squared. The second step above eliminates $C'(t)(1+r)^t$ since $C'(t) = 0$. In the third step we multiply by a well-chosen one given by $P/P$ to conclude that bond fluctuations are equal to $-DP/(1+r)$. The symbol $D$ denotes a very important concept in bond analysis called *duration* and given by

$$D = \frac{\sum_{t=1}^{M} \frac{tC(t)}{(1+r)^t}}{P}. \tag{4.13}$$

The concept of duration in (4.13) plays a significant role in the optimal hedging of interest sensitive assets. Let $dP_i$ denote changes in the price of the cash market instrument due to changes in its yield to maturity $dr_i$, while $dP_F$ and $dr_F$ denotes changes in the price of the futures instruments and its yield respectively. To hedge against unexpected changes in the cash market instrument, suppose that $N$ number of futures contracts are required for each cash instrument so that during the hedging period

$$dP_i + NdP_F = 0. \tag{4.14}$$

Solve for $N$ and use (4.12) to replace $dP_i$ and $dP_F$ to get

$$N = -\frac{dP_i}{dP_F} = -\frac{-D_iP_i\dfrac{dr_i}{1+r_i}}{-D_FP_F\dfrac{dr_F}{1+r_F}}. \tag{4.15}$$

This last equation gives the optimal number of futures contracts needed to hedge the cash market instrument. It is called price sensitive method and was developed by Kolb and Chiang (1981) who illustrate it with various examples. Further illustrations are found in Kolb and Gay (1982), who apply this method to bond portfolio and bank immunization.

Going beyond interest rate hedging, the significant topic of market efficiency is studied in two important papers by Elton, Gruber and Rentzler (1984) for the Treasury Bill futures market and by Klemkosky and Lasser (1985) for the Treasury Bond futures market. Both studies conclude that some inefficiencies exist.

Finally D'Arcy and France (1992) offer a useful introduction to insurance futures. These are very recent developments initiated by the Chicago Board of Trade.

**Foreign currency**
The daily trading activity in cash foreign currencies and their derivatives is significantly greater than that of all the other financial instruments and their derivatives. World trade, foreign investments and international capital flows certainly contribute to this trading activity. More importantly, however, financial deregulation along with technological advances in electronic transfer have offered traders the opportunity to seek the highest return adjusted for risk globally, thus causing a continuous twenty-four-hour trading in foreign currencies.

The large volume of currency trading, along with volatile currency prices, offer both speculative opportunities and also demand for hedging. The Ederington (1979) portfolio approach to hedging can be applied to foreign currencies because both the cash and futures instruments are similar. For example a US firm that anticipates an invoice to be paid in Japanese Yen and wishes to minimize the risk of the Yen's variability may take a long futures position in Yen traded at the International Monetary Market of the Chicago Mercantile Exchange.

According to the portfolio theory approach to hedging, the hedge ratio and the measure of hedging effectiveness correspond to the regression coefficient $\beta$, and the coefficient of determination, $R^2$, obtained from regressing the spot price changes on futures price changes. The coefficients $\beta$ and $R^2$ have been extensively examined. However, previous studies of hedging performance of futures markets are subject to a certain criticism because they are based on the assumption that the regression coefficient, which corresponds to the hedge ratio, is stable over the whole sample period. Indeed, Grammatikos and Saunders (1983) find that the hedge ratio for five major foreign currency futures is unstable over time.

Malliaris and Urrutia (1991a) claim and empirically test the hypothesis that the hedge ratio $\beta$ and the measure of hedging effectiveness $R^2$ follow a random walk process in the case of foreign currencies.

The concept of a random walk is much more precise in financial analysis than the notion of instability. Authors such as Grammatikos and Saunders use the term 'unstable hedge ratios' to mean that these ratios are not constant over time. In mathematical economic analysis the notion of instability is given a more precise meaning. Intuitively, one can say that the sequence of hedge ratios $\beta_0, \beta_1, \beta_2, \beta_3 \ldots$ is unstable if the absolute deviations of these hedge ratios from the equilibrium hedge ratio become large after a certain time period. Clearly, it is difficult to test this notion of instability for at least two reasons: first, one needs a very long sequence and second, a precise meaning of 'equilibrium hedge ratio' needs to be established.

Attention is devoted in Malliaris and Urrutia (1991a) to the nonconstant behaviour of hedge ratios and coefficients of hedging effectiveness in terms of random walk, a notion familiar to financial analysts. Random walk may eventually lead to instability, but instability need not necessarily imply random walk. One reason for studying the random walk behaviour is the methodological clarification it provides for the time series behaviour of the hedge ratio and coefficient of hedging effectiveness.

There are additional reasons for interest in random walk. First, in an efficient market, changes of spot prices over time are random and reflect the arrival of new information. In other words, price changes on any particular day are uncorrelated with past historical price changes. Empirical research in futures markets suggests that futures price changes also follow a random walk, reflecting efficiency in futures markets as well. The hedge ratio is the ratio of dollar amounts invested in a spot asset and a futures contract. It is reasonable to assume that the behaviour of this ratio reflects the behaviour of these prices. Therefore, given that prices follow a random walk process, one can also expect the hedge ratio to vary randomly over time. A detailed and penetrating analysis of the asset pricing framework for pricing foreign currency futures and statistical tests is given by McCurdy and Morgan (1992).

Second, the random walk behaviour of the hedge ratio may be caused by differences in the microstructure of cash and futures markets. Spot prices are determined in dealership markets while futures prices are formulated in open outcry auction markets. There is an increasing literature that emphasizes the role of different trading mechanisms with special emphasis given to the role of 'noise' and 'feedback' traders on price formulation and the time series properties of such prices. It seems reasonable to postulate that such differences in the microstructure of cash and futures markets and dissimilarities in trading mechanisms and types of traders may cause hedge ratios to vary randomly over time.

Using weekly spot and futures prices of the British Pound, German Mark, Japanese Yen and Swiss Franc for the time period from 4 March 1980 through 27 December 1988 as well as two random walk methodologies, the empirical tests confirm the hypothesis that the hedge ratios and the measures of hedging effectiveness follow a random walk. One way of interpreting these results is to think in terms of market efficiency. In this sense, the findings reinforce previous research confirming market efficiency in both spot and futures markets. The major implication of this random walk hypothesis is that hedgers cannot consistently place perfect hedges and need to continuously readjust their hedges in foreign currencies. This can be done by using appropriate computational methods that take into account the variable nature of the hedge ratio and the measure of hedging effectiveness.

Malliaris and Urrutia (1991b) further explore the consequences of the random walk behaviour of betas and $R^2$. Their motivation is twofold: first, the effect of changes in the length of the estimation period on the effectiveness of the hedge is examined. It is postulated that if hedge ratios are constant over time, then a longer estimation period should give a better estimate of the futures beta and improve the effectiveness of the hedge. If, on the other hand, hedge ratios are changing over time, then using data from long ago may lead to a poorer estimate of the futures beta and worsen the effectiveness of the hedge. In other words, if betas are unstable, the use of shorter estimation periods is advisable because they should give better hedges. Shorter estimation periods also save time and money because smaller data samples are easier to analyse.

Second, the length of the hedging horizon is examined to see if it impacts on the effectiveness of the hedge. It is postulated that if shorter hedges are more effective than longer ones, then hedgers are better off hedging their cash position for shorter periods of time, recomputing their hedge ratios, and rolling the hedges over rather than keeping the hedge for longer periods of time. If the opposite is true, then longer hedging horizons are advisable.

There are no theoretical guidelines in addressing the impact of the length of the estimation period and the length of the hedging horizon on the effectiveness of a hedge. The modern portfolio theory approach to futures hedging derives the optimal hedge as the beta of a specific regression but offers no clues as to the length of the estimation period nor the appropriate length of the hedging horizon. Obviously, foreign exchange hedgers consider both issues of great practical significance.

Using similar data to Malliaris and Urrutia (1991a) and following ex post and ex ante hedging methodologies, a twenty-six-week and 104-week estimation periods and one-week and four-week hedging horizon, Malliaris and Urrutia (1991b) conclude:

1. Ex post hedge ratios are less than one and show instability over time. However, it is found that, on average, betas are not significantly different from one.
2. Measures of hedging effectiveness are large, indicating that foreign currency futures contracts are good hedging devices.
3. For ex post hedges, it is found that longer hedges (one-month hedging horizons) are more effective than shorter hedges (one-week hedging horizons).
4. The length of the estimation period, used for computing the betas and the $R^2$s by means of OLS regressions, does not appear to have an impact on the effectiveness of the hedge both on an ex post hedging (evaluated in terms of $R^2$) and on an ex ante hedging (evaluated in terms of the returns). This result provides some empirical evidence in favour of the hypothesis that hedge ratios are unstable over time.
5. For ex ante hedges, it is found that shorter hedges (weekly hedging horizons) are

more effective than longer hedges (monthly hedging horizons). This finding is the opposite of the one obtained for the ex post hedges, but not necessarily contradictory, since the ex post and ex ante methodologies utilize different criteria.

## Summary

During the past twenty-five years and in particular during the past ten years, financial futures have experienced a phenomenal growth both in the USA and in several foreign exchanges. This chapter identifies deregulation and taxation as the key factors that contributed to this global innovation. There is also a third rather obvious factor: the computer revolution.

Each of the three broad categories of financial futures has its unique characteristics. Stock index futures provide enormous speculative opportunities and hedging services. These speculative opportunities are often expressed as arbitrage activity between cash and futures stock indexes and usually account for about 10 per cent of the volume of shares traded at the New York Stock Exchange. On the other hand, hedging with stock index futures and options is one form of portfolio insurance.

Interest rate futures have offered similar speculative and hedging activities to traders of interest rate sensitive instruments. Speculation is often driven by anticipation of changes in the yield curve. Hedging is made possible by recently developed methods, such as the price sensitive approach which uses the concept of duration.

Finally, foreign currency cash and derivatives instruments constitute a significantly larger market than stock indexes or interest rate sensitive contracts. Several country treasury and banking authorities are often active participants in foreign currency markets. Large swings in exchange rates are not unusual. Such volatility necessitates hedging and one way to implement it is by using the portfolio approach to hedging.

## References

Antoniou, A. and I. Garrett (1993), 'To what extent did stock index futures contribute to the October 1987 stock market crash?', *The Economic Journal*, **103**, 1441–61.

Bookstaber, R. and J.A. Langsam (1988), 'Portfolio insurance trading rules', *The Journal of Futures Markets*, **8**, 15–31.

Brennan, M.J. and E.S. Schwartz (1988), 'Time-invariant portfolio insurance strategies', *The Journal of Finance*, **43**, 283–99.

Brennan, M.J. and E.S. Schwartz (1990), 'Arbitrage in stock index futures', *Journal of Business*, **63**, S7–S31.

Cornell, Bradford and Kenneth R. French (1983), 'The pricing of stock index futures', *The Journal of Futures Markets*, **3**, 1–14.

D'Arcy, Stephen and Virginia G. France (1992), 'Catastrophe futures: a better hedge for insurers', *The Journal of Risk and Insurance*, **59**, 575–600.

Ederington, L.H. (1979), 'The hedging performance of the new futures markets', *Journal of Finance*, **34**, 157–70.

Elton, Edwin, Martin Gruber and Joel Rentzler (1984), 'Intra-day tests of the efficiency of the treasury bill futures market', *Review of Economics and Statistics*, **62**, 129–37.

Figlewski, Stephen (1984), 'Hedging performance and basis risk in stock index futures', *The Journal of Finance*, **39**, 657–69.

Grammatikos, T. and A. Saunders (1983), 'Stability and the hedging performance of foreign currency futures', *The Journal of Futures Markets*, **3**, 295–305.

Grossman, S.J. (1988), 'Program trading and stock and futures price volatility', *The Journal of Futures Markets*, **8**, 413–19.

Hardouvelis, G. (1988), 'Margins requirements and stock market volatility', *Quarterly Review, Federal Reserve Bank of New York*, Summer, 80–9.

Harris, L. (1989), 'The October 1987 S&P 500 stock-futures basis', *The Journal of Finance*, **44**, 77–99.

Hsieh, David and Merton Miller (1990), 'Margin regulation and stock market volatility', *The Journal of Finance*, **45**, 3–29.

Kaldor, N. (1939), 'Speculation and economic stability', *Review of Economic Studies*, **7**, 1–27.

Kawaller, I.G., P.D. Koch and T.W. Koch (1987), 'The temporal price relationship between S&P 500 futures and the S&P 500 index', *The Journal of Finance*, **42**, 1309–29.

Klemkosky, R. and D. Lasser (1985), 'An efficiency analysis of the T-bond futures market', *The Journal of Futures Markets*, **5**, 607–20.

Kolb, R.W. and R. Chiang (1981), 'Improving hedging performance using interest rate futures', *Financial Management*, **10**, 72–9.

Kolb, R.W. and G.D. Gay (1982), 'Immunizing bond portfolios with interest rate futures', *Financial Management*, Summer, 81–9.

Kupiec, P.H. (1991), 'Noise traders, excess volatility, and a securities transaction tax', Board of Governors of the Federal Reserve System, FEDS working paper, no. 166.

MacKinlay, C. and K. Ramaswamy (1988), 'Index-futures arbitrage behavior of stock index futures prices', *The Review of Financial Studies*, **1**, 137–58.

Malliaris, A.G. and J. Urrutia (1991a), 'Tests of random walk of hedge ratios and measures of hedging effectiveness for stock indexes and foreign currencies', *The Journal of Futures Markets*, **11**, 55–68.

Malliaris, A.G. and J.L. Urrutia (1991b), 'The impact of the lengths of estimation periods and hedging horizons on the effectiveness of a hedge: evidence from foreign currency futures', *The Journal of Futures Markets*, **11**, 271–89.

McCurdy, Thomas and Ieuan Morgan (1992), 'Evidence of risk premiums in foreign currency futures markets', *The Review of Financial Studies*, **5**, 65–84.

Merrick Jr, J.J. (1988), 'Portfolio insurance with stock index futures', *The Journal of Futures Markets*, **8**, 441–55.

Miller, M.H. (1986), 'Financial innovation: the last twenty years and the next', *Journal of Financial and Quantitative Analysis*, **21**, 459–71.

Santoni, G.J. (1988), 'The October crash: some evidence on the cascade theory', *Review of The Federal Reserve Bank of Saint Louis*, May–June, 18–33.

Stoll, H.R. and R.E. Whaley (1990), 'The dynamics of stock index and stock index futures returns', *Journal of Financial and Quantitative Analysis*, **25**, 441–68.

Subrahmanyam, Avanidhar (1991), 'A theory of trading in stock index futures', *The Review of Financial Studies*, **4**, 17–51.

Taussig, F.W. (1921), 'Is market price determinate?', *Quarterly Journal of Economics*, **35**, 394–411.

Working, H. (1953), 'Futures trading and hedging', *American Economic Review*, **18**, 314–43.

Yadav, P.K. and P.E. Pope (1990), 'Stock index futures arbitrage: international evidence', *Journal of Futures Markets*, **10**, 573–603.

# PART II

# METHODS

SIAM REVIEW
Vol. 23, No. 4, October 1981

# MARTINGALE METHODS IN FINANCIAL DECISION-MAKING*

A. G. MALLIARIS†

**Abstract.** This paper presents an introduction to martingale theory by stating some basic definitions and presenting some probabilistic examples. Afterwards, we illustrate the use of martingale methods in economics and finance. In particular, we present applications of martingale methods in futures pricing, in stochastic present discounted value of capitalization and in intertemporal stochastic optimization. The main conclusion of this paper is that martingale methods have been applied as useful techniques in decision-making problems in economics and finance.

**1. Introduction.** Martingale theory, like various other areas of probability theory, has its origins in notions of gambling in the following sense. Let $X_1, X_2, \cdots$ be a sequence of random variables defined on a common probability space $(\Omega, \mathscr{F}, P)$. Within the gambling context, these random variables denote the gambler's total winnings after $1, 2, \cdots, n, \cdots$ trials in a succession of games. The gambler's expected fortune after trial $n+1$, given that he has completed $n$ trials already, is denoted as $E[X_{n+1}|X_1, \cdots, X_n]$. Observe that $E[X_{n+1}|X_1, \cdots, X_n]$ denotes the expectation of $X_{n+1}$ conditioned upon the $\sigma$-field generated by the random variables $X_1, \cdots, X_n$. Intuitively, the $\sigma$-field generated by $X_1, \cdots, X_n$ contains all the past information of the gambler's fortune up to and including the $n$th trial. If a game is fair then the gambler after the $(n+1)$st trial will expect on the average to be neither wealthier nor poorer than he is before this trial; i.e.,

$$(1) \qquad E[X_{n+1}|X_1, \cdots, X_n] = X_n.$$

Stated differently, (1), called the *martingale property*, states that in a *fair* game, the gambler's fortune on the next play is on the average his current fortune and is not otherwise affected by the previous history.

If instead of $=$ in (1) we put $\geqq$ or $\leqq$, then the game is favorable or unfavorable, respectively. With this motivation we state the definition of a martingale following Billingsley [1].

**2. Definitions.** Let $X_1, X_2, \cdots$ be a sequence of random variables defined on a common probability space $(\Omega, \mathscr{F}, P)$, and let $\mathscr{F}_1, \mathscr{F}_2, \cdots$ be a sequence of $\sigma$-fields all belonging to $\mathscr{F}$. The sequence $\{(X_n, \mathscr{F}_n), n = 1, 2, \cdots\}$ is a *martingale* if for each $n$ it satisfies the four conditions below:

1. $\mathscr{F}_n \subset \mathscr{F}_{n+1}$;
2. $X_n$ is measurable $\mathscr{F}_n$;
3. $E(|X_n|) < \infty$;
4. $E[X_{n+1}|\mathscr{F}_n] = X_n$ with probability 1, (w.p.1).

Condition 1 states that $\{\mathscr{F}_n\}$, $n = 1, 2, \cdots$ is an increasing sequence of $\sigma$-fields in $\mathscr{F}$. Intuitively, the requirement of an increasing $\{\mathscr{F}_n\}$ implies that the amount of information contained in the sequence of $\sigma$-fields $\{\mathscr{F}_n\}$ is increasing. This is called the *monotoneity property* of the $\sigma$-fields $\{\mathscr{F}_n\}$ in $\mathscr{F}$, and it attempts to capture the practical idea that the past to time $n + 1$ includes more events, information and/or history than the past to time $n$. The overall informational structure represented by the monotonically increasing sequence $\{\mathscr{F}_n\}$ captures the concept of *learning without forgetting*. In

* Received by the editors February 29, 1980, and in revised form October 3, 1980. An earlier version of this paper was presented at the Midwest Conference of the American Institute for Decision Sciences, April 17–18, 1980, Dayton, Ohio.

† Director, The Graduate School of Business, Loyola University of Chicago, Chicago, Illinois 60611.

some applications $\mathcal{F}_n$ is the $\sigma$-field generated by the random variables $X_1, \cdots, X_n$, or perhaps some other sequence of random variables, say, $Y_1, \cdots, Y_n$. In such applications, instead of $E[X_{n+1}|\mathcal{F}_n]$ we write $E[X_{n+1}|X_1, \cdots, X_n]$ or $E[X_{n+1}|Y_1, \cdots, Y_n]$, as the case may be.

The *measurability property* stated in Condition 2 means that, for each $n$, $X_n$ has as its domain the measurable space $(\Omega, \mathcal{F}_n)$ and as its target space $(R, \mathcal{R})$. Some authors, such as Meyer [9, p. 77], use the terminology that $X_n$ is adapted to the $\sigma$-field $\mathcal{F}_n$. As was remarked in the previous paragraph, when $\{\mathcal{F}_n\}$ are taken to be the $\sigma$-fields generated by $X_1, X_2, \cdots, X_n$, i.e., $\mathcal{F}_n = \sigma(X_1, \cdots, X_n)$, then the measurability condition is automatically satisfied. Recall that $\sigma(X_1, \cdots, X_n)$, the $\sigma$-field generated by $X_1, \cdots, X_n$, is the smallest $\sigma$-field making $X_1, \cdots, X_n$ measurable. Suppose that $Y$ is a random variable defined on the same space and consider the $\sigma$-field generated by $Y, X_1, \cdots, X_n$ and denoted by $\sigma(Y, X_1, \cdots, X_n)$. We have that

$$\sigma(X_1, \cdots, X_n) \subset \sigma(Y, X_1, \cdots, X_n),$$

and $X_1, \cdots, X_n$ continue to be measurable with respect to the new $\sigma$-field $\sigma(Y, X_1, \cdots, X_n)$. It is theoretically natural and many applications require it practically to allow $\sigma$-fields $\{\mathcal{F}_n\}$ to be larger than the minimal ones $\sigma(X_1, \cdots, X_n)$. Fama [3] has used various sizes of $\sigma$-fields to denote various degrees of information.

Condition 3, called the *integrability property*, says simply that $X_n$ is integrable, i.e., that the expectation of $X_n$ is finite. Finally, the *martingale property* expressed in Condition 4 says that $X_n$ is a version of $E[X_{n+1}|\mathcal{F}_n]$, and in a gambling context this condition indicates that the game is fair. Note that Condition 4 is equivalent to

$$(2) \qquad \int_A E[X_{n+1}|\mathcal{F}_n]\, dP = \int_A X_n\, dP$$

for $A \in \mathcal{F}_n$, $n = 1, 2, \cdots$. Observe, however, that from the definition of conditional expected value

$$(3) \qquad \int_A E[X_{n+1}|\mathcal{F}_n]\, dP = \int_A X_{n+1}\, dP$$

for $A \in \mathcal{F}_n$. Using (2) and (3), we conclude that

$$(4) \qquad \int_A X_{n+1}\, dP = \int_A X_n\, dP$$

for $A \in \mathcal{F}_n$. Therefore Condition 4 and (4) are equivalent. The same reasoning used inductively yields

$$\int_A X_n\, dP = \int_A X_{n+1}\, dP = \cdots = \int_A X_{n+k}\, dP$$

for $A \in \mathcal{F}_n \subset \mathcal{F}_{n+1} \subset \cdots \subset \mathcal{F}_{n+k}$ and $k \geq 1$. This means that $X_n$ is a version of $E[X_{n+k}|\mathcal{F}_n]$, and therefore the martingale property in Condition 4 can also be written as

$$E[X_{n+k}|\mathcal{F}_n] = X_n.$$

Some additional definitions are appropriate. Condition 4 still makes sense for nonnegative $X_n$ which do not satisfy Condition 3. For such nonnegative $X_n$ which satisfy Conditions 1, 2 and 4 but not necessarily Condition 3, we say that $\{(X_n, \mathcal{F}_n), n = 1, 2, \cdots\}$ is a *generalized martingale*. The sequence $\{(X_n, \mathcal{F}_n), n = 1, 2, \cdots\}$ is a submartingale if it satisfies Conditions 1, 2, 3 and

4a.  $E[X_{n+1}|\mathcal{F}_n] \geq X_n$   w.p. 1.

If instead of $\geq$ in Condition 4a we put $\leq$, then $\{(X_n, \mathcal{F}_n), n = 1, 2\}$ is called a *super-martingale*. Using (4) we state that $\{(X_n, \mathcal{F}_n), n = 1, 2, \cdots\}$ is a *submartingale* if and only if

$$(5) \qquad \int_A X_{n+1}\,dP \geq \int_A X_n\,dP$$

for $A \in \mathcal{F}_n$ and $\{(X_n, \mathcal{F}_n), n = 1, 2, \cdots\}$ is a *supermartingale* if and only if

$$(6) \qquad \int_A X_{n+1}\,dP \leq \int_A X_n\,dP$$

for $A \in \mathcal{F}_n$.

**3. Probabilistic examples.** With the above notions stated we give some examples of a probabilistic nature before we illustrate the application of martingale theory in economics and finance.

*Example* 1. Suppose $Y$ is an integrable random variable on $(\Omega, \mathcal{F}, P)$ and $\{\mathcal{F}_n\}$ is a nondecreasing sequence of $\sigma$-fields in $\mathcal{F}$. Define $X_n$ as

$$X_n = E[Y|\mathcal{F}_n];$$

that is, $X_n$ is the conditional expectation of $Y$ conditioned on the $\sigma$-field $\mathcal{F}_n$. From the very definition of conditional probability, $X_n$ is both measurable and integrable. Furthermore, Condition 4 holds since

$$E[X_{n+1}|\mathcal{F}_n] = E[E[Y|\mathcal{F}_{n+1}]|\mathcal{F}_n] = E[Y|\mathcal{F}_n] = X_n.$$

Thus $\{(X_n, \mathcal{F}_n), n = 1, 2, \cdots\}$ is a martingale, obtained from successive conditional expectations of $Y$ as we know more and more. We note that this example illustrates a fundamental property of Bayesian theory.

*Example* 2. This example supposes that $Y_0, Y_1, Y_2, \cdots$ are independent random variables with $Y_0 = 0, E(|Y_n|) < \infty$ and $E(Y_n) = 0$ for all $n \geq 1$. Define $X_0 = Y_0$ and $X_n = Y_1 + \cdots + Y_n$ for $n \geq 1$. Then $X_n$ is a martingale with respect to the $\sigma$-field generated by $Y_n$. Condition 1 holds because the $\sigma$-field generated by $Y_1, \cdots, Y_n$, denoted by $\sigma(Y_1, \cdots, Y_n)$, is contained in the $\sigma$-field generated by $Y_1, \cdots, Y_{n+1}$, denoted by $\sigma(Y_1, \cdots, Y_{n+1})$; that is,

$$\sigma(Y_1, \cdots, Y_n) \subset \sigma(Y_1, \cdots, Y_{n+1}).$$

Condition 2 holds since measurability is preserved by addition. Condition 3 follows from

$$E(|X_n|) \leq E(|Y_1|) + \cdots + E(|Y_n|) < \infty.$$

Finally, Condition 4 holds since

$$\begin{aligned}
E[X_{n+1}|Y_0, \cdots, Y_n] &= E[X_n + Y_{n+1}|Y_0, \cdots, Y_n] \\
&= E[X_n|Y_0, \cdots, Y_n] + E[Y_{n+1}|Y_0, \cdots, Y_n] \\
&= X_n + E(Y_{n+1}) \\
&= X_n.
\end{aligned}$$

In establishing Condition 4, note that $E[Y_{n+1}|Y_0, \cdots, Y_n] = E(Y_{n+1})$ follows from the assumption that $Y_0, Y_1, \cdots$ are independent random variables.

In this same example, if we assume that $E(Y_n) \geq 0$ for $n \geq 1$, we conclude that $X_n$ is a submartingale, and assuming that $E(Y_n) \leq 0$ we obtain that $X_n$ is a supermartingale.

*Example* 3. As an example of a submartingale assume that $\{(X_n, \mathscr{F}_n), n = 1, 2, \cdots\}$ is a martingale. We claim that $\{(|X_n|, \mathscr{F}_n), n = 1, 2, \cdots\}$ is a submartingale. Condition 1 holds trivially since we consider the same family of $\sigma$-fields, while Conditions 2 and 3 hold because measurability and integrability of $X_n$ imply the same for $|X_n|$. Condition 4a holds because

$$E[|X_{n+1}| \,|\, \mathscr{F}_n] \geq |E[X_{n+1}|\mathscr{F}_n]| = |X_n|.$$

For additional examples the reader is referred to Doob [2].

**4. Applications in finance and economics.** The concept of a martingale and various martingale methods have found several applications in economics and finance. Below we present some such applications to illustrate the decision-theoretic aspects of martingale theory.

*Application* 1. *Futures pricing.* In this application we follow Samuelson [12], with minor modifications, to show that *futures pricing*, under certain conditions, is a martingale.

Let $\cdots, X_t, X_{t+1}, \cdots, X_{t+T}, \cdots$ represent a sequence of bounded random variables defined on a probability space $(\Omega, \mathscr{F}, P)$. For example, this sequence may represent a time sequence of prices, say spot prices of wheat or gold. $X_t$ denotes the present spot price and $X_{t+T}$ denotes the spot price that is to prevail $T$ units of time from now. The assumption of boundedness of the random variables is not too restrictive because commodity prices are always finite. An economic agent is assumed to know at least today's price as well as the past prices. In the language of probability, we assume that the economic agent knows all the available information generated by the process which is in the $\sigma$-field $\mathscr{F}_t$, where

(7) $$\mathscr{F}_t = \sigma(X_0, X_1, \cdots, X_t).$$

Note that $\mathscr{F}_t$ contains, in particular, the past price realizations of the process. These prices denoted by $x_0, x_1, \cdots, x_{t-1}, x_t$ are specific values of the process for a specific $\omega \in \Omega$, where

$$X_0(\omega) = x_0, \quad \cdots, \quad X_{t-1}(\omega) = x_{t-1}, \quad X_t(\omega) = x_t.$$

The economic agent cannot know with certainty tomorrow's price $X_{t+1}$, or any future price $X_{t+T}$. However, as time goes on his information increases because he observes additional price realizations. Needless to say, $\mathscr{F}_t$ is a monotone increasing sequence by the definition in (7). Parenthetically we mention that Fama [3] introduced the terminology *weak*, *semi-strong* and *strong information sets* to describe information sets $\mathscr{F}_t$ which include past values of the process, all publicly available past information and all past information (both public and internal to an economic agent), respectively. In this present example $\mathscr{F}_t$ contains at least weak information which guarantees the measurability of $X_t$.

Now consider today's futures price quotation for the actual spot price that will prevail $T$ periods from now. We use the notation $Y(T, t)$ to write the futures price that will prevail $T$ periods from period $t$ and quoted at $t$. Let another period pass; then the new quotation for the *same* futures price is written as $Y(T-1, t+1)$. Thus we have a sequence,

(8)        $Y(T, t), Y(T-1, t+1), \cdots, Y(T-n, t+n), \cdots, Y(1, t+T-1).$

Samuelson's fundamental assumption [12] is that a futures price is to be set by competitive bidding at the *now-expected level of the terminal spot price*. This is similar to Muth's [10] *rational expectations* hypothesis, and can be written as

(9)                          $Y(T, t) = E[X_{t+T}|\mathscr{F}_t]$

for $T = 1, 2, \cdots$. Note that (9) makes sense because the conditional expectation of $X_{t+T}$ with respect to $\mathscr{F}_t$ exists; this is so because $X_{t+T}$ is integrable. The integrability of $X_{t+T}$ follows from the assumption of the boundedness of $X_{t+T}$ made at the beginning of this application.

Now we are ready to establish that (8) is a martingale. The $\sigma$-fields associated with (8) are $\mathscr{F}_t, \mathscr{F}_{t+1}, \cdots, \mathscr{F}_{t+n}, \cdots \mathscr{F}_{t+T-1}$. Such $\sigma$-fields defined in (7) form a monotone increasing sequence which satisfies the first condition of a martingale. The measurability and integrability conditions of (8) follow from (9) and the properties of conditional expectation of $X_{t+T}$. More precisely, $E[X_{t+T}|\mathscr{F}_t]$ is measurable by $\mathscr{F}_t$ and by (9) so is $Y(T, t)$. Furthermore $E[X_{t+T}|\mathscr{F}_t]$ is integrable and

(10)                $\int_A E[X_{t+T}|\mathscr{F}_t]\,dP = \int_A X_{t+T}\,dP < \infty$

for $A \in \mathscr{F}_t$; so is $Y(T, t)$, by (9). The right-hand side of (10) follows from the boundedness assumption of $X_{t+T}$. Thus, we only need to establish the martingale property,

(11)                      $E[Y(T-1, t+1)|\mathscr{F}_t] = Y(T, t).$

Equation (11) is easy to establish by using equation (10). More specifically,

$$E[Y(T-1, t+1)|\mathscr{F}_t] = E[E[X_{t+T}|\mathscr{F}_{t+1}]|\mathscr{F}_t] = E[X_{t+T}|\mathscr{F}_t] = Y(T, t).$$

Thus futures pricing under the assumptions stated is a martingale.

The theoretical paper of Samuelson [12] summarized in this application and the work of Mandelbrot [8] generated great interest in econometric testing of the properties of stock prices. Although Samuelson's paper establishes the martingale property for futures pricing rather than for an equity asset, a share of a stock may be regarded as a sequence of futures claims due to mature at successive intervals. Thus, the martingale property properly applied to stock prices may be used as a measure of capital market efficiency. A capital market is *efficient* if the prices of the securities incorporate all the available information. Here we briefly report some findings of Jensen [6] and refer the interested reader to Fama [3] for a detailed survey of the theory and empirical findings on efficient capital markets. Jensen distinguishes between weak and strong information and he proceeds to test the strong martingale hypothesis, where the expectation of prices $T$ periods from $t$, denoted by $X_{t+T}$, is conditioned upon all information available at $t$. As stated earlier, such information includes the past values of the process and information both public and internal to the firm. Notationally, Jensen [6] writes $\theta_t$ for $\sigma$-fields that contain all such information. Then the strong martingale hypothesis is written as

(12)                          $E[X_{t+T}|\theta_t] = f(T)X_t,$

where, according to Jensen, $f(T)$ represents the *normal accumulation rate* which depends on the length of the period $T$. Note that (12) actually represents a submartingale for the sequence $X_t, X_{t+1}, \cdots, X_{t+T}$, since

(13)                    $$E[X_{t+T}|\theta_t] \geq X_t$$

holds for $f(T) \geq 1$. Jensen's empirical analysis [6] of 115 mutual funds shows that current prices of securities incorporate all available information, and therefore the best forecast of future prices is the present prices plus a normal expected return over the period $T$.

We close this application with a remark on Samuelson's [12] sequences $\cdots, X_t, \cdots, X_{t+T}, \cdots$, and their unconditional expectations in (8). Note that these sequences are assumed to be given exogenously. LeRoy [7] has attempted to derive the martingale property when the assumption of exogenously given sequences is relaxed. He analyzes the relation between the riskiness of a stock and the constant *absolute risk aversion* of investors to formally derive endogenously probability distributions of rates of return. LeRoy [7, p. 437] concludes, "not that any particular systematic departure from the martingale property is to be expected, but only that under risk aversion no rigorous theoretical justification for an exact martingale property is available." Ohlson [11], in commenting on LeRoy's 1973 paper, shows that the martingale property holds when investors have constant *relative risk aversion*[1] and the percentage change in dividends is stationary.

*Application 2. Generalized futures pricing.* The application of futures pricing as a martingale can be generalized following Samuelson [12]. Let $\alpha = (1+r)^{-1}$, where $r > 0$ is a measure of foregone risk-free interest rate, say the rate on U.S. Treasury Bills, and postulate

(14)                    $$Y(T, t) = \alpha^T E[X_{t+T}|\mathcal{F}_t]$$

instead of (9). That is, we allow the conditional expectation of the spot price, $T$ periods from now, to be appropriately discounted. Then the sequence $Y(T, t), \cdots, Y(T-n, t+n), \cdots$, which satisfies the axiom of present discounted expected value in (14), is a submartingale with respect to the $\sigma$-fields $\mathcal{F}_t, \cdots, \mathcal{F}_{t+n}, \cdots$. Here we assume that the $\sigma$-fields include at least weak information.

To establish that the sequence is a submartingale we only check the submartingale property. Conditions 1, 2 and 3 are easily established as in the previous application. Note that in the economics and finance literature Conditions 1, 2 and 3 are seldom checked carefully. The reader, however, may use the analysis in the previous example as a model in establishing the monoteneity, measurability and integrability conditions.

The submartingale condition is established using (14) as follows:

$$E[Y(t+1, T-1)|\mathcal{F}_{t+1}] = E[\alpha^{T-1}E[X_{t+T}|\mathcal{F}_{t+1}]|\mathcal{F}_t]$$
$$= \alpha^{T-1}E[E[X_{t+T}|\mathcal{F}_{t+1}]|\mathcal{F}_t] = \alpha^{T-1}E[X_{t+T}|\mathcal{F}_t]$$
$$= \alpha^{T-1}\alpha^{-T}Y(t, T) = \alpha^{-1}Y(t, T)$$
$$= (1+r)Y(t, T) \geq Y(t, T).$$

In this application the discounted futures price will rise in each period by a percentage equal to $r$. Samuelson [12] uses this application to provide a rational

---

[1] The general definition of two terms, *absolute risk aversion* denoted by AR $(W)$ and *relative risk aversion* denoted by RR $(W)$, is as follows: let $W$ be the level of wealth and suppose that $U(W)$ is the investor's real-valued utility function; then

$$AR(W) = -U''(W)/U'(W), \qquad RR(W) = -U''(W)W/U'(W).$$

The primes denote first and second derivatives of $U$.

explanation of the doctrine of *normal backwardation*, which hypothesizes that the futures price is less than the expected spot price.

The overall moral of the two applications is this: the martingale property of futures pricing establishes that all methods used to read out of the past sequence of known prices any profitable pattern of prediction are doomed to failure. Thus the martingale concept and its statistical verification in specific applications has definite implications in financial decision-making.

*Application 3. Stochastic rule of capitalization.* In this application we follow Samuelson [13] to show that, under certain conditions, stocks that are capitalized at their expected present discounted values satisfy the martingale property. Although our purpose is to establish the martingale property, before we do so in this application, we generalize the familiar *present discounted-value rule of capitalization.*

Let $x_t, \cdots, x_{t+T}$ be a sequence of dividends of a given stock paid out at time $t, \cdots, t+T$, on each dollar invested at time $t, \cdots, t+T$. Suppose that the discount rate is $r$ and remains constant. Allowing $r$ to change per unit of time does not add any new insights into the analysis; it just complicates the notation. Initially, we assume that $x_t, \cdots, x_{t+T}$ are nonrandom and we write the familiar equation

$$(15) \qquad V_t = \sum_{T=1}^{\infty} \frac{x_{t+T}}{(1+r)^T},$$

where $V_t$ is the value of the stock at time $t$ obtained from the present discounted-value rule of capitalization. Using (15) we can obtain the value of the stock next period, $V_{t+1}$, as follows,

$$(16) \qquad V_{t+1} = \sum_{T=1}^{\infty} \frac{x_{t+1+T}}{(1+r)^T} = \sum_{T=2}^{\infty} \frac{x_{t+T}}{(1+r)^{T-1}}.$$

From (15) and (16) it follows that

$$V_t - \frac{V_{t+1}}{1+r} = \frac{x_{t+1}}{1+r},$$

which can be written as

$$(17) \qquad V_{t+1} = (1+r)V_t - x_{t+1}.$$

Equation (17) is useful because it expresses the value of the stock next period as a function of its current price $V_t$, the discount rate $r$ and the stock's dividend at the end of next period, $x_{t+1}$. As a special case, if $rV_t = x_{t+1}$, then $V_{t+1} = V_t$, which means that if the discount rate is equal to the rate of return, $x_{t+1}/V_t$, then the value of the stock will remain the same.

With the above review we now generalize (15) and (17) to make them stochastic. Let $(\Omega, \mathcal{F}, P)$ be a probability space and let $x_t(\omega), \cdots, x_{t+T}(\omega)$ be a sequence of random variables denoting stock dividends. In what follows we delete the $\omega$'s to simplify the notation. For each random variable $x_{t+T}$, $T = 1, 2, \cdots$, we assume the existence of a distribution and of a conditional expectation. The sequence of $\sigma$-fields in $\mathcal{F}$ is denoted by $\mathcal{F}_{t+T}$ and it contains at least weak information, that is, $\sigma(x_t, \cdots, x_{t+T}) \subset \mathcal{F}_{t+T}$. In words, this means that the investor knows at least the dividend history of the stock.

At this point we can immediately generalize (15) by writing it as

$$(18) \qquad v_t \equiv E[V_t | \mathcal{F}_t] = E\left[ \sum_{T=1}^{\infty} \frac{x_{t+T}}{(1+r)^T} \,\bigg|\, \mathcal{F}_t \right] = \sum_{T=1}^{\infty} \left( E\left[ \frac{x_{t+T}}{(1+r)^T} \,\bigg|\, \mathcal{F}_t \right] \right).$$

Note that the stochastic generalization of (17) is also easy. As a first step, compute $v_{t+1}$ using (16) and (17):

$$(19) \qquad v_{t+1} \equiv E[V_{t+1}|\mathscr{F}_{t+1}] = E\left[ \sum_{T=2}^{\infty} \frac{x_{t+T}}{(1+r)^{T-1}} \,\Big|\, \mathscr{F}_{t+1} \right].$$

Next, observe that from (18) and (19) we get

$$(20) \qquad \begin{aligned} E[v_{t+1}|\mathscr{F}_t] &= E\left[ E\left[ \sum_{T=2}^{\infty} \frac{x_{t+T}}{(1+r)^{T-1}} \,\Big|\, \mathscr{F}_{t+1} \right] \Big| \mathscr{F}_t \right] \\ &= E\left[ \sum_{T=2}^{\infty} \frac{x_{t+T}}{(1+r)^{T-1}} \,\Big|\, \mathscr{F}_t \right] = E\left[ \pm x_{t+1} + \sum_{T=2}^{\infty} \frac{x_{t+T}}{(1+r)^{T-1}} \,\Big|\, \mathscr{F}_t \right]. \end{aligned}$$

Finally, multiplying both sides by $1/(1+r)$ and using the definition of $v_t$ in (18), we conclude

$$(21) \qquad \begin{aligned} E[v_{t+1}|\mathscr{F}_t] &= (1+r)E\left[ \sum_{T=1}^{\infty} \frac{x_{t+T}}{(1+r)^{T}} \,\Big|\, \mathscr{F}_t \right] - E[x_{t+1}|\mathscr{F}_t] \\ &= (1+r)v_t - E[x_{t+1}|\mathscr{F}_t]. \end{aligned}$$

Equation (21) is the stochastic generalization of (17), and it can be used to help us decide under what conditions the sequence $v_t, \cdots, v_{t+T}$ is a martingale. In other words, we ask under what conditions $E[v_{t+1}|\mathscr{F}_t] = v_t$. The answer is when $rv_t = E[x_{t+1}|\mathscr{F}_t]$. This means that the martingale condition holds when the discount rate is equal to the conditional expected return of the stock.

We conclude therefore that the sequence $v_t, v_{t+T}, T = 1, 2, \cdots$ of discounted expected values of a stock is a martingale, provided

$$(22) \qquad r = E[x_{t+1}|\mathscr{F}_t]/v_t.$$

From this last equation we can at once decide that $v_t, v_{t+T}, \cdots, T = 1, 2, \cdots$ is a submartingale if in (22) instead of $=$ we have $\geqq$. This is so because (21) with (22) having $\geqq$ instead of $=$ yields

$$E[v_{t+1}|\mathscr{F}_t] = v_t + \left( r - \frac{E[x_{t-1}|\mathscr{F}_t]}{v_t} \right) v_t \geqq v_t.$$

The submartingale property says that the conditional expected value of the stock next period is greater than or equal to its current value. This is so because the conditional expected rate of return is smaller than or equal to the discount rate.

We close this application with a remark. Recall that in this application we assumed the existence of conditional expectation for the sequence $x_t, \cdots, x_{t+T}$ but we did not explain the way the individual investor forms his expectations. A more complete analysis would proceed as follows. Let an individual investor form his *subjective* expectations $y_t, \cdots, y_{t+T}$ as a sequence of random variables, where $y_{t+T}, T = 1, 2, \cdots$ denotes the investor's expected dividends of a given stock to be paid out $T$ periods from now. After he has done so, a relationship needs to be established between $y_{t+T}$ and $x_{t+T}$. A natural candidate is the relationship

$$(23) \qquad y_{t+T} = E[x_{t+T}|\mathscr{F}_t],$$

which is Samuelson's [12] *axiom of expectation formation* or Muth's [10] *rational expectation hypothesis*. Equation (23) links the investor's *subjective* expectations to the markets' *objective* conditional expectations. Thus, we may start with an investor and his subjective expectations $y_{t+T}$, use (23) to link the subjective expectations to the objective ones and proceed from there using $x_{t+T}$ as was done above.

*Application* 4. *Stochastic optimization.* In this final application we follow Hall [5] to study a simple model of *intertemporal stochastic optimization* to obtain a martingale property for the marginal utility of consumption.

Consider an individual with a strictly concave one-period utility function $u(\cdot)$, whose problem is given by

$$(24) \qquad \max E\left[ \sum_{T=0}^{N} \frac{u(c_{t+T})}{(1+\delta)^T} \middle| \mathscr{F}_t \right]$$

subject to the condition

$$(25) \qquad \sum_{T=0}^{N} \frac{c_{t+T} - w_{t+T}}{(1+r)^T} \equiv A_t.$$

In (24) and (25) the notation used is: $c_{t+T}$, $T = 0, 1, \cdots, N$ is consumption, $\delta$ is the rate of subjective time preference, $r$ is the real rate of interest, $w_{t+T}$ is earnings and $A_t$ is the value of assets at time $t$. The individual considers the problem today, at time $t$, and his length of economic life is $t + N$ periods. The problem described by (24) and (25) is usually called the consumer's life-cycle consumption problem under uncertainty, that is to say, in an environment of uncertain outcomes how a consumer can maximize his expected total utility by selecting appropriately his consumption spending today for each period of the rest of his lifetime. Such a maximization is constrained by the consumer's earnings and accumulated wealth (we do not allow for borrowing); we also postulate that current consumption is preferred to future consumption. The $\sigma$-fields $\mathscr{F}_t, \mathscr{F}_{t+1}, \cdots, \mathscr{F}_{t+N}$ each include information, at least, about the sequence of consumption and the sequence of marginal utility of such consumption, respectively at $t, \cdots, t + N$.

Hall [5] derives a necessary condition for this maximization problem of the form

$$(26) \qquad E[u'(c_{t+1})|\mathscr{F}_t] = \frac{1+\delta}{1+r} u'(c_t),$$

where $u'(\cdot)$ denotes marginal utility, which is the derivative of $u$. If we assume $\delta = r$, (26) says that the sequence of marginal utilities satisfies the martingale property. If we assume that $r < \delta$, then (26) says that the sequence of marginal utilities is a sub-martingale.

Hall [5] also shows that if the stochastic change in marginal utility from one period to the next is small, then consumption itself is a submartingale, written as

$$(27) \qquad E[c_{t+1}|\mathscr{F}_t] = \lambda_t c_t \geq c_t,$$

where $\lambda_t$ is given by

$$(28) \qquad \lambda_t = \left( \frac{1+\delta}{1+r} \right)^{u'(c_t)/c_t u''(c_t)}.$$

From (28) we obtain that $\lambda_t \geq 1$ because $u'' < 0$ and $r$ is assumed to be greater than $\delta$. This is an interesting result which says that the consumer expects his consumption tomorrow conditioned upon his consumption expenditures history to be at least as large as today's consumption. Such a hypothesis seems quite appropriate as judged by our individual experiences as consumers.

Before we close this application we mention that Foldes [4] has obtained martingale conditions for a dynamic discrete time model of stochastic optimal saving.

**5. Conclusion.** This analysis leads to one basic conclusion: the martingale concept can be used as a tool in business decision-making under uncertainty. The few examples discussed in this paper illustrate that martingale theory can be applied to specific business problems to characterize conditions under which the martingale property holds. This enables the researcher to better understand the problem and thus to make better decisions. Although martingale theory has already been used in finance and economics, a large number of already discovered mathematical results in this area remain to be used in business applications. Both the use of martingale methods in formulating financial behavior hypotheses and the design of statistical methods for testing them will continue to interest quantitative financial researchers.

REFERENCES

[1] P. BILLINGSLEY, *Probability and Measure*, John Wiley, New York, 1979.

[2] J. L. DOOB, *What is a martingale?*, Amer. Math. Monthly, 78 (1971), pp. 451–462.

[3] E. F. FAMA, *Efficient capital markets: A review of theory and empirical work*, J. Finance, 25 (1970), pp. 383–417.

[4] L. FOLDES, *Martingale conditions for optimal saving—discrete time*, J. Math. Econ., 5 (1978), pp. 83–96.

[5] R. E. HALL, *Stochastic implications of the life cycle-permanent income hypothesis: Theory and evidence*, J. Pol. Econ., 86 (1978), pp. 971–987.

[6] M. C. JENSEN, *Risk, the pricing of capital assets, and the evaluation of investment portfolios*, J. Bus., 42 (1969), pp. 167–248.

[7] S. LeROY, *Risk aversion and the martingale property of stock prices*, Int. Econ. Rev., 14 (1973), pp. 436–446.

[8] B. B. MANDELBROT, *Forecasts of future prices, unbiased markets and martingale models*, J. Bus., 39 (1966), pp. 242–255.

[9] P. A. MEYER, *Probability and Potentials*, Blaisdell, Waltham, MA, 1966.

[10] J. F. MUTH, *Rational expectations and the theory of price movements*, Econometrica, 29 (1961), pp. 315–335.

[11] J. A. OHLSON, *Risk aversion and the martingale property of stock prices: Comments*, Internat. Econ. Rev., 18 (1977), pp. 229–234.

[12] P. A. SAMUELSON, *Proof that properly anticipated prices fluctuate randomly*, Ind. Man. Rev., 6 (1965), pp. 41–49.

[13] ———, *Proof that properly discounted present values of assets vibrate randomly*, Bell J. Econ. Man. Sci., 4 (1973), pp. 369–374.

SIAM Review
Vol. 25, No. 4, October 1983

© 1983 Society for Industrial and Applied Mathematics
0036-1445/83/2504-0002 $01.25/0

# ITÔ'S CALCULUS IN FINANCIAL DECISION MAKING*

A. G. MALLIARIS†

**Abstract.** This paper presents an introduction to Itô's stochastic calculus by stating some basic definitions, theorems and mathematical examples. Afterwards, the use of Itô's calculus in modern financial theory is illustrated by expositing a few representative applications. The main observation of this paper is that Itô's calculus which was developed from purely mathematical questions originating in Wiener's work has found unexpectedly important applicability in the theory of finance from the perspective of continuous time.

**1. Introduction.** Uncertainty and its modeling have played an important role in economic analysis. It is the purpose of this paper to demonstrate how certain relatively recent mathematical discoveries have enabled economists to formulate clearly and solve successfully several significant problems in financial economics. The mathematical theory we have in mind is known as *Itô's calculus* and includes stochastic integration, stochastic differentials, rules of stochastic differentiation, and stochastic differential equations.

The development of Itô's calculus was motivated by purely mathematical questions originating in Wiener's [35] work of 1923 on stochastic integrals. At no time did Itô or the other pioneering mathematicians working in this area realize the impact of their results on economic analysis. During the last two decades economists have used Itô's differential equation

$$(1) \qquad dX(t) = f(t, X(t))\, dt + \sigma(t, X(t))\, dZ(t)$$

to describe the behavior of stock prices, the stochastic rate of inflation, the stochastic spot rate of interest, and other economic variables. The availability of Itô's theory was not in itself sufficient for the formulation and solution of various economic problems. It had to be supplemented by appropriate breakthroughs in financial modeling. More on this issue will be said later on as the applications are explored. However, there is no doubt that Itô's calculus was necessary for the solution of several major economic problems.

Before we proceed to expound on Itô's calculus and to present some of its applications in financial economics, we should first say roughly why we consider stochastic models in economic analysis. In general, probability theory is introduced in economic analysis in cases when we are faced with an uncertain situation. As a researcher attempts to model the uncertain future behavior of an economic variable, probabilistic reasoning becomes appropriate by embedding a particular situation in a collection of like situations. Arrow [2] argues that the uncertainties about economics are rooted in our need for a better understanding of the economics of uncertainty. Such a better understanding of economic uncertainty is supplied by using Itô's methods.

More specifically, Merton [25] and [27] has argued that (1) is a satisfactory approximation of the actual behavior of certain economic variables. Furthermore, by using (1) to describe the stochastic behavior of economic variables and by assuming that trading takes place continuously in time, Merton states the benefits of such an analysis. The benefits include sharper results that are easier to interpret than those of the discrete time analysis and extensive mathematical literature on stochastic calculus which allows one to analyze rather complex economic models and still get quantitative results. In brief, stochastic models are considered because they lead to generalized results which are richer in theoretical content and more fruitful in empirical analysis.

---

*Received by the editors March 25, 1982, and in revised form January 12, 1983.

†Graduate School of Business, Loyola University of Chicago, Chicago, Illinois 60611.

In what follows we give the mathematical meaning of (1), we define the concepts of stochastic differential and stochastic differential equation, we state Itô's lemma and we give some mathematical examples. Then we proceed to formulate and solve two representative economic problems to illustrate the use of Itô's theory in modern financial decision making. We conclude with a few historical comments, bibliographical references and the basic remark that sometimes mathematical theories, no matter how pure or abstract, may eventually play a crucial part in applied problem solving.

**2. Stochastic integration.** Consider a probability space $(\Omega, \mathcal{F}, P)$ on which both a real-valued stochastic process $X(t, \omega):[0, \infty) \times \Omega \to R$ and a real-valued Wiener process with unit variance $Z(t, \omega):[0, \infty) \times \Omega \to R$ are defined. Equation (1) can be transformed into an integral equation to obtain

$$(2) \qquad X(t) = X(0) + \int_0^t f(s, X(s))\, ds + \int_0^t \sigma(s, X(s))\, dZ(s).$$

Note that $X(0)$ is the initial condition which is a random variable. As a rule, the first integral in the right-hand side of (2) can be understood as a Riemann integral or in more general cases as a Lebesgue integral. However, the second integral presents a problem because $dZ(t)$ does not exist. Putting it differently, although the Wiener process $Z(t)$ is continuous with probability 1 (w.p.1), it is a function of unbounded variation w.p.1 and therefore the second integral cannot be interpreted as a Riemann–Stieltjes integral. Thus, unless we define the second integral in (2), the process $X(t)$ has no meaning. The elements of stochastic integration are presented next to provide an appropriate meaning for the process $X(t)$ in (2).

Let $\{Z(t), t \geq 0\}$ be a Wiener process defined on a probability space $(\Omega, \mathcal{F}, P)$. A family of $\sigma$-fields $\mathcal{F}_t$ in $\mathcal{F}$ for $t \geq 0$ is said to be *nonanticipating* with respect to $Z(t)$ if it satisfies the following three conditions:

1. $\mathcal{F}_s \subset \mathcal{F}_t$ for $0 \leq s \leq t$.
2. $\mathcal{F}_t$ contains the $\sigma$-field generated by $Z(s)$ for $0 \leq s \leq t$.
3. $\mathcal{F}_t$ is independent of the $\sigma$-field generated by the increment $Z(u) - Z(t)$, $t \leq u < \infty$.

Condition 1 requires a monotonicity property to hold while condition 2 means that $Z(t)$ is measurable with respect to $\mathcal{F}_t$ for every $t \geq 0$. Condition 3 means that for $h = u - t, t \leq u < \infty$, the process $Z(t + h) - Z(h)$ is independent of any of the events of the $\sigma$-field $\mathcal{F}_h$. In particular, condition 3 means that $\mathcal{F}_0$ can contain only events that are independent of the process $Z(t)$ for $t \geq 0$.

Consider now a function $\sigma(t, \omega) : [0, T] \times \Omega \to R$ which is assumed to be measurable in $(t, \omega)$ with $[0, T] \subset [0, \infty)$, and let $\mathcal{F}_t, t \geq 0$, be a nonanticipating family of $\sigma$-fields with respect to $Z(t)$. A function $\sigma(t, \omega)$ is said to be *nonanticipating* with respect to a family of $\sigma$-fields $\mathcal{F}_t$ if it satisfies two conditions:

1. The sample path $\sigma(t, \cdot)$ is $\mathcal{F}_t$-measurable for all $t \in [0, T]$.
2. The integral

$$(3) \qquad \int_0^T |\sigma(t, \omega)|^2\, dt$$

is finite w.p.1.

Note that for a function $\sigma(t, \omega)$ with continuous sample paths w.p.1, the last integral is an ordinary Riemann integral. In more general cases (3) is taken to be a Lebesgue integral.

A special class of nonanticipating functions is the class of nonanticipating step functions. A nonanticipating function $\sigma(t, \omega)$ is called a *step function* if there exists a partition of the interval $[0, T] \subset [0, \infty)$, say

(4) $$0 = t_0 < t_1 < \cdots < t_n = T < \infty,$$

such that $\sigma(t, \omega) = \sigma(t_i, \omega)$ for $t \in [t_i, t_{i+1})$ for $i = 0, 1, 2, \cdots, n - 1$. We remark that the points $t_i$ are independent of $\omega$. For such step functions we now define Itô's stochastic integral.

Let $(\Omega, \mathcal{F}, P)$ be a probability space, $\sigma(t, \omega) : [0, T] \times \Omega \to R$ a nonanticipating step function for a partition of the form of (4) and $Z(t, \omega) : [0, T] \times \Omega \to R$ a Wiener process. The *stochastic integral* of a nonanticipating step function $\sigma$ with respect to $Z(t)$ over the interval $[0, T]$ is a real-valued random variable denoted by $I(\sigma)$ and defined as

(5)
$$I(\sigma) = \sum_{1}^{n} \sigma(t_{i-1}, \omega)[Z(t_i, \omega) - Z(t_{i-1}, \omega)]$$
$$= \sum_{1}^{n} \sigma(t_{i-1})[Z(t_i) - Z(t_{i-1})] = \sum_{0}^{n-1} \sigma(t_i)[Z(t_{i+1}) - Z(t_i)].$$

The presence of $\omega \in \Omega$ emphasizes the fact that Itô's integral is a random variable; $\omega$ is sometimes omitted for notational convenience. It is important to remark that in the definition of the step function, and consequently in the definition of stochastic integral, the left-hand endpoints of the subintervals are used for evaluation. This definition is easily generalized to give Itô's stochastic integral for an arbitrary nonanticipating function $\sigma(t)$.

More specifically, let $(\Omega, \mathcal{F}, P)$ be a probability space, and consider a Wiener process $Z(t)$ and an arbitrary nonanticipating function $\sigma(t, \omega)$, both defined on $[0, T] \times \Omega$ and both real-valued. *Itô's stochastic integral* of $\sigma(t)$ with respect to $Z(t)$ over the interval $[0, T]$, denoted by $I(\sigma)$, is a random variable defined as the *limit in probability* (denoted $\xrightarrow{P}$) of the stochastic Cauchy sequence $\{\int_0^T \sigma_n(t)\, dZ(t)\}$, that is,

(6) $$\int_0^T \sigma_n(t, \omega)\, dZ(t, \omega) \xrightarrow{P} \int_0^T \sigma(t, \omega)\, dZ(t, \omega) \equiv I(\sigma).$$

Here, $\{\sigma_n(t)\}$ is a sequence of nonanticipating step functions that approximates $\sigma$ in the sense of convergence in probability, that is,

(7) $$\int_0^T |\sigma(t, \omega) - \sigma_n(t, \omega)|^2\, dt \xrightarrow{P} 0.$$

We observe that $I(\sigma)$ is unique w.p.1 and independent of the choice of the sequence $\{\sigma_n(t)\}$ and we remark that Gikhman and Skorokhod [11, pp. 378–385] prove in detail, first, (7) and then (6).

Having defined Itô's stochastic integal we next define the indefinite integral. Suppose that $\chi_{[0,t]}$ is the characteristic function of the interval $[0, t] \subset [0, T]$ and let $\sigma$ be a nonanticipating function on $[0, t]$ for each $t$, where $0 \le t \le T$, and where $T$ is as before an arbitrarily large positive real number. The *indefinite integral* of a nonanticipating function $\sigma(t)$ with respect to $Z(t)$ is a stochastic process $I(t)$ defined as follows:

(8) $$I(t) = \int_0^T \sigma(s, \omega) \chi_{[0,t]}\, dZ(s, \omega).$$

Note that $I(t)$ is a real-valued $\mathcal{F}_t$-measurable stochastic process defined uniquely up to stochastic equivalence for $t \in [0, T]$ with $I(0) = \int_0^0 \sigma(s)\, dZ(s) = 0$, w.p.1.

The above brief analysis clarifies the meaning of (2). Itô's definite and indefinite integrals satisfy various important properties which are presented in Gikhman and Skorokhod [11, pp. 378–385]. For the purpose of our exposition these properties are not needed and therefore we proceed with additional concepts of Itô's calculus.

**3. Stochastic differentiation.** In this section we define the concept of stochastic differential and we present the main result of stochastic differentiation which is the celebrated Itô's lemma. The various applications which follow demonstrate the immediate usefulness of these concepts.

Consider a probability space $(\Omega, \mathcal{F}, P)$, a stochastic process $X(t, \omega) : [0, T] \times \Omega \rightarrow R$ that is measurable, for $t \in [0, T]$, with respect to a nonanticipating family of $\sigma$-fields $\mathcal{F}_t$, and a Wiener process $Z(t, \omega) : [0, T] \times \Omega \rightarrow R$. Assume that $\sigma(t, \omega) : [0, T] \times \Omega \rightarrow R$ is a nonanticipating function on $[0, T]$ and also that $f(t, \omega) : [0, T] \times \Omega \rightarrow R$ is measurable for each $t \in [0, T]$ with respect to $\mathcal{F}_t$ and also that $\int_0^T |f(t, \omega)| \, dt < \infty$, w.p.1. Let $0 \leqq r < s \leqq T$ and suppose

$$(9) \qquad X(s) - X(r) = \int_r^s f(t, \omega) \, dt + \int_r^s \sigma(t, \omega) \, dZ(t, \omega).$$

The *stochastic differential of the process* $X(t)$ is defined to be the quantity $f(t) \, dt + \sigma(t) \, dZ(t)$ and is denoted as $dX(t)$, that is,

$$(10) \qquad dX(t) = f(t) \, dt + \sigma(t) \, dZ(t).$$

A question naturally arises: Given a stochastic process $X(t)$ with respect to a Wiener process $Z(t)$ as in (9) if $Y(t) = u(t, X(t))$ be a new process, what is the stochastic differential of $Y(t)$ with respect to the *same* Wiener process? This question is important for both mathematical analysis and applications. The answer is provided below.

LEMMA 1 (Itô). *Let* $u(t, x) : [0, T] \times R \rightarrow R$ *be a continuous nonrandom function with continuous partial derivatives* $u_t$, $u_x$ *and* $u_{xx}$. *Suppose that* $X(t) : [0, T] \times \Omega \rightarrow R$ *is a process with stochastic differential*

$$dX(t) = f(t) \, dt + \sigma(t) \, dZ(t).$$

*Let* $Y(t) = u(t, X(t))$. *Then the process* $Y(t)$ *has a differential on* $[0, T]$ *given by*

$$(11) \qquad \begin{aligned} dY(t) &= [u_t(t, X(t)) + u_x(t, X(t)) f(t) + \tfrac{1}{2} u_{xx}(t, X(t)) \sigma^2(t)] \, dt \\ &\quad + u_x(t, X(t)) \sigma(t) \, dZ(t). \end{aligned}$$

The proof is presented in Gikhman and Skorokhod [11, pp. 387–389] and extensions of this lemma may be found in Arnold [1, pp. 90–99]. Here we limit our analysis by making three remarks.

First, Itô's lemma is a useful result because it allows us to compute stochastic differentials of arbitrary functions having as an argument a stochastic process which itself is assumed to possess a stochastic differential. In this respect Itô's formula is as useful as the chain rule of ordinary calculus.

Second, given an Itô stochastic process $X(t)$ with respect to a given Wiener process $Z(t)$ and letting $Y(t) = u(t, X(t))$ be a new process, Itô's formula gives us the stochastic differential of $Y(t)$, where $dY(t)$ is given with respect to the same Wiener process.

Third, an inspection of the proof of Itô's lemma reveals that it consists of an application of Taylor's theorem of advanced calculus and several probabilistic arguments to establish the convergence of certain quantities to appropriate integrals. Therefore, the reader may obtain Itô's formula by applying Taylor's theorem instead of remembering the specific result in (11). More specifically, the differential of $Y(t) = u(t, X(t))$, where $X(t)$ is a stochastic process with differential given by (10), may be computed by using Taylor's theorem and the following multiplication rules

$$(12) \qquad dt \times dt = 0, \quad dZ \times dZ = dt, \quad dt \times dZ = 0,$$

as below:

$$dY(t) = u_t dt + u_x dX(t) + \tfrac{1}{2} u_{xx}[dX(t)]^2$$

(13)
$$= u_t dt + u_x[f(t)\, dt + \sigma(t)\, dZ(t)]$$

$$+ \tfrac{1}{2} u_{xx}[f(t)\, dt + \sigma(t)\, dZ(t)]^2.$$

Carrying out the multiplications in (13), using the rules in (12) and rearranging terms, we obtain Itô's results in (11).

We close this section by defining Itô's stochastic differential equation. Let us write the stochastic differential

(14)
$$dX(t) = f(t, X(t))\, dt + \sigma(t, X(t))\, dZ(t),$$

which is exactly as (1) and suppose that the initial condition is given by

(15)
$$X(0, \omega) = X_0.$$

An equation of the form (14) with initial condition as in (15) for $t \in [0, T]$ is called an *Itô stochastic differential equation*. A stochastic process $X(t)$ is called a solution of (14) given (15) on the interval $[0, T]$ if $X(t)$ satisfies the following three properties:

1. $X(t)$ is $\mathcal{F}_t$-measurable, that is, nonanticipating for $t \in [0, T]$.
2. Both integrals satisfy w.p.1

$$\int_0^T |f(t, X(t, \omega))|\, dt < \infty,$$

$$\int_0^T |\sigma(t, X(t, \omega))|^2\, dt < \infty.$$

3. The integral equation

$$X(t) = X(0) + \int_0^t f(s, X(s))\, ds + \int_0^t \sigma(s, X(s))\, dZ(s)$$

is satisfied for every $t \in [0, T]$ w.p.1.

**4. Mathematical examples.** Here we give two examples of a mathematical nature to illustrate the application of Itô's lemma before we present applications from financial economics.

*Example* 1. Suppose that $Y(t) = u(X(t)) = e^{X(t)}$, where

$$dX(t) = -\tfrac{1}{2} dt + dZ(t)$$

and $X(0) = 0$. Applying Itô's lemma, we obtain

$$dY(t) = u_t dt + u_x dX(t) + \tfrac{1}{2} u_{xx}[dX(t)]^2$$

$$= e^{X(t)}[-\tfrac{1}{2} dt + dZ(t)] + \tfrac{1}{2} e^{X(t)}[-\tfrac{1}{2} dt + dZ(t)]^2$$

$$= e^{X(t)}\, dZ(t).$$

This example illustrates that given the stochastic differential equation

(16)
$$dY(t) = e^{X(t)}\, dZ(t) = Y(t)\, dZ(t)$$

with initial condition $Y(0) = e^{X(0)} = 1$, its solution is

(17)
$$Y(t) = \exp[-\tfrac{1}{2} t + Z(t)].$$

This result illustrates the difference between ordinary differential equations and stochastic differential equations. Observe that if (16) were an ordinary differential equation its solution would be $Y(t) = \exp Z(t)$, which is different from (17).

*Example* 2. Suppose $Y(t) = u(X(t)) = u(Z(t))$, where $u$ is assumed to be twice continuously differentiable with respect to $x$; let $X(0) = Z(0) = 0$ and $dX(t) = dZ(t)$. Itô's lemma gives

(18)
$$dY(t) = u_t dt + u_x dX(t) + \tfrac{1}{2} u_{xx}[dX(t)]^2$$
$$= u'(Z(t))dZ(t) + \tfrac{1}{2} u''(Z(t))\, dt.$$

Here prime denotes ordinary derivative. If we write (18) in integral form, it becomes

(19)     $$Y(t) = u(Z(t)) = u(0) + \int_0^t u'(Z(s))\, dZ(s) + \frac{1}{2} \int_0^t u''(Z(s))\, ds.$$

From (19), solving for the second term in the right-hand side, we get

(20)     $$\int_0^t u'(Z(s))\, dZ(s) = u(Z(t)) - u(Z(0)) - \frac{1}{2} \int_0^t u''(Z(s))\, ds.$$

Equation (20) is called the fundamental theorem of calculus for Itô's stochastic integral and it expresses the integral in the left-hand side only in terms of an ordinary integral.

We now proceed to illustrate the use of Itô's calculus in financial economics.

**5. The pricing of an option.** An *option* is a contract giving the right to buy or sell an asset within a specified period of time subject to certain conditions. The simplest kind of an option is the *European call option* which is a contract to buy a share of a certain stock at a given date for a specified price. The date the option expires is called the expiration date or maturity date and the price that is paid for the stock when the option is exercised is called the exercise price or the striking price.

In terms of economic analysis several propositions about option pricing seem clear. The value of an option increases as the price of the stock increases. If the stock price is much greater than the exercise price, it is almost sure that the option will be exercised, and analogously, if the price of the stock is much less than the exercise price, the value of the option will be near zero and the option will expire without being exercised. If the expiration date is very far in the future, the value of the option will be approximately equal to the price of the stock. If the expiration date is very near, the value of the option will be approximately equal to the stock price minus the exercise price, or zero, if the stock price is less than the exercise price. In general the value of the option is more volatile than the price of the stock and the relative volatility of the option depends on both the stock price and maturity.

The first rigorous formulation and solution of the problem of option pricing was achieved by Black and Scholes [5] and Merton [24]. Consider a stock option denoted by A, whose price at time $t$ can be written as

(21)                               $$W(t) = F(t, S(t))$$

where $F$ is a twice continuously differentiable function. Here $S(t)$ is the price of some other asset denoted by B, for example, the stock upon which the option is written. The price of $B$ is assumed to follow Itô's stochastic differential equation,

$$dS(t) = f(t, S(t))\, dt + \eta(t, S(t))\, dZ(t),$$
$$S(0) = S_0 \text{ given.}$$

Assume as a simplifying special case that $f(t, S(t)) = \alpha S(t)$ and that $\eta(t, S(t)) = \sigma S(t)$ where $\alpha$ and $\sigma$ are constants. The last equation can be written as

$$(22) \qquad dS(t) = \alpha S(t)\, dt + \sigma S(t)\, dZ(t).$$

Consider an investor who builds up a portfolio of three assets, $A$, $B$ and a riskless asset, such as a government bond, denoted by $C$. We assume that $C$ earns the riskless competitive rate of return $r(t)$. The nominal value of the portfolio is

$$(23) \qquad P(t) = N_1(t)S(t) + N_2(t)W(t) + Q(t),$$

where $N_1$ denotes the number of shares of $B$, $N_2$ the number of $A$, and $Q$ is the number of dollars invested in the riskless asset $C$. Assume that $B$ pays no dividends or other distributions. By Itô's lemma using (21) and (22), we compute

$$
\begin{aligned}
dW &= F_t dt + F_S dS + \tfrac{1}{2}F_{SS}(dS)^2 \\
(24) \qquad &= [F_t + F_S\alpha S + \tfrac{1}{2}F_{SS}\sigma^2 S^2]\, dt + F_S\sigma S dZ \\
&= \alpha_W W dt + \sigma_W W dZ.
\end{aligned}
$$

Note that in (24) we let

$$(24a) \qquad \alpha_W W = F_t + F_S\alpha S + \tfrac{1}{2}F_{SS}\sigma^2 S^2,$$

$$(24b) \qquad \sigma_W W = F_S\sigma S,$$

in order to simplify the notation. The change in the nominal value of the portfolio, $dP$, results from the change in the prices of the assets because at a point in time the quantities of option and stock are given, that is, $dN_1 = dN_2 = 0$. More precisely,

$$
\begin{aligned}
(25) \qquad dP &= N_1(dS) + N_2(dW) + dQ \\
&= (\alpha dt + \sigma dZ)N_1 S + (\alpha_W dt + \sigma_W dZ)N_2 W + rQ dt.
\end{aligned}
$$

Set $w_1 = N_1 S/P$, $w_2 = N_2 W/P$, $w_3 = Q/P = 1 - w_1 - w_2$. Then (25) becomes

$$(26) \qquad \frac{dP}{P} = (\alpha dt + \sigma dZ)w_1 + (\alpha_W dt + \sigma_W dZ)w_2 + (rdt)w_3.$$

At this point the notion of economic equilibrium (also called risk-neutral or preference-free pricing) is introduced in the analysis. This notion plays an important role in modeling financial behavior and its appropriate formulation is considered to be a major break-through in financial analysis.

More specifically, design the proportions $w_1$, $w_2$ so that the position is riskless for all $t \geq 0$, that is, let $w_1$ and $w_2$ be such that

$$(27) \qquad \mathrm{Var}_t\left(\frac{dP}{P}\right) = \mathrm{Var}_t(w_1\sigma dZ + w_2\sigma_W dZ) = 0.$$

In the last equation $\mathrm{Var}_t$ denotes variance conditioned on $S(t)$, $W(t)$ and $Q(t)$. In other words, choose $(w_1, w_2) = (\overline{w}_1, \overline{w}_2)$ so that

$$(28) \qquad \overline{w}_1\sigma + \overline{w}_2\sigma_W = 0.$$

Then from (26), because the portfolio is riskless, it follows that

$$(29) \qquad E_t\left(\frac{dP}{P}\right) = [\alpha\overline{w}_1 + \alpha_W\overline{w}_2 + r(1 - \overline{w}_1 - \overline{w}_2)]\, dt = r(t)\, dt.$$

Equations (28) and (29) yield the Black–Scholes–Merton equations

$$(30) \qquad \frac{\overline{w}_1}{\overline{w}_2} = -\frac{\sigma_W}{\sigma}$$

and

$$(31) \qquad r = \alpha \overline{w}_1 + \alpha_W \overline{w}_2 - r\overline{w}_1 - r\overline{w}_2 + r,$$

which simplify to

$$(32) \qquad \frac{\alpha - r}{\sigma} = \frac{\alpha_W - r}{\sigma_W}.$$

Equation (32) says that the net rate of return per unit of risk must be the same for the two assets and describes an appropriate concept of *economic equilibrium* in this problem. Using (32) and making the necessary substitutions from (24a) and (24b), the partial differential equation of the pricing of an option is obtained.

$$(33) \qquad \tfrac{1}{2}\sigma^2 S^2 F_{SS}(t,S) + rSF_S(t,S) - rF(t,S) + F_t(t,S) = 0.$$

**6. A reexamination of option pricing.** To illustrate the notion of economic equilibrium once again we present a modified exposition. Consider the nominal value of a portfolio consisting of a stock and a call option on this stock and write

$$(34) \qquad P(t) = N_1(t)S(t) + N_2(t)W(t)$$

using the same notation as in section 5. Equation (34) differs from (23) by having deleted the term $Q(t)$. Here we concentrate on the two assets of the portfolio, that is, the stock and call option. Using (34) and (24), the change in the value of the portfolio is given by

$$(35) \qquad dP = N_1\,dS + N_2\,dW = N_1\,dS + N_2[(F_t + \tfrac{1}{2}F_{SS}\sigma^2 S^2)\,dt + F_S\,dS].$$

Note that $dN_1 = dN_2 = 0$, since at any given point in time the quantities of stock and option are given. For arbitrary quantities of stock and option, (35) shows that the change in the nominal value of the portfolio, $dP$, is stochastic because $dS$ is a random variable expressed in (22). Suppose the quantities of stock and call option are chosen so that

$$(36) \qquad \frac{N_1}{N_2} = -F_S.$$

Then $N_1\,dS + N_2 F_S\,dS = 0$, and inserting (36) into (35) yields

$$(37) \quad dP = -N_2 F_S\,dS + N_2[(F_t + \tfrac{1}{2}F_{SS}\sigma^2 S^2)\,dt + F_S\,dS] = N_2(F_t + \tfrac{1}{2}F_{ss}\sigma^2 S^2)\,dt.$$

Let $N_2 = 1$ in (37) and observe that in equilibrium the rate of return of the riskless portfolio must be the same as the riskless rate $r(t)$. Therefore we write

$$(38) \qquad \frac{dP}{P} = r\,dt.$$

Equation (38) can be used to derive the partial differential equation for the value of the option. Making the necessary substitutions in (38), obtain

$$(39) \qquad \frac{(F_t + (1/2)F_{SS}\sigma^2 S^2)\,dt}{-F_S S + W} = r\,dt,$$

which upon rearrangement gives (33). Note that the option pricing equation in (33) is a second-order linear partial differential equation of the parabolic type. The boundary conditions of (33) are determined by the specification of the asset. For the case of an option which can be exercised only at the expiration date $t^*$ with an exercise price $E$, the boundary conditions are

(40a) $$F(t, S = 0) = 0,$$

(40b) $$F(t = t^*, S) = \max [0, S - E].$$

Observe that (40a) says that the call option price is zero if the stock price is zero at any date $t$; (40b) says that the call option price at the expiration date $t = t^*$ must equal the maximum of either zero or the difference between the stock price and the exercise price.

The solution of the option pricing equation subject to the boundary conditions is given by Black and Scholes [5] and Merton [24] as:

(41) $$F(T, S, \sigma^2, E, r) = S\Phi(d_1) - \frac{E}{e^{rT}} \Phi(d_2),$$

where $\Phi$ denotes the cumulative normal distribution, namely,

$$\Phi(y) = \frac{1}{\sqrt{2\pi}} \int_{-\infty}^{y} e^{-x^2/2} dx.$$

In (41), $T = t^* - t$, namely, $T$ is time to expiration (measured in years) and $d_1$ and $d_2$ are given by

(42) $$d_1 = \frac{\ln (S/E) + (r + \sigma^2/2) T}{\sigma \sqrt{T}},$$

(43) $$d_2 = \frac{\ln (S/E) + (r - \sigma^2/2) T}{\sigma \sqrt{T}}.$$

It can be shown that

$$\frac{\partial F}{\partial T} > 0, \quad \frac{\partial F}{\partial S} > 0, \quad \frac{\partial F}{\partial \sigma^2} > 0, \quad \frac{\partial F}{\partial E} < 0, \quad \frac{\partial F}{\partial r} > 0.$$

These partial derivatives justify the intuitive behavior of the price of an option as was indicated in the beginning of 5. More specifically, these partials show that as the stock price rises so does the option price; as the variance rate of the underlying stock rises so does the option price; with a higher exercise price, the expected payoff decreases; the value of the option increases as the interest rate rises; and finally, with a longer time to maturity the price of the option is greater.

**7. An example.** Equation (41) indicates that the Black–Scholes option pricing model is a function of only five variables: T, the time to expiration; S, the stock price; $\sigma^2$, the instantaneous variance rate on the stock price; E, the exercise price; and, r, the riskless interest rate. From these five variables, only the variance rate must be estimated; the other four variables are directly observable. A simple example is presented to illustrate the use of (41). The values of the observable variables are taken from the *Wall Street Journal*.

On Friday, December 10, 1982, the IBM stock price was $92.875. To estimate the call option price with expiration date the third Friday in April 1983, with an exercise price $95, the riskless rate and the instantaneous variance need to be estimated. The riskless rate is estimated by using the average of the bid and ask quotes on U.S. Treasury bills of approximately the same maturity as the option. The results of the Monday, December 13, 1982, auction show a riskless rate of 7.995% for U.S. Treasury bills maturing in 13 weeks. The only missing piece of information is the instantaneous variance of the stock price.

There are several different techniques which have been suggested for estimating the instantaneous variance. In this regard the work of Latané and Rendleman [20] must be mentioned; they derive standard deviations of continuous price relative returns which are implied in actual call option prices on the assumption that investors behave as if they price options according to the Black–Scholes model. In our example we calculate the implicit variance by using the actual April 1983 call price of an IBM option with an exercise price of $90 to solve for an estimate of the instantaneous variance. More specifically, a numerical search is used to approximate the standard deviation implied by the Black–Scholes formula with parameters: price of the stock, $S = 92.875$; exercise price, $E = 90$; time to expiration, $T = 126/365 = .345$; riskless rate, $r = .08$; and call option price, $F = 9.875$. The approximated implicit standard deviation is found to be $\sigma = .35$.

After the above clarifications are made, the example is this: given $S = 92.875$, $E = 95$, $T = .345$, $r = .08$ and $\sigma = .35$, use (41) to compute $F$. Using (42) and (43) we calculate

$$d_1 = \frac{\ln (92.875/95) + [.08 + (1/2)(.35)^2](.345)}{.35\sqrt{.345}} = .127004,$$

$$d_2 = \frac{\ln (92.875/95) + [.08 - (1/2)(.35)^2](.345)}{.35\sqrt{.345}} = -.078575.$$

From statistical tables, giving the area of a standard normal distribution, we obtain $\Phi(.127004) = .550532$ and $\Phi(-.078575) = .46867$. Finally,

$$F = (92.875)(.550532) - \frac{95}{e^{(.08)(.345)}} (.46867) = 7.819.$$

The calculated call option price of $7.819 is very close to the actual call price of $7.875 reported in the *Wall Street Journal* on Monday December 13, 1982.

This simple example shows how to use the Black–Scholes model to price a call option under the assumptions of the model. The example is presented for illustrative purposes only and it relies heavily on the implicit estimate of the variance, its constancy over time and all the remaining assumptions of the model. The appropriateness of estimating the instantaneous variance implicitly is ultimately an empirical question, as is the entire Black–Scholes pricing formula. Boyle and Ananthanarayanan [6] study the implications of using an estimate of the variance in option valuation models and show that this procedure produces biased option values. However, the magnitude of this bias is not large.

One additional remark must be made. The closeness in this example of the calculated call option price to the actual call price is not necessarily evidence of the validity of the Black–Scholes model. Extensive empirical work has taken place to investigate how market prices of call options compare with prices predicted by Black and Scholes. The interested reader is referred to Macbeth and Merville [21] and Bhattacharya [4].

**8. Remarks on option pricing.** It is beyond the scope of this paper to review the voluminous literature on option pricing. For such a review the reader is referred to the two papers by Smith [31] and [32]. It is appropriate, however, to make a few remarks on the Black–Scholes option pricing model to clarify its significance and its limitations.

First, the Black–Scholes model for a European call as derived in [5] and [24] and as reported here is based on several simplifying assumptions: the stock price follows an Itô equation; the market operates continuously; there are no transaction costs in buying or selling the option or the underlying stock; there are no taxes; the riskless rate is known and constant; and finally, there are no restrictions on short sales. Several researchers have extended the original Black-Scholes model by modifying these assumptions. Merton [24] generalizes the model to include dividend payments, exercise price changes and the case of a stochastic interest rate. Roll [29] has solved the problem of valuing a call option that can be exercised prior to its expiration date when the underlying stock is assumed to make known dividend payments before the option matures. Ingersoll [13] studies the effect of differential taxes on capital gains and income while Scholes [30] determines the effects of the tax treatment of options on the pricing model. Furthermore, Merton [26] and Cox and Ross [8] have shown that if the stock price movements are discontinuous, under certain assumptions, the valuation model still holds. These, and some other modifications of the original Black–Scholes analysis, have shown the model to be quite robust regarding the relaxation of its foundational assumptions.

Second, it is worth repeating that the use of Itô's calculus and the important insight concerning the appropriate concept of an equilibrium by creating a riskless hedge portfolio have led Black and Scholes to obtain a closed form solution for option pricing. In this closed form solution several variables do not appear, such as: the expected rate of return on the stock, the expected rate of return on the option, a measure of investor's risk preference, investor expectations and equilibrium conditions for the entire capital market.

Third, the Black–Scholes pricing model has found numerous applications. We mention a few such as: pricing the debt and equity of a firm; the effects of corporate policy and, specifically, the effect of mergers, acquisitions and scale expansions on the relative values of the debt and equity of the firm; the pricing of convertible bonds; the pricing of underwriting contracts; the pricing of leases; and the pricing of insurance. Smith in [31] and [32] summarizes most applications and indicates the original references.

Finally, three important papers by Harrison and Kreps [12], Kreps [17] and [18] consider some foundational issues that arise in conjunction with the arbitrage theory of option pricing. The important point to consider is this: the ability to trade securities frequently can enable a few multiperiod securities to span many states of nature. In the Black–Scholes theory there are two securities and uncountably many states of nature, but because there are infinitely many trading opportunities and because uncertainty resolves nicely, markets are effectively complete. Thus, even though there are far fewer securities than states of nature, nonetheless, markets are complete and risk is allocated efficiently.

### 9. Term structure of interest rates.

The *term structure of interest rates* measures the relationship among the yields on default free securities that differ only in their term to maturity. The determinants of this relationship have long been an area of active research for economists. By offering a complete schedule of interest rates across time, the term structure embodies the market's anticipations of future events. Therefore, an explanation of the term structure gives researchers a way to extract this information and encourages them to develop testable theories.

Previous theories of the term structure have assumed as their starting point a world of certainty and have proceeded by examining stochastic generalizations of the certainty equilibrium relationships. The literature in this area is voluminous and a reexamination of several traditional theories, while employing recent advances in the theory of valuation of contingent claims, can be found in Cox, Ingersoll and Ross [7]. Here, we present a term structure model developed by Vasicek [34].

Consider a market in which investors issue and buy default free claims on a specified sum of money to be delivered at a given future date. Such a claim will be called a *discount bond*.

Let $P(t, s)$ denote the price at time $t$ of a discount bond maturing at time $s$, with $t \le s$. The bond is assumed to have a maturity value of one unit, that is,

$$(44) \qquad\qquad P(s, s) = 1.$$

The *yield to maturity* denoted by $R(t, T)$ is the internal rate of return at time $t$ on a bond with maturity date $s = t + T$, and is given by

$$(45) \qquad\qquad R(t, T) = -\frac{1}{T} \ln P(t, t + T), \qquad T > 0.$$

From (45), the rates $R(t, T)$ considered as a function of $T$ will be referred to as *the term structure at time t*. We use (45) to define the *spot rate* as the instantaneous borrowing and lending rate, $r(t)$, given by

$$(46) \qquad\qquad r(t) = R(t, 0) = \lim_{T \to 0} R(t, T).$$

At any time $t$, the current value $r(t)$ of the spot rate is known. However, the subsequent future values are not necessarily certain. It is natural to expect that the price of a discount bond will be determined over its term solely by the spot interest rate. More accurately, we assume that the price $P(t, s)$ of the discount bond is determined by the assessment at time $t$ of the spot rate process $\{r(u), t \le u \le s\}$ over the term of the bond. We write

$$(47) \qquad\qquad P(t, s) = P(t, s, r(t))$$

to indicate that the price $P(t, s)$ of the discount bond is a function of the spot rate $r(t)$. To complete the model we need to postulate the behavior of the spot rate process. It is assumed that the stochastic dynamics of the spot rate can be described by an Itô stochastic differential equation given by

$$(48) \qquad\qquad dr(t) = f(t, r(t))\, dt + \rho(t, r(t))\, dZ(t).$$

Finally, assume that there are no transaction costs, information is available to all investors simultaneously and that investors act rationally, that is, assume that the market is efficient. This last assumption implies that no profitable riskless arbitrage is possible.

From (47) and (48) by using Itô's lemma obtain the stochastic differential equation

$$(49) \qquad\qquad dP = P\mu(t, s, r(t))\, dt - P\sigma(t, s, r(t))\, dZ$$

which describes the bond price changes. In (49) the functions $\mu$ and $\sigma$ are defined as follows,

$$(50) \qquad\qquad \mu(t, s, r) \equiv \frac{1}{P(t, s, r)} \left[ \frac{\partial}{\partial t} + f \frac{\partial}{\partial r} + \frac{1}{2} \rho^2 \frac{\partial^2}{\partial r^2} \right] P(t, s, r),$$

$$(51) \qquad\qquad \sigma(t, s, r) \equiv -\frac{1}{P(t, s, r)} \rho \frac{\partial}{\partial r} P(t, s, r).$$

Consider now the quantity $q(t, r(t))$ given by

$$(52) \qquad\qquad q(t, r) = \frac{\mu(t, s, r) - r}{\sigma(t, s, r)}, \qquad t \le s,$$

which is called the *market price of risk* and which specifies the increase in expected instantaneous rate of return on a bond per an additional unit of risk. Substitute the expressions of $\mu$ and $\sigma$ from (50) and (51) into (52), make the necessary rearrangements to obtain the *term structure equation* given by

$$
(53) \qquad \frac{\partial P}{\partial t} + (f + pq)\frac{\partial P}{\partial r} + \frac{1}{2}p^2\frac{\partial^2 P}{\partial r^2} - rP = 0.
$$

Observe that (53) is a partial differential equation whose solution $P$ may be obtained once the spot rate process $r(t)$ and market price of risk $q(t, r)$ are specified. The boundary condition of (53) is

$$
(54) \qquad P(s, s, r) = 1.
$$

Knowing $P(t, s, r)$ as a solution of (53) subject to (54) allows one to obtain the term structure from (45).

Vasicek uses techniques presented in Friedman [10] to write a representation for the bond price as a solution to the term structure equation, given by

$$
(55) \quad P(t, s) = E_t \exp\left[ -\int_t^s r(u)\,du - \frac{1}{2}\int_t^s q^2(u, r(u))\,du + \int_t^s q(u, r(u))\,dZ(u) \right],
$$

$$t \leq s.$$

To obtain some economic insight in (55), construct a portfolio consisting of a bond whose maturity approaches infinity, called a long bond, and lending or borrowing at the spot rate, with proportions $\lambda(t)$ and $1 - \lambda(t)$ respectively. Define $\lambda(t)$ as

$$
\lambda(t) = \frac{\mu(t, \infty) - r(t)}{\sigma^2(t, \infty)},
$$

that is,

$$
(56) \qquad \lambda(t)\sigma(t, \infty) = q(t, r(t)).
$$

The price, $Q(t)$, of such a portfolio satisfies the equation

$$
(57) \qquad dQ = \lambda Q[\mu(t, \infty)\,dt - \sigma(t, \infty)\,dZ] + (1 - \lambda)Qr\,dt.
$$

Equation (57) can be integrated by evaluating the differential of $\ln Q$ and using (56) to yield

$$
d(\ln Q) = \lambda\mu(t, \infty)\,dt - \lambda\sigma(t, \infty)\,dZ + (1 - \lambda)r\,dt - \tfrac{1}{2}\lambda^2\sigma^2(t, \infty)\,dt
$$

$$
= r\,dt + \tfrac{1}{2}q^2\,dt - q\,dZ.
$$

Therefore, we conclude that

$$
\frac{Q(t)}{Q(s)} = \exp\left[ -\int_t^s r(u)\,du - \frac{1}{2}\int_t^s q^2(u, r(u))\,du + \int_t^s q(u, r(u))\,dZ \right].
$$

Using this last equation we can rewrite (55) as

$$
P(t, s) = E_t \frac{Q(t)}{Q(s)}, \qquad t \leq s.
$$

This means that the price of any bond measured in units of the value of a portfolio $Q$ follows a martingale,

$$
\frac{P(t, s)}{Q(t)} = E_t \frac{P(u, s)}{Q(u)}, \qquad t \leq u \leq s.
$$

Therefore, we conclude that if the bond price at time $t$ is a certain fraction of the value of the portfolio $Q$, then the same will hold in the future. Further applications of the martingale concept in financial economics are presented in Malliaris [22] and an arbitrage model of the term structure of interest rates may be found in Richard [28].

**10. Concluding remarks.** In this final section we collect various remarks, historical notes and additional bibliographical references.

Stochastic integration was developed by Itô [14] as he generalized a stochastic integral first introduced in 1923 by Wiener [35]. Parts of Itô's original work were presented initially by Doob [9] and later by Gikhman and Skorokhod [11]. Our presentation on stochastic integration follows Gikhman and Skorokhod [11, pp. 378–385], Bharucha-Reid [3, pp. 221–226], Arnold [1, pp. 64–75], Friedman [10, pp. 55–72] and Ladde and Lakshmikanthan [19, pp. 114–122].

It is useful to remark that Itô's stochastic integral is not related to the various nonstochastic integrals of ordinary calculus and measure theory. Doob [9, p. 444] shows that if $Z(t, \omega)$ is a Wiener process with unit variance, then Itô's stochastic integral yields

$$\int_a^b Z(t, \omega)\, dZ(t, \omega) = \frac{1}{2} [Z^2(b, \omega) - Z^2(a, \omega)] - \frac{1}{2} (b - a),$$

which is different from the ordinary Riemann integral for a continuous nonstochastic function $Z(t)$, which is

$$\int_a^b Z(t)\, dZ(t) = \frac{1}{2} [Z^2(b) - Z^2(a)].$$

Since Itô's calculus is based on Itô's stochastic integral, it is not surprising that Itô's rules of stochastic differentiation are not the same as the rules of ordinary calculus. Furthermore, Itô's stochastic differential and integral equations differ from the ordinary ones. Therefore, it may be concluded that Itô's calculus is an independent, self-consistent mathematical theory which is not connected to ordinary calculus. In other words, Itô's calculus cannot be formulated as an extension, in some mathematical sense, of ordinary calculus.

Stratonovich [33] has defined a new stochastic integral as a mean square limit of a symmetrized sum which preserves the rules of ordinary calculus. However, the economics and finance literature relies almost exclusively on Itô's stochastic integral and Itô's calculus in general for several reasons. The expectations of the Itô integral are easier to compute than the Stratonovich integral; the Itô has the important property of being a martingale; the Itô stochastic differential equation exhibits a nonanticipating property which is the appropriate way to model economic uncertainty; the solutions of Itô equations have nice properties, that is, they are Markov process and under certain conditions they are diffusion processes; and finally, virtually all the mathematical theory of stochastic control and stability is developed using the Itô integral.

Itô's lemma first appeared in Itô [15] and later in Itô [16]. In our presentation we follow Gikhman and Skorokhod [11, pp. 387–389] and Arnold [1, pp. 96–99]. The mathematical examples and financial applications presented in this paper illustrate the usefulness of Itô's lemma. Note also that Itô's lemma has found further applications in financial economics in areas such as: first, the formulation of appropriate stochastic budget constraints and, second, the stochastic control problems of optimum consumption and portfolio decisions. A detailed presentation of these topics may be found in Malliaris and Brock [23].

**Acknowledgments.** The ideas discussed in this paper were presented in some detail at a Finance Seminar at The University of Texas at Austin in June 1981. I am thankful to all members of this seminar for their interest and in particular to Professors Stephen Magee, Sam Cox, Wayne Lee, George Morgan, Stephen Smith and Robert Witt for helpful discussions. I am also thankful to Carol Ross for research and computational assistance. A briefer version of this paper was presented at the Midwest Conference of the American Institute for Decision Sciences, April 7–9, 1982, Milwaukee, Wisconsin.

## REFERENCES

[1] L. ARNOLD, *Stochastic Differential Equations: Theory and Applications*, John Wiley, New York, 1974.

[2] K. J. ARROW, *Limited knowledge and economic analysis*, Amer. Econ. Rev., 64 (1974), pp. 1–10.

[3] A. T. BHARUCHA-REID, *Random Integral Equations*, Academic Press, New York, 1972.

[4] M. BHATTACHARYA, *Empirical properties of the Black–Scholes formula under ideal conditions*, J. Fin. Quant. Anal., 15 (1980), pp. 1081–1105.

[5] F. BLACK AND M. SCHOLES, *The pricing of options and corporate liabilities*, J. Pol. Econ., 81 (1973), pp. 637–654.

[6] P. P. BOYLE AND A. L. ANANTHANARAYANAN, *The impact of variance estimation in option valuation models*, J. Fin. Econ., 5 (1977), pp. 375–387.

[7] J. C. COX, J. E. INGERSOLL, JR. AND S. A. ROSS, *A re-examination of traditional hypotheses about the term structure of interest rates*, J. Fin., 36 (1981), pp. 769–799.

[8] J. C. COX AND S. A. ROSS, *The valuation of options for alternative stochastic processes*, J. Fin. Econ., 3 (1976), pp. 145–166.

[9] J. L. DOOB, *Stochastic Processes*, John Wiley, New York, 1953.

[10] A. FRIEDMAN, *Stochastic Differential Equations and Applications*, Academic Press, New York, 1975.

[11] I. GIKHMAN AND A. V. SKOROKHOD, *Introduction to the Theory of Random Processes*, Saunders, Philadelphia, 1969.

[12] J. M. HARRISON AND D. M. KREPS, *Martingales and arbitrage in multiperiod securities markets*, J. Econ. Th., 20 (1979), pp. 381–408.

[13] J. E. INGERSOLL, *A theoretical and empirical investigation of the dual purpose funds: An application of contingent claims analysis*, J. Fin. Econ., 3 (1976), pp. 83–123.

[14] K. ITÔ, *Stochastic integrals*, Proc. Imperial Academy, 20 (1944), pp. 519–524.

[15] ———, *On a formula concerning stochastic differentials*. Nagoya Math. J., 3 (1951), pp. 55–65.

[16] ———, *Lectures on Stochastic Processes*, Tata Institute of Fundamental Research, India, 1961.

[17] D. M. KREPS, *Arbitrage and equilibrium in economies with infinitely many commodities*, J. Math. Econ., 8 (1981), pp. 15–35.

[18] ———, *Multiperiod securities and the efficient allocation of risk: A comment on the Black–Scholes option pricing model*, The Economics of Information and Uncertainty, J.J. McCall, ed., Univ. Chicago Press, Chicago, 1982.

[19] G. S. LADDE AND V. LAKSHMIKANTHAM, *Random Differential Inequalities*, Academic Press, New York, 1980.

[20] H. A. LATANÉ AND R. J. RENDLEMAN, JR., *Standard deviations of stock price ratios implied in option prices*, J. Fin., 31 (1976), pp. 369–381.

[21] J. D. MACBETH AND L. J. MERVILLE, *An empirical examination of the Black–Scholes call option pricing model*, J. Fin., 34 (1979), pp. 1173–1186.

[22] A. G. MALLIARIS, *Martingale methods in financial decision-making*, this Review, 23 (1981), pp. 434–443.

[23] A. G. MALLIARIS AND W. A. BROCK, *Stochastic Methods in Economics and Finance*, North-Holland, Amsterdam, 1982.

[24] R. C. MERTON, *Theory of rational option pricing*, Bell J. Econ. Man. Sci., 4 (1973), pp. 141–183.

[25] ———, *Theory of finance from the perspective of continuous time*, J. Fin. Quant. An., 10 (1975), pp. 659–674.

[26] ———, *Option pricing when underlying stock returns are discontinuous*, J. Fin. Econ., 3 (1976), pp. 125–144.

[27] ———, *On the mathematics and economic assumptions of continuous time models*, Financial Economics: Essays in Honor of Paul Cootner, W.F. Sharpe and C.M. Cootner eds., North-Holland, Amsterdam, 1982.

[28] S. F. RICHARD, *An arbitrage model of the term structure of interest rates,* J. Fin. Econ., 6 (1978), pp. 33–57.

[29] R. ROLL, *An analytic valuation formula for unprotected American call options on stocks with known dividends,* J. Fin. Econ., 5 (1977), pp. 251–258.

[30] M. SCHOLES. *Taxes and the pricing of options,* J. Fin., 31 (1976), pp. 319–332.

[31] C. W. SMITH, JR., *Option pricing: A review,* J. Fin. Econ., 3 (1976), pp. 3–51.

[32] ———, *Applications of option pricing analysis,* Handbook of Financial Economics, J.L. Bicksler, ed., North-Holland, Amsterdam, 1979.

[33] R. L. STRATONOVICH, *A new representation for stochastic integrals and equations,* SIAM J. Control, 4 (1966), pp. 362–371.

[34] O. VASICEK, *An equilibrium characterization of the term structure,* J. Fin. Econ., 4 (1977), pp. 177–188.

[35] N. WIENER, *Discontinuous boundary conditions and the Dirichlet problem,* Trans. Amer. Math. Soc., 25 (1923), pp. 307–314.

# [7]

## Random Walk vs. Chaotic Dynamics
## in Financial Economics

A. G. MALLIARIS

*Department of Economics, Loyola University of Chicago*

*820 N. Michigan Avenue, Chicago, IL 60611*


G. PHILIPPATOS

*College of Business Administration, The University of Tennessee*

*432 Stokely Management Center, Knoxville, TEN 27990*

## 1. INTRODUCTION

During the past three decades, financial economists have studied in detail the behavior of stock market prices and the prices of derivative securities issued on such stocks. By price behavior we mean the dynamic, period by period, change in the price level of a given stock, such as, the daily closing price of an IBM share and the daily settlement price of the corresponding put or call. The extensive literature that addresses these twin problems is known as the market efficiency theory and the option pricing theory. Both theories constitute significant pillars of modern financial economics and despite various puzzles and anomalies, such as the October 1987 stock market crash, that cannot be explained by market efficiency, there are currently no competing theories that are widely accepted.

We do not wish to review here market efficiency or option pricing. Both are well known and can be found readily in textbooks such as Lee, Finnerty, and Wort (1990). Ross (1987) gives an insightful and comprehensive overview of the field of finance and dedicates a significant portion of his essay on efficient markets and options. Rather, we propose to contrast the random walk behavior of stock prices and of derivative securities to chaotic dynamics. Although we plan to give a precise definition of chaotic dynamics later on, the methodological intuition of this concept is motivated by the notion that stock prices follow a deterministic, dynamic and nonlinear process which generates a very complex time series that although it looks like the random walk it actually is not.

In other words, in this essay we address the question: is it possible for stock prices and their derivative instruments to appear to be random but not to be really random? Put differently, we ask:  do there exist <u>nonrandom</u> functions whose time series characteristics are similar to random walk?  We hasten to inform the reader that the answer to both questions is affirmative.  In other words, there are nonrandom functions whose time characteristics appear as complicated as those of the random walk and by implication it is, at least theoretically, possible for stock prices to be generated by such functions.

In section 2 we describe the meaning of random walk and reformulate the two questions in a technically more precise way.  In section 3 we give an example of a deterministic (nonstochastic) dynamic (indexed by time) and nonlinear function whose time series not only appears (visually) to be random, but actually fails to reject the null hypothesis of a random walk.  We also give a precise definition of chaotic dynamics and explain it in detail.  We dedicate section 4 to some recent techniques used in distinguishing between random and nonrandom time series and report some available empirical evidence.  In this section we also address the theoretical and practical implications of these two alternative modelling approaches to asset pricing.  The last section summarizes our ideas and offers suggestions for future research.

## 2. RANDOM WALK

Random walk is a statistical term which financial economics uses to describe the dynamic behavior of stock market and other asset prices.  In its simplest formulation we define the sequence of prices, denoted by $\{p(t) : t = 0, 1, 2, ...\}$, to follow a random walk if

$$p(t + 1) = p(t) + \epsilon(t + 1), \tag{2.1}$$

where $\epsilon(t + 1)$ is the value obtained from sampling with replacement from a given distribution with a given population mean $\mu_\epsilon$ and a variance of $\sigma^2_\epsilon$ .  In (2.1) we express tomorrow's price as a random departure from today's price, or equivalently, we express the price change between today and tomorrow, i.e. $p(t + 1)$ - $p(t)$, as random.  It is usually assumed that $\mu_\epsilon = 0$.  In our analysis we concentrate on price changes denoted as $dp(t + 1) = p(t + 1) - p(t)$.

As a mathematical model, the notion of random walk has its methodological foundation in probability theory.  Recall that probability theory analyzes events whose outcome is uncertain in contrast to deterministic calculus where the relationship between the dependent and independent variable is exact.  Long before the efficient market hypothesis was conceived, formulated and tested, the random walk model in (2.1) was utilized to convey the notion that stock prices cannot be systematically forecasted.  Over fifty years ago Cowles (1933) asked rhetorically the question: can stock market forecasters forecast?  Roberts (1959) reviews several early papers on stock market price behavior and challenges the relevance of technical analysis in anticipating price changes.

Roberts uses the term technical analysis to describe the search for patterns in stock market prices and argues that such patterns may actually be nothing more than statistical artifacts. Although Roberts does not use the term random walk, he constructs a "chance model" and argues that weekly changes of a typical stock market index behave as if they were independent sample observations from a normal distribution with mean + 0.5 and standard deviation 5.0.

The early observations of the random behavior of stock market prices and their modelling using the random walk paradigm, eventually directed finance researchers to seek explanations for such a statistical phenomenon. Thus, the efficient market hypothesis was developed to rationalize the random walk behavior claiming that the current price $p(t)$ fully and correctly reflects all relevant information and because the flow of information between now and next period cannot be anticipated, price changes are serially uncorrelated. Fama (1970) skillfully reviews the earlier theoretical and empirical literature on efficient capital markets.

During the last twenty years, the theory of market efficiency has been refined analytically, mathematically and statistically. Analytically, the concept of information was made precise and its meaning was clarified. Mathematically, the notion of random walk was generalized to martingales and Itô processes; and finally, numerous sophisticated statistical tests were employed to test the theory. In such an intense scientific activity it was not surprising to find, along with numerous studies confirming market efficiency, several studies rejecting it.

This rapid overview allows us to conclude that currently, the random walk behavior of stock market price changes is the orthodoxy of financial economics. Needless to say, this orthodoxy is not undisputed, nor have analysts given up their search for alternative modelling. Actually we wish to propose such an alternative modelling here and in order to do so we claim that Figure 1 can be utilized as a metaphor of the random walk and the market efficiency theory. This figure illustrates a sequence of 101 random numbers between 0 and 1. Obviously, market price changes range over a much larger subset of the real numbers rather than the subset of [0, 1]. However, this is a simple issue of scaling. What matters in Figure 1 and in the theory of market efficiency is not so much the range of price changes but the fact that knowing, let us say, the first 10 numbers, does not enable us to predict the 11th number and in general knowing all the numbers up to a given number does not allow us to predict the next one. Thus, Figure 1 is a numerical representation of the random walk and what market efficiency theory does is to provide a rationale for such a statistical behavior.[1]

---

[1]The 101 numbers in Figure 1 were obtained from the random number generator of LOTUS 1-2-3. Their mean and variance are .502435 and .076573 respectively. Each element of the set $\{\epsilon(t) : t = 0, 1, 2, ..., 100\}$ represents a numerical random price change. Note that if instead of the simple random walk in (2.1) an Itô equation were used to describe price changes of the form $dp(t) = \mu dt + \sigma dZ(t)$, assuming $\mu$ and $\sigma$ as constant parameters, it would also generate a graph similar to the one in Figure 1. This is so because an Itô equation is driven by its random term $dZ$ which in discrete time is approximated by sampling from a normal distribution with zero mean and variance equal to one. Therefore, there is no loss of generality in analyzing the random walk in its numerical representation in Figure 1 instead of Itô processes or martingales. A methodological analysis of martingales is presented in Malliaris (1981) and of Itô processes in Malliaris (1990).

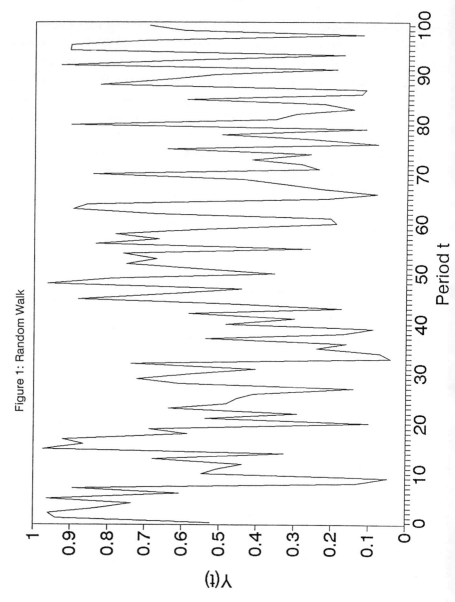

Figure 1: Random Walk

Focusing on Figure 1 we now ask the question: can a graph similar to the one in Figure 1 be constructed from a nonrandom methodology? In other words, does there exist a deterministic (nonrandom) function with an exact relationship between dependent and independent variable that generates a graph like the one in Figure 1? These are purely mathematical questions with significant implications for market efficiency. In sharp contrast to the random walk, the existence of an exact, deterministic equation would imply perfect predictability of all future prices. Market efficiency would argue that such a clairvoyant knowledge would alter today's price because market participants would take appropriate positions today to benefit from such knowledge about the future and in so doing would alter this deterministic equation. In other words a deterministic equation and market efficiency are not compatible, provided that the deterministic stock price model is common across investors and furthermore, it is common knowledge.

To briefly recapitulate, consider the random behavior in Figure 1 as a paradigm of stock market price changes. On the basis of casual observation and more formally, on the basis of traditional statistical tests, can we manufacture a similar graph from a nonrandom equation? This is the topic presented in the next section.

## 3. CHAOTIC DYNAMICS

Consider the nonlinear deterministic equation

$$dp(t + 1) = 3.89\, dp(t)\, [1 - dp(t)], \tag{3.1}$$

with initial condition $dp(0) = .52$. The value selected for the initial condition is that of the first value of the random walk in Figure 1. It is used to coordinate the starting value of the random walk and the logistic map and has no significance. Any value in $[0, 1]$ will yield similar results.

Suppose that stock price changes are generated by (3.1). How does the time series of such price changes look like? Figure 2 illustrates such a time series for $t = 0, 1, 2, ...100$. Notice that for each $t = 1, 2, ...100$, equation (3.1) precisely yields a stock price change denoted as $dp(t)$. Furthermore, all that is needed to calculate the stock price change next period is the current price change. Randomness does not enter equation (3.1) and therefore we can say that stock price changes are not uncertain. Knowing today's price change, (3.1) allows us to calculate all future price changes precisely.

We do not propose that (3.1) is an actual mathematical expression of stock price changes. We simply wish to illustrate that (3.1) generates a time series that exhibits complex dynamics that resemble actual stock price changes. If Figure 2 appeared in a business publication it would not surprise anyone; yet its time series comes from an exact, deterministic, nonrandom, and nonlinear

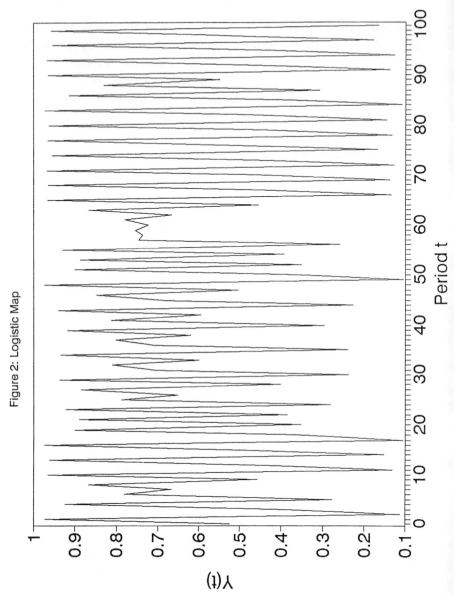

Figure 2: Logistic Map

equation that generates random-like behavior.

Obviously the existence of a deterministic equation such as (3.1) does not disprove that stock market price changes follow a random walk, it only casts a strong doubt that the random walk cannot be the only and exclusive mathematical model for such price changes. It is true, that the random walk is supported by an elaborate theory of efficient markets and by numerous empirical studies. However, the existence of an alternative mathematical paradigm invites our intellectual consideration.

At this point we could digress to explain the chaotic dynamics associated with (3.1). Brock and Malliaris (1989) give an introduction to chaos and explain how the work of physicists on turbulence has offered financial economists new ways of modelling complicated time series. Hsieh (1991) gives a detailed analysis of chaos and nonlinear dynamics in financial markets. It suffices for our purpose to simply say that (3.1) is a specific example of a chaotic function, known as the logistic map, and that it has been studied extensively not only by physicists but has also been reviewed in economics by Baumol and Benhabib (1989) and in futures markets by Savit (1988). The remarkable characteristic of the logistic map is not so much its exact quadratic (therefore nonlinear) expression but, rather, the fact that by changing the values of the coefficient 3.89 in (3.1), this equation can generate a rich variety of time series behavior. Figures 3a and 3b give a small sample of few time series obtained by simply changing the coefficient **w** in

$$dp(t + 1) = w\,dp(t)\,[1 - dp(t)]. \tag{3.2}$$

Savit (1988) and Baumol and Benhabib (1989) devote essentially their entire articles in analyzing, illustrating and explaining the behavior of (3.2) for parameter values[2] of **w** in various subintervals of **[0, 4]**. The important point, however, is that (3.1) as a special case of (3.2) invites the financial analyst to reflect on the question: could it be that actual stock price changes are generated by nonlinear, deterministic, dynamic equations? As much as our intuition, guided by the orthodoxy of efficient market theory[3], might object such a consideration, academic curiosity encourages us to proceed.

The logical way to proceed in the analysis of chaotic dynamics is to give a precise definition. The definition we give is purely mathematical and can be found in several books such as Devaney

---

[2]The important paper that proposed the use of differential equations depending upon a parameter for the modelling of turbulence is Ruelle and Takens (1971). For an elegant review of the mathematical properties of the logistic map and of other maps known to mathematicians for their complicated time series see May (1976). In Figures 3a and 3b we illustrate how the behavior of (3.2) and its graphical representation change as the parameter value changes. For **w** = 3 we obtain a series that is convergent; for **w** = 3.3 the map generates a two-period cycle while for **w** = 3.4495 we have a four-period cycle. For **w** = 3.5 we generate a long cycle while for **w** = 3.935 and **w** = 3.99 we obtain chaotic behavior. More specifically note that for **w** ≤ 3, the system is stable while for 3 < **w** ≤ 3.57 the system is periodic. Finally, for 3.57 < **w** < 4, the system is mostly chaotic.

[3]Notice that our approach is to contrast the paradigms of random walk and that of chaotic dynamics instead of attacking the efficient market hypothesis. For a recent attack see Shleifer and Summers (1990).

# Figure 3a: Selected Logistic Maps

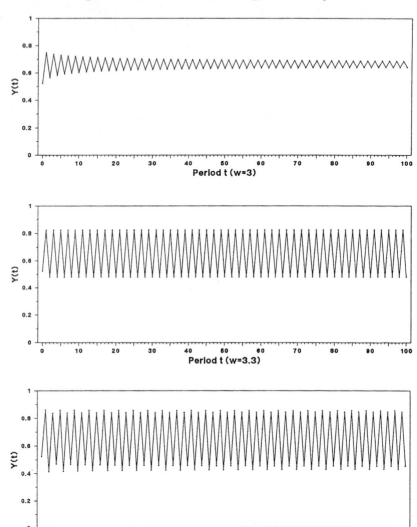

# Figure 3b: Selected Logistic Maps

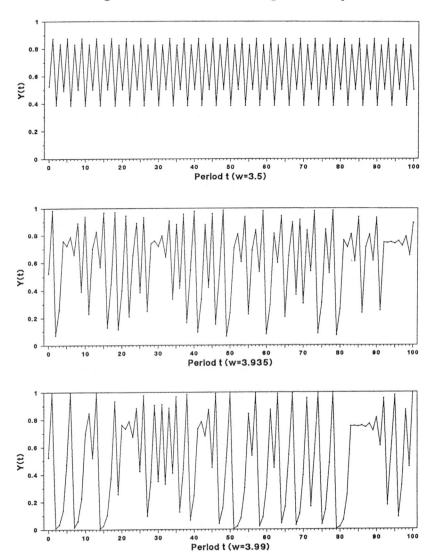

(1986). It requires, first, to explain a few terms. We do this next.

Consider a real-valued function **f : R → R**. We are interested in the time series generated by this function starting from some arbitrary $x_0 \in$ **R**. Denote by $f^2 \equiv f[f(x)] \equiv f \circ f(x)$ where o means composition and in general let $f^n = f \circ f \circ ... \circ f(x)$ mean **n** compositions. The time series takes the values

$$x_o, \; f(x_o), \; f^2(x_o), \; ..., f^n(x_o), \; ...,  \qquad (3.3)$$

for **t = 0, 1, 2,..., n**. For (3.3) to describe a chaotic function it must satisfy three requirements.

First it must sample infinitely many values. To make this idea precise we say that **f : R → R** is <u>topologically</u> <u>transitive</u> if for any pair of open sets **U** and **V** in the real line **R** there is an integer **k > 0** such that $f^k(U) \cap V \neq \phi$.

The second requirement is sensitive dependence on initial conditions. We say that the function **f : R → R** has <u>sensitive dependence</u> on initial conditions if there exists a $\delta > 0$ such that for any $x \in$ **R** and any neighborhood **N** of x, there is a y $\in$ **N** and an integer **n > 0** such that

$$| f^n(x) - f^n(y) | > \delta . \qquad (3.4)$$

This condition says that there are time series that start very close to each other but diverge exponentially fast from each other.

The third requirement involves a property of the periodic points of the function **f**, namely that these periodic points are dense in **R**. We say that a point $x \in$ **R** is <u>periodic</u> if for **n > 0**, $f^n(x)$ = x. The least positive integer **n** for which $f^n(x)$ = x is called the <u>prime period</u> of x.

We can summarize our analysis by giving the definition of a chaotic function. We say that a function **f : R → R** is <u>chaotic</u> if it satisfies three conditions:

1. f is topologically transitive.
2. f has sensitive dependence on initial conditions.
3. f has periodic points that are dense in the real numbers.

Observe that this is a precise mathematical definition which is not motivated by stock market price behavior. Yet, each condition can be given a financial interpretation. The first condition requires the time series dynamics to be rich in the sense that (3.1) takes infinitely many different values. This condition makes a chaotic map similar to random walk because each value is different from all the previous ones. Of course, in random walk this happens because we are sampling from an infinite population. On the other hand, in chaotic dynamics we do not have sampling; instead we have a nonlinear equation that generates many different values. Note that for both the random walk and for the chaotic dynamics it is possible for certain values to occur more than once in the time series. What we are emphasizing is that such a repetition is very unlikely. Put differently the first condition of topological transitivity, requires the time series to be rich in the sense that it takes infinitely many different values. Intuitively, such a map can move under iteration, i.e. through time, from one arbitrarily small neighborhood to any other. Since the space cannot be decomposed into two disjoint open sets which are invariant under the map (by definition) the points not only can wander anywhere (since they can't be blocked) but actually will wander everywhere.

The second condition casts serious difficulties in forecasting. Although a chaotic map is deterministic and knowing today's value immediately allows one to compute tomorrow's price, the same exact equation can generate very dissimilar time series if we are uncertain about when the series got started and at what initial value $x_o$. To contrast with a random walk, recall that the past and future values are independent because we are sampling from an infinite population of values. The inability to forecast is due precisely to this statistical independence. In a chaotic function, however, we know exactly the relationship between the past and the future but we are unable to predict because we cannot be sure as to when we started and with what value. Put differently, in a chaotic function, only if we know exactly $x_0$ can we then generate the sequence (3.1). Figure 4 illustrates the time series of errors generated from a very small error in the initial value for the logistic map. In this graph the top two time series, $y(t)$ and $v(t)$, are generated with the same parameter value $w = 3.89$ but two slightly different initial conditions, $y(0) = .52$ and $v(0) = .51$. The third graph depicts the deviations due to the insignificant difference in the initial value. It should be, however, noted that not all points near $x_0$ need eventually separate from $x_0$ under iteration; rather it must be emphasized that there must be at least one such point in every neighborhood of $x_0$.

The third condition gives a chaotic function structure. It essentially requires that the chaotic function exhibit important regularities. However, these regularities are hidden in the sense that no researcher could explore the infinitely many patterns of the periodic points and their limits. In an analogous manner, the random walk can be said to have some structure given to it by the properties of the distribution that characterizes the population. Again, no researcher could explore the infinitely many sample paths that a random walk process can generate. This analogy between the structure of a chaotic function and a random walk should not be understood as meaning that both have exactly the same structure. Although we do not know how to compare correctly the structure of a chaotic function to that of a random walk, it suffices to remark that (3.1) involves infinitely many iterations of a nonlinear function and therefore its structure could be viewed as being more complex compared to the structure of a random walk generated from a simple equation as (2.1). More technically, one can argue that in chaotic dynamics because the set of periodic points is dense in **R**, for any point in **R**, there exists a sequence of periodic points which converges to this point. Thus, it appears intuitively that not only a structure exists because of the mere existence of the periodic points, but moreover because they are clustered around each point in the domain. Therefore, due to the fact that periodic points are dense, each point in the domain can be identified

## Figure 4: Sentitive Dependence on Initial Conditions

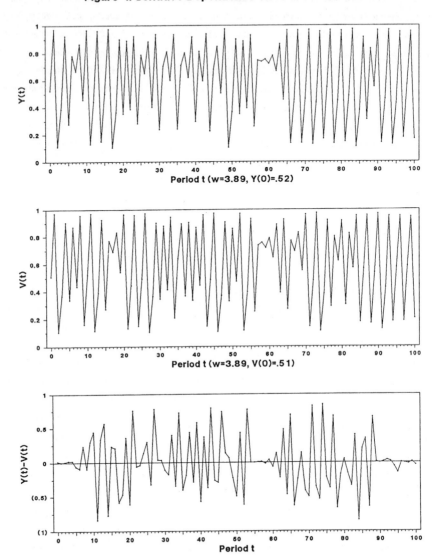

by a sequence of periodic points, which converges to it. However, in the random walk case, each point is identified by its probability of occurrence which is described by the normal density function.

Having presented and explained the definition of a chaotic function, there are at least two ways to proceed. First, one can take the road of mathematics and present theorems about chaotic dynamics. The second possibility is to return immediately to financial economics and reflect the appropriateness of chaotic dynamics in representing stock market price changes and price changes of derivative assets. The first possibility, although informative, becomes rapidly very technical. The second possibility has limited potential because we only have one tool: the definition of a chaotic process. Therefore we suggest a third alternative: we will describe an interesting mathematical result instead of rigorously stating and proving theorems, and use it for our main purpose of contrasting the methodologies of random walk vs. chaotic dynamics in financial economics.

The mathematical result that makes chaotic dynamics very interesting is the existence of strange attractors. In studying various chaotic maps, mathematicians discovered that as time increases, despite the turbulent behavior of such maps that looks like random, the time series values indeed converge to a set. Furthermore, the set which, of course, depends on the specific map is not one of the standard sets of stability theory such as a point, a circle, or a torous. Because the attractors of chaotic maps are not as the regular attractors of ordinary differential equations, they were named strange.

A precise mathematical definition of a strange attractor is given in Guckenheimer and Holmes (1983) along with several beautiful illustrations. We will use a simple definition and say that a strange attractor of a chaotic dynamical system is a compact set, denoted $S$, such that almost all initial conditions in the neighborhood of $S$ converge to $S$. The neighborhood of $S$ from where almost all initial conditions yield time series that converge to $S$ is called the basin of the strange attractor.

Instead of reproducing graphically strange attractors of famous chaotic maps we generated 5000 points of the logistic map and graphed in Figure 5 not the time series $\{y(t) : t = 0, 1, 2, 5000\}$ but instead its phase diagram, that is $\{[y(t), y(t + 1)] : t = 0, 1, 2, ..., 5000\}$. Observe that although Figure 2 shows that the logistic map with $w = 3.89$ as in (3.1) behaves randomly (only the first 101 points are illustrated but the same is true for the entire time series) as time increases the values of this map stay within a set that has a specific shape and looks like a parabola. From a mathematical standpoint we cannot decide the strange attractor with only 5000 iterations but it is nevertheless instructive that even so early the limit set begins to take shape.

In sharp contrast to Figure 5 now examine Figure 6. It is generated from a random walk with 5001 drawings. As in Figure 1, which depicts the first 101 points we continued the process for 5001 drawings and then graphed the pairs $\{[y(t), y(t + 1)], t = 0, ... 5000\}$ as explained in footnote 1. Figure 5 illustrates that chaotic maps settle down to structured sets while Figure 6 illustrates that

## Figure 5: Strange Attractor
### Y(0)=.52, w=3.89

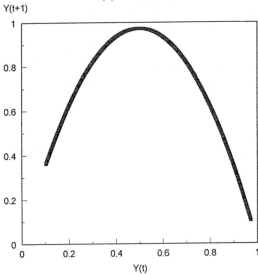

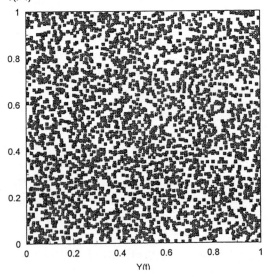

## Figure 6: Random Walk - Scatter Diagram

random walks do not settle down. One conclusion we can draw from the examination of Figures 5 and 6 is that a random walk fills all the space and continues to wander around (as time increases) while chaotic dynamics (despite their appearance as random and turbulent) fill much less space and have strange attractors.

## 4. DETECTING CHAOTIC DYNAMICS

The reader has by now, most likely, understood our message: given a time series of actual stock price changes how can it be analytically modelled? We have argued that the random walk paradigm, despite its wide popularity is only one way. Another model is chaotic dynamics. Furthermore we have contrasted the definitions and graphical representations of these two approaches and concluded that the random walk wanders for ever while chaotic dynamics wanders also but in a narrower range. Put differently, the randomness of random walk has no structure while the randomness of chaotic dynamics has significant hidden structure. In other words, random walk describes uncertainty in a more extreme way than chaotic dynamics. Naturally, the important question is: Given a time series how can we distinguish whether it is generated by a random walk or a chaotic process?

In an important paper Brock (1986) reviewed an extensive literature in physics that addresses precisely this question. He also evaluated the various methods used by the physicists and reported some preliminary results using such methods in economic and financial data. Brock and Malliaris (1989, Chapter 10) present a pedagogical exposition of some similar ideas.

What we plan to do in this section is to intuitively explain one method, i.e. correlation dimension[4], for detecting whether the data are random or chaotic and then apply it to the two sets of data that generated Figures 5 and 6. Since we manufactured both sets and already know from these two figures the nature and structure of these data, our procedure would allow us to evaluate the effectiveness of the detecting methodology.

The correlation dimension was originally proposed by Grassberger and Procaccia (1983). We first give an intuitive motivation and then proceed to describe the methods more carefully. The intuition behind this method is guided by Figures 5 and 6. A system that is random is space filling as in Figure 6 while a system that is chaotic has a strange attractor that fills less space. Instead of just examining pairs $\{[y(t), y(t + 1)] : t = 0, 1, 2, ...\}$ in two dimensional figures as in 5 and 6, suppose that we consider triplets $\{[y(t), y(t + 1), y(t + 2)] : t = 0, 1, 2, ...\}$ and in general M-

---

[4]There are at least three methods used by nonlinear scientists in distinguishing random from deterministic systems: correlation dimension, Liapunov exponents and Kolmogorov entropy. These methods are reviewed and evaluated in Eckmann and Ruelle (1985), Brock (1986) and Brock and Malliaris (1989). There is general agreement that the correlation dimension has emerged as the most useful method, among these three.

histories $\{[y(t), y(t + 1), ... y(t + M - 1)] : t = 0, 1, 2, ...\}$. The same way the pairs of a random walk filled the 2-dimensional space, one would expect the M-histories of a random walk to fill the M-dimensional space while the chaotic system's attractor may not spread over too many dimensions. In other words the dimension of a chaotic system tends to stabilize.

Let us now translate this intuition into careful analysis. Suppose that we are given a time series of price changes $\{dp(t) : t = 0, 1, 2, ... T\}$. Suppose that T is large enough so that a strange attractor has begun to take shape. Use this time series to create pairs, i.e. $dP^2(t) \equiv \{[dp(t), dp(t + 1)] : t = 0, 1, 2, ... T\}$ and then triplets and finally M-histories, i.e. $dp^M(t) \equiv \{[dp(t), ... dp(t + M - 1)] : t = 0, 1, 2, ... T\}$. In other words we convert the original time series of singletons into vectors of dimension 2, 3, ... M. In generating these vectors we allow for overlapping entries. For example if M = 3 we have a set of the form $\{[dp(0), dp(1), dp(2)], [dp(1), dp(2), dp(3)], ..., dp(T - 2), dp(T - 1), dp(T)\}$. Such a set will have $(T + 1) - (M - 1)$ vectors. Mathematically, the process of creating vectors of various dimension from the original series is called an <u>embedding</u>.

Suppose that for a given embedding dimension, say M, we wish to measure if these M-vectors fill the entire M-space or only a fraction. For a given $\epsilon > 0$ define the <u>correlation integral</u>, denoted by

$$C^M(\epsilon) = \frac{\text{the number of pairs } (s, t) \text{ whose distance } \| dp^M(s) - dp^M(t) \| < \epsilon}{T^2_M}$$
$$= \frac{\text{the number of } (s, t),\ 1 \leq t,\ s \leq T,\ \| dp^M(s) - dp^M(t) \| < \epsilon}{T^2_M}, \tag{4.1}$$

where $T_M = (T + 1) - (M - 1)$, and as before

$$dp^M(t) = [dp(t), dp(t + 1), ..., dp(t + M - 1)].$$

Observe that $\| \cdot \|$ in (4.1) denotes vector norm. Using the correlation integral we can define the <u>correlation dimension</u> for an embedding dimension M as

$$D^M = \lim_{\substack{\epsilon \to 0 \\ T \to \infty}} \frac{\ln C^M(\epsilon)}{\ln \epsilon}. \tag{4.2}$$

In (4.2) ln denotes natural logarithm. Finally, the correlation dimension D is given by

$$D = \lim_{M \to \infty} D^M. \tag{4.3}$$

We remark that technical accuracy requires that $D^M$ in (4.2) is a double limit, first in terms of $T \to \infty$ and then in terms of $\epsilon \to 0$. However, in practice T is usually given and it is impossible to increase it to infinity. Thus the limit $T \to \infty$ is meaningless in practice and moreover M is practically bounded by T. Therefore, we only consider the limit $\epsilon \to 0$ in (4.2).

Tables 1 and 2 illustrate the use of (4.1), (4.2) and (4.3). For our two sets of data, each with 5001 points, we proceed as follows. Since T is fixed, our two variables are the embedding

## TABLE 1: CORRELATION DIMENSION FOR LOGISTIC DATA

| | | VALUES OF $\epsilon$ | | | | |
|---|---|---|---|---|---|---|
| | | $\epsilon$ (.3366) | $\epsilon^2$ (.1133) | $\epsilon^3$ (.03814) | $\epsilon^4$ (.01284) | $\epsilon^5$ (.004321) |
| **E** | 2 | 1.00 | .94 | .93 | .93 | .92 |
| **M** | 3 | 1.34 | 1.16 | 1.09 | 1.05 | 1.02 |
| **B** | 4 | 1.67 | 1.36 | 1.22 | 1.14 | 1.10 |
| **E** | | | | | | |
| **D** | 5 | 1.99 | 1.55 | 1.35 | 1.25 | 1.19 |
| **D** | | | | | | |
| **I** | 6 | 2.28 | 1.73 | 1.48 | 1.34 | 1.27 |
| **N** | | | | | | |
| **G** | 7 | 2.60 | 1.92 | 1.60 | 1.44 | 1.35 |
| **D** | 8 | 2.88 | 2.10 | 1.73 | 1.54 | 1.42 |
| **I** | | | | | | |
| **M** | 9 | 3.16 | 2.27 | 1.85 | 1.63 | 1.50 |
| **E** | | | | | | |
| **N** | 10 | 3.44 | 2.45 | 1.97 | 1.73 | 1.59 |
| **S** | | | | | | |
| **I** | | | | | | |
| **O** | 11 | 3.72 | 2.62 | 2.10 | 1.82 | 1.66 |
| **N** | | | | | | |

dimension **M** and the distance of neighboring points. We consider the values of **M** = 2, 3, ..., 11. Obviously one could consider many more. For $\epsilon$ we consider the first five powers of the standard deviation of the original data sets. Therefore the entries in Table 1 correspond to specific values of (4.1). The limit (4.2) corresponds to the limit of a given row of this Table, while **D** corresponds to the limit of the last column.[5]

A review of tables 1 and 2 is quite revealing. Table 1 presents in a matrix form the correlation dimension calculated for a given embedding dimension and a given value of $\epsilon$ for the 5001 points of the logistic map. For example, for **M** = 2 and $\epsilon$ = .3366 the calculations in (4.1) yield **1.00**, while for **M** = 10 and $\epsilon^4$ = .01284 the value of (4.1) is **1.73**. Notice that for a given embedding dimension as $\epsilon \to 0$ the values converge so that $\mathbf{D^M}$ in (4.2) has a limit. Also notice that as we hold $\epsilon$ or its powers fixed and increase the embedding dimension the numbers increase very slowly, again implying convergence. From our limited calculations we conclude that the correlation dimension **D** in (4.3) approaches **1.66** which is a small and finite number.

In contrast to Table 1, observe the results generated using the 5001 random data with a very similar mean and standard deviation to those of the logistic map. For a given embedding dimension as $\epsilon \to 0$, (4.1) now yields values that diverge. Furthermore, as you examine the values in a given cell as the embedding dimension increases holding $\epsilon$ or its powers fixed there is an increase which is faster than that of the logistic data. In conclusion, Table 2 shows that because random data fills the space even as the embedding dimension increases the correlation dimension **D** in (4.2) is not defined. In other words, the quantitative description of figures 5 and 6 is given quantitative expressions in calculating **D** in (4.3) confirming that the correlation dimension of the strange attractor is smaller than that of the random set.

Thus far the correlation dimension was applied to the 5001 points of the two sets: random and logistic. Actually, the entire article is an exposition of these two paradigms. However, we wish now to briefly report that the same methodology has been applied to actual data[6]. Scheinkman and LeBaron (1989) present preliminary evidence that indicates the presence of chaotic dynamics in stock market data. They used an initial data set of at least 5200 daily returns on the value-weighted portfolio of the Center for Research in Security Prices at the University of Chicago (CRSP). Because daily returns are usually noisy, these authors constructed a weekly return series of 1226 observations. Using embedding dimension from **M** = 1, 2, ... 14 and letting their $\epsilon \to 0$ they observe that the correlation dimension **D** in (4.3) is about **6.3**. Of course this number is small but one cannot be absolutely confident that this is conclusive evidence of chaos. The authors provide,

---

[5]All the calculations in Tables 1 and 2 were performed using Professor Dechert's software for calculating BDS statistics. We thank Professor Dechert for supplying us with his helpful program.

[6]It is of historical significance to note that two decades ago Philippatos and Wilson (1971, 1972, 1974), Philippatos and Martell (1974) and Philippatos and Nawrocki (1973) used entropy measures to study time dependency in stock market prices.

## TABLE 2: CORRELATION DIMENSION FOR RANDOM DATA

| | | VALUES OF $\epsilon$ | | | | |
|---|---|---|---|---|---|---|
| | | $\epsilon$ (.2902) | $\epsilon^2$ (.08422) | $\epsilon^3$ (.02444) | $\epsilon^4$ (.0071) | $\epsilon^5$ (.002058) |
| **E M B E D D I N G   D I M E N S I O N** | 2 | 1.14 | 1.48 | 1.63 | 1.72 | 1.77 |
| | 3 | 1.71 | 2.21 | 2.45 | 2.50 | 2.74 |
| | 4 | 2.28 | 2.94 | 3.26 | * | * |
| | 5 | 2.84 | 3.66 | 4.11 | * | * |
| | 6 | 3.41 | 4.38 | * | * | * |
| | 7 | 3.97 | 5.07 | * | * | * |
| | 8 | 4.53 | 6.04 | * | * | * |
| | 9 | 5.09 | * | * | * | * |
| | 10 | 5.65 | * | * | * | * |
| | 11 | 6.21 | * | * | * | * |

* : An asterisk denotes that calculations do not yield a finite number.

however, a yardstick for comparison: they create scrambled data in the following manner. First, returns were regressed on past returns. Then, they sampled with replacement from the residuals and rebuilt the data set using the estimated linear system and the same initial values as the real data. This way they created data that seemed much more random than the initial 1226 observations. For the scrambled data, they found that the correlation dimension almost doubled in value to **11.2**. Furthermore, Scheinkman and LeBaron (1989) compute the correlation dimension of Abbot Labs and find that for both the original data of this stock and for the scrambled data the numbers are higher than for the index. One implication of these findings is that individual stock returns could be more random than the value-weighted index.[7]

Although these early findings are encouraging, much more work needs to be done. A tentative conclusion is that as research reveals that the random walk paradigm is extreme, such findings would encourage financial economists to reformulate the theories of market efficiency[8].

## 5.  SUMMARY AND CONCLUSIONS

We have contrasted two paradigms of stock market price changes:  random walk and chaotic dynamics.  The analysis emphasized the definitions of these two concepts and graphical presentations illustrated their behavior.  Instead of casting the analysis in a form of a debate by attacking the random walk model, we chose to clarify the issues involved.  Namely, both random walk and chaotic dynamics are mathematical concepts whose time series generate graphical representations resembling actual stock market price changes.  However the scientific foundations of these two models are radically different:  one is probabilistic while the other is deterministic.

Because chaotic dynamics is a relatively new concept it is developed here in a little more detail and the method of correlation dimension is explained and illustrated with two data sets. Our conclusions include the following.

First, despite its general acceptability, substantial empirical evidence and analytical simplicity, the random walk model of stock price changes does not command currently the popularity it once had.  Therefore the profession is searching for alternative models.

Second, various generalizations of the random walk, theoretically such as martingales and Itô processes or empirically, such as ARCH, GARCH, bilinear models, or theoretical deviations

---

[7]Ramsey and Yuan (1989) and Ramsey, Sayers and Rothman (1988) evaluate the Scheinkman and LeBaron results using various simulations. Brock, Dechert and Scheinkman (1986) develop a test that is better grounded on statistical theory. For details see these references and Brock, Hsieh and LeBaron (1991). Finally, applications of chaotic techniques to derivative and other financial markets is currently available. Few representative studies among several others are: Savit (1989) for options, Hsieh (1989) for foreign currencies, Blank(1991) for futures markets and Van Der Ploeg (1986) for bonds.

[8]Brock (1988) discusses the theoretical implications of chaotic dynamics in economics and finance.

from market efficiency, such as noise trading, share common probabilistic foundations and therefore are not radical departures from the old methodology.

Third, chaotic dynamics offers an important alternative paradigm. The time series of a chaotic dynamic system appears random but actually contains significant structure. In other words its randomness is not extreme. Financial economists can learn a great deal from physicists who have researched this area extensively.

Fourth, random walk is supported by an elaborate theory of market efficiency. Chaotic dynamics has no companion theory. Market efficiency is inconsistent with the deterministic foundation of chaos and nonlinearity. For chaotic dynamics to gain further ground, appropriate theories of market behavior must be developed to offer theoretical support.

Fifth, initial empirical evidence of actual stock market data has provided partial support for chaotic dynamics and nonlinearity. A further challenge for chaotic dynamics is the development of an appropriate theory of statistical inference. The work of Brock, Dechert, and Scheinkman is very encouraging. See also the forthcoming book of Brock, Hsieh and LeBaron (1992).

Finally, the use of the logistic map or other well known chaotic maps, only serves as a metaphor of the actual map that drives stock market price changes. The actual map, if it is chaotic, is unknown. Even worst, the nonlinear scientist has currently no methods for discovering it. Available methods only distinguish between chaos and randomness. Simply put, we may have more models of the behavior of stock market but the "market is still a fascinating mystery."

## ACKNOWLEDGEMENT

We owe a significant intellectual debt to Professor William Brock for his pioneering work in this area, for his continued support and valuable comments on an earlier draft. Parts of this paper were presented by A. G. Malliaris at the Citicorp Seminar of the Economics Department at Brown University. We wish to thank Professor Jerome Stein and various seminar participants for their valuable comments. We are grateful to Professor L. Geronazzo for the invitation to contribute this paper to the present volume. All errors are our own responsibility.

## BIBLIOGRAPHY

Baumol, W., and J. Benhabib, (1989), "Chaos:    Significance, Mechanism, and Economic Applications", Journal of Economic Perspectives, Vol. 3,  77-105.

Blank, S., (1991), "Chaos In Futures Markets?  A Nonlinear Dynamical Analysis", Journal of Futures Markets, 11,  711-728.

Brock,W., (1986), "Distinguishing Random and Deterministic Systems: Abridged Version", Journal of Economic Theory, Vol. 40,  168-194.

Brock, W., (1988), "Nonlinearity and Complex Dynamics in Economics and Finance", in THE ECONOMY AS AN EVOLVING COMPLEX SYSTEM, SFI Studies in the Sciences of Complexity, Addison-Wesley Publishing Company.

Brock, W., W. Dechert, and J. Scheinkman, (1986), "A Test for Independence Based on the Correlation Dimension",   Working Paper, Department of Economics,   University of Wisconsin, University of Chicago and University of Houston.

Brock, W.,   D. Hsieh and B. LeBaron (1991), NONLINEAR DYNAMICS, CHAOS AND INSTABILITY : STATISTICAL THEORY AND ECONOMIC EVIDENCE, Cambridge, Massachusetts : The MIT Press.

Brock, W., and A.G. Malliaris, (1989), DIFFERENTIAL EQUATIONS, STABILITY AND CHAOS IN DYNAMIC ECONOMICS. Advanced Textbooks in Economics, North-Holland Publishing Company, Amsterdam.

Brock, W., and C. Sayers,(1988), "Is the Business Cycle Characterized by Deterministic Chaos", Journal of Monetary Economics, Vol. 22, 71-90.

Cowles, A., (1933), "Can Stock Market Forecasters Forecast?", Econometrica, Vol. 1, 309-324.

Devaney, R., (1986), AN INTRODUCTION TO CHAOTIC DYNAMICAL SYSTEMS, Menlo Park, California, Benjamin/Cummings Publishing.

Eckmann, J., and D. Ruelle, (1985), "Ergodic Theory of Chaos and Strange Attractors", Review of Modern Physics, Vol. 57, 617-656.

Fama, E., (1970), "Efficient Capital Markets: A Review of Theory and Empirical Work", Journal of Finance, Vol. 25, 383-417.

Frank, M., and T. Stengos, (1989), "Measuring the Strangeness of Gold and Silver Rates of Return", Review of Economic Studies, Vol. 56, 553-567.

Grassberger, P. and I. Procaccia, (1983), "Measuring the Strangeness of Strange Attractors", Physics, Vol. 9-D, 189-208.

Guckenheimer, J., and P. Holmes, (1983), NONLINEAR OSCILLATIONS, DYNAMICAL SYSTEMS AND BIFURCATIONS OF VECTOR FIELDS, Springer-Verlag, New York.

Helms, B., and T. Martell, (1985), "An Examination of the Distribution of Futures Price Changes", The Journal of Futures Markets, Vol. 5, 259-272.

Hsieh, D., (1989), "Testing for Nonlinear Dependence in Daily Foreign Exchange Rates", Journal of Business, Vol. 62, 339-368.

Hsieh, D. (1991), "Chaos and Nonlinear Dynamics : Application to Financial Markets", The Journal of Finance, Vol. 46, 1839-1877.

Lee, C., J. Finnerty, and D. Wort, (1990), SECURITY ANALYSIS AND PORTFOLIO MANAGEMENT, Scott, Foresman/Little, Brown Higher Education, Glenview, Illinois.

Malliaris, A.G., (1981), "Martingale Methods in Financial Decision-Making", Society for Industrial and Applied Mathematics, Vol. 23, 434-443.

Malliaris, A.G., (1990), "Itô's Calculus: Derivation of the Black-Scholes Option-Pricing Model", in SECURITY ANALYSIS AND PORTFOLIO MANAGEMENT by C.F. Lee, J. Finnerty and Donald Wort, 737-763.

May, R., (1976),"Simple Mathematical Models With Very Complicated Dynamics", Nature, Vol. 261, 459-467.

Melese, F., and W. Transue, (1986), "Unscrambling Chaos Through Thick and Thin", The Quarterly Journal of Economics, Vol. 101, 419-423.

Philippatos, G., and T. Martell, (1974), "Adaptation, Information, and Dependence in Commodity Markets", The Journal of Finance, Vol. 29, 493-498.

Philippatos, G., and D. Nawrocki, (1973), "The Information Inaccuracy of Stock Market Forecasts: Some New Evidence of Dependence of the New York Stock Exchange", Journal of Financial Quantitative Analysis, 445-458.

Philippatos, G., and C. Wilson, (1971), "Entropy As A Measure of Dispersion in The Portfolio Selection Problem", American Institute for Decision Sciences, 142-152.

Philippatos, G., and C. Wilson, (1972), "Entropy, Market Risk, and The Selection of Efficient Portfolios", Applied Economics, Vol. 4, 209-220.

Philippatos, G., and C. Wilson, (1974), "Information Theory and Risk in Capital Markets", Omega, The International Journal of Management Science, Vol. 2, 523-532.

Ramsey, J. B., C. Sayers, and P. Rothman (1988), "The Statistical Properties of Dimension Calculations using Small Data Sets : Some Economic Applications", International Economic Review, Vol. 31, 991-1020.

Ramsey, J. B., and H. Yuan, (1989), "Bias and Error Bars in Dimension Calculations and their Evaluation in Some Simple Models", Physics Letters A, Vol. 134, 287-297.

Roberts, V., (1959), "Stock-Market 'Patterns' and Financial Analysis: Methodological Suggestions", The Journal of Finance, Vol. 14, 1-10.

Ross, S., (1987), "Finance", in THE NEW PALGRAVE, Vol. II.

Ruelle, D., and F. Takens, (1971), "On the Nature of Turbulence", Communications of Mathematical Physics, Vol. 20, 167-192.

Savit, R., (1988), "When Random is Not Random: An Introduction to Chaos in Market Prices",

122

The Journal of Futures Markets, Vol. 8, 271-289.

Savit, R., (1989), "Nonlinearities and Chaotic Effects in Options Prices", The Journal of Futures Markets, Vol. 9, no. 6, 507-518.

Scheinkman, J., and B. LeBaron, (1989), "Nonlinear Dynamics and Stock Returns", Journal of Business, Vol. 62, 311-337.

Sheifer, A., and L. Summers, (1990), "The Noise Trader Approach to Finance", The Journal of Economic Perspectives, 4, 19-33.

Van der Ploeg, F., (1986), "Rational Expectations, Risk and Chaos in Financial Markets", The Economic Journal, 151-162.

# [8]

R. Jarrow et al., Eds., *Handbooks in OR & MS, Vol. 9*

Chapter 1

# Portfolio Theory

## G.M. Constantinides

*Graduate School of Business, University of Chicago, 1101 East 58th Street, Chicago, IL 60637, U.S.A.; and NBER*

## A.G. Malliaris

*School of Business Administration, Loyola University of Chicago, 820 North Michigan Avenue, Chicago, IL 60611, U.S.A.*

## 1. Introduction

Consider a consumer with a given amount of income. Such a consumer typically faces two important economic decisions. First, how to allocate his or her current consumption among goods and services. Second, how to invest among various assets. These two interrelated consumer or household problems are known as the consumption-saving decision and the portfolio selection decision.

Beginning with Adam Smith, economists have systematically studied the first decision. Arguing that a consumer will choose commodities and services that offer the greatest marginal utility relative to price, a theory of value was developed that combines subjective notions from consumer utility with objective notions from the production theory of the firm. By the beginning of the twentieth century, neoclassical economists had developed a static theory of consumer behavior as part of an analysis of market pricing under conditions of perfect competition and certainty.

The asset allocation decision was not adequately addressed by neoclassical economists, probably because they treated savings as the supply of loanable funds in developing a theory of interest rate determination instead of portfolio selection. More importantly, however, these two decisions, although closely interrelated, require substantially different methodologies. The methodology of deterministic calculus is adequate for the decision of maximizing a consumer's utility subject to a budget constraint. Portfolio selection involves making a decision under uncertainty. The probabilistic notions of expected return and risk become very important. Neoclassical economists did not have such a methodology available to them and despite some very early attempts by probabilists, like Bernoulli [1738] to define and measure risk, or Irving Fisher [1906] to describe asset returns in terms of a probability distribution, the twin concepts of expected return and risk had not yet been fully integrated. An early and important attempt to do that was made by

Marschak [1938] who expressed preferences for investment by indifference curves in the mean–variance space.[1]

The methodological breakthrough of treating axiomatically the theory of choice under uncertainty was offered by von Neumann & Morgenstern [1947] and it was only a few years later that Markowitz [1952, 1959] and Tobin [1958], used this theory to formulate and solve the portfolio selection problem.

In this essay we plan to exposit portfolio theory with a special emphasis on its historical evolution and methodological foundations. In Section 2, we describe the early work of Markowitz [1952, 1959] and Tobin [1958] to illustrate the individual contributions of these authors. Following these general remarks about the early beginning of portfolio theory, we define and solve the mean–variance portfolio problem in Section 3 and relate it to its most famous intellectual first fruits, namely the two-fund separation and the capital asset pricing theory of Sharpe [1964] and Lintner [1965] in Sections 4, 5 and 6. In particular, a portion of Section 6 is devoted to the presentation of Roll's [1977] critique of the asset pricing theory's tests and the interplay of analysis and empirical testing. This leads to an analysis of the foundational assumptions of portfolio theory with respect to investor preferences and asset return distributions, both reviewed in Section 7. The contrast of methodologies is illustrated in Sections 8 and 9 where stochastic calculus and stochastic control techniques are used to generalize the consumption-investment problem to an arbitrary number of periods. Market imperfections are addressed in Section 10. The last section identifies several extensions and refers the reader to several articles, some included in this volume. It also contains our summary and conclusions.

## 2. The early contributions

Markowitz [1952] marks the beginning of modern portfolio theory, where for the first time, the problem of portfolio selection is clearly formulated and solved. Earlier contributions of Keynes [1936], Marschak [1938] and others only tangentially analyze investment decisions. Markowitz's focus is the explanation of the phenomenon of portfolio diversification.

Before Markowitz could propose the "expected returns–variance of returns" rule, he first had to discredit the then widely accepted principle that an investor chooses a portfolio by selecting securities that maximize discounted expected returns.[2] Markowitz points out that if an investor follows this rule, his or her

---

[1] Marschak [1938, p. 312] recognizes that "the unsatisfactory state of Monetary Theory as compared with General Economics is due to the fact that the principle of determinateness so well established by Walras and Pareto for the world of perishable consumption goods and labor services has never been applied with much consistency to durable goods and, still less, to claims (securities, loans, cash)". In our modern terminology we could replace the names Monetary Theory and General Economics with Financial Economics and Microeconomic Theory, respectively.

[2] Markowitz refers the reader to a standard investments textbook by Williams [1938] that elaborates the notion that portfolio choice is guided by the rule of maximizing the discounted

portfolio will consist of only one stock, namely the one that has the highest discounted expected return which is contrary to the observed phenomenon of diversification. Therefore a rule of investor behavior which does not yield portfolio diversification must be rejected. Furthermore, the rejection of this rule holds no matter how expectations of future returns are formed and how discount rates are selected. Markowitz then proposes the expected mean returns–variance of returns M–V rule. He concludes that the M–V rule not only implies diversification, it actually implies the right kind of diversification for the right reason. In trying to reduce the portfolio variance, it is not enough to just invest in many securities. It is important to diversify across securities with low return covariances. In 1959, Markowitz published a monograph on the same topic. In the last part (consisting of four chapters) and in an appendix, portfolio selection is grounded firmly as rational choice under uncertainty.

In contrast to Markowitz's contributions which may be viewed as microeconomic, Tobin [1958] addresses a standard Keynesian macroeconomic problem, namely liquidity preference. Keynes [1936] used the concept of liquidity preference to describe an inverse relationship between the demand for cash balances and the rate of interest. This aggregative function was postulated by Keynes without a formal derivation. Tobin derives the economy's liquidity preference by developing a theory that explains the behavior of the decision-making units of the economy.[3]

Numerous contributions followed. To mention just a few, Sharpe [1970], Merton [1972], Gonzalez-Gaverra [1973], Fama [1976] and Roll [1977], are important references. Ziemba & Vickson [1975] have collected numerous classic articles on both static and dynamic models of portfolio selection. The recent books by Ingersoll [1987], Huang & Litzenberger [1988], and Jarrow [1988] also contain a useful analysis of the mean–variance portfolio theory. Our exposition relies heavily on Roll [1977].

---

value of future returns. It is not correct to deduce that earlier economists completely ignored the notion of risk. They simply were unsuccessful in developing a precise microeconomic theory of investor behavior under conditions of risk. The typical way risk was accounted for in Keynes' [1936] marginal efficiency of investment or Hicks' [1939] development of the investment decisions of a firm was by letting expected future returns include an allowance for risk or by adding a risk premium to discount rates.

[3] One may wonder what is the connection between liquidity preference and portfolio theory. You may recall that Keynes identified three motives for holding cash balances: transactions, precautionary and speculative. Furthermore, while the transactions and precautionary motives were determined by income, the amount of cash balances held for speculative purposes was influenced by the rate of interest. Tobin analyzes this speculative motive of investors to offer a theoretically sound foundation of the interest elasticity of the liquidity preference. Because he wishes to explain the demand for cash, he considers an investor whose portfolio selection includes only two assets: cash and consoles. Of course, the yield of cash is zero while the yield of consoles is positive. Tobin posits and solves a two-asset portfolio selection problem using a quadratic expected utility function. He justifies his choice of a quadratic utility function by arguing that the investor considers two parameters in his or her portfolio selection: expected return and risk (measured by the standard deviation of the portfolio return). Finally, having developed his portfolio selection theory, he applies it to show that changes in real interest rates affect inversely the demand for cash, which is what Keynes had conjectured without offering a proof.

4                            *G.M. Constantinides, A.G. Malliaris*

### 3. Mean–variance portfolio selection

In the formulation of the mean–variance portfolio we use the following notation: $x$ is an $n$-column vector whose components $x_1, \ldots x_n$ denote the weight or
proportion of the investor's wealth allocated to the $i$th asset in the portfolio with
$i = 1, 2, \ldots n$. Obviously the sum of weights is equal to 1, i.e. $\sum_1^n x_i = 1$; $\mathbf{1}$ is an
$n$-column vector of ones and superscript T denotes the transpose of a vector or a
matrix. $R$ is an $n$-column vector of mean returns $R_1, \ldots, R_n$ of the $n$ assets, where
it is assumed that not all elements of $R$ are equal, and $\mathbf{V}$ is the $n \times n$ covariance
matrix with entries $\sigma_{ij}$, $i, j = 1, 2, \ldots n$. We assume that $\mathbf{V}$ is nonsingular. This
essentially requires that none of the asset returns is perfectly correlated with the
return of a portfolio made up of the remaining assets; and that none of the assets
or portfolios of the assets is riskless. The case where one of the assets is riskless
will be treated separately at a later stage. Observe that $\mathbf{V}$ is symmetric and positive
definite being a covariance matrix. We say that an $n \times n$ matrix $\mathbf{V}$ is *positive definite*,
if for any nonzero $n$-vector $x$, it follows that $x^T\mathbf{V}x > 0$. In our case the property
of positive definiteness of $\mathbf{V}$ follows from the fact that variances of risky portfolios
are strictly positive. The mean returns and covariance matrix of the assets are
assumed to be known. We do not specify if $n$ denotes the entire population or just
a sample of assets. Finally, for a given portfolio $p$, its variance, denoted by $\sigma_p^2$, is
given by $x^T\mathbf{V}x$, while the portfolio mean, denoted by $R_p$, is given by $R_p = x^TR$.

Much in the spirit of Markowitz's [1952] formulation[4] the portfolio selection
problem can be stated as

$$\text{minimize} \quad \sigma_p^2 = x^T\mathbf{V}x$$

$$\text{subject to} \quad x^T\mathbf{1} = 1 \qquad\qquad\qquad (3.1)$$

$$x^TR = R_p.$$

In problem (3.1) we minimize the portfolio variance $\sigma_p^2$ subject to two constraints: first, the portfolio weights must sum to unity, which means that all the
wealth is invested, and second the portfolio must earn an expected rate of return
equal to $R_p$. Technically, we minimize a convex function subject to linear constraints. Observe that $x^T\mathbf{V}x$ is convex because $\mathbf{V}$ is positive definite and also note
that the two linear constraints define a convex set. Therefore, the problem has a
unique solution and we only need to obtain the first-order conditions.

Two remarks are appropriate. First, the investor's preferences, as represented
by a utility function, do not enter explicitly in (3.1). We only assume that a utility
function exists which is defined over the mean and variance of the portfolio return
and which has the further property of favoring higher mean and smaller variance.
Second, unlike Tobin who explicitly considers cash in his portfolio selection

---

[4] Markowitz [1952] considers only three securities because he solves the same problem as (3.1)
using geometric methods. He does not allow short sales in order to simplify the analysis. In (3.1)
short sales are permitted, which means that portfolio weights are allowed to be negative.

problem, (3.1) does not include a riskless asset. A riskless asset will be included in Section 5.

Form the Lagrangian function

$$L = x^{\mathsf{T}}Vx - \lambda_1(x^{\mathsf{T}}R - R_p) - \lambda_2(x^{\mathsf{T}}1 - 1). \tag{3.2}$$

The first-order conditions are

$$\frac{\partial L}{\partial x} = 2Vx - \lambda_1 R - \lambda_2 1 = 0, \tag{3.3}$$

where $0$ in (3.3) is an $n$-vector of zeros, and

$$\frac{\partial L}{\partial \lambda_1} = R_p - x^{\mathsf{T}}R = 0, \tag{3.4}$$

$$\frac{\partial L}{\partial \lambda_2} = 1 - x^{\mathsf{T}}1 = 0. \tag{3.5}$$

From equation (3.3) we obtain

$$x = \frac{1}{2}V^{-1}(\lambda_1 R + \lambda_2 1) = \frac{1}{2}V^{-1}[R\ 1]\begin{bmatrix} \lambda_1 \\ \lambda_2 \end{bmatrix}. \tag{3.6}$$

In this last equation the term $\lambda_1 R + \lambda_2 1$ is written in a matrix form because we will use (3.4) and (3.5) to solve for $\begin{bmatrix} \lambda_1 \\ \lambda_2 \end{bmatrix}$. Doing this we write (3.4) and (3.5) as

$$[R\ 1]^{\mathsf{T}}x = \begin{bmatrix} R_p \\ 1 \end{bmatrix}. \tag{3.7}$$

Premultiply both sides of (3.6) by $[R\ 1]^{\mathsf{T}}$ and use (3.7) to obtain

$$[R\ 1]^{\mathsf{T}}x = \frac{1}{2}[R\ 1]^{\mathsf{T}}V^{-1}[R\ 1]\begin{bmatrix} \lambda_1 \\ \lambda_2 \end{bmatrix} = \begin{bmatrix} R_p \\ 1 \end{bmatrix}. \tag{3.8}$$

For notational convenience denote by

$$A \equiv [R\ 1]^{\mathsf{T}}V^{-1}[R\ 1] \tag{3.9}$$

the $2 \times 2$ symmetric matrix with entries

$$\begin{bmatrix} a & b \\ b & c \end{bmatrix} = \begin{bmatrix} R^{\mathsf{T}}V^{-1}R & R^{\mathsf{T}}V^{-1}1 \\ R^{\mathsf{T}}V^{-1}1 & 1^{\mathsf{T}}V^{-1}1 \end{bmatrix}. \tag{3.10}$$

We need to establish that $A$ is positive definite. For any $y_1, y_2$ such that at least one of the elements $y_1, y_2$ is nonzero, observe that

$$[R\ 1]\begin{bmatrix} y_1 \\ y_2 \end{bmatrix} = [y_1 R + y_2 1]$$

is a nonzero $n$-vector because, by assumption, the elements of $R$ are not all equal.

Then $\mathbf{A}$ is positive definite because

$$[y_1 \ y_2]\mathbf{A}\begin{bmatrix} y_1 \\ y_2 \end{bmatrix} = [y_1 \ y_2][\mathbf{R} \ \mathbf{1}]^T\mathbf{V}^{-1}[\mathbf{R} \ \mathbf{1}]\begin{bmatrix} y_1 \\ y_2 \end{bmatrix}$$

$$= [y_1\mathbf{R} + y_2\mathbf{1}]^T\mathbf{V}^{-1}[y_1\mathbf{R} + y_2\mathbf{1}] > 0$$

by the positive definiteness of $\mathbf{V}^{-1}$.

Substitute the newly defined $\mathbf{A}$ in (3.9) to get

$$\frac{1}{2}\mathbf{A}\begin{bmatrix} \lambda_1 \\ \lambda_2 \end{bmatrix} = \begin{bmatrix} R_p \\ 1 \end{bmatrix}$$

from which we can immediately solve for the multipliers since $\mathbf{A}$ is nonsingular and its inverse exists. Thus

$$\frac{1}{2}\begin{bmatrix} \lambda_1 \\ \lambda_2 \end{bmatrix} = \mathbf{A}^{-1}\begin{bmatrix} R_p \\ 1 \end{bmatrix}. \tag{3.11}$$

From these manipulations we obtain the desired result using (3.11) and (3.6). Thus, the $n$-vector of portfolio weights $x$ that minimizes portfolio variance for a given mean return is

$$x = \frac{1}{2}\mathbf{V}^{-1}[\mathbf{R} \ \mathbf{1}]\begin{bmatrix} \lambda_1 \\ \lambda_2 \end{bmatrix} = \mathbf{V}^{-1}[\mathbf{R} \ \mathbf{1}]\mathbf{A}^{-1}\begin{bmatrix} R_p \\ 1 \end{bmatrix}. \tag{3.12}$$

The result of this analysis can be stated as:

**Theorem 3.1** (Mean–variance portfolio selection). *Let $\mathbf{V}$ be the $n \times n$ positive definite covariance matrix and $\mathbf{R}$ be the $n$-column vector of mean returns of the $n$ assets where it is assumed that not all elements of $\mathbf{R}$ are equal. Then the minimum variance portfolio with given mean return $R_p$ is unique and its weights are given by (3.12).*

Let us compute the variance of any minimum variance portfolio with a given mean $R_p$. Using the definitions of the variance $\sigma_p^2$, matrix $\mathbf{A}$ in (3.9) and the solution of weights in (3.12), calculate

$$\sigma_p^2 = x^T\mathbf{V}x = [R_p \ 1]\mathbf{A}^{-1}[\mathbf{R} \ \mathbf{1}]^T\mathbf{V}^{-1}\mathbf{V}\mathbf{V}^{-1}[\mathbf{R} \ \mathbf{1}]\mathbf{A}^{-1}\begin{bmatrix} R_p \\ 1 \end{bmatrix}$$

$$= [R_p \ 1]\mathbf{A}^{-1}\begin{bmatrix} R_p \\ 1 \end{bmatrix}$$

$$= [R_p \ 1]\frac{1}{(ac - b^2)}\begin{bmatrix} c & -b \\ -b & a \end{bmatrix}\begin{bmatrix} R_p \\ 1 \end{bmatrix} \tag{3.13}$$

$$= \frac{a - 2bR_p + cR_p^2}{(ac - b^2)}.$$

In (3.13) the relation between the variance of the minimum variance portfolio $\sigma_p^2$ for any given mean $R_p$ is expressed as a parabola and is called the *minimum variance portfolio frontier* or *locus*. In mean–standard-deviation space the relation is expressed as a hyperbola.

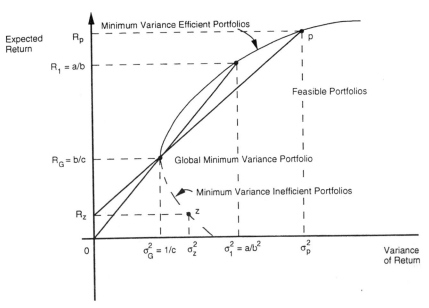

Fig. 1. Portfolios of $n$ risky assets.

Figure 1 graphs equation (3.13) and distinguishes between the upper half (solid curve) and the bottom half (broken curve). The upper half of the minimum variance portfolio frontier identifies the set of portfolios having the highest return for a given variance; these are called mean–variance *efficient portfolios*. The portfolios on the bottom half are called *inefficient portfolios*. The mean–variance efficient portfolios are a subset of the minimum variance portfolios. Portfolios to the right of the parabola are called *feasible*. For a given variance the mean return of a feasible portfolio is less than the mean return of an efficient portfolio and higher than the mean return of an inefficient one, both having the same variance.

Figure 1 also identifies the *global minimum variance portfolio*. This is the portfolio with the smallest possible variance for any mean return. Its mean, denoted by $R_G$ is obtained by minimizing (3.13) with respect to $R_p$, to yield

$$R_G = \frac{b}{c} \tag{3.14}$$

and its variance, denoted by $\sigma_G^2$, is calculated by inserting (3.14) into the general equation (3.13) to obtain

$$\sigma_G^2 = \frac{a - 2bR_G + cR_G^2}{ac - b^2} = \frac{a - 2b(b/c) + c(b/c)^2}{ac - b^2} = \frac{1}{c}. \tag{3.15}$$

Similarly, by inserting $R_G$ from (3.14) into (3.12) we find the weights of the global minimum variance portfolio, denoted by $x_G$,

$$x_G = V^{-1}[R\ 1]A^{-1}\begin{bmatrix} R_G \\ 1 \end{bmatrix} = \frac{V^{-1}[R\ 1]\begin{bmatrix} c & -b \\ -b & a \end{bmatrix}\begin{bmatrix} b/c \\ 1 \end{bmatrix}}{(ac - b^2)} = \frac{V^{-1}\ 1}{c}.$$

$$(3.16)$$

An additional notion that will be used later in this section and which is illustrated in Figure 1 also, is the concept of an orthogonal portfolio. We say that two minimum variance portfolios $x_p$ and $x_z$ are *orthogonal* if their covariance is zero, that is,

$$x_z^T V x_p = 0. \tag{3.17}$$

We want to show that for every minimum variance portfolio, except the global minimum variance portfolio, we can find a unique orthogonal minimum variance portfolio. Furthermore, if the first portfolio has mean $R_p$, its orthogonal one has mean $R_z$ with

$$R_z = \frac{a - bR_p}{b - cR_p}. \tag{3.18}$$

To establish (3.18), let first $p$ and $z$ be two arbitrary minimum variance portfolios with weights $x_p$ given by (3.12) and $x_z$ given by

$$x_z = V^{-1}[R\ 1]A^{-1}\begin{bmatrix} R_z \\ 1 \end{bmatrix}. \tag{3.19}$$

The covariance between portfolios $p$ and $z$, being zero implies

$$0 = x_z^T V x_p = [R_z\ 1]A^{-1}\begin{bmatrix} R_p \\ 1 \end{bmatrix}, \tag{3.20}$$

from which (3.18) follows.

In Figure 1, we also illustrate the geometry of orthogonal portfolios. Given an arbitrary efficient portfolio $p$ on the efficient portfolio frontier, the line passing between $p$ and the global minimum variance portfolio can be shown to intersect the expected return axis at $R_z$. Once $R_z$ is known, then the orthogonal portfolio $z$ can be uniquely identified on the minimum variance portfolio frontier. Note that if a portfolio $p$ is efficient and therefore lies on the positively sloped segment of the portfolio frontier, as in Figure 1, then its orthogonal portfolio $z$ is inefficient and lies on the negatively sloped segment. In general, orthogonal portfolios lie on opposite-sloped segments of the portfolio frontier.

## 4. Two-fund separation

We now present the important property of two-fund separation. The mathematics of this property is straightforward; its economic implications however are significant because the following theorem establishes that the minimum variance portfolio frontier can be generated by any two distinct frontier portfolios.

**Theorem 4.1** (Two-fund separation). *Let $x_a$ and $x_b$ be two minimum variance portfolios with mean returns $R_a$ and $R_b$ respectively, such that $R_a \neq R_b$.*

*(a) Then every minimum variance portfolio $x_c$ is a linear combination of $x_a$ and $x_b$.*

*(b) Conversely, every portfolio which is a linear combination of $x_a$ and $x_b$, i.e, $\alpha x_a + (1 - \alpha) x_b$, is a minimum variance portfolio.*

*(c) In particular, if $x_a$ and $x_b$ are minimum variance efficient portfolios, then $\alpha x_a + (1 - \alpha) x_b$ is a minimum variance efficient portfolio for $0 \leq \alpha \leq 1$.*

**Proof.** (a) Let $R_c$ denote the mean return of the given minimum variance portfolio $x_c$. Choose parameter $\alpha$ such that

$$R_c = \alpha R_a + (1 - \alpha) R_b \tag{4.1}$$

that is, choose $\alpha$ given by

$$\alpha = \frac{R_c - R_b}{R_a - R_b}. \tag{4.2}$$

Note that $\alpha$ exists and is unique because by hypothesis $R_a \neq R_b$.

We claim that

$$x_c = \alpha x_a + (1 - \alpha) x_b. \tag{4.3}$$

To establish (4.3) use first (3.12) and next (4.1) to write

$$
\begin{aligned}
x_c &= V^{-1}[R\ 1]A^{-1}\begin{bmatrix} R_c \\ 1 \end{bmatrix} \\
&= V^{-1}[R\ 1]A^{-1}\begin{bmatrix} \alpha R_a + (1 - \alpha) R_b \\ \alpha + (1 - \alpha) \end{bmatrix} \\
&= \alpha V^{-1}[R\ 1]A^{-1}\begin{bmatrix} R_a \\ 1 \end{bmatrix} + (1 - \alpha) V^{-1}[R\ 1]A^{-1}\begin{bmatrix} R_b \\ 1 \end{bmatrix} \\
&= \alpha x_a + (1 - \alpha) x_b.
\end{aligned}
\tag{4.4}
$$

(b) Consider portfolio $x_c$ which is a linear combination of $x_a$ and $x_b$ as in (4.3). Then

$$
\begin{aligned}
x_c &= \alpha x_a + (1 - \alpha) x_b \\
&= \alpha V^{-1}[R\ 1]A^{-1}\begin{bmatrix} R_a \\ 1 \end{bmatrix} + (1 - \alpha) V^{-1}[R\ 1]A^{-1}\begin{bmatrix} R_b \\ 1 \end{bmatrix} \\
&= V^{-1}[R\ 1]A^{-1}\begin{bmatrix} \alpha R_a + (1 - \alpha) R_b \\ 1 \end{bmatrix}
\end{aligned}
$$

By (3.12) we conclude that $x_c$ is the minimum variance portfolio with expected return $\alpha R_a + (1 - \alpha) R_b$.

(c) This is proved as in (b) noting that the restriction $0 \leq \alpha \leq 1$ implies, $R_a \leq \alpha R_a + (1 - \alpha) R_b \leq R_b$, if $R_a \leq R_b$.

This completes the proof.   $\square$

It is of historical interest that this fact was discovered by Tobin [1958]. Tobin uses only two assets (riskless cash and a risky consol), and demonstrates that nothing essential is changed if there are many risky assets. He argues that the risky assets can be viewed as a single composite asset (mutual fund) and investors find it optimal to combine their cash with a specific portfolio of risky assets. In particular, Theorem 4.1 shows that any mean variance efficient portfolio can be generated by two arbitrary distinct mean–variance efficient portfolios. In other words, if an investor wishes to invest in a mean–variance efficient portfolio with a given expected return and variance, he or she can achieve this goal by investing in an appropriate linear combination of any two mutual funds which are also mean–variance efficient. Practically this means that the $n$ original assets can be purchased by only two mutual funds and investors then can just choose to allocate their wealth, not in the original $n$ assets directly but in these two mutual funds in such a way that the investment results (mean–variance) of the two actions (portfolios) would be identical.

There is, however, an additional implication from part (c) of the two-fund separation theorem. Suppose that utility functions are restricted so that all investors choose to invest in mean–variance efficient portfolios and choose $x_a$ and $x_b$ to be the investment proportions of two distinct mean–variance efficient portfolios that generate all the others. In particular $x_a$ and $x_b$ can be used to generate the *market portfolio*, that is, the wealth weighted sum of the portfolio holdings of all investors.[5] This implies that the market portfolio is also mean–variance efficient. Black [1972] employs this result in deriving the capital asset pricing model.

Having shown that any two distinct portfolios can generate all other portfolios, it is of practical interest to select two portfolios whose means and variances are easy to compute. One such portfolio is the global minimum variance portfolio with $R_G$, $\sigma_G^2$ and $x_G$ given in the previous section. The other one is identified in Figure 1, with $R_1 = a/b$, $\sigma_1^2 = a/b^2$, and

$$x_1 = \frac{V^{-1} R}{b}. \tag{4.5}$$

---

[5] To clarify the concept of market portfolio, it is helpful to proceed inductively. Suppose that investors 1 and 2 have wealth $w_1$ and $w_2$ invested in minimum variance efficient portfolios with weights $x_1$ and $x_2$. Then the sum of their holdings is a portfolio with wealth $w_1 + w_2$ and portfolio weights $\alpha x_1 + (1 - \alpha) x_2$ where $\alpha = w_1/(w_1 + w_2)$. Since $0 \leq \alpha \leq 1$, from Theorem 4.1(c), the sum total of their holdings is also an efficient portfolio. Next suppose that the wealth $w_n$ of $n$ investors is invested in an efficient portfolio with weights $x_n$ and investor $n + 1$ has wealth $w_{n+1}$ invested in an efficient portfolio with weights $x_{n+1}$. Again from Theorem 4.1(c) the sum total of the holdings of all $n + 1$ investors is an efficient portfolio. Proceeding in this manner we conclude that the sum total of all the investors' portfolios is an efficient portfolio. By definition, however, this is the market portfolio. Thus we conclude that the market portfolio is efficient.

Observe from Figure 1 that this second portfolio's orthogonal portfolio has an expected return of zero. Theorem 4.2 below uses these two portfolios $x_G$ and $x_1$.

We state a theorem about the relation of individual asset parameters which will be useful in the analysis of the capital asset pricing model.

**Theorem 4.2.** *For a given portfolio $x_p$, the covariance vector of individual assets with respect to portfolio $p$ is linear in the vector of mean returns $R$ if and only if $p$ is a minimum variance portfolio.*

**Proof.** Let $x_p$ be the weights of a minimum variance portfolio which can be written as (3.12). The vector of covariances between individual assets and $x_p$ is given by

$$\mathbf{V}x_p = \mathbf{V}\mathbf{V}^{-1}[R \ 1]A^{-1}\begin{bmatrix} R_p \\ 1 \end{bmatrix} = [R \ 1]A^{-1}\begin{bmatrix} R_p \\ 1 \end{bmatrix} \tag{4.6}$$

which verifies the linearity between the covariance vector and the vector of expected returns, $R$.

Conversely, let the vector of covariances with an arbitrary portfolio $x_p$ be expressed linearly as

$$\mathbf{V}x_p = gR + h\mathbf{1} \tag{4.7}$$

where $g$ and $h$ are arbitrary constants. From (4.7), solving for $x_p$ we get

$$x_p = g\mathbf{V}^{-1}R + \mathbf{V}^{-1}\mathbf{1} = gbx_1 + hcx_G. \tag{4.8}$$

Note that in this last equation $x_p$ is generated by two distinct efficient portfolios $x_1$ and $x_G$. Recall that $x_G$ is the vector of investment proportions of the global minimum variance portfolio and $x_1$ is the vector of investment proportions described in (4.5). Since both $x_G$ and $x_1$ are investment proportions, they satisfy $x_G^T\mathbf{1} = x_1^T\mathbf{1} = 1$ which combined with the property that $x_p^T\mathbf{1} = 1$ allows us to conclude that $gb + hc = 1$. Thus we conclude from Theorem 4.1 that $x_p$ is a minimum variance portfolio. This completes the proof. $\square$

We close this section by expressing (4.6) in a way that will be useful in the discussion of the capital asset pricing model in Section 6. From (4.6) write

$$\begin{aligned} \text{cov}\,(R_i, R_p) &= [0 \ \ldots \ 1 \ \ldots \ 0]\mathbf{V}x_p \\ &= [0 \ \ldots \ 1 \ \ldots \ 0][R \ 1]A^{-1}\begin{bmatrix} R_p \\ 1 \end{bmatrix} \\ &= [R_i \ 1]A^{-1}\begin{bmatrix} R_p \\ 1 \end{bmatrix}, \end{aligned} \tag{4.9}$$

where the 1 in the row vector is placed in the position of the $i$th asset. Let $x_z$ be orthogonal to $x_p$ and calculate their covariance as in (3.20). Subtract (3.20) from (4.9) to get

$$\text{cov}\,(R_i, R_p) = [r_i \ 0]A^{-1}\begin{bmatrix} R_p \\ 1 \end{bmatrix} = \gamma r_i \tag{4.10}$$

where the two new variables $r_i$ and $\gamma$ are defined as

$$r_i = R_i - R_z,$$  (4.11)

and

$$\gamma = \frac{cR_p - b}{ac - b^2}.$$  (4.12)

Observe that (4.10) holds for each $i$ and must therefore hold for all assets, i.e.

$$\operatorname{cov}(R_p, R_p) = \sigma_p^2 = \gamma r_p,$$  (4.13)

where $r_p$ expresses the excess mean return of portfolio $p$ from its orthogonal $z$. From this last equation obtain $\gamma = \sigma_p^2/r_p$ and substitute in (4.10) to conclude that

$$r_i = \frac{\operatorname{cov}(R_i, R_p)}{\sigma_p^2} r_p = \beta_i r_p$$  (4.14)

which expresses the excess mean return of the $i$th asset as a proportion of its beta, $\beta_i$, with respect to portfolio $p$, where

$$\beta_i = \frac{\operatorname{cov}(R_i, R_p)}{\sigma_p^2}.$$  (4.15)

These mathematical manipulations show that (4.14), which has a capital asset pricing appearance, holds true for any minimum variance portfolio, in general, and for any minimum variance efficient portfolio, in particular.


## 5. Mean–variance portfolio with a riskless asset

The previous two sections presented and solved the portfolio selection problem for $n$ risky assets, and then established the two fund separation theorem. We now return to Tobin's original idea of introducing a riskless asset. The portfolio selection problem with n risky assets and one riskless, i.e. a total of $(n + 1)$ assets can easily be formulated and solved. Let there be $n + 1$ assets, $i = 0, 1, 2, \ldots, n$, where 0 denotes the riskless asset with return $R_0$. The vector of expected excess returns has elements defined as $r_i = R_i - R_0$, $i = 1, 2, \ldots, n$, and is denoted by $r$. Wealth is now allocated among $(n + 1)$ assets with weights $w_0, w_1, \ldots, w_n$. In the various calculations we denote the vector of weights $w_1, \ldots, w_n$ as $w$ and write $w_0 = 1 - w^T \mathbf{1}$.

For a given portfolio $p$, the mean excess return is

$$r_p = w^T R + (1 - w^T \mathbf{1}) R_0 - R_0 = w^T r.$$  (5.1)

The variance of $p$ is

$$\sigma_p^2 = w^T V w,$$  (5.2)

where in (5.1) and (5.2), $R$ and $V$ are as in Section 3. Note that in (5.2) the riskless asset does not contribute to the variance.

The mean–variance portfolio selection problem with a riskless asset can be stated as

$$\text{minimize} \quad w^T V w$$

$$\text{subject to} \quad w^T r = r_p. \tag{5.3}$$

In (5.3), the variance of the $n$-risky assets is minimized subject to a given excess return $r_p$. Note that $w^T \mathbf{1} = 1$ is not a constraint because the wealth need not all be allocated to the $n$-risky assets; some may be held in the riskless asset.

Following the method of (3.1) one obtains the solution

$$w = \left( \frac{r_p}{r^T V^{-1} r} \right) V^{-1} r \tag{5.4}$$

which gives the variance of the minimum-variance portfolio with excess mean $r_p$ as

$$
\begin{aligned}
\sigma_p^2 &= w^T V w \\
&= \left( \frac{r_p}{r^T V^{-1} r} \right)^2 r^T V^{-1} V V^{-1} r \\
&= \frac{r_p^2}{r^T V^{-1} r}.
\end{aligned}
\tag{5.5}
$$

The Sharpe's measure of portfolio $p$, defined as the ratio of its excess mean return to the standard deviation of its return, is obtained from (5.5) as

$$\frac{r_p}{\sigma_p} = \left\{ \begin{array}{ll} (r^T V^{-1} r)^{1/2}, & \text{if } r_p \geq 0 \\ -(r^T V^{-1} r)^{1/2}, & \text{if } r_p < 0 \end{array} \right\}. \tag{5.6}$$

The tangency portfolio $T$ is the minimum-variance portfolio for which

$$\mathbf{1}^T w_T = 1. \tag{5.7}$$

Combining equations (5.4) and (5.7) we obtain

$$r_T = \frac{r^T V^{-1} r}{\mathbf{1}^T V^{-1} r} \gtrless 0. \tag{5.8}$$

It is economically plausible to assert that the riskless return is lower than the mean return of the global minimum variance portfolio of the risky assets, that is, $R_0 < R_G$. We may then prove that $\mathbf{1}^T V^{-1} r > 0$. Also $r^T V^{-1} r > 0$ by the positive definiteness of the matrix $V$. It then follows that $r_T > 0$ and the slope of the tangency line in Figure 2 is positive. This positively-sloped line is the capital market line and defines the set of minimum variance efficient portfolios. For an actual calculation of Figure 2, see Ziemba, Parkan & Brooks-Hill [1974].

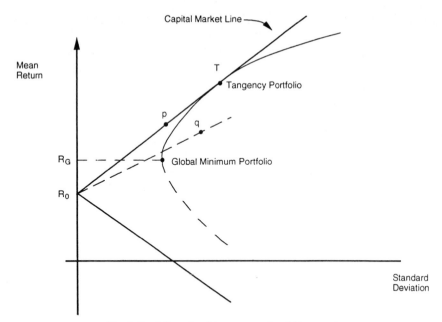

Fig. 2. Portfolios of $n$-risky assets and a riskless asset.

The correlation coefficient of the return of any portfolio $q$, with weights $w_q$, and any portfolio $p$ on the efficient segment of the minimum-variance frontier is

$$
\begin{aligned}
\rho(p, q) &= \frac{w_q^T V w_p}{\sigma_q \sigma_p} \\
&= \frac{r_p r_q}{(r^T V^{-1} r) \sigma_q \sigma_p} \\
&= \frac{r_q / \sigma_q}{r_p / \sigma_p} \\
&= \frac{\text{Sharpe's measure of portfolio } q}{\text{Sharpe's measure of portfolio } p}
\end{aligned}
\tag{5.9}
$$

Referring to Figure 2, the correlation $\rho(p, q)$ is the ratio of the slope of the line from $R_0$ to $q$ to the slope of the efficient frontier.

## 6. The capital asset pricing model

Markowitz's approach to portfolio selection may be characterized as normative. The analysis of Sections 3, 4 and 5 concentrates on a typical investor and by making several simplifying assumptions, solves the investor's portfolio selection problem. Recall the assumptions: (i) the investor considers only the first two moments of the probability distribution of returns; (ii) given the mean portfolio return, the investor chooses a portfolio with the lowest variance of returns; and (iii) the investment horizon is one period. There are also a few additional assumptions that are implicit: (i) the investor's individual decisions do not affect market prices; (ii) fractional shares may be purchased (i.e. investments are infinitely divisible); (iii) transaction costs and taxes do not exist, and (iv) investors can sell assets short.

It is historically worth observing that six years had to elapse before the normative results of portfolio selection could be generalized into a positive theory of capital markets. Brennan [1989] claims that "[t]he reason for delay was undoubtedly the boldness of the assumption required for progress, namely that all investors hold the same beliefs about the joint distribution of a security[6]". Indeed, Sharpe [1964] emphasizes that in order to obtain equilibrium conditions in the capital market the *homogeneity of investor expectations*[7] assumption must be made.

Under these assumptions we have demonstrated that all investors hold mean–variance efficient portfolios. With the added homogeneity assumption, Theorem 4.1 shows that a portfolio which consists of two (or more) mean–variance efficient portfolios is mean variance efficient. Therefore the market portfolio is mean variance efficient. Therefore, the mean asset returns are linear in their covariance with the market return as shown in Theorem 4.2. This simple, yet powerful argument due to Black [1972] does not rely on the existence of a riskless asset, unlike the original derivation of the Capital Asset Pricing Model (CAPM) by Sharpe [1964]. From equation (4.14) we may write the CAPM as

$$R_i - R_z = \beta_i (R_M - R_z) \tag{6.1}$$

where $R_M$ is the mean return of the market portfolio, $\beta_i$ is $\text{cov}(R_i, R_M)/\text{var}(R_M)$ and $R_z$ is the mean return of a minimum variance portfolio which is orthogonal to the market portfolio. In the special case that a riskless asset exists, $R_z$ must equal the riskless rate of return. Ferson [1994] surveys in this volume both the theory and testing of the capital asset pricing model.

Fama [1976] and Roll [1977] pointed out that testing the capital asset pricing model is equivalent to testing the market's mean–variance efficiency. If the only testable hypothesis of the capital asset pricing theory is that the market portfolio is mean–variance efficient, then such testing is infeasible. The infeasibility is due to our ignorance of the exact composition of the true market portfolio. In other words, the capital asset pricing theory is not testable unless all individual assets are included in the market. Using a proxy for the true market portfolio does not solve the problem for two reasons: first, the proxy itself may be mean–variance

---

[6] See Brennan [1989, p. 93].

[7] Two brief remarks are in order. First, Sharpe attributes the term of homogeneity of investor expectations to one of the referees of his paper. Second, he acknowledges that this assumption is highly restrictive and unrealistic but defends it because of its implication, i.e. attainment of equilibrium. See also Lintner [1965] and Mossin [1966]. Numerous papers have appeared which have relaxed some of the stated assumptions. For example see Levy & Samuelson [1992]

efficient even when the true market portfolio is not; second, the chosen proxy may be inefficient even though the true market portfolio is actually efficient.

We conclude this section by pointing out that the empirical methodologies of testing for the mean–variance efficiency of a given portfolio may be applied in testing a broad class of asset pricing models. Absence of arbitrage among n assets with returns represented by the random variables, $\tilde{R}_i$ $i = 1, \ldots, n$, implies the existence of a strictly positive pricing kernel represented by the random variable $\tilde{m}$ such that

$$E[\tilde{m}\ \tilde{R}_i] = 1, \qquad i = 1, \ldots, n. \tag{6.2}$$

For example, in the consumption asset pricing model, $\tilde{m}$ stands for the marginal rate of substitution in consumption between the beginning and end of the period.

Let $x$ denote the weights of a portfolio of $n$ assets which has return maximally correlated with the pricing operator $\tilde{m}$. Then we can write $\tilde{m}$ as

$$\tilde{m} = \alpha \sum_{j=1}^{n} x_j \tilde{R}_j + \tilde{\varepsilon} \tag{6.3}$$

where $\alpha$ is a constant. The property of maximal correlation implies that $\text{cov}(\tilde{\varepsilon}, \tilde{R}_j) = 0$, $j = 1, \ldots, n$. Combining equations (6.2) and (6.3) we obtain

$$1 = E[\tilde{m}\ \tilde{R}_i] = E[\tilde{m}]E[\tilde{R}_i] + \alpha \, \text{cov}\left(\sum_{j=1}^{n} x_j \tilde{R}_j, \tilde{R}_i\right), \quad i = 1, \ldots, n. \tag{6.4}$$

This implies that the $n$ assets' covariances with the portfolio $x$ are linear in their mean returns. By Theorem 4.2 we conclude that the portfolio $x$ must lie on the minimum-variance frontier of the $n$ assets, a property which can be tested by the methodologies which test for the efficiency of a given portfolio. For further discussion of these issues see the papers of Hansen & Jagannathan [1991] and Ferson [1995].

## 7. Theoretical justification of mean–variance analysis, mutual fund separation and the CAPM

In this section we first address the following question: what set of assumptions is needed on the investor's utility function or distribution of asset returns so that the investor chooses a mean–variance efficient portfolio?

Tobin [1958] uses a quadratic utility function represented by

$$u(c) = c - B\frac{c^2}{2}, \qquad B > 0 \tag{7.1}$$

and defined only for $c \leq 1/B$, where $c$ denotes consumption. Arrow [1971] has remarked that quadratic utility exhibits increasing absolute risk aversion which implies that risky assets are inferior goods in the context of the portfolio selection problem. It can be easily shown that utility is increasing in the mean and decreasing in the variance, and that moments higher than the variance do not matter. Therefore only mean–variance efficient portfolios will be selected by expected quadratic utility maximizing investors.

Next note that multivariate normality is a special distribution of asset returns for which mean–variance analysis is consistent with expected utility maximization without assuming quadratic utility. To show this recall that the distribution of any portfolio is completely specified by its mean and variance. This follows from the basic property that any linear combination of multivariate normally distributed variables has a distribution in the same family.

Chamberlain [1983a] shows that the most general class of distributions that allow investors to rank portfolios based on the first two generalized moments is the family of *elliptical distributions*. A vector $x$ of n random variables is said to be elliptically distributed if its density function is of the form

$$f(x) = |\Omega|^{-1/2} g[(x - \mu)^T \Omega^{-1}(x - \mu); \, x] \tag{7.2}$$

where $\Omega$ is an $n \times n$ positive definite dispersion matrix and $\mu$ is the vector of medians. From (7.1) Ingersoll [1987] obtains as special cases both the multivariate normal and the multivariate Student-$t$ distributions.

Having presented a theoretical justification for mean–variance analysis[8] we can now ask a second and broader question: which is the class of utility functions that imply two-fund separation? Without assuming the existence of a riskless asset, Cass & Stiglitz [1970] prove that a necessary and sufficient condition for two-fund separation is that preferences are either quadratic or of the constant-relative-risk-aversion family, $u(c) = (1 - A)^{-1} c^{1-A}$, $A > 0$, $A \neq 1$ (with $u(c) = \ln c$ corresponding to the case $A = 1$). Actually constant relative risk aversion implies the stronger property of one-fund separation. If a riskless asset is assumed to exist, the necessary and sufficient condition for two-fund separation is either quadratic preferences or HARA preferences defined as $u(c) = (1 - A)^{-1}(c - \hat{c})^{1-A}$, $A > 0$, $A \neq 1$ (with $u(c) = \ln(c - \hat{c})$ corresponding to the case $A = 1$). Their main conclusion is that utility-based conditions under which separation holds are very restrictive. But more to the point, utility-based two-fund separation, with the exception of quadratic utility, does not imply mean–variance choice and does not imply the CAPM.

Ross [1978] establishes the necessary and sufficient conditions on the stochastic structure of asset returns such that two-fund portfolio separation would obtain for any increasing and concave von Neumann–Morgenstern utility function. More specifically, a vector of asset returns $R$ is said to exhibit two-fund separability if

---

[8] Ingersoll [1975] and Kraus & Litzenberger [1976] address the interesting question of how portfolios are formed when either the utility function or the distribution of returns are not of the type that imply mean–variance analysis. In particular, Kraus & Litzenberger [1976] extend the portfolio selection problem to include the effect of skewness. The rate of return on the investor's portfolio is assumed to be nonsymmetrically distributed and the investor's utility function considers the first three moments of such a distribution. See also Ziemba [1994], Ohlson & Ziemba [1976], and Kallberg & Ziemba [1983].

there are two mutual funds $\alpha$ and $\beta$ of $n$ assets such that for any portfolio $q$ there exists a portfolio weight $\lambda$ such that

$$E[u(\lambda R_\alpha + (1 - \lambda)R_\beta)] \geq E[u(R_q)] \tag{7.3}$$

for each monotone increasing and concave utility functions $u(\cdot)$. Observe that (7.3) captures analytically the intuitive notion that portfolios generated by the two funds are preferred to arbitrary portfolios. There is an extensive literature that deals with this important issue of comparing portfolios for a class of investor preferences known as *stochastic dominance*. Ingersoll [1987] or Huang & Litzenberger [1988] give a general overview of these ideas and Rothschild & Stiglitz [1970] offer a detailed analysis.

From the above definition, Ross [1978, p. 267] proves that two-fund separability is equivalent to the following conditions: there exist random variables $\tilde{R}$, $\tilde{Y}$ and $\tilde{\varepsilon}$ and weights $x_i$, $x_i^M$ and $x_i^z$, $i = 1, 2, \ldots, n$, such that

$$\tilde{R}_i = \tilde{R} + b_i \tilde{Y} + \tilde{\varepsilon}_i \qquad \text{for all } i \tag{7.4}$$

$$E[\tilde{\varepsilon}_i \mid \tilde{R} + \xi \tilde{Y}] = 0 \qquad \text{for all } i, \xi \tag{7.5}$$

$$\sum_i w_i^M = 1, \qquad \sum_i w_i^z = 1 \tag{7.6}$$

$$\sum_i w_i^M \tilde{\varepsilon}_i = 0, \qquad \sum_i w_i^z \tilde{\varepsilon}_i = 0 \tag{7.7}$$

$$\text{and either } b_i = b \text{ for all } i, \text{ or } \sum_i w_i^M b_i \neq \sum_i w_i^z b_i. \tag{7.8}$$

Observe that conditions (7.4)–(7.8) represent the most general form of distribution of returns which permits two-fund separation. In particular, Ross [1978, p. 273] shows that all multivariate normally distributed random variables satisfy condition (7.7). But, more to the point Ross shows that, if asset returns are drawn from the family of two-fund separating distributions, and if asset variances are finite, then the CAPM holds.

Having reviewed the assumptions needed on asset distributions for mean–variance portfolio theory and two-fund separation to hold, we close with a brief evaluation of these assumptions. Osborne [1959], Mandelbrot [1963], Fama [1965a, b], Boness, Chen & Jatusipitak [1974] and numerous other studies have shown that there are substantial deviations from normality in the distribution of actual stock prices. Although actual returns are not normally distributed and the use of quadratic utility cannot be supported empirically, the mean–variance portfolio theory remains theoretically useful and empirically relevant. Actually, portfolio theory is a prime example of Milton Friedman's assertion that a theory should not be judged by the relevance of its assumptions, but rather, by the realism of its predictions.[9]

---

[9] Stiglitz [1989] evaluates the various assumptions placed on investor preferences, and Markowitz [1991] in his Nobel Lecture supports the appropriateness of the approximation. See also Levy & Markowitz [1979] and Markowitz [1987].

## 8. Consumption and portfolio selection in continuous time

Mean–variance portfolio theory addresses the investor's asset selection problem for an investment horizon of one period. Progress in portfolio theory came as financial economists relaxed this restrictive assumption. In so doing, however, they were faced with the twin decisions discussed in the introduction: consumption-saving and portfolio selection. The relaxation of the single-period assumption proceeded along two lines: first, in discrete time multiperiod models by Samuelson [1969], Hakansson [1970], Fama [1970], Rubinstein [1976], Long [1974] and others, and second, in continuous time models by Merton [1969, 1971, 1973], Breeden [1979, 1986], Cox, Ingersoll & Ross [1985a, b], and others. Ingersoll [1987] presents a detailed overview of discrete time models. Here, we follow Merton [1973] to develop and solve a continuous-time intertemporal portfolio selection problem.[10]

Assume that there exist continuously trading markets for all $n + 1$ assets and that prices per share $P_i(t)$ are generated by Itô processes, i.e.

$$\frac{\mathrm{d}P_i}{P_i} = \alpha_i(x, t)\,\mathrm{d}t + \sigma_i(x, t)\,\mathrm{d}z_i(t), \qquad i = 1, \ldots, n+1 \tag{8.1}$$

where $\alpha_i$ is the conditional arithmetic expected rate of return and $\sigma_i^2\,\mathrm{d}t$ is the conditional variance of the rate of return of asset $i$. We either assume zero dividends on the stock or, more plausibly, we assume that the dividends are continuously reinvested in the stock and $P_i$ represents the price of one share plus the value of the reinvested dividends. The random variable $z_i(t)$ is a Wiener process. The variance of the increment of the Wiener process is $\mathrm{d}t$. The processes $z_i(t)$ and $z_j(t)$ have correlated increments and we denote

$$\mathrm{cov}\left[\sigma_i \mathrm{d}z_i(t), \sigma_j \mathrm{d}z_j(t)\right] = \sigma_{ij}\mathrm{d}t.$$

In the particular case (not assumed hereafter) where $\alpha_i$ and $\sigma_i$ are constants, the price $P_i(t)$ is lognormally distributed.

The conditional mean and variance of the rate of return are functions of the random variable $x(t)$, assumed here to be a scalar solely for expositional ease. The random variable $x(t)$, referred to here as the *state variable*, is an Itô process

$$\mathrm{d}x = m(x, t)\mathrm{d}t + s(x, t)s\hat{\mathrm{d}z}(t). \tag{8.2}$$

The covariance $\mathrm{cov}[s\hat{\mathrm{d}z}(t), \sigma_i \mathrm{d}z_i(t)]$ is denoted by $\sigma_{ix}\mathrm{d}t$.

---

[10] The appropriateness of the continuous-time approach to the intertemporal portfolio selection problem in particular, and to problems of financial economics in general, is skillfully evaluated in Merton [1975, 1982]. He argues that the use of stochastic calculus methods in finance allows the financial theorist to obtain important generalizations by making realistic assumptions about trading and the evolution of uncertainty. These methods are briefly exposited in Ingersoll [1987] or more extensively in Malliaris & Brock [1982]. The remainder of this paper assumes some familiarity with these techniques.

An investor has wealth $W(t)$ at time $t$. The investor consumes $C(t)dt$ over $[t, t + dt]$ and invests fraction $w_i(t)$ of the wealth in asset $i$, $i = 1, \ldots, n, n + 1$. The budget constraint, or wealth dynamics, is

$$dW(t) = dy(t) - Cdt + \sum_{i=1}^{n+1} w_i \frac{dP_i}{P_i} W \tag{8.3}$$

where $dy(t)$ is the labor income, or generally the exogenous endowment income over the infinitesimal interval $[t, t + dt]$.

For expositional simplicity we assume that the labor income is zero. We also assume that the $(n + 1)$st asset is riskless, i.e. $\sigma_{n+1} = 0$ and we denote $\alpha_{n+1}$ by $r$, the instantaneously riskless rate of interest. Then the wealth dynamics equation simplifies to

$$\begin{aligned} dW &= -Cdt + rW(1 - \sum_{i=1}^{n} w_i)dt + \sum_{i=1}^{n} w_i W(\alpha_i dt + \sigma_i dz_i) \\ &= -Cdt + rWdt + \sum_{i=1}^{n} w_i W[(\alpha_i - r)dt + \sigma_i dz_i]. \end{aligned} \tag{8.4}$$

We assume that the investor makes sequential consumption and investment decisions with the objective to maximize the von Neumann–Morgenstern expected utility i.e.

$$\max E_0 \left[ \int_0^\infty u(C, x, t)\, dt \right] \tag{8.5}$$

where $u$ is monotone increasing and concave in the consumption flow $C$. Note that in the above representation of preferences utility is time-separable but nonstate separable since preferences depend on $x$. The case of nontime-separable preferences is discussed in Sundaresan [1989], Constantinides [1990], and Detemple & Zapatero [1991].

To derive the optimal consumption and investment policies we define

$$J(W, x, t) = \max_{\{C, w\}} E_t \left[ \int_t^\infty u(C, x, \tau)\, d\tau \right].$$

Assuming sufficient regularity conditions as presented in Fleming & Richel [1975], so that a solution exists, the derived utility of wealth, $J$, satisfies the equation derived by Merton [1971, 1973]

$$0 = \max_{\{C, w\}} \left[ u(C, x, t) + \left\{ -C + rW + W \sum_{i=1}^{n} w_i(\alpha_i - r) \right\} J_W + m J_x + J_t + \right. $$
$$\left. + \frac{1}{2} W^2 J_{WW} \sum_{i=1}^{n} \sum_{j=1}^{n} w_i w_j \sigma_{ij} + W J_{Wx} \sum_{i=1}^{n} w_i \sigma_{ix} + \frac{s^2}{2} J_{xx} \right]. \tag{8.6}$$

The first-order conditions with respect to $C$ and $w_i$ are

$$u_C - J_W = 0 \tag{8.7}$$

and

$$W(\alpha_i - r)J_W + W^2 J_{WW} \sum_{j=1}^{n} w_j \sigma_{ij} + W J_{Wx}\sigma_{ix} = 0, \quad i = 1, \ldots, n. \tag{8.8}$$

The concavity of the utility function implies that $J$ is concave in $W$; hence the second-order conditions are satisfied.

Under appropriate regularity conditions which are not discussed here a verification theorem can be stated to the effect that the solution of the partial differential equation is unique, and therefore is the solution of the original optimal consumption and investment problem.

Since the topic of this essay is the portfolio problem we focus on the first-order conditions (8.8) implied by optimal investment which we write in matrix notation as

$$(\alpha - r\mathbf{1})J_W + W J_{WW}\mathbf{w}^\mathsf{T}\mathbf{V} + J_{Wx}\sigma_x = 0, \tag{8.9}$$

where $\mathbf{V}$ is the $n \times n$ covariance matrix with $i \times j$ element $\sigma_{ij}$ and $\sigma_x$ is a vector with $i$th element $\sigma_{ix}$. Solving for the optimal portfolio weights we obtain

$$\mathbf{w} = \left(\frac{-J_W}{W J_{WW}}\right)\mathbf{V}^{-1}(\alpha - r\mathbf{1}) - \frac{J_{Wx}}{W J_{WW}}\mathbf{V}^{-1}\sigma_x. \tag{8.10}$$

Before we analyze the optimal portfolio decision in its full generality, consider first the important special case where the term $[J_{Wx}/(W J_{WW})]\mathbf{V}^{-1}\sigma_x$ is a vector of zeros. We will shortly discuss three cases where this occurs. Then we may write equation (8.10) as

$$\mathbf{w} = \left(\frac{-J_W}{W J_{WW}}\right)\left[\mathbf{1}^\mathsf{T}\mathbf{V}^{-1}(\alpha - r\mathbf{1})\right]\mathbf{w}_\mathsf{T} \tag{8.11}$$

where

$$\mathbf{w}_\mathsf{T} = \frac{\mathbf{V}^{-1}(\alpha - r\mathbf{1})}{\mathbf{1}^\mathsf{T}\mathbf{V}^{-1}(\alpha - r\mathbf{1})}. \tag{8.12}$$

From our discussion in Section 5, we recognize $\mathbf{w}_\mathsf{T}$ as the vector of portfolio weights of the tangency portfolio on the frontier of minimum variance portfolios generated by the $n$ risky assets. We also interpret $(-J_W / W J_{WW})^{-1}$ as the relative risk aversion (RRA) coefficient of the investor. Then equation (8.11) states that the investor invests in just two portfolios, namely the riskless asset and the tangency portfolio. The extent of the investment in the tangency portfolio depends on the investor's RRA coefficient. Thus we have proved that there is two-fund separation with the two funds being the riskless asset and the tangency portfolio. From here it is a small step, outlined in Section 9, to show that the CAPM holds.

We present three sets of conditions each of which implies two-fund separation and the CAPM:

(a) Logarithmic utility. Then we may show that the derived utility $J(W, x)$ is the sum of a function of $W$ and a function of $x$. Hence the cross-derivative $J_{Wx}$ equals zero and the second term in equation (8.10) becomes a vector of zeros.

(b) All assets' returns are uncorrelated with the change in $x$, i.e. $\sigma_{ix} = 0$, $i = 1, \ldots, n$.

(c) All assets have distributions of returns which are independent of $x$, i.e. $\alpha_i$, $\sigma_i$ are independent of $x$ for $i = 1, \ldots, n$.

We now return to the general case where none of the assumptions (a)–(c) hold and the term $[J_{Wx}/(W J_{WW})]V^{-1}\sigma_x$ is not a vector of zeros. Define by $w_H$ the weights of a portfolio

$$w_H = \frac{V^{-1}\sigma_x}{1^T V^{-1}\sigma_x}.$$

Then we may write equation (8.10) as

$$w = \left(\frac{-J_W}{W J_{WW}}\right)\left[1^T V^{-1}(\alpha - r1)\right]w_T + \left(\frac{-J_{Wx}}{W J_{WW}}\right)\left[1^T V^{-1}\sigma_x\right]w_H. \quad (8.13)$$

We observe that three-fund portfolio separation obtains: The investor invests in the riskless asset, the tangency portfolio $w_T$ and the hedging portfolio $w_H$. The weights which the investor assigns to each portfolio depend on his/her preferences and are, therefore, investor-specific.

We may further interpret the hedging portfolio by solving the following maximization problem: Choose vector $y$ such that $1^T y = 1$ (i.e. $y$ is the vector of a portfolio's weights) to maximize the correlation of $dx$ and $\sum_{i=1}^n y_i(dP_i/P_i)$. The solution to this problem is easily shown to be $y = w_H$. That is, the hedging portfolio is the portfolio of the risky assets with returns maximally correlated with the change in the state variable $x$.

Note that $x$ enters into the decision problem through $\alpha_i$ and $\sigma_i$, that is, it causes changes in the investment opportunity set and through the utility of consumption, $u(C, x, t)$, that is, it causes shifts in tastes. We may interpret the three fund separation result as follows: The investor invests in the riskless asset and in the tangency portfolio, as in the mean–variance case, but modifies his or her portfolio investing in (or selling short) a third portfolio which has returns maximally correlated with changes in the variable $x$ which represents shifts in the investment opportunity set and tastes.

As we stated earlier we have chosen $x$ to be a scalar solely for expositional ease. If instead, $x$ is a vector with $m$ elements we obtain $(m + 2)$-fund separation where the investor invests in the riskless asset, the tangency portfolio and the $m$ hedging portfolios.

In evaluating Merton's [1971, 1973] intertemporal continuous-time portfolio theory at least two important contributions need to be identified: first, its generalization of the static mean–variance theory is achieved by considering both the consumption and portfolio selection over time and by dropping the quadratic utility assumption; and second, its realism and tractability compared to the discrete-time portfolio theories which assume normally distributed asset prices implying a nonzero probability of negative asset prices. By replacing the assumption of normally distributed asset prices with the assumption that prices follow (8.1), the continuous-time portfolio theory becomes more realistic as well as more tractable in view of the extensive mathematical literature on diffusion processes.

Merton's work was extended in several directions. Among them, Breeden [1979] and Cox, Ingersoll & Ross [1985a, b] consider a generalization of the intertemporal continuous-time portfolio theory in a general equilibrium model with production. Another contribution was made by Breeden [1979] who shows that Merton's [1973] multi-beta pricing model can be expressed with a single beta measured with respect to changes in aggregate consumption assuming that consumption preferences are time separable. One interesting result of Breeden's work is that, in an intertemporal economy, the portfolio that has the highest correlation of returns with aggregate real consumption changes is mean–variance efficient.

Several authors have considered equation (8.1) which is the most significant assumption of continuous-time portfolio theory and have asked the question: under what conditions is a price system representable by Itô processes such as (8.1)? Huang [1985a, b] shows that when the information structure is a Brownian filtration then any arbitrage-free price system is an Itô process. The arbitrage-free concept is analyzed in Harrison & Kreps [1979] and Harrison & Pliska [1981] who make a connection to a martingale representation theorem. The role of information is analyzed in Duffie & Huang [1986].

Finally, in contrast to the stochastic dynamic programming approach to the continuous time consumption and portfolio problem, Pliska [1986] and Cox & Huang [1989], among others have used the martingale representation methodology. In the martingale approach, first, the dynamic consumption and portfolio problem is transformed and solved as a static utility maximization problem to find the optimal consumption and, second, the martingale representation theorem is applied to determine the portfolio trading strategy which is consistent with the optimal consumption. It is usually assumed that markets are dynamically complete which allows for the determination of a budget constraint and the solution of the static utility maximization. The case when markets are dynamically incomplete with the dimension of the Brownian motion driving the security prices being greater than the number of risky securities is presented in He & Pearson [1991].

## 9. The Intertemporal Asset Pricing Model (ICAPM) and the Arbitrage Pricing Theory (APT)

In the last section we solved for the optimal weights of the portfolio of risky assets held by an investor with given preferences. If all consumers in the economy have identical preferences and endowments then the above optimal portfolio may be identified as the market portfolio of risky assets. The condition that consumers have identical preferences and endowments may be relaxed under conditions which imply demand aggregation as in Rubinstein [1974] and Constantinides [1980] or under complete markets as in Constantinides [1982]. Hereafter we assume that either through demand aggregation or through complete markets we can claim that the optimal portfolio in (8.10) is indeed the market portfolio of risky assets. We denote the weights of this portfolio by $w^M$ and its return by

$$\frac{dP_M}{P_M} = \sum_{i=1}^{n} w_i^M \frac{dP_i}{P_i}$$

We should stress that, in general, the market portfolio does not coincide with the tangency portfolio. In the last section we discussed conditions under which the two portfolios coincide but these conditions will not be imposed here.

To derive the intertemporal capital asset pricing model (ICAPM), we rewrite equation (8.8) as

$$\alpha_i - r = \left( -\frac{W J_{WW}}{J_W} \right) \sum_{j=1}^{n} w_j^M \sigma_{ij} + \left( -\frac{J_{Wx}}{J_W} \right) \sigma_{ix}$$

$$= \lambda_M \beta_{iM} + \lambda_x \beta_{ix} \qquad i = 1, \ldots, n. \tag{9.1}$$

where

$$\beta_{iM} = \frac{\text{cov}(dP_i/P_i, dP_M/P_M)}{\text{var}(dP_M/P_M)}$$

$$\lambda_M = -\frac{W J_{WW}}{J_W} \frac{\text{var}(dP_M/P_M)}{dt}$$

$$\beta_{ix} = \frac{\text{cov}(dP_i/P_i, dx)}{\text{var}(dx)}$$

and

$$\lambda_x = -\frac{J_{Wx}}{J_W} \frac{\text{var}(dx)}{dt}.$$

This result generalizes in a routine fashion to the case where the state variable is a vector.

We conclude this section by discussing the empirically testable implications of the theory, along with the arbitrage pricing theory of Ross [1976a, b]. The common starting point of both the ICAPM and the APT is a linear multivariate regression of the $n \times 1$ vector of asset returns, $\tilde{R}$, on a $k \times 1$ vector of state variables (in the ICAPM) or factors (in the APT), $\tilde{f}$:

$$\tilde{R} = R + B(\tilde{f} - f) + \tilde{\varepsilon} \tag{9.2}$$

where $R \equiv E[\tilde{R}]$, $f \equiv E[\tilde{f}]$ and $E[\tilde{\varepsilon}] = 0$. In both theories the elements of $\tilde{f}$ are assumed to have finite variance. The covariance matrix $\Omega \equiv E[\tilde{\varepsilon}\tilde{\varepsilon}^T]$ is assumed to have finite elements. Furthermore, in the APT the elements of $\tilde{f}$ are assumed to be factors in the sense that the largest eigenvalue of $\Omega$ remains bounded as $n \to \infty$ [see Chamberlain, 1983b].

The pricing restriction implied by the ICAPM is that there exist a constant, $\lambda_0$, and a $k \times 1$ vector of risk "premia", $\lambda$, such that

$$R = \lambda_0 1 + B\lambda \tag{9.3}$$

where $1$ is the $n \times 1$ vector of ones as before. The pricing restriction implied by the APT is

$$\lim_{n \to \infty} (R - \lambda_0 1 - B\lambda)^{\mathrm{T}} (R - \lambda_0 1 - B\lambda) = A, \qquad A < \infty \tag{9.4}$$

which, in empirical work (where $n$ is finite), is interpreted to imply (9.3).

If the proxies for state variables in the ICAPM or factors in the APT are portfolios of the $n$ assets, the ICAPM or APT pricing restrictions, (9.3), state that there exists a portfolio of these proxy portfolios which has mean and variance on the mean–variance, minimum-variance frontier. See Jobson & Korkie [1985], Grinblatt & Titman [1987] and Huberman, Kandel & Stambaugh [1987]. Therefore the econometric methods for testing that a given portfolio lies on the minimum-variance frontier may be extended to test the ICAPM and the APT. See Kandel & Stambaugh [1989] and the Connor & Korajczyk [1995] essay in this volume.

## 10. Market imperfections

Market imperfections were suppressed in our earlier discussion by implicitly assuming that (i) transaction costs are zero, (ii) the capital gains tax is zero (or, capital gains and losses are realized and taxed in every period), and (iii) the assets may be sold short with full use of the proceeds which, in the case of a riskless asset, implies that the borrowing rate equals the lending rate. How sensitive are our conclusions on portfolio selection and equilibrium asset pricing to the presence of these imperfections? Whereas a comprehensive discussion of these issues is beyond the scope of this essay, we discuss briefly one instance of market imperfections.

Consider first the discrete-time intertemporal investment and consumption problem with proportional transaction costs. The agent maximizes the expectation of a time-separable utility function where the period utility is of the convenient power form. The agent consumes in every period and invests the remaining wealth in only two assets. The agent enters period $t$ with $x_t$ units of account of the first asset and $y_t$ units of account of the second asset. If the agent buys (or, sells) $v_t$ units of account of the second asset, the holding of the first asset becomes $x_t - v_t - \max[k_1 v_t, -k_2 v_t]$, net of transaction costs where the constants $k_1, k_2$ satisfy $0 \le k_1 \le 1$ and $0 \le k_2 \le 1$. The optimal investment policy, described in terms of two parameters $\underline{\alpha}_t$ and $\overline{\alpha}_t$, $\underline{\alpha}_t \le \overline{\alpha}_t$, is to refrain from transacting as long as the portfolio proportions, $x_t/y_t$, lie within the interval $[\underline{\alpha}_t, \overline{\alpha}_t]$; and transact to the closer boundary, $\underline{\alpha}_t$ or $\overline{\alpha}_t$, of the region of no transactions whenever the portfolio proportions lie outside this interval (provided, of course, that this is feasible). The parameters $(\underline{\alpha}_t, \overline{\alpha}_t)$ are functions of time and of the state variables which define the conditional distribution of the assets' return. This general form of the optimal portfolio policy also holds in a model with continuous trading under additional assumptions on the distribution of asset returns. See Kamin [1975], Constantinides [1979], Taksar, Klass & Assaf [1988] and Davis & Norman [1990].

In numerical solutions of the portfolio problem with even small proportional transaction costs one finds that the region of no transactions is wide. We conclude from these examples and extrapolate in more general cases with transaction costs that even small transaction costs distort significantly the optimal portfolio policy which is optimal in the absence of transaction costs. See Constantinides [1986], Dumas & Luciano [1991], Fleming, Grossman, Vila & Zariphopoulou [1990] and Gennotte & Jung [1991]. An encouraging finding, however, is that transaction costs have only a second-order effect on equilibrium asset returns: investors accommodate large transaction costs by drastically reducing the frequency and volume of trade. It turns out that the agent's utility is insensitive to deviations of the asset proportions from those proportions which are optimal in the absence of transaction costs. Therefore, a small liquidity premium is sufficient to compensate an agent for deviating significantly from the target portfolio proportions. These results need to be qualified as they apply to the case where the only motive for trade is portfolio rebalancing. Transaction costs may have a first-order effect on equilibrium asset returns in cases where the investors receive exogenous income or trade on the basis of inside information.

## 11. Concluding remarks

Portfolio theory is the analysis of the real world phenomenon of diversification. This paper has exposited this theory in its historical evolution, from the early work on static mean–variance mathematics to its generalization of dynamic consumption and portfolio rules. In its intellectual development portfolio theory has benefitted from empirical work which came from capital asset pricing tests and from statistical investigations of the distributions of asset prices. Furthermore, as more powerful techniques were developed, such as stochastic calculus, portfolio theory became dynamic and many results were generalized.

Because the topic of our paper is theoretical, we have not mentioned any issues related to real world portfolio management. Interested readers can find such topics in standard graduate textbooks such as Lee, Finnerty & Wort [1990] or papers in this volume on performance evaluation by Grinblatt & Titman [1995], on market microstructure by Easley & O'Hara [1995], and on world wide security market regularities by Hawawini & Keim [1995], among others. Although our topic was on portfolio theory, numerous important theoretical developments are not mentioned. Fortunately again, some are treated in this volume such as futures and options markets by Carr & Jarrow [1995], market volatility by LeRoy

& Steigerwald [1995], and the extension of portfolio theory from national to international markets by Stulz [1995]. A useful companion survey is presented in Constantinides [1989], where theoretical issues of financial valuation are presented in a unified way.

### Acknowledgements

We thank Wayne Ferson, Brian Kennedy and Bill Ziemba for several useful comments.

### References

Arrow, K.J. (1971). *Essays on the Theory of Risk-Bearing*, Markham, Chicago.

Bernoulli, D. (1738). Exposition of a new theory of the measurement of risk, translated by L. Sommer and published in 1954 in *Econometrica* 22, 23–36.

Black, F. (1972). Capital market equilibrium with restricted borrowing. *J. Bus.* 45, 444–455.

Boness, A.J., A. Chen and S. Jatusipitak (1974). Investigations on nonstationarity in prices. *J. Bus.* 47, 518–537.

Breeden, D.T. (1979). An intertemporal asset pricing model with stochastic consumption and investment opportunities. *J. Financ. Econ.* 7, 265–296.

Breeden, D.T. (1986). Consumption, production, inflation, and interest rates: A synthesis. *J. Financ. Econ.* 16, 3–39.

Brennan, M.J. (1989). Capital asset pricing model, in: J. Eatwell, M. Milgate and P. Newman (eds.), *The New Palgrave Dictionary of Economics*, Stockton Press, New York, NY.

Carr, P., and R.A. Jarrow (1995). A discrete time synthesis of derivative security valuation using a term structure of futures prices, in: R. Jarrow, V. Maksimovic and W.T. Ziemba (eds.), *Finance*, Elsevier, Amsterdam, pp. (this volume).

Cass, D., and J. Stiglitz (1970). The structure of investor preferences and asset returns, and separability in portfolio selection: A contribution to the pure theory of mutual funds. *J. Econ. Theory* 2, 122–160.

Chamberlain, G. (1983a). A characterization of the distributions that imply mean–variance utility functions. *J. Econ. Theory* 29, 185–201.

Chamberlain, G. (1983b). Funds, factors, and diversification in arbitrage pricing models. *Econometrica* 51, 1305–1323.

Connor, G, and R. Korajczyk (1995). The arbitrage pricing theory, and multifactor models of asset returns, in: R. Jarrow, V. Maksimovic and W.T. Ziemba (eds.), *Finance*, Elsevier, Amsterdam, pp. 65–122 (this volume).

Constantinides, G.M. (1979). Multiperiod consumption and investment behavior with convex transaction costs. *Manage. Sci.* 25, 1127–1137.

Constantinides, G.M. (1980). Admissible uncertainty in the intertemporal asset pricing model. *J. Financ. Econ.* 8, 71–86.

Constantinides, G.M. (1982). Intertemporal asset pricing with heterogeneous consumers and without demand aggregation. *J. Bus.* 55, 253–267.

Constantinides, G.M. (1986). Capital market equilibrium with transaction costs. *J. Polit. Econ.* 94, 842–862.

Constantinides, G.M. (1989). Theory of valuation: Overview and recent developments, in: S. Bhattacharya and G.M. Constantinides (eds.), *Theory of Valuation*, Rowman & Littlefield, Totowa, NJ.

Constantinides, G.M. (1990). Habit formation: A resolution of the equity premium puzzle. *J. Polit. Econ.* 98, 519–543.

Cox, J.C, and C.F. Huang (1989). Optimal consumption and portfolio policies when asset prices follow a diffusion process. *J. Econ. Theory* 49, 33–83.

Cox, J.C., J.E. Ingersoll, and S.A. Ross (1985a). A theory of the term structure of interest rates. *Econometrica* 53, 385–407.

Cox, J.C., J.E. Ingersoll, and S.A. Ross (1985b). An intertemporal general equilibrium model of asset prices. *Econometrica* 53, 363–384.

Davis, M.H.A., and A.R. Norman (1990). Portfolio selection with transactions costs. *Math. Oper. Res.* 15, 676–713.

Detemple, J.B., and F. Zapatero (1991). Asset prices in an exchange economy with habit formation. *Econometrica* 59, 1633–1657.

Dumas, B., and E. Luciano (1991). An exact solution to a dynamic portfolio choice problem under transactions costs. *J. Finance* 46, 577–595.

Duffie, D, and C. Huang (1986). Multiperiod securities markets with differential information: Martingales and resolution times. *J. Math. Econ.* 15, 283–303.

Easley, M, and M. O'Hara (1995). Market microstructure, in: R. Jarrow, V. Maksimovic and W.T. Ziemba (eds.), *Finance*, Elsevier, Amsterdam, pp. 357–384 (this volume).

Fama, E.F. (1965a). Portfolio analysis in a stable Paretian market. *Manage. Sci.* 11, 409–419.

Fama, E.F. (1965b). The behavior of stock market prices. *J. Bus.* 38, 34–105.

Fama, E.F. (1970). Multiperiod consumption-investment decisions. *Am. Econ. Rev.* 60, 163–174.

Fama, E.F. (1976). *Foundations of Finance*, Basic Books, New York, NY.

Ferson, W. (1995). Theory and empirical testing of asset pricing models, in: R. Jarrow, V. Maksimovic and W.T. Ziemba (eds.), *Finance*, Elsevier, Amsterdam, pp. 145–200 (this volume).

Fisher, I. (1906). *The Nature of Capital and Income*, Macmillan, New York, NY.

Fleming, W, and R. Richel (1975). *Deterministic and Stochastic Optimal Control*, Springer-Verlag, New York, NY.

Fleming, W.H.S., S.G. Grossman, J.L. Vila, and T. Zariphopoulou (1990). Optimal portfolio rebalancing with transactions costs. Working paper, Brown University.

Gennotte, G, and A. Jung (1991). Investment strategies under transaction costs: The finite horizon case. Working paper, University of California at Berkeley.

Gonzalez-Gaverra, N. (1973). Inflation and capital asset market prices: Theory and tests. Unpublished PhD Dissertation, Stanford University.

Grinblatt, M, and S. Titman (1987). The relation between mean–variance efficiency and arbitrage pricing. *J. Bus.* 60, 97–112.

Grinblatt, M, and S. Titman (1995). Performance evaluation, in: R. Jarrow, V. Maksimovic and W.T. Ziemba (eds.), *Finance*, Elsevier, Amsterdam, pp. 581–610 (this volume).

Hakansson, N. (1970). Optimal investment and consumption strategies under risk for a class of utility functions. *Econometrica* 38, 587–607.

Hakansson, N. (1974). Convergence in multiperiod portfolio choice. *J. Financ. Econ.* 1, 201–224.

Hansen, L.P, and R. Jagannathan (1991). Implications of security market data for models of dynamic economies. *J. Polit. Econ.* 99, 225–262.

Harrison, M, and D. Kreps (1979). Martingales and arbitrage in multiperiod securities markets. *J. Econ. Theory* 20, 381–408.

Harrison, M, and S. Pliska (1981). Martingales and stochastic integrals in the theory of continuous trading. *Stoch. Process Appl.* 11, 215–260.

Hawawini, G, and D. Keim (1995). On the predictability of common stock returns: world-wide evidence, in: R. Jarrow, V. Maksimovic and W.T. Ziemba (eds.), *Finance*, Elsevier, Amsterdam, pp. (this volume).

He, H, and N.D. Pearson (1991). Consumption and portfolio policies with incomplete markets and short-sale constraints: The infinite dimensional case. *J. Econ. Theory* 54, 259–304.

Hicks, J.R. (1939). *Value and Capital*, Oxford University Press, New York, NY.

Huang, C. (1985a). Information structure and equilibrium asset prices. *J. Econ. Theory* 35, 33–71.

Huang, C. (1985b). Information structure and viable price systems. *J. Math. Econ.* 14, 215–240.

Huang, C.F, and R.H. Litzenberger (1988). *Foundations for Financial Economics*, North Holland, Amsterdam.

Huberman G., S. Kandel, and R.F. Stambaugh (1987). Mimicking portfolios and exact arbitrage pricing. *J. Finance* 42, 1–9.

Ingersoll, Jr., J.E. (1975). Multidimensional security pricing. *J. Financ. Quant. Anal.* 10, 785–798.

Ingersoll, Jr., J.E. (1987). *Theory of Financial Decision Making*, Rowman and Littlefield, Totowa, NJ.

Jarrow, R.A. (1988). *Finance Theory*, Prentice Hall, Englewood Cliffs, NJ.

Jobson, J.D., and B. Korkie (1985). Some tests of linear asset pricing with multivariate normality. *Can. J. Adm. Sci.* 2, 114–138.

Kallberg, J.G, and W.T. Ziemba (1983). Comparison of alternative utility functions in portfolio selection problems. *Manage. Sci.* 29, 1257–1276.

Kamin, J. (1975). Optimal portfolio revision with a proportional transactions cost. *Manage. Sci.* 21, 1263–1271.

Kandel, S., and R.F. Stambaugh (1989). A mean–variance framework for tests of asset pricing models. *Rev. Financ. Studies* 2, 125–156.

Keynes, J.L. (1936). *The General Theory of Employment, Interest and Money*, Harcourt Brace and Company, New York, NY.

Kraus, A, and R. Litzenberger (1976). Skewness preference and the valuation of risk assets. *J. Finance* 31, 1085–1100.

Lee, C.F., J.E. Finnerty and D.H. Wort (1990). *Security Analysis and Portfolio Management*, Scott, Foresman and Company, Glenview, IL.

LeRoy, S, and D. Steigerwald (1995). Volatility, in: R. Jarrow, V. Maksimovic and W.T. Ziemba (eds.), *Finance*, Elsevier, Amsterdam, pp. 411–434 (this volume).

Levy, H, and H.M. Markowitz (1979). Approximating expected utility by a function of mean and variance. *Am. Econ. Rev.* 69, 308–317.

Levy, H, and P.A. Samuelson (1992) The capital asset pricing model with diverse holding periods. *Manage. Sci.* 38, 1529–1542.

Lintner, J. (1965). The valuation of risk assets and the selection of risky investments in stock portfolios and capital assets. *Rev. Econ. Stat.* 47, 13–37.

Long, J.B. (1974). Stock prices, inflation, and the term structure of interest rates. *J. Financ. Econ.* 2, 131–170.

Malliaris, A.G, and W.A. Brock (1982). *Stochastic Methods in Economics and Finance*, North Holland, Amsterdam.

Mandelbrot, B. (1963). The variation of certain speculative prices. *J. Bus.* 36, 394–419.

Markowitz, H. (1952). Portfolio selection. *J. Finance* 7, 77–91.

Markowitz, H. (1959). *Portfolio Selection: Efficient Diversification of Investments*, Wiley, New York, NY.

Markowitz, H.M. (1987). *Mean–Variance Analysis in Portfolio Choice and Capital Markets*, Basil Blackwell, Oxford.

Markowitz, H.M. (1991). Foundations of portfolio theory. *J. Finance* 46, 469–477.

Marschak, J. (1938). Money and the theory of assets. *Econometrica* 6, 311–325.

Merton, R.C. (1969). Lifetime portfolio selection under uncertainty: The continuous time case. *Rev. Econ. Stat.* 51, 247–257.

Merton, R.C. (1971). Optimum consumption and portfolio rules in a continuous time model. *J. Econ. Theory* 3, 373–413.

Merton, R.C. (1972). An analytical derivation of the efficient portfolio frontier. *J. Financ. Quant. Anal.* 7, 1851–1872.

Merton, R.C. (1973). An intertemporal capital asset pricing model. *Econometrica* 41, 867–887.

Merton, R.C. (1975). Theory of finance from the perspective of continuous time. *J. Financ. Quant. Anal.* 10, 659–674.

Merton, R.C. (1980). On estimating the expected return on the market: An explanatory investigation. *J. Financ. Econ.* 8, 323–361.

Merton, R.C. (1982). On the mathematics and economics assumptions of continuous-time models, in: W.F. Sharpe and C.M. Cootner (eds.), *Financial Economics: Essays in Honor of Paul Cootner*, Prentice Hall, Englewood Cliffs, NJ.

Mossin, J. (1966). Equilibrium in a capital asset market. *Econometrica* 35, 768–783.

Mossin, J. (1969). Optimal multiperiod portfolio policies. *J. Bus.* 41, 215–229.

Ohlson, J.A, and W.T. Ziemba (1976). Portfolio selection in a lognormal market when the investor has a power utility function. *J. Financ. Quant. Anal.* 11, 393–401.

Osborne, M.F.M. (1959). Brownian motion in the stock market. *Oper. Res.* 7, 145–173.

Pliska, S. (1986). A stochastic calculus model of continuous trading: Optimal portfolios. *Math. Oper. Res.* 11, 371–382.

Roll, R. (1977). A critique of the asset pricing theory's tests: Part I. *J. Financ. Econ.* 4, 129–176.

Rothschild, M, and J. Stiglitz (1970). Increasing risk. I. A definition. *J. Econ. Theory* 2, 225–243.

Ross, S.A. (1976a). Return, risk and arbitrage, in: I. Friend and J. Bicksler (eds.), *Risk and Return in Finance*, Ballinger, Cambridge, MA.

Ross, S.A. (1976b). The arbitrage theory of capital asset pricing. *J. Econ. Theory* 13, 341–360.

Ross, S.A. (1978). Mutual fund separation in financial theory — The separating distributions. *J. Econ. Theory* 17, 254–286.

Rubinstein, M. (1974). An aggregation theorem for security markets. *J. Financ. Econ.* 1, 225–244.

Rubinstein, M. (1976). The valuation of uncertain income streams and the pricing of options. *Bell J. Econ. Manage. Sci.* 7, 407–425.

Samuelson, P. (1969). Lifetime portfolio selection by dynamic stochastic programming. *Rev. Econ. Stat.* 57, 239–246.

Sharpe, W.F. (1964). Capital asset prices: A theory of market equilibrium under conditions of risk. *J. Finance* 19, 425–442.

Sharpe, W.F. (1970). *Portfolio Theory and Capital Markets*, McGraw-Hill, New York, NY.

Stiglitz, J.E. (1989). Discussion: Mutual funds, capital structure, and economic efficiency, in: S. Bhattacharya and G.M. Constantinides (eds.), *Theory of Valuation*, Rowman & Littlefield Publishers, Totowa, NJ.

Stulz, R. (1995). International portfolio choice and asset pricing: an integrative survey, in: R. Jarrow, V. Maksimovic and W.T. Ziemba (eds.), *Finance*, Elsevier, Amsterdam, pp. 201–224 (this volume).

Sundaresan, S.M. (1989). Intertemporal dependent preferences and the volatility of consumption and wealth. *Rev. Financ. Studies* 2, 73–90.

Taksar, M., M. Klass, and D. Assaf (1988). A diffusion model for optimal portfolio selection in the presence of brokerage fees. *Math. Oper. Res.* 13, 277–294.

Tobin, J. (1958). Liquidity preference as behavior toward risk. *Rev. Econ. Studies* 25, 65–86.

Von Neumann, J, and O. Morgenstern (1947). *Theory of Games and Economic Behavior*, 2nd edition, Princeton University Press, Princeton.

Williams J.B. (1938). *The Theory of Investment Value*, Harvard University Press, Cambridge, MA.

Ziemba W.T., C. Parkan and R. Brooks-Hill (1974). Calculation of investment portfolios with risk free borrowing and lending. *Manage. Sci.* 21, 209–222.

Ziemba, W.T. (1974). Choosing investment portfolios when returns have stable distributions, in: P.L. Hammer and G. Zoutendijk (eds.), *Mathematical Programming in Theory and Practice*, North-Holland, Amsterdam, pp. 443–482.

Ziemba, W.T, and R.G. Vickson, editors (1975). *Stochastic Optimization Models in Finance*, Academic Press, New York, NY.

# PART III

# AGRICULTURAL FUTURES

# [9]

# LINKAGES BETWEEN
# AGRICULTURAL
# COMMODITY FUTURES
# CONTRACTS

## A. G. MALLIARIS
## JORGE L. URRUTIA

## INTRODUCTION

Two distinct methodologies are used in price determination: partial equilibrium analysis and general equilibrium analysis. The former emphasizes supply and demand conditions for a specific good or service, assuming all other factors are the same, while the latter explicitly recognizes the interdependence of all prices. This study empirically tests the independence of the futures prices of the six agricultural commodities traded at the Chicago Board of Trade. The working hypothesis is that the prices of the six agricultural commodities move independently.

Although the null hypothesis is formulated in terms of price independence between any two of the six agricultural commodities (in the spirit of a partial equilibrium analysis) there are important economic reasons that would make one expect rejection of this hypothesis. These reasons are discussed next.

An earlier version was presented at the Midwest Finance Association Meetings, March 24–26, 1994, in Chicago, and was selected as the outstanding Chicago Board of Trade article in the area of Futures and Options. We acknowledge with thanks the prize offered to us by the Chicago Board of Trade. We also wish to express our gratitude to Ms. M. Kathryn Jennings who offered us her expertise on the important variables which may explain the linkages among agricultural commodities. All errors are our responsibility.

- A.G. Malliaris is the Walter F. Mullady, Sr. Professor of Business Administration in the Department of Economics, Loyola University of Chicago.
- Jorge L. Urrutia is a Professor in the Department of Finance, Loyola University of Chicago.

The Journal of Futures Markets, Vol. 16, No. 5, 595–609 (1996)
© 1996 by John Wiley & Sons, Inc.                    CCC 0270-7314/96/ 050595-15

Microeconomic theory postulates that there are two key economic linkages between any two commodities—substitutability and complementarity. For example, if the price of corn increases, cattle feeders may use soybean meal as a substitute, and vice versa. The relationship here is one of substitutability. On the other hand, if the price of soybean oil increases dramatically and soybeans are crushed to supply such oil, this process also produces soybean meal and may result in a drop in the price of soybean meal. The relationship here is one of complementarity. Substitutability and complementarity can be present simultaneously among the six agricultural commodities traded at the Chicago Board of Trade. For example, both corn and soybean meal are used for animal and chicken feeding. While substitutability exists between the two, some degree of complementarity is also at play. While soybean meal is high in protein, corn is high in nutrients and vitamins. Soybean meal and corn are usually mixed in certain proportions which are determined by economic and nutritional considerations. Oats and wheat can be used along with soybean meal and corn in various proportions. Thus, substitutability and complementarity are not strictly mutually exclusive among soybean meal, corn, oats, and wheat.

Given that corn, wheat, and soybeans are grown in a relatively concentrated geographical area, weather and general climatological factors affect the national supply of these crops in a similar way. Although corn is grown in over 40 of the contiguous United States, approximately 84% of the corn crop is grown in 17 states. Iowa, Illinois, Nebraska, Minnesota, Indiana, and Ohio produce the most corn. Figures vary somewhat from year to year. Total corn acres planted during the time period, 1981–1991, averaged 83 million acres per year; harvested corn acres averaged 73.7% to 89% of annual planted acreage for the 1981–1991 time period. Most of this acreage is concentrated in the "corn belt" where planting begins in early April and is completed in northern areas by late May. Following a period of slow growth, the corn plant grows rapidly provided that ample supply of moisture and soil nutrients are available.

Soybeans were grown in 20 states and planted on approximately 63 million acres of farmland per year during the 1981–1991 time period. In general, wheat is grown in more states than any other commodity and planted on approximately 76 million acres a year. Oats are grown in approximately 12 north central states and planted an average of 14 million acres per year.

The importance of the effects of weather on the futures prices of agricultural commodities is well documented. Stevens (1991) has found evidence for a weather persistence effect on corn, wheat, and soybean contract prices. Similar results are reported in Teigen and Singer (1989), Westcott (1989) and others. A much larger literature exists that relates weather conditions to seasonal price dynamics. Anderson and Danthine (1983) and Anderson (1985) review aspects of grain production seasonality effects.

As important as the weather and general climatological factors are, recall that every farmer (whether an individual or a large corporate entity) attempts to plant crops that allow maximization of profit under the uncertain conditions of weather and future spot prices. The farmer knows with some degree of accuracy when to plant and when to harvest, what and how much fertilizer to use, and what is the expected crop yield under certain conditions. For example, corn must be planted very early in June to have time to grow and mature during the hot late summer months. Cool weather delays maturity and a possible early frost could cause serious crop damage. On the other hand, soybeans can still be planted mid- to late June and are less sensitive to early fall frost damage than is corn. However, soybean yield is much less that corn yield. Thus, the supply of these crops is ultimately dependent on the profit-maximizing behavior of farmers under conditions of weather and price uncertainty.

Crop production costs are different from region to region, and from county to county. The farmer must determine the costs of seed, fertilizer, chemicals, fuel, land/rent, labor, taxes, and capital and weigh those costs against projected income based upon estimated yield and estimated futures prices. After land costs, fertilizer is the second greatest expense unique to corn production due to the nitrogen requirements of the corn plant. The nitrogen requirements contribute to corn's reputation for being the highest cost grain to produce. On the other hand, the corn plant has the highest yield per bushel of any of the grain or soy alternatives. During the 1981–1991 time period, the average corn yield was 129 bushels per acre; 2 times the yield of soybeans, 1.7 times the yield of wheat, and over 2.25 times the yield of oats.

Beyond the supply and demand considerations that affect the interdependence of agricultural commodities, one should mention exogenous shocks such as the Soviet Union grain policy shift of the early 1970s and the European Economic Community's emphasis on self-sufficiency in the 1980s. Reinhart and Wickham (1994) give an exhaustive list of factors affecting world commodity prices with emphasis on policy issues, such as stabilization funds, agricultural boards, international commodity agreements, external compensatory finance, and others. Furthermore, over a longer term, technological advances and population growth also affect agricultural prices.

Pindyck and Rotemberg (1990) offer numerous statistical tests which confirm that prices of several commodities such as wheat, cotton, copper, gold, crude oil, lumber and cocoa, have a persistent tendency to move together. They maintain that a possible explanation for such excess comovement "is that commodity price movements are to some extent the result of herd behavior." By herd behavior, they mean that traders are alternatively bullish or bearish across all commodity markets with no justification provided by economic fundamentals.

Finally, agricultural commodities are linked via the trading strategy called spreading. When traders find soybeans cheap, they buy soybeans and they sell soybean oil and soybean meal; or they buy corn and sell soybeans, often in various ratios. Their actions are motivated by perceived mispricings between the products. Spreading, as an arbitrage activity, acts as a mechanism that restores proper relationships.

## DATA DESCRIPTION

This study uses daily settlement prices for the nearby contract for the six agricultural futures contracts traded at the Chicago Board of Trade (CBOT): corn, wheat, oats, soybean, soybean meal, and soybean oil. The time period is from January 2, 1981, to October 24, 1991, for a total of 2734 observations. The data are provided by the CBOT. A few daily prices are missing. Missing daily observations are replaced by the average of the previous and subsequent prices.

## METHODOLOGY

The error correction model (ECM) of Engle and Granger (1987) is used. Since the ECM is based on the concept of Granger causality and the notion of cointegration, these two tests are described first.

### Granger Causality Tests

Granger causality tests are tests of the prediction ability of time series models. Specifically, $Y$ is said to cause or lead $X$ provided some coefficient, $a_i$, is not zero in the following equation:

$$X_t = c_0 + \sum_{i=1}^{m} a_i Y_{t-i} + \sum_{j=1}^{m} b_j X_{t-j} + \varepsilon_t \qquad (1)$$

Similarly, $X$ is causing or leading $Y$ if some coefficient, $a_i$, is not zero in eq. (2) below:

$$Y_t = \gamma_0 + \sum_{i=1}^{m} a_i X_{t-i} + \sum_{j=1}^{m} \beta_j Y_{t-j} + \mu_t \tag{2}$$

If both of these events occur, there is feedback.[1] Regressions (1) and (2) can be used to test for the existence of a short-term relationship between the variables $X$ and $Y$. The test for causality is based on an $F$-statistic that is computed by running the regressions in both the unconstrained form (full model) and the constrained form (reduced model). The reduced model is obtained from eqs. (1) and (2) by dropping the lagged values of the independent variables. The $F$-statistic is given by

$$F_1 = \frac{(SSE_r - SSE_f)/m}{SSE_f/(T - 2m - 1)} \tag{3}$$

where $SSE_r$ and $SSE_f$ are the sum of squares of residuals of the reduced and full models, respectively; $m$ is the number of lags; and $T$ is the number of observations.

## Tests of Stationarity and Cointegration

If variables, $X_t$ and $Y_t$, are both non-stationary in levels, but the first differences of the variables are stationary, then variables, $X_t$ and $Y_t$ are integrated of order one, denoted by $I(1)$. The ECM requires the variables to be $I(1)$. The stationarity of the time series is investigated with the Augmented Dickey–Fuller (1979) (ADF) test:

$$\ln X_t - \ln X_{t-1} = b_0 + b_1 \ln X_{t-1}$$
$$+ \sum_{i=1}^{m} c_i (\ln X_{t-i} - \ln X_{t-i-1}) + \varepsilon_t \tag{4}$$

where $X$ represents the level or the first difference of the variable. The null hypothesis of non-stationarity is $b_1 = 0$.

When two variables are $I(1)$, their linear combinations, $Z_t = X_t - aY_t$, is generally $I(1)$. However, if there is an $a$ such that $Z_t$ is integrated of order zero, $I(0)$, the linear combination of $X_t$ and $Y_t$ is stationary, and it is said that the two variables are cointegrated. Cointegration is a property of two non-stationary time series and the relationship, $Z_t = X_t - aY_t$, represents a long-run equilibrium relationship. Thus, the cointegra-

---

[1]The several testable forms of Granger's causality are described in Pierce and Haugh (1977), Guilkey and Salemi (1982), and Geweke, Meese, and Dent (1983).

tion factor, $Z_t$, can be used to measure long-term linkages between variables, $X_t$ and $Y_t$.

Engle and Granger suggest the following method for estimating the value of $a$. First run the regression:

$$X_t = a + aY_t + \varepsilon_t \tag{5}$$

Then, the estimate of $a$ obtained from (5) is plugged into eq. (6):

$$\hat{Z}_t = X_t - (\hat{a} + \hat{a}Y_t), \tag{6}$$

where $\hat{Z}_t$ represents an estimate of the cointegration factor.

### Error Correction Model

By integrating the concept of causality in the Granger sense with the notion of cointegration, it is possible to develop a model which tests for the presence of both short-term and long-term relationships between the variables, $X_t$ and $Y_t$. This model is the ECM, proposed by Engle and Granger. In (7), the ECM model investigates the potential long-run and short-run impact of the variable, $Y_t$, on the variable, $X_t$:

$$X_t - X_{t-1} = a_0 + a_1\hat{Z}_{t-1} + \sum_{i=1}^{m} c_i(Y_{t-i} - Y_{t-i-1})$$

$$+ \sum_{j=1}^{m} d_j(X_{t-j} + X_{t-j-1}) + \varepsilon_t. \tag{7}$$

The ECM represented by eq. (7) decomposes the dynamic adjustments of the dependent variable, $X_t$, to changes in the independent variable, $Y_t$, into two components: first, a long-run component given by the cointegration term, $a_1\hat{Z}_{t-1}$, also known as the error-correction term; and, second, a short-term component given by the first summation term in the right-hand side of eq. (7). In other words, a long-run relationship refers to one established by (7) during the entire sample of January 2, 1981, to October 24, 1991. On the other hand, a short-term relationship is shown in (7) by the lagged values of the dependent and independent variables. Three lags are used in this study.

Similarly, the long-run and short-run impact of $X_t$ on $Y_t$ can be captured by the following ECM:

$$Y_t - Y_{t-1} = \beta_0 + \beta_1 \hat{Z}_{t-1} + \sum_{i=1}^{m} \phi_i(X_{t-i} - X_{t-i-1})$$

$$+ \sum_{j=1}^{m} \theta_j(Y_{t-j} + Y_{t-j-1}) + \varepsilon_t. \tag{8}$$

From eqs. (7) and (8) one may deduce that the variables, $X_t$ and $Y_t$, exhibit long-run movements when at least one of the coefficients, $a_1$ or $\beta_1$, is different from zero. If $a_1$ is statistically different from zero, but $\beta_1$ is not; then, the implication is that $X_t$ follows and adjusts to $Y_t$ in the long run. The opposite occurs when $\beta_1$ is statistically different from zero but $a_1$ is not. If both coefficients, $a_1$ and $\beta_1$, are statistically different from zero, a feedback relationship exists, implying that variables, $X_t$ and $Y_t$, adjust to one another over the long run.

The coefficients, $c_i$'s and $\phi_i$'s, in eqs. (7) and (8), respectively, represent the short-term relationships between the variables, $X_t$ and $Y_t$. If the $c_i$'s are not all zero in a statistical sense but all $\phi_i$'s are; then, $Y_t$ is leading or causing $X_t$ in the short run. The reverse case occurs when the $\phi_i$'s are not all zero in a statistical sense, but all $c_i$'s are. If both events occur, then there is a feedback relationship and the variables, $X_t$ and $Y_t$, affect each other in the short run.

The empirical results of this study's investigation of short-term and long-term relationships between the six agricultural futures contracts are discussed next.

## RESULTS OF THE TESTS OF STATIONARITY

The results of the ADF tests of stationarity for the level and first difference of the natural logarithm of the agricultural futures prices are presented in Tables I and II, respectively. For the price level, the null hypothesis of non-stationarity cannot be rejected for all contracts at the 5% of confidence level. However, the null of non-stationarity is rejected for all contracts for the price first difference. Thus, the prices of the six agricultural futures contracts under analysis are integrated of order one, $I(1)$.

## RESULTS OF THE TESTS OF COINTEGRATION

Since the several tests of cointegration suggested by Engle and Granger differ in terms of power and sensitivity, three different tests are conducted: the Durbin Watson, the Dickey and Fuller (DF), and the ADF.

**TABLE I**

Augmented Dickey–Fuller Tests
Agricultural Futures Price Levels

| Commodity | $b_0$ | $b_1$ | $b_2$ | $b_3$ | $b_4$ | $R^2$ |
|---|---|---|---|---|---|---|
| Corn | 0.032 | −0.003 | 0.057 | 0.024 | 0.007 | 0.006 |
| | $(2.391)^a$ | $(-2.402)$ | $(2.954)^a$ | $(-1.230)$ | $(0.365)$ | $(3.876)^a$ |
| Wheat | 0.061 | −0.006 | −0.018 | −0.052 | 0.001 | 0.007 |
| | $(3.066)^a$ | $(2.400)$ | $(-0.947)$ | $(-2.718)^a$ | $(0.070)$ | $(4.629)^a$ |
| Oats | 0.039 | −0.004 | 0.056 | −0.027 | 0.030 | 0.007 |
| | $(2.470)^a$ | $(-2.483)$ | $(2.932)^a$ | $(-1.384)$ | $(1.569)$ | $(4.441)^a$ |
| Soybean | 0.048 | −0.004 | 0.006 | −0.035 | 0.009 | 0.004 |
| | $(2.507)^a$ | $(-2.515)$ | $(0.296)$ | $(-1.816)$ | $(0.485)$ | $(2.548)^a$ |
| Soybean meal | 0.040 | −0.004 | 0.016 | −0.033 | 0.006 | 0.004 |
| | $(2.469)^a$ | $(-2.475)$ | $(0.842)$ | $(-1.715)$ | $(0.302)$ | $(2.489)^a$ |
| Soybean oil | 0.024 | −0.003 | 0.073 | −0.054 | 0.009 | 0.009 |
| | $(2.095)^a$ | $(-2.105)$ | $(3.823)^a$ | $(-2.813)^a$ | $(0.451)$ | $(6.353)^a$ |

Notes: The model is:

$$\ln P_t - \ln P_{t-1} = b_0 + b_1 \ln P_{t-1} + b_2 (\ln P_{t-1} - \ln P_{t-2}) + b_3 (\ln P_{t-2} - \ln P_{t-3}) + b_4 (\ln P_{t-3} - \ln P_{t-4}) + \varepsilon_t$$

The null hypothesis is $b_1 = 0$ (price levels are non-stationary) and is not rejected. The critical $t$-statistic for the $b_1$ coefficient at the 5% level is −2.86 [from Dickey-Fuller (1979), Table 8.5.2].
[a]Indicates the individual regression coefficient is statistically significantly different from zero at the 5% level.

The results presented in Table III indicate that cointegration is rejected by the Durbin Watson test but it is strongly confirmed by the more powerful tests of DF and ADF. Therefore, it is concluded that the time series of agricultural commodity futures prices are cointegrated and the use of the error correction model is appropriate in testing for short-term and long-term relationships between agricultural commodities.

## ECM RESULTS

The results of the ECM are reported in Table IV. The main rows contain the regression coefficients, $a_1$'s and $c_i$'s, given by eq. (7), or the regression coefficients, $\beta_1$'s and $\phi_i$'s, given by eq. (8). The corresponding $t$-statistics are given in parenthesis in the second rows. The last three columns to the right of Table IV contain the $F$-statistics which test for long-term, short-term, and long-term or short-term relationships, respectively. There is unidirectional long-term causality from corn to: wheat, oats, soybean, soybean meal, and soybean oil; from wheat to oats, soybean and soybean meal; from soybean to wheat and soybean meal; from soybean oil to

**TABLE II**

Augmented Dickey–Fuller Tests
First Difference of Agricultural Futures Prices

| Commodity | $b_0$ | $b_1$ | $b_2$ | $b_3$ | $b_4$ | $R^2$ |
|---|---|---|---|---|---|---|
| Corn | −0.013 | −0.982 | −0.037 | 0.012 | 0.019 | 0.474 |
| | (−0.474) | (−26.428)[a] | (1.158) | (0.462) | (0.994) | (611.526)[b] |
| Wheat | −0.013 | −1.089 | 0.069 | 0.014 | 0.013 | 0.511 |
| | (−0.424) | (−27.268)[a] | (2.003)[b] | (6.505)[b] | (0.671) | (711.704)[b] |
| Oats | −0.019 | −0.974 | 0.029 | −0.001 | 0.029 | 0.475 |
| | (−0.493) | (−26.279)[a] | (0.898) | (−0.007) | (1.538) | (614.976)[b] |
| Soybean | −0.015 | −1.013 | 0.016 | −0.020 | −0.013 | 0.499 |
| | (−0.535) | (−26.056)[a] | (0.479) | (−0.736) | (−0.660) | (678.137)[b] |
| Soybean meal | −0.010 | −1.036 | 0.050 | 0.015 | 0.020 | 0.494 |
| | (−0.340) | (−26.889)[a] | (1.511) | (0.575) | (1.036) | (664.829)[b] |
| Soybean oil | −0.09 | −0.953 | 0.025 | −0.029 | −0.023 | 0.468 |
| | (−0.298) | (−25.584)[a] | (0.783) | (−1.104) | (−1.218) | (598.205)[b] |

Notes: The model is:

$$R_t - R_{t-1} = b_0 + b_1 R_{t-1} + b_2 (R_{t-1} - R_{t-2}) + b_3 (R_{t-2} - R_{t-3}) + b_4 (R_{t-3} - R_{t-4}) + \varepsilon_t$$

where

$$R_t = 100 \ln (P_t/P_{t-1})$$

The null hypothesis is $b_1 = 0$ (Price first differences are non-stationary). The critical $t$-statistic for the $b_1$ coefficient at the 5% level is −2.88 [from Dickey–Fuller (1979), Table 8.5.2].
[a] Indicates rejection of the null hypothesis of non-stationarity.
[b] Indicates the individual regression coefficient is statistically significantly different from zero at the 5% level.

wheat, oats, soybean and soybean meal; and from oats to soybean meal. There is feedback in the long-term relationship between wheat and oats, wheat and soybean, and soybean and oats. The long-term linkages are strong and present in almost every pair of contracts. On the other hand, little short-term causality is detected. Finally, the hypothesis of neither long-term nor short-term unidirectional causality is rejected in 20 of the 30 cases.

In general, the results of the ECM reported in Table IV confirm the long-term interdependence of agricultural commodity futures. The economic rationale for this long-term interdependence can be found in the several theoretical reasons described in the introduction. That is, the substitutability and complementarity of the agricultural commodities, geographical and climatological factors, global demand shocks due to government policies both at home and abroad, and the excess comovement hypothesis.

**TABLE III**

Tests of Cointegration

| Dependent Variable | Independent Variable | Durbin Watson Test (1) | Dickey Fuller Test (2) | Augmented Dickey Fuller Test (3) |
|---|---|---|---|---|
| Wheat | Corn | 0.014369 | −52.26189[a] | −30.12145[a] |
| Corn | Wheat | 0.009165 | −52.21620[a] | −29.91296[a] |
| Oats | Corn | 0.007707 | −52.20759[a] | −29.28114[a] |
| Corn | Oats | 0.005001 | −52.22821[a] | −29.95998[a] |
| Soybean | Corn | 0.001845 | −52.23562[a] | −29.93037[a] |
| Corn | Soybean | 0.008373 | −52.24120[a] | −29.95983[a] |
| Soybean meal | Corn | 0.008724 | −52.17515[a] | −29.58511[a] |
| Corn | Soybean meal | 0.006034 | −52.10741[a] | −29.49466[a] |
| Soybean oil | Corn | 0.010841 | −52.22683[a] | −29.96488[a] |
| Corn | Soybean oil | 0.009368 | −52.22040[a] | −29.93878[a] |
| Oats | Wheat | 0.015934 | −52.15556[a] | −29.22252[a] |
| Wheat | Oats | 0.018432 | −52.22925[a] | −30.12490[a] |
| Soybean | Wheat | 0.013952 | −52.19921[a] | −29.91429[a] |
| Wheat | Soybean | 0.015684 | −52.22321[a] | −30.05781[a] |
| Soybean meal | Wheat | 0.013595 | −52.17447[a] | −30.02778[a] |
| Wheat | Soybean meal | 0.016112 | −52.17388[a] | −29.97973[a] |
| Soybean oil | Wheat | 0.006891 | −52.118435[a] | −29.98776[a] |
| Wheat | Soybean oil | 0.010623 | −52.21108[a] | −30.06295[a] |
| Soybean | Oats | 0.013572 | −52.21487[a] | −29.90226[a] |
| Oats | Soybean | 0.012806 | −52.16034[a] | −29.20106[a] |
| Soybean meal | Oats | 0.014519 | −52.17772[a] | −30.15126[a] |
| Oats | Soybean meal | 0.014530 | −52.16615[a] | −29.21062[a] |
| Soybean oil | Oats | 0.006183 | −52.22409[a] | −29.98051[a] |
| Oats | Soybean oil | 0.007417 | −52.15125[a] | −29.26256[a] |
| Soybean meal | Soybean | 0.026209 | −52.61152[a] | −30.90135[a] |
| Soybean | Soybean meal | 0.26995 | −52.21353[a] | −30.38700[a] |
| Soybean oil | Soybean | 0.006119 | −52.19815[a] | −29.95631[a] |
| Soybean | Soybean oil | 0.008118 | −52.19837[a] | −29.94611[a] |

Among the various statistically significant relationships presented in Table IV, it is worth noticing that the highest significant statistics in the last column of the table involve corn as the independent variable. This leading role of corn can be explained by noting that the average annual corn crop during the period, 1981–1991 was the highest among the other crops; 7.3 billion bushels of corn was produced versus 1.9 billion bushels of soybeans, and even lower quantities of wheat and oats. During the period, 1981–1991, corn exports amounted to 1.8 billion bushels, followed by soybean exports that totaled 716 million bushels. The leading

**TABLE III (Continued)**

Tests of Cointegration

| Dependent Variable | Independent Variable | Durbin Watson Test (1) | Dickey Fuller Test (2) | Augmented Dickey Fuller Test (3) |
|---|---|---|---|---|
| Soybean oil | Soybean meal | 0.006216 | −52.22677[a] | −30.07316[a] |
| Soybean meal | Soybean oil | 0.007432 | −52.16634[a] | −30.13913[a] |

Notes: (1) The cointegration equation is:

$$\ln Y_t = a + b \ln X_t + \varepsilon_t$$

The null hypothesis is: $H_0: b = 0$ (No cointegration).
The Durbin Watson critical value for rejection of the null hypothesis of no cointegration, at the 5% level, is 0.386 (Engle and Granger 1987).
(2) The model is the following:

$$\ln Y_t = c_0 + \sum_{i=1}^{3} a_i \ln Y_{t-i} + \sum_{j=1}^{3} b_j \ln X_{t-j} + \mu_t$$

$$\mu_t - \mu_{t-1} = a + \phi\mu_{t-1} + \varepsilon_t$$

The null hypothesis is: $H_0: \phi = 0$ (No cointegration).
The critical value for rejection of the null hypothesis of no cointegration, at the 5% level, is −3.37. (Engle and Granger, 1987).
(3) The model is the following:

$$\ln Y_t = c_0 + \sum_{i=1}^{3} a_i \ln Y_{t-i} + \sum_{j=1}^{3} b_j \ln X_{t-j} + \mu_t$$

$$\mu_t - \mu_{t-1} = a + \phi_1\mu_{t-1} + \phi_2(\mu_{t-1} - \mu_{t-2}) + \phi_3(\mu_{t-2} - \mu_{t-3}) + \varepsilon_t$$

The null hypothesis is: $H_0: \phi_1 = 0$ (No cointegration).
The critical value for rejection of the null hypothesis of no cointegration, at the 5% level, is −3.17. [Engle and Granger (1987)]
[a]Indicates rejection of the null hypothesis.

role of corn is also evidenced by the decision of the Chicago Board of Trade to introduce new products tied to corn contracts, such as the Iowa Corn Crop Yield Insurance futures and option contracts.

## SUMMARY AND CONCLUSIONS

This study investigates long-term and short-term relationships among the six agricultural futures contracts traded at the CBOT: corn, wheat, oats, soybean, soybean meal, and soybean oil. The data correspond to daily settlement prices for the nearby contract. The time period under analysis extends from January 2, 1981, to October 24, 1991, and involves 2734 observations for each contract.

Tests of stationarity find that prices are non-stationary in levels but stationary in the first differences. That is, prices are integrated of order

**TABLE IV**

Error Correction Model (ECM) for Testing for Long-Term (LT) and Short-Term (ST) Relationship for Prices of Agricultural Futures Contracts

| Dependent Variable | Independent Variable | $a_1, \beta_1$ | $c_1, \phi_1$ | $c_2, \phi_2$ | $c_3, \phi_3$ | No LT Impact | No ST Impact | No LT or ST Impact |
|---|---|---|---|---|---|---|---|---|
| Wheat | Corn | 0.0092 (3.632)[c] | −0.0130 (−0.579) | −0.0191 (−0.854) | −0.0518 (−2.319)[c] | 13.220[a] | 2.224 | 5.005[a] |
| Corn | Wheat | 0.0001 (0.051) | 0.356 (1.763) | −0.0013 (−0.065) | 0.0273 (1.371) | 0.005 | 1.603 | 1.206 |
| Oats | Corn | 0.0049 (2.684)[c] | −0.0873 (−3.094)[c] | 0.0048 (0.171) | 0.0361 (1.278) | 7.219[a] | 3.796[a] | 4.648[a] |
| Corn | Oats | 0.0006 (0.387) | 0.0395 (2.575)[c] | −0.0107 (−0.698) | −0.0007 (−0.048) | 0.147 | 2.324 | 1.766 |
| Soybean | Corn | 0.0091 (3.461)[c] | 0.0037 (0.160) | 0.0310 (1.327) | 0.0246 (1.057) | 12.006[a] | 1.013 | 3.726[a] |
| Corn | Soybean | −0.0010 (−0.488) | 0.0251 (1.011) | −0.0417 (−1.681) | −0.0098 (−0.393) | 0.239 | 1.359 | 1.067 |
| Soybean meal | Corn | 0.0049 (2.677)[c] | 0.0013 (0.054) | 0.0033 (0.134) | 0.0082 (0.337) | 7.179[a] | 0.046 | 3.846[a] |
| Corn | Soybean meal | −0.0001 (−0.048) | 0.0038 (0.179) | −0.0567 (−2.650)[c] | −0.0120 (−0.561) | 0.001 | 2.469 | 1.854 |
| Soybean oil | Corn | 0.0047 (2.127)[c] | −0.0104 (−0.431) | 0.0200 (0.828) | 0.0373 (1.541) | 4.534[b] | 1.120 | 3.915[a] |
| Corn | Soybean oil | 0.0023 (1.196) | 0.0420 (2.160)[c] | −0.0284 (−1.456) | 0.018 (0.094) | 1.433 | 2.162 | 1.963 |
| Oats | Wheat | 0.0067 (2.945)[c] | −0.0129 (−0.498) | −0.0333 (−1.290) | 0.0353 (1.366) | 8.693[a] | 1.307 | 3.192[b] |
| Wheat | Oats | 0.0059 (2.213)[c] | 0.0182 (1.153) | 0.0173 (1.095) | 0.0103 (0.649) | 4.909[b] | 1.037 | 3.231[b] |
| Soybean | Wheat | 0.0063 (2.733)[c] | 0.0169 (0.893) | 0.0010 (0.053) | 0.0343 (1.810) | 7.487[a] | 1.315 | 2.750[b] |
| Wheat | Soybean | 0.0054 (2.124)[c] | −0.0236 (−1.038) | −0.0222 (−0.980) | 0.0049 (0.214) | 4.521[b] | 0.702 | 3.266[b] |
| Soybean meal | Wheat | 0.0062 (3.073)[c] | 0.0228 (1.122) | −0.0090 (−0.443) | 0.0300 (1.474) | 9.468[a] | 1.185 | 3.239[b] |
| Wheat | Soybean meal | 0.0033 (1.400) | −0.0152 (−0.754) | −0.0255 (−1.260) | 0.0081 (0.402) | 1.967 | 0.782 | 1.158 |
| Soybean oil | Wheat | 0.0025 (1.516) | −0.0199 (−0.943) | −0.0128 (−0.608) | 0.0373 (1.766) | 2.302 | 1.511 | 1.709 |
| Wheat | Soybean oil | 0.0051 (2.453)[c] | −0.0102 (−0.531) | −0.0374 (−1.948) | 0.0068 (0.357) | 6.027[b] | 1.443 | 2.608[b] |
| Soybean | Oats | 0.0053 (2.183)[c] | 0.0207 (1.350) | 0.0099 (0.645) | 0.0222 (1.451) | 4.777[b] | 1.525 | 2.683[b] |
| Oats | Soybean | 0.0047 (2.032)[c] | −0.1110 (−3.720)[c] | −0.0305 (−1.020) | 0.0459 (1.534) | 4.136[b] | 5.929[a] | 5.647[a] |
| Soybean meal | Oats | 0.0054 (2.584)[c] | 0.0181 (1.105) | 0.0084 (0.511) | 0.00040 (0.245) | 6.692[a] | 0.548 | 2.634[b] |
| Oats | Soybean meal | 0.0031 (1.464) | −0.0898 (−3.400)[c] | −0.0216 (−0.818) | 0.0465 (1.756) | 2.150 | 5.283[a] | 4.612[a] |
| Soybean oil | Oats | 0.0022 (1.391) | −0.0052 (−0.308) | 0.01200 (0.705) | 0.0281 (1.663) | 1.937 | 1.173 | 1.314 |

**TABLE IV (Continued)**

Error Correction Model (ECM) for Testing for Long-Term (LT) and Short-Term
(ST) Relationship for Prices of Agricultural Futures Contracts

| Dependent Variable | Independent Variable | $a_1, \beta_1$ | $c_1, \phi_1$ | $c_2, \phi_2$ | $c_3, \phi_3$ | $H_0$: No Relationship No LT Impact | No ST Impact | No LT or ST Impact |
|---|---|---|---|---|---|---|---|---|
| Oats | Soybean oil | 0.0042 (2.322)$^c$ | −0.0398 (−1.589) | −0.0644 (−2.860)$^c$ | 0.0188 (0.750) | 5.401$^b$ | 3.142$^b$ | 3.904$^a$ |
| Soybean meal | Soybean | 0.0071 (2.369)$^c$ | 0.0203 (0.560) | −0.0376 (−1.034) | −0.0411 (−1.134) | 5.624$^b$ | 0.879 | 2.716$^b$ |
| Soybean | Soybean meal | 0.0018 (0.581) | 0.0710 (2.364)$^c$ | 0.0240 (0.798) | 0.0452 (1.502) | 0.337 | 2.658$^b$ | 2.623$^b$ |
| Soybean oil | Soybean | 0.0012 (0.574) | −0.0185 (−0.602) | −0.0020 (−0.065) | 0.0572 (1.858) | 0.330 | 1.301 | 1.048 |
| Soybean | Soybean oil | 0.0058 (2.402)$^c$ | 0.0459 (1.969)$^c$ | −0.0097 (−0.415) | 0.0030 (0.128) | 5.781$^b$ | 1.330 | 2.422$^b$ |
| Soybean oil | Soybean meal | 0.0022 (1.404) | −0.0398 (−1.756) | −0.0014 (0.059) | 0.0409 (1.808) | 1.977 | 2.184 | 2.136 |
| Soybean meal | Soybean oil | 0.0039 (2.286)$^c$ | −0.0524 (−2.528)$^c$ | 0.0173 (−0.830) | 0.0008 (0.040) | 5.240$^b$ | 2.561 | 3.177$^b$ |

Notes: The data are natural logarithms of daily closing prices for six nearby agricultural futures contracts: corn, wheat, oats, soybean, soybean meal, and soybean oil. The data cover the time period from January 2, 1981, to October 24, 1991. The variable $Z_t$, which tests for long-term relationship, is estimated using a procedure suggested by Engle and Granger (1987). When $X_t$ is the dependent variable in the ECM, the regression used is $X_t = a_0 + \hat{a}_1 Y_t + \varepsilon_t$. $\hat{Z}_t$ is computed from $\hat{Z}_t = X_t − \hat{a}_1 Y_t$. The roles of $X_t$ and $Y_t$ are reversed when $Y_t$ is the dependent variable in the ECM. The following ECMs used are

$$\ln X_t − \ln X_{t-1} = a_0 + a_1 \hat{Z}_{t-1} + \sum_{i=1}^{m} c_i (\ln Y_{t-i} − \ln Y_{t-i-1}) + \sum_{j=1}^{m} d_j (\ln X_{t-j} − \ln X_{t-j-1}) + \varepsilon_t$$

and

$$\ln Y_t − \ln Y_{t-1} = \beta_0 + \beta_1 \hat{Z}_{t-1} + \sum_{i=1}^{m} \Phi_i (\ln X_{t-i} − \ln X_{t-i-1}) + \sum_{j=1}^{m} \Theta_j (\ln Y_{t-j} + \ln Y_{t-j-1}) + \varepsilon_t$$

These two models test if the independent variable, $Y(X)$, has long-term (LT), short-term (ST), and long-term or short-term (LT or ST) impact on the dependent variable, $X(Y)$. The null hypotheses of no-impact are tested with $F$-statistics. $^{a,b}$Indicates rejection of the null hypothesis of no-LT, no-ST or no LT or no ST impact at the 1%, or 5% level, respectively. $^c$Indicates the individual regression coefficient is statistically significantly different from zero at the 5% level or better.

one, $I(1)$. The time series of prices are also cointegrated. The empirical results of the ECM show strong, statistically significant, long-term relationships between the six commodity futures contracts but no short-term causality. These results reject the working hypothesis that the prices of the six agricultural products move independently. Such rejection is consistent with economic thought on substitutability and complementarity between agricultural commodities. It is believed, also, that rejection of the working hypothesis is due to the effects of specific factors, such as climate and geography, global demand shocks due to government farm policies at home and abroad, and the excess comovement hypothesis of Pindyck and Rotemberg (1990).

The very essence of futures markets is the opportunity they offer for price discovery. The results of this study suggest that the price discovery function of a commodity futures contract signals valuable information that is relevant to other related commodity futures contracts. For example, the results indicate that corn prices have a long-run impact on wheat, soybeans, and soybean meal. This means that the price discovery process generated in corn futures markets offers valuable information not only to corn cash markets but also to the spot markets of wheat, soybean, and soybean meal. This information incorporates several possible factors such as substitutability, complementarity, weather and climatological factors, world agricultural demand and supply shocks, even herd trends. No analyst could evaluate the impact of all these factors in the absence of a futures market. The price discovery mechanism of a well-functioning futures market allows the quantification of such information and its use across economically linked markets.

The findings have further implications in terms of cross hedging and cross speculation and offer justification for the introduction of the new crop yield futures and option contracts. In other words, if significant linkages are known to exist between two agricultural products, cross hedging opportunities become possible. For example, if corn and soybeans are economically linked for the various reasons explained above, a soybean position could be hedged in the much more liquid corn futures market. Similarly, linkages between agricultural markets could offer cross speculation opportunities.

## BIBLIOGRAPHY

Anderson, R. W. (1985): "Some Determinants of the Volatility of Futures Prices," *The Journal of Futures Markets,* 11:331–348.

Anderson, R. W., and Danthine, J. (1983): "The Time Pattern of Hedging and the Volatility of Futures Prices," *Review of Economic Studies,* 50:249–266.

Dickey, D. A., and W. A. Fuller (1979): "Distribution of the Estimators for Autoregressive Time Series with a Unit Root," *Journal of the American Statistical Association,* 74, pp: 427–431.

Engle, R. F., and C. W. J. Granger (1987): "Cointegration and Error Correction: Representation, Estimation, and Testing," *Econometrica,* 55, pp:251–276.

Geweke, J., R. Meese, and W. Dent (1983): "Comparing Alternative Tests of Causality in Temporal Systems," *Journal of Econometrics,* 21, pp:161–194.

Guilkey, D. K., and M. K. Salemi (1982): "Small Sample Properties of Three Tests for Granger Causal Ordering in a Bivariate Stochastic System", *The Review of Economics and Statistics,* 64, pp:668–680.

Pierce, D. A., and L. D. Haugh (1977): "Causality in Temporal Systems: Characterizations and a Survey," *Journal of Econometrics*, 5, pp:265–293.

Pindyck, R. and J. Rotemberg (1990): "The Excess Comovement of Commodity Prices," *Economic Journal*, 100, pp:1173–1189.

Reinhart, C. and P. Wickham (1994): "Commodity Prices: Cyclical Weakness or Secular Decline?" *IMF Staff Papers*, 41, pp.:175–213.

Stevens, S.C. (1991): "Evidence for a Weather Persistence Effect on the Corn, Wheat, and Soybean Growing Season Price Dynamics", *The Journal of Futures Markets*, 11, pp:81–88.

Teigen, L. D., and F. Singer (1989): "Weather in U.S. Agriculture: Monthly Temperature and Precipitation by State and Farm Production Region, 1950–88," USDA, ERS, SB789, November.

Westcott, P. C. (1989): "An Analysis of Factors Influencing Corn Yield," *Feed Outlook and Situation Report*, USDA, ERS, FdS-310, May:27–31.

# [10]

# SEARCHING FOR FRACTAL STRUCTURE IN AGRICULTURAL FUTURES MARKETS

**MARCO CORAZZA**
**A. G. MALLIARIS**
**CARLA NARDELLI**

The four parameters of the Pareto stable probability distribution for six agricultural futures are estimated. The behavior of these estimates for different time-scaled distributions is consistent with the conjecture that the stochastic processes generating these agricultural futures returns are characterized by a fractal structure. In particular, it is empirically verified that the six futures returns satisfy the property of statistical self-similarity. Moreover, the same time series is analyzed by using the so-called rescaled range analysis. This analysis is able to detect both the fractal structure and the presence of long-term dependence within the observations. The Hurst exponent with the use of two methods, the classical and modified rescaled analysis, is estimated and tested. Finally, with the use of Mandelbrot's result on the existence of a link between the characteristic ex-

We are grateful to two anonymous referees for extensive comments and to Professor Giovanni Zambruno, Department of Mathematics and Statistics, University of Milan (Italy), for his useful suggestions. We are also thankful to the editor, Dr. Mark Powers, for his support and encouragement.

- *Marco Corazza is a researcher in the Department of Applied Mathematics and Computer Science at Ca' Foscari University of Venice.*
- *A. G. Malliaris is a Professor of Economics in the Department of Economics at Loyola University of Chicago.*
- *Carla Nardelli is a Researcher in the Department of Applied Mathematics and Computer Science at Ca' Foscari University of Venice.*

The Journal of Futures Markets, Vol. 17, No. 4, 433–473 (1997)
CCC 0270-7314/97/040433-41

ponent of a stable distribution and the Hurst exponent, further empirical confirmation is found that the processes generating agricultural futures returns are fractal.

## INTRODUCTION

Despite the early contributions of Working (1934) about the random behavior of futures prices, financial economists have studied systematically the behavior of asset pricing only during the past three decades. Asset pricing is assumed to mean the dynamic, period-by-period, change in the price level of an asset, such as the closing price of a given stock or the settlement price of a certain futures contract. The exhaustive literature on the random walk behavior of asset prices is known as market efficiency. Despite the existence of several puzzling and conflicting results, in general, and in futures markets in particular, the theory of efficient markets remains a central pillar of modern financial economics.

Samuelson (1965) developed the efficient market hypothesis to rationalize the random walk behavior, whereby the current price, $P(t)$, fully reflects all relevant information. Because the flow of such information between now and the next period cannot be anticipated, efficient market price changes are serially uncorrelated. In other words, the randomness in price changes originates in the random flow of unanticipated information.

During the past 20 years, the theory of market efficiency has been refined analytically, mathematically and statistically; the concept of information has been made more precise; and the notion of random walk has been generalized to martingales and Itô processes. Numerous sophisticated statistical tests were employed to test the theory. Moreover, a very large literature has been developed concerning the statistical distribution of the changes in spot or futures prices: Are they log-normal, or are they leptokurtic and if leptokurtic, how fat are the tails?

The actual distribution of spot or futures price changes or returns is an issue of great importance to financial economists. In an efficient market it follows that such returns are random. Furthermore, these random returns are postulated to be normally distributed. The theoretical foundations underlying these studies are not always clear. Grossman and Stiglitz (1980) addressed several important analytical issues of the theory of efficient markets. They argued that the notion of market efficiency is inconsistent with the reality of costly arbitrage. They developed a simple model with a constant absolute risk-aversion utility function and showed that costless information is both necessary and sufficient for prices to fully reflect all available information. Efficient markets theorists realize that costless information is a sufficient condition for market efficiency. However, they are not always clear that it is also a necessary condition. The cost of acquiring and acting on new information means that prices in a competitive market need not follow a random walk. Tomek (1994) explained well how persistence in price behavior can occur in rational markets.

It is not surprising to find that along with numerous studies confirming market efficiency, there are numerous studies rejecting it, and that there is no agreement concerning the statistical distribution functions of price changes. Nevertheless, the most convenient and widely acceptable paradigm postulates that returns are normally distributed, which means that asset prices follow log-normal distributions. Both modern portfolio theory and the Black–Scholes methodology of pricing derivative assets are founded on such a paradigm.

Although market efficiency remains the central theory of financial economics, numerous studies question its twin foundations: random walk and log-normal distribution of asset prices. Notice, however, that it is not enough to reject randomness or log-normality. To make scientific progress, alternatives to randomness and log-normality must be specified.

The purpose of this paper is to investigate these twin issues of randomness and log-normality by empirically examining the behavior of six agricultural futures prices.

It is shown that returns are neither log-normally distributed nor statistically independent.

The classical approach of time-series analysis concerning financial markets [initiated by Bachelier (1900)] investigates the distribution of security price increments. Most models are based on the hypothesis of a normal distribution for the variation of such prices; that is,

$$P(t + dt) - P(t) \sim N(\mu \, dt, \sigma^2 \, dt) \tag{1}$$

As a result of the empirical work of Osborne (1959), such normal distributions were replaced by the notion that asset prices are independent and log-normally distributed as

$$\log[P(t + dt)] - \log[P(t)] = \log[P(t + dt)/P(t)] \sim N(\mu \, dt, \sigma^2 \, dt) \tag{2}$$

This idea had an important impact on financial theory. The Black–Scholes option pricing model is one of its most celebrated results. However, as the following review describes, several studies showed that (2) does not hold empirically, primarily because of reasons such as fatter tails, the instability in the variance level (accounting for the relatively many outliers), and issues of asymmetry. The Pareto–Lévy stable distribution family is proposed as a way of correcting for these realities.

## HYPOTHESIS

This study's hypothesis rejects the null hypothesis that the distribution of agricultural futures prices is log-normal, as was postulated by Helms and Martell (1985). Then the four parameters of the characteristic function of the stable random variable are estimated with the use of U.S. agricultural futures data. The behavior of the values of the estimates for different time-scaled distributions leads to the formulation of the hypothesis: The stochastic-process underlying futures returns are characterized by a fractal structure, as proposed by Peters (1989, 1991a, 1991b and 1994) and Walter (1990).

This hypothesis is analyzed also with the use of the so-called rescaled range analysis proposed by Hurst (1951) to detect both a possible fractal structure and long-run dependence in the observations. In particular, the memory effect emphasizes the existence of a nonzero temporal linear or nonlinear correlation among the observations, contradicting the usual hypothesis of their independence by the efficient market hypothesis. The fractality and the dependence within the observations is measured with the use of the Hurst exponent.

The Hurst exponent is estimated by two methods: the classical R/S analysis and the modified R/S one, proposed by Lo (1991), which adjusts the classical rescaled range statistic mainly for short-term dependence. Then, the goodness fit of the estimate of the Hurst exponent is checked with the use of an asymptotic test proposed also by Lo (1991). Finally, with the use of the Mandelbrot and Taqqu (1979) result on the existence of a link between the characteristic exponent of the Pareto–Lévy stable distribution and the Hurst exponent, it is confirmed that the processes generating the six agricultural futures returns are fractal.

## REVIEW OF THE LITERATURE

A brief review of the literature on randomness and log-normality follows. Only a few key references are discussed, because these ideas are generally well known.

The two fundamental reviews are Fama (1970) and (1991), and the book by Guimaraes, Kingsman, and Taylor (1989). These apply to asset prices in general, rather than to futures prices, in particular. Studies that deal with the appropriateness of the random walk or the martingale model in futures markets include: the investigation of the treasury bill and treasury bond futures markets by Chance (1985), Klemkosky and Lasser (1985), Cole, Impson, and Reichenstein (1991), and MacDonald and Hein (1993); the investigation of the agricultural commodities by Bigman, Goldfarb, and Schechtman (1983), Canarella and Pollard (1985), Maberly (1985), Bird (1985), Elam and Dixon (1988); the investigation of the metal futures market by Gross (1988); and the investigation of the foreign currency markets by Glassman (1987), Saunders and Mahajan (1988), Harpaz, Krull, and Yagil (1990).

Many of these studies hold positive opinions on market efficiency. Chance (1985) believes that the treasury bond futures market correctly anticipates the information contained in the announcement of the rate of change of the Consumer Price Index. MacDonald and Hein (1993) comment that the T-bill futures market may not be as inefficient as once presumed in terms of weak form efficiency, though it does not provide optimal forecasts. Maberly (1985) demonstrates that, in the grains, the inference that the market is inefficient for more distant futures contracts is due to the bias that results from using ordinary least squares to estimate parameters. Elam and Dixon (1988) attack the inefficiency grain market argument by conducting several Monte Carlo experiments to find out that very often the $F$ test tends to wrongly reject the true model. The research of Canarella and Pollard (1985) suggests that the efficient market hypothesis cannot be rejected for corn, wheat, soybeans, and soybean oil. Gross (1988) claims that the hypothesis of efficient copper and aluminum markets cannot be rejected on the evidence of his semistrong efficiency tests. Saunders and Mahajan (1988) show that the index futures pricing is efficient.

However, numerous authors offer negative evidence on market efficiency. Bird (1985) discovers that for coffee and sugar the efficient market hypothesis is invalid, and for cocoa there is some evidence of inefficiency, but of limited economic significance. Harpaz et al. (1990) perform tests for efficiency of the USDX futures contracts during the period, 1985–1988, which result in their rejection of the null hypothesis that the USDX futures market is efficient during that period.

Finally, quite a few authors, instead of totally supporting or rejecting the efficient market hypothesis, offer different answers under different situations. Bigman et al. (1983) believe that the market can be generally characterized as efficient for the futures contracts on wheat, soybeans, and corn six weeks before delivery or less. For longer-term futures contracts, their tests reject the efficiency hypothesis. The results of the T-bond market efficiency tests of Klemkosky and Lasser (1985) do not agree totally with the conclusions drawn from earlier studies. Glassman (1987) reports evidence of multimarket and joint multimarket inefficiency in foreign currency futures markets during some of the 38 contract periods studied. Much of the inefficiency appeared to be short term in duration (one week or less). Cole et al. (1991) conclude that the T-bill futures rates provide rational one- and two-quarters-ahead forecasts of futures spot rates, which are the forecast horizons that seem to be of most interest to the public. However, they believe the rationality of four-quarters-ahead futures forecasts should be rejected.

The various empirical studies that have rejected the theory of market efficiency have encouraged financial economists to seek alternative explanations for the time-series behavior of asset returns. This literature is known as the *chaotic dynamics* approach to asset returns, and several studies, such as Decoster, Labys, and Mitchell (1992) offer evidence that futures prices appear to follow low dimensional chaotic dynamics.

Observe that the majority of research concentrates on stock returns. After the seminal articles by Osborne (1959), Fama (1965), Mandelbrot (1963), Fama and Roll (1968 and 1971), and Mandelbrot and Taylor (1967), numerous other articles have followed. These are carefully reviewed in Akgiray and Booth (1988). Although most articles reject the normal distribution in favor of the stable Lévy–Paretian, studies exist that reject the stable Lévy–Paretian distribution, but not in favor of normality.

Earlier, Stevenson and Bear (1970) and Dusak (1973) offered evidence in support of the stable Lévy–Paretian distribution. More recently, Helms and Martell (1985), using data for all commodities traded on the Chicago Board of Trade, conclude that returns on futures prices, although they are not normally distributed, are closer to normal than to any other member of the family of Pareto distributions. Contrary to their results, Cornew, Town, and Crowson (1984) claim that the stable Lévy–Paretian distribution offers a better fit for futures returns of several contracts than the normal distribution. So (1987) confirms that currency futures and spot returns are stable Lévy–Paretian, whereas Hall, Brorsen, and Irwin (1989) and Hudson, Leuthold, and Sarassoro (1987) claim that futures returns are not stable Lévy–Paretian. Finally, Gribbin, Harris, and Lau (1992) use a newly developed statistical methodology to conclude that futures prices are not stable Lévy–Paretian distributed. Their methodology, however, is not powerful enough to distinguish a stable distribution from other distributions. Simulation results show that the method will almost always reject any stable distribution.

## DATA

The data used in this study correspond to returns of daily settlement prices for the time period, January 2, 1981 to October 24, 1991, for the following six agricultural futures contracts: corn, oats, soybeans, soybean meal, soybean oil, and wheat. These contracts are traded at the Chicago Board of Trade.

## FRACTAL PARETO–LÉVY STABLE DISTRIBUTIONS: THEORETICAL ASPECTS

Lévy (1925) introduced the stable distributions as a generalization of the Brownian motion. Recall that a Brownian motion is simply a continuous-time random walk. Falconer (1990) gives the following definition regarding the stable process.

**Definition 5.1.** A random process $X(t)$, with $t \in [0, +\infty)$, is stable if the increments $X(t + \Delta t) - X(t)$ are stationary; that is, they depend only on $\Delta t$, and independent; that is, for all $0 < t_1 < t_2 < \cdots < t_{2m}$, the increments $X(t_2) - X(t_1), \ldots, X(t_{2m}) - X(t_{2m-1})$ are independent.

This class of distributions allows a generalization of the central limit theorem under weaker hypotheses. In particular, the stable distribution represents a generalization of the normal one when the moment of order 2 or the moments of order 1 and 2 do not exist.

Generally speaking, it is not possible to give a closed form for the density functions of the stable class. This family can be characterized by its characteristic function:

$$\phi(t) = \exp\{i\,\delta t - |\gamma t|^\alpha [1 + j\beta\,sgn(t)\omega(t,\alpha)]\} \tag{3}$$

where

$$j = \begin{cases} -i, & \text{if } \alpha \neq 1 \\ +i, & \text{if } \alpha = 1 \end{cases}$$

$$\omega(t,\alpha) = \begin{cases} \tan(\alpha\pi/2), & \text{if } \alpha \neq 1 \\ (2/\pi)\log(t), & \text{if } \alpha = 1 \end{cases}$$

Note that (3) is characterized by four parameters $\alpha$, $\beta$, $\gamma$, and $\delta$. In particular:

1. $\alpha \in (0,2]$ is the characteristic exponent that accounts for the relative importance of the tails. If $\alpha = 2$, then (3) corresponds to the normal distribution with finite mean and variance. When $\alpha \in (1,2]$, the random variable has only finite mean.

2. $\beta \in [-1,1]$ is a skewness parameter. In particular, when $\beta = 0$, the distribution is symmetric.

3. $\gamma \in (0, +\infty)$ is a scale parameter. In particular, some authors use $c = \gamma^\alpha$ (when $\alpha = 2$, the distribution has variance $2c$),

4. $\delta \in (-\infty, +\infty)$ is a location parameter. When $\alpha \in (1,2]$, $\delta$ is the mean of the distribution and when $\beta = 0$, $\delta$ is the median of the distribution.

The density probability function of the stable distribution can be written in the following integral form:

$$f(x) = \frac{1}{\pi} \int_0^{+\infty} \cos[-xt + \delta t - (\gamma t)^\alpha \beta \omega(t, \alpha)] \exp[-(\gamma t)^\alpha] \, dt. \quad (4)$$

Using *Definition 5.1* of the stable distribution, Falconer (1990) and Peters (1991b) cite an important theorem that gives a property of this distribution, namely, that the stable distribution is fractal. Falconer (1990) offers a detailed mathematical definition of fractal and then summarizes it intuitively as follows. A set, $F$, is fractal if it satisfies four conditions:

1. $F$ has a fine structure. This means the set is very detailed on arbitrary small scales.

2. $F$ is too irregular both locally and globally.

3. $F$ has some form of self-similarity; that is, parts of $F$ resemble the whole $F$ in some way.

4. The fractal dimension of $F$, defined in some way, is greater than its topological dimension.

5. $F$ is often described recursively.

The interest in fractal objects is motivated by the central question of financial economics; that is, what is the behavior of asset prices? To show that asset prices follow fractal processes is to show more than random walk. Fractal processes generalize random walks because, in addition to their irregularity they are also self-similar, and the dimension of the set can be computed. In other words, fractal processes have a fine structure that often cannot be detected by various low-power tests of random walk. Furthermore, because fractal processes are quite complex and cannot be detected easily, they are consistent with the paradigm of market efficiency.

To characterize the fractal nature of a Pareto–Lévy stable distribution, Falconer (1990) and Peters (1991b) give the following theorem.

***Theorem 5.1.*** Let $X(t)$, with $t \in [0, +\infty)$, be a Pareto–Lévy stable stochastic process with characteristic exponent, $\alpha$, and let $S_{X(t)} = \{X(t_i),$ $t_i \in [0, +\infty), i \in \{1, \ldots, T\}\}$ be its time series. Then, with probability 1, the $\dim(S_{X(t)})$, is equal to $\alpha$.

Moreover, to point out another property of the stochastic fractal objects; that is, the self-similarity, Mandelbrot and Taqqu (1979), Feder (1988), and Falconer (1990) give the following definition.

***Definition 5.2.*** Let $X(t)$, with $t \in [0, +\infty)$, be a continuous stochastic process. This process is called self-similar if, for fixed $t$, it has the same distribution as $\lambda^{-K}X(\lambda t)$, with $K \in (-\infty, +\infty)$ and $\lambda \in (0, +\infty)$.

Notice that the characteristic functions of these two random variables must depend on the same parameters. Therefore, the random variable, $X(t)$, is affected neither by an expansion of the time scale ($\lambda t$) nor by the contemporaneous homothety of the space scale, ($\lambda^{-K}$). In particular, if the random variable is Pareto–Lévy stable, Mandelbrot and Taqqu (1979) prove that $K = 1/\alpha$.

## FRACTAL PARETO–LÉVY STABLE DISTRIBUTIONS: EMPIRICAL RESULTS

To obtain the values of the four parameters and to verify the statistical self-similarity property, the time series of the daily settlement prices of the six agricultural futures contracts are used to compute scaled returns

$$X_{t,n} = \lambda^{-1/\alpha} \log[P(t + n)/P(t)] \tag{5}$$

where $n = \lambda t$ is a time scale, with $t = 1$ and $\lambda > 0$. $P(t)$ is the settlement price at time $t$. Notice that, if $n = 1$, then $X_{t,n}$ is the usual logarithmic return of daily settlement prices.

Possible dependence in the data must be eliminated. Of course, the true autocorrelative relationship characterizing each time series is not known, so it is approximated by an autoregressive model of order $q$ (AR($q$)). From this the corresponding uncorrelated residuals time series is obtained by fitting an ordinary least-squares (OLS) regression. In this OLS regression a crucial role is played by $q$, and the Andrews (1991) data-dependent rule, $q = \text{Int}\{(3T/2)^{1/3}[\mu/(1 - \mu^2)]^{2/3}\}$, where $T$ is the time series size and $\mu$ is its sample first-order autocorrelation coefficient, is used to detect it. Notice that this data-dependent rule is mainly able to detect the short-term autocorrelative length and so, by using it, a second source of approximation is introduced. The results obtained by using the Andrews' rule are the following: $q = 3$ for corn, $q = 3$ for oats, $q =$

**TABLE I**

Tests for Log-Normality Using a $\chi^2(g)$ test; $g$ Denotes Degrees of Freedom

| Futures | $\chi_0^2(13)$ | $\chi_q^2(13)$ | $\chi_0^2(27)$ | $\chi_q^2(27)$ |
|---|---|---|---|---|
| Corn | 450.337 | 425.461 | 477.513 | 455.028 |
| Oats | 249.722 | 231.980 | 286.482 | 262.884 |
| Soybeans | 248.087 | 248.087 | 276.800 | 276.800 |
| Soybean meal | 310.154 | 305.477 | 336.552 | 325.947 |
| Soybean oil | 158.493 | 143.318 | 173.902 | 165.264 |
| Wheat | 352.703 | 352.218 | 368.403 | 369.448 |

**TABLE II**

Estimates of the Four Parameters of the Stable Distribution
Assuming Independence

| Futures | $\alpha_{1.0}$ | $R_\alpha^2$ | $\bar{R}_\alpha^2$ | $\beta_{1.0}$ | $R_\beta^2$ | $\bar{R}_\beta^2$ | $c_{1.0}$ | $\delta_{1.0}$ |
|---|---|---|---|---|---|---|---|---|
| Corn | 1.64 | 1.00 | 1.00 | 0.05 | 0.91 | 0.90 | 0.01 | 0.00 |
| Oats | 1.77 | 1.00 | 1.00 | -0.02 | 0.99 | 0.99 | 0.01 | 0.00 |
| Soybeans | 1.74 | 1.00 | 1.00 | -0.17 | 1.00 | 1.00 | 0.01 | 0.00 |
| Soybean meal | 1.73 | 1.00 | 1.00 | 0.15 | 0.96 | 0.96 | 0.01 | 0.00 |
| Soybean oil | 1.81 | 1.00 | 1.00 | 0.17 | 0.97 | 0.96 | 0.01 | 0.00 |
| Wheat | 1.77 | 1.00 | 1.00 | 0.18 | 0.92 | 0.92 | 0.01 | 0.00 |

**TABLE III**

Estimates of the Four Parameters Assuming Dependence

| Futures | $\alpha_{1,q}$ | $R_\alpha^2$ | $\bar{R}_\alpha^2$ | $\beta_{1,q}$ | $R_\beta^2$ | $\bar{R}_\beta^2$ | $c_{1,q}$ | $\delta_{1,q}$ |
|---|---|---|---|---|---|---|---|---|
| Corn | 1.64 | 1.00 | 1.00 | 0.05 | 0.95 | 0.94 | 0.01 | 0.00 |
| Oats | 1.77 | 1.00 | 1.00 | 0.01 | 0.98 | 0.98 | 0.01 | 0.00 |
| Soybean | 1.74 | 1.00 | 1.00 | -0.17 | 1.00 | 1.00 | 0.01 | 0.00 |
| Soybean meal | 1.73 | 1.00 | 1.00 | 0.15 | 0.97 | 0.97 | 0.01 | 0.00 |
| Soybean oil | 1.82 | 1.00 | 1.00 | 0.16 | 0.98 | 0.98 | 0.01 | 0.00 |
| Wheat | 1.77 | 1.00 | 1.00 | 0.18 | 0.93 | 0.92 | 0.01 | 0.00 |

0 for soybeans, $q = 1$ for soybean meal, $q = 4$ for soybean oil, and $q = 1$ for wheat.

Next the null hypothesis that the distribution of daily price changes of the agricultural futures contracts is log-normal is rejected. Specifically, this study tests for log-normality using an $\chi_q^2$ $(g)$ distributed fit test, where $g$ are the degrees of freedom, assuming both independence $(q = 0)$ and dependence as previously described. The results of this test are presented in Table I.

In Tables II and III the estimates, $\alpha_{n,q}$, $\beta_{n,q}$, $c_{n,q}$ and $\delta_{n,q}$, are reported with the time scale, $n = 1$, assuming both independence and dependence as previously described. To estimate these parameters, the method developed by Koutrouvelis (1980, 1981) is used, where the starting values of the parameters are determined by the MacCulloch method (1986) instead of by the simple Fama and Roll one (1971). The algorithm for the estimation of these parameters using the Koutrouvelis' methodology is found in Canestrelli, Cipriani, and Corazza (1993). In particular, the MacCulloch method eliminates some restrictions arising from the (strong) *a priori* hypotheses assumed by the Fama and Roll method, that is, the symmetry of the probability distribution ($\beta = 0$) and the existence of a mean ($\alpha \in (1,2]$).

To detect the statistical self-similarity, following the *Definition 5.2*, it is empirically verified if the four estimated parameters are affected by an expansion of the time scale on the contemporaneous homothety of the space scale. In particular, the time scale from 1 day ($n = 1$) to about 1 month ($n = 25$) is considered. Notice that, for every fixed time scale, $n$, it is possible to extract $n$ different sequences from the original time series. To get better estimates, the value of each parameter is determined by calculating the mean of the different sequences. The results of this analysis are reported in Figures 1–6.

From Tables I–III and Figures 1–6 one can deduce the following.

First, the analyzed time series are significantly nonnormal because of the (wide) rejection of the null hypothesis that the sample distribution of daily (i.e., $n = 1$) price changes is normal (see Table I). In particular, the results of the test are qualitatively the same assuming both independence ($q = 0$) and dependence; therefore, one can conjecture that the influence of the simple autocorrelative structure assumed earlier is negligible. Moreover, the estimated characteristic exponent for different time-scaled distributions (i.e., from $n = 1$ to $n = 25$) are, in general, less than 2 and, so, nonnormal.

Second, the values of the statistics, $R^2$ and $\bar{R}^2$, associated with both the characteristic exponents and the skewness parameters of every analyzed time series, are elevated ($R_\alpha^2 = 1.00$, $\bar{R}_\alpha^2 = 1.00$, $R_\beta^2 \in [0.91, 1.00]$ and $\bar{R}_\beta^2 \in [0.90, 1.00]$). Notice that, because the characteristic exponent is greater than 1, the location parameter gives the sample mean of the distribution and, in particular, it is close to 0 for all the analyzed time series. Notice also that, because the characteristic exponent is less than 2, the probability distribution does not have finite variance, so, one can-

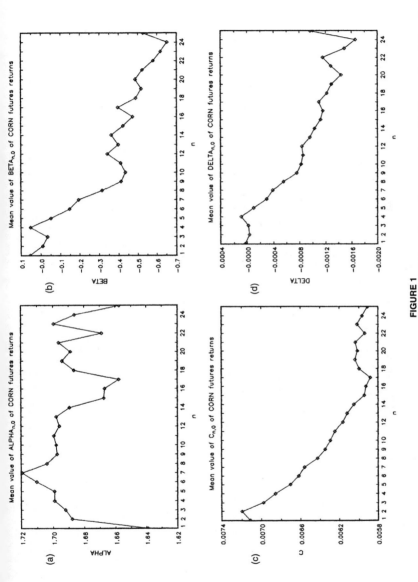

**FIGURE 1**

(a) Mean value of $ALPHA_{n,0}$ of corn futures returns. (b) Mean value of $BETA_{n,0}$ of corn futures returns. (c) Mean value of $C_{n,0}$ of corn futures returns. (d) Mean value of $DELTA_{n,0}$ of corn futures returns.

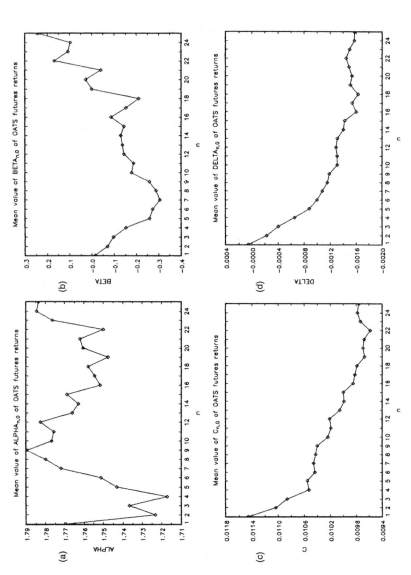

**FIGURE 2**

(a) Mean value of $ALPHA_{n,0}$ of oats futures returns. (b) Mean value of $BETA_{n,0}$ of oats futures returns. (c) Mean value of $C_{n,0}$ of oats futures returns. (d) Mean value of $DELTA_{n,0}$ of oats futures returns.

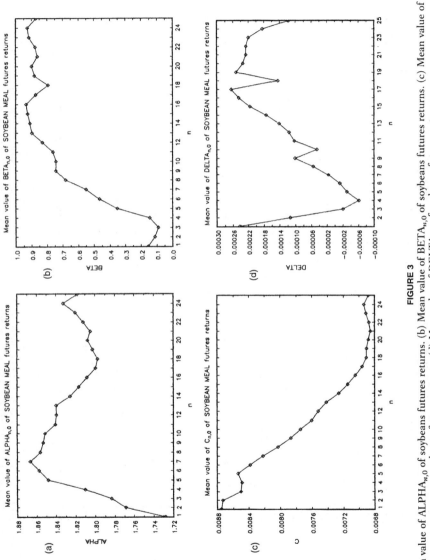

**FIGURE 3**

(a) Mean value of ALPHA$_{n,0}$ of soybeans futures returns. (b) Mean value of BETA$_{n,0}$ of soybeans futures returns. (c) Mean value of $C_{n,0}$ of soybeans futures returns. (d) Mean value of DELTA$_{n,0}$ of soybeans futures returns.

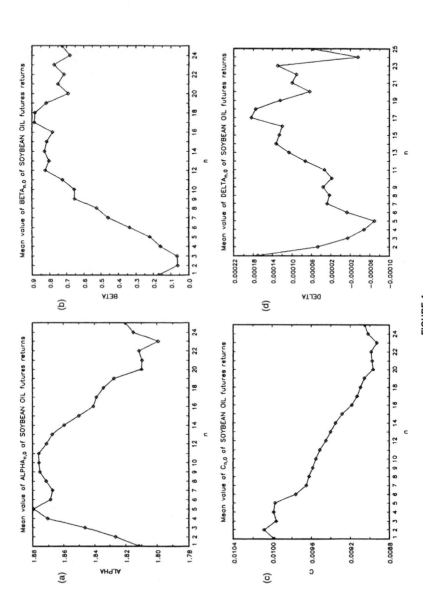

**FIGURE 4**

(a) Mean value of $ALPHA_{n,0}$ of soybean meal futures returns. (b) Mean value of $BETA_{n,0}$ of soybean meal futures returns. (c) Mean value of $C_{n,0}$ of soybean meal futures returns. (d) Mean value of $DELTA_{n,0}$ of soybean meal futures returns.

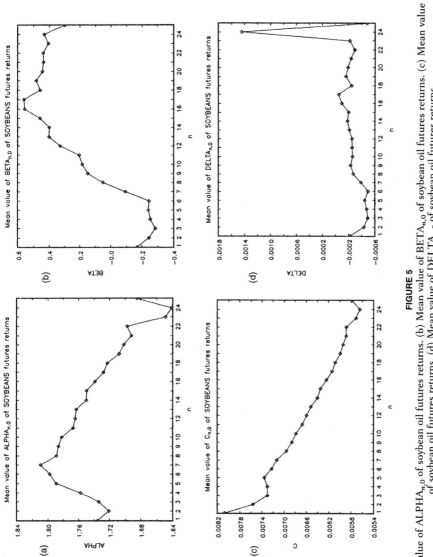

**FIGURE 5**

(a) Mean value of $ALPHA_{n,0}$ of soybean oil futures returns. (b) Mean value of $BETA_{n,0}$ of soybean oil futures returns. (c) Mean value of $C_{n,0}$ of soybean oil futures returns. (d) Mean value of $DELTA_{n,0}$ of soybean oil futures returns.

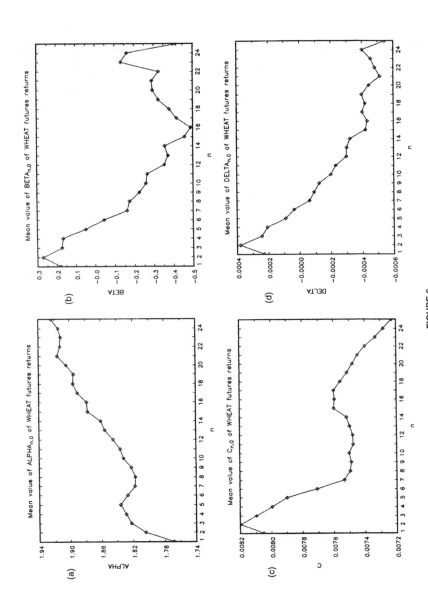

**FIGURE 6**

(a) Mean value of $ALPHA_{n,0}$ of wheat futures returns. (b) Mean value of $BETA_{n,0}$ of wheat futures returns. (c) Mean value of $C_{n,0}$ of wheat futures returns. (d) Mean value of $DELTA_{n,0}$ of wheat futures returns.

not use the volatility as a proper index of risk. Nevertheless, because the probability distribution has finite mean, it is always possible to define an index of variability based on the first-order moment, like, for instance, the mean absolute error (i.e., $[\Sigma_{i=1}^{T}|x_i - \delta|]/T$).

Third, the estimates of the four parameters are quite similar assuming both independence ($q = 0$) and dependence (see Tables II and III), so one can conjecture also the negligibility of the sample autocorrelative structure assumed in section 6.

Because of $\alpha_{1,q} \in [1.64, 1.82]$ (see Tables II and III), following *Theorem 5.1*, it is confirmed empirically that the dimensions of all time series analyzed are not integer. It is a first confirmation of the fractal nature of the process generating the returns.

Following *Definition 5.2* and the expression (6), one can deduce empirically the property of the invariability by time-scale change, or statistical self-similarity, for corn, oats, soybeans, soybean meal, and soybean oil (see Figures 1–5) because their estimated characteristic exponents are between 1.64 and 1.81, as $n$ goes from 1 to 25. This variability range is similar to the one ($\alpha_{n,0} \in [1.6, 1.8]$) found by Walter (1990), by which he accepted the statistical self-similarity property for the French stock market. On the other hand, only the variability range concerning wheat (see Figure 6) is wider than the others. Notice that the characteristic exponents of the different time series analyzed do not show the same behavior when $n$ increases from 1 to 25. In particular, for soybeans it shows a decreasing behavior, for corn, oats, soybean meal, and soybean oil they show an oscillating one, and for wheat they show an increasing one, taking values progressively closer to 2 as $n$ increases. Furthermore, the presence of invariability by time scale change for all time series analyzed is confirmed empirically by the steadiness of their scale and location parameters behavior. Only in the skewness parameter behavior are significant differences found among the analyzed time series, probably due to the estimation method [for more details see Walter (1990)]. Indeed, such behaviors are characterized by a variability range equaling 40% of its domain. In particular, for corn and wheat the skewness parameter shows a decreasing behavior and for oats, soybeans, soybean meal, and soybean oil it shows an increasing one.

From an economics point of view, the empirical results verify the invariability by time-scale change property. This means that the analyzed agricultural futures markets are characterized by (self-) similar liquidity, risk, and trading levels. It implies the contemporaneous presence of investors with different time horizons (probably due to different evaluations of the same new information arriving to the market). Moreover, it makes the matching between supply and demand easier, and, consequently, makes the market able to avoid panics and/or stampedes when the supply and demand become imbalanced. Peters (1994) calls this property, the fractal market hypothesis.

## HURST EXPONENT *H*: THEORETICAL ASPECTS

Hurst (1951) discovered that a large class of natural phenomena show a behavior over time that can be described through a particular biased stochastic process. Such a process was called fractional Brownian motion (FBM) by Mandelbrot and van Ness (1968). This process implies the presence of some long-term dependence in its realizations. Falconer (1990) defines the FBM as follows.

*Definition 7.1.* A real stochastic process $X(t)$, with $t \in [0, +\infty)$, is a fractional Brownian motion with index $H \in (0,1)$, called the Hurst exponent, if

(a) $X(0) = 0$ with probability one,

(b) $X(t)$ is continuous almost everywhere for all $t \in [0, +\infty)$,

(c) The increments $X(t + \Delta t) - X(t)$ are normally distributed with mean zero and variance $\Delta t^{2H}$ for all $t \in [0, +\infty)$ and $\Delta t \in [0, +\infty)$.

This means that, if $H \neq 0.5$, the increments of the FBM are stationary but dependent random variables. In particular, it is not the short-term (Markovian-like) memory, but the long-term memory that is influenced the most by the latest increments.

Notice that for FBM the Hurst exponent, $H$, provides double information on the underlying stochastic process. Indeed, remembering *Definition 5.2*, it is possible to prove that $H$ is also equal to the statistical self-similarity parameter, $K$. This result is found in Mandelbrot and Taqqu (1979). Notice, also, that the Hurst exponent, $H$, qualifies the nature of the long-term memory. In particular, for $H \in (0, 0.5)$ there is a negative dependence between the increments; that is, if the graph of $X(t)$ increases/decreases for $t_0 \geq 0$, then it probably decreases/increases for some $t > t_0$. In this case the process has an antipersistent behavior and the time series of the realizations is qualified as ergodic or mean reverting. For $H \in (0.5, 1)$ there is a positive dependence between the increments; that is, if the graph of $X(t)$ increases/decreases for $t_0 \geq 0$, then it probably continues to increase/decrease for some $t > t_0$. In this case the process has a persistent or trend-reinforcing behavior.

The case, $H = 0.5$, is the standard Brownian motion (sBm) with independent increments. Moreover, the Hurst exponent, $H$, also gives a kind of measure of the long-term memory intensity; that is, the period and the strength of the antipersistent/persistent behavior increases as $H$ approaches to 0/1. In particular, for a FBM, it is possible to quantify the link between the Hurst exponent, $H$, and the long-term dependence by the following autocorrelation function:

$$C(H) = 2^{2H-1} - 1$$

$$\begin{cases} <0 & \text{if } H \in (0,0.5), \quad C(H) \to -0.5 \text{ as } H \to 0 \\ =0 & \text{if } H = 0.5 \\ >0 & \text{if } H \in (0.5,1), \quad C(H) \to 1 \text{ as } H \to 1 \end{cases} \tag{7}$$

To determine the value of the Hurst exponent, $H$, Hurst used the R/S analysis, based on the range of partial sums of deviations of a time series from its mean, rescaled by its standard deviation. From a qualitative point of view it gives a standardized measure of the path length covered over a given time interval by the stochastic process. It is a statistical method used to study a wide range of phenomena. Mandelbrot and Wallis (1969) show that the R/S analysis is robust to highly nonnormal distribution of the process generating the considered time series. Moreover, it is possible to prove its almost-sure convergence for stochastic process with infinite variance [for more details see Mandelbrot and Taqqu (1979)]. In particular, it is possible to prove the following link between the R/S statistic and the Hurst exponent, $H$. [For more details see Cutland, Kopp, and Willinger (1993) and Peters (1994).]

$$\lim_{T \to +\infty} E[R_T/S_T]/(aT^H) = 1 \tag{8}$$

where

$R_T$ is the range of the partial sums of deviations of the time series from its sample mean

$S_T$ is the sample standard deviation of the original time series

$a \in (0, +\infty)$ is a constant.

From this link, it is possible to obtain the approximate relationship

$$\ln\{E[R_T/S_T]\} \simeq \ln(a) + H\ln(T). \tag{9}$$

In particular, some techniques proposed by Greene and Fielitz (1977), Mandelbrot and Taqqu (1979), Feder (1988), and Peters (1991b) are improved upon and coordinated. The algorithm used can be summarized as follows:

*Step 1.* Consider the original time series, $Y = \{y_i, i = 1, \ldots, T\}$.

*Step 2.* Fix subtime series of length, $N = N_0 \leq T$.

*Step 3.* Determine all possible nonoverlapping subtime series, $Y_{1,N} = \{y_1, \ldots, y_N\}$, $Y_{2,N} = \{y_{N+1}, \ldots, y_{2N}\}$, $\ldots$, $Y_{i,N} = \{y_{(i-1)N+1}, \ldots, y_{iN}\}$, $\ldots$, $Y_{i,Z} = \{y_{(i-1)Z+1}, \ldots, y_{iZ}\}$, where Z is the integer part of the ratio, $T/N$.

*Step 4.* For every subtime series, $Y_{i,N}$, $i = 1, \ldots, Z$, calculate the sample mean, $m_{i,N}$, determine subtime series, $X_{i,N}$, of the cumulative sums of deviations

$$X_{i,N} = \{x_{(i-1)N+t} = \sum_{j=1}^{t} (y_{(i-1)N+j} - m_{i,N}), t = 1, \ldots, N\} \quad (10)$$

compute the sample variation range, $R_{i,N}$,

$$R_{i,N} = \max_{1 \leq t \leq N} X_{i,N} - \min_{1 \leq t \leq N} X_{i,N} \quad (11)$$

and calculate its standard deviation, $S_{i,N}$, and ratio, $R_{i,N}/S_{i,N}$.

*Step 5.* Calculate the mean value, $R_N/S_N$, from $R_{i,N}/S_{i,N}$.

*Step 6.* Set new subtime series length, N by $N_{Ser} = N + S$ $(S > 0)$ and $N = N_{Ser}$.

*Step 7.* If $N \leq T$, then go to *Step 3*; otherwise, go to *Step 8*.

*Step 8.* Fit OLS regression between $\{\log(R_1/S_1), \ldots, \log(R_j/S_j)\}$ and $\{\log(1), \ldots, \log(j)\}$ for every $j = 2, \ldots, Z$.

*Step 9.* Determine the unique value of the Hurst exponent, H, among the Z-2 estimates making joined use of the graphic approach proposed in Peters (1989 and 1991b) and of the statistical one proposed in Lo (1991).

Notice that, if the time series possesses a natural cycle of length M [called *mean orbital period* (MOP)], R/S analysis identifies it. In particular, it is possible to show that the Hurst exponent, H, tends to 0.5 as T becomes greater than M and tends to $+\infty$; it indicates that, for such a large time lag, the stochastic process is losing its long-term memory.

Finally, to point out another property of the stochastic fractal objects, Greene and Fielitz (1977) report that the (fractal) dimension of a process probability distribution is $1/H$, with $H \in [0.5,1)$. Notice that, if $H = 0.5$ (i.e., sBm) the corresponding dimension is 2. Moreover, it is possible to prove the existence of the following relationship between the statistical self-similarity of a FBM ($K = H$) and one of a Pareto–Lévy stable process; that is, $K = 1/\alpha$ [for more details see Mandelbrot and Taqqu (1979)]:

$$H = 1/\alpha, \qquad H \in (0, 0.5) \tag{12}$$

It means that, although the two considered stochastic processes are quite different, their behaviors, from a fractal point of view, are the same.

Lo (1991) proposes a modification of the classical $R/S$ analysis mainly because of its sensitivity to short-term dependence. Indeed, it is possible to prove that, because of such a sensitivity, the long-term memory results from the classical $R/S$ method can merely be due to short-term memory. In particular, the modified statistic is robust to both short-term dependence and highly nonnormal innovations and its behavior is invariant over a general class of short-term memory processes but deviates for long-term memory processes. Moreover, unlike the classical $R/S$ statistics, it has well-defined distribution properties.

Lo modified the classical statistic $R/S$ by using $R/\tilde{S}$, with

$$\tilde{S}^2 = S^2 + 2\sum_{i=1}^{q} w_i(q)\gamma_i, \qquad q < T \tag{13}$$

where

$w_i(q) = 1 - i/(q + 1), i = 1, \ldots, q$ are weights depending on the short-term memory length $q$

$$\gamma_i = \sum_{j=i+1}^{T} (Y_j - m_N)(Y_{j-1} - m_N)$$

$i = 1, \ldots, q$ are autocorrelation estimators.

Observe that the $R/\tilde{S}$ statistic differs from the $R/S$ one only in its modified standard deviation, which is the square root of a correct and consistent estimator of the sample variance. In fact, if the analyzed time series is characterized by short-term dependence, the modified variance also includes the autocovariances weighted up to lag $q$. In particular, to detect $q$ the Andrews data-dependent rule is used and to determine the weights, the Newey and West proposal (1987) is used, always yielding a nonnegative $\tilde{S}^2$. Moreover, Lo (1991) determines the distribution properties of the modified statistic and identifies some link between it and the classical one. In particular, he proves the following asymptotic relationship for the modified statistics

$$Q_T(q) = \frac{1}{\sqrt{T}} R/S \sim V \qquad (14)$$

where

the tilde denotes weak convergence
V is a random variable with the following probability distribution

$$F_v(v) = 1 + 2 \sum_{K=1}^{+\infty} (1 - 4k^2v^2)\exp(-2k^2v^2). \qquad (15)$$

Lo (1991) also proves the asymptotic relationship for the classical statistics

$$Q_T(0) = \frac{1}{\sqrt{T}} R/S \sim \xi V, \qquad (16)$$

where $\xi$ is a function depending on the short-time memory structure

Finally, by using the fractiles of the distribution of $Q_T(q)$ [also calculated by Lo (1991)], it is possible to determine the values for different levels of significance to test the null hypothesis of no long-term dependence.[1]

## HURST EXPONENT *H* IN THE FUTURES RETURNS

To determine the values of the Hurst exponent, $H$, the time series of the futures returns are used. Tables IV and V report the values of $H_{n,q}$ obtained with the use of the algorithm summarized in the previous section, with the time scale, $n = 1, 5$, and 25, assuming both independence; that is, $q = 0$ (classical Hurst exponent) and dependence (modified Hurst exponent). Notice that, for time scale $n = 5$ and 25, $q = 0$ (independence) is used because it is found that $0 \leq q \leq 4$ for all analyzed time series. Notice also that, because the stability of the results depends on the nonoverlapping subtime series, N (see *Steps 2, 6,* and 7), and because detection of the MOP requires that the Hurst exponent tends to 0.5, in general, a time series of sufficient size is necessary.

Second, the same tables report the results obtained from testing the null hypothesis of no long-term dependence by the statistic, $Q_T(q)$, $q = 0$ and $q \neq 0$ [see relationship (14)].

---

[1]Notice that a rejection of such a null hypothesis does not necessarily imply that long-range memory is present, but merely that the underlying stochastic process does not satisfy simultaneously all the conditions stated by Lo (1991).

**TABLE IV**

Estimates of $H_{n,q}$ for $n = 1$, $q = 0$, and $q \neq 0$ with Estimates of Corresponding
Mean Orbital Periods

| Futures | $H_{1,0}$ | | MOP | $H_{1,q}$ | | MOP |
|---|---|---|---|---|---|---|
| Corn | 0.60 | Lo | 1000 | 0.57 | Lo | 950 |
| Corn | 0.61 | – | 1250 | 0.59 | – | 1300 |
| Oats | 0.55 | Me | 1450 | 0.53 | Me | 1450 |
| Oats | 0.57 | – | 1350 | 0.55 | – | 1350 |
| Soybeans | ?? | ?? | ?? | ?? | ?? | ?? |
| Soybeans | 0.62 | – | 1350 | 0.62 | – | 1350 |
| S. Meal | ?? | ?? | ?? | ?? | ?? | ?? |
| S. Meal | 0.59 | – | 1200 | 0.59 | – | 1200 |
| S. Oil | 0.65 | Me | 1100 | 0.62 | Me | 1100 |
| S. Oil | 0.65 | – | 1150 | 0.62 | – | 1200 |
| Wheat | 0.43 | Hi | 1800 | 0.43 | Hi | 1800 |
| Wheat | 0.42 | – | 1950 | 0.42 | – | 1950 |

*Note:* The first row for each commodity contract reports estimates of the classical or modified Hurst exponent from eq. (19) for which the null hypothesis of no long-term dependence is rejected. Hi denotes rejection at the 95% or 99% confidence level, Me denotes rejection at the 90%, and Lo rejection at the 80% confidence level. If the null hypothesis of no long-term dependence is not rejected, the row is filled with question marks. The second row reports the descriptive results from the rescaled range analysis obtained from the graphical approach for which no hypothesis testing can be performed.

**TABLE V**

Estimates of $H_{n,q}$ for $n = 5$, $25$ and $q = 0$, with Estimates of Corresponding
Mean Orbital Periods

| Futures | $H_{5,0}$ | | MOP | $H_{25,0}$ | | MOP |
|---|---|---|---|---|---|---|
| Corn | ?? | ?? | ?? | ?? | ?? | ?? |
| Corn | 0.66 | – | 1300 | 0.76 | – | 1200 |
| Oats | 0.60 | Me | 1450 | 0.66 | Me | 1500 |
| Oats | 0.62 | – | 1300 | 0.70 | – | 1250 |
| Soybeans | ?? | ?? | ?? | 0.60 | Lo | 2700 |
| Soybeans | 0.68 | – | 1250 | 0.74 | – | 1250 |
| Soybean meal | ?? | ?? | ?? | ?? | ?? | ?? |
| Soybean meal | 0.65 | – | 1050 | 0.76 | – | 900 |
| Soybean oil | 0.71 | Lo | 1150 | ?? | ?? | ?? |
| Soybean oil | 0.71 | – | 1150 | 0.80 | – | 1150 |
| Wheat | 0.50 | Hi | 1750 | 0.60 | Hi | 1500 |
| Wheat | 0.50 | – | 1750 | 0.65 | – | 1300 |

*Note:* The first row for each commodity contract reports estimates of the classical Hurst exponent from eq. (19) for which the null hypothesis of no long-term dependence is rejected. Hi denotes rejection at the 95% or 99% confidence level, Me denotes rejection at the 90%, and Lo rejection at the 80% confidence level. If the null hypothesis of no long-term dependence is not rejected, the row is filled with question marks. The second row reports the descriptive results from the rescaled range analysis obtained from the graphical approach for which no hypothesis testing can be performed.

**TABLE VI**

Estimates of $\alpha_{n,q}H_{n,q}$ for $n = 1, 5, 25$, $q = 0$, and $q \neq 0$

| Futures | $\alpha_{1,0}H_{1,0}$ | $\alpha_{1,q}H_{1,q}$ | $\alpha_{5,0}H_{5,0}$ | $\alpha_{25,0}H_{25,0}$ |
|---|---|---|---|---|
| Corn | 0.98 | 0.93 | 1.12 | 1.26 |
| Oats | 0.97 | 0.94 | 1.04 | 1.24 |
| Soybeans | 1.08 G | 1.03 G | 1.22 | 1.01 |
| Soybean meal | 1.02 G | 1.02 G | 1.20 G | 1.38 G |
| Soybean oil | 1.18 | 1.13 | 1.33 | 1.46 G |
| Wheat | ?? | ?? | 0.92 | 1.15 |

*Note:* The row for each commodity contract reports the empirical verification of the relationship (12) by using the $H_{n,q}$ values obtained from the statistical analysis when the null hypothesis of no long-term memory is rejected and by using the $H_{n,q}$ values obtained from the graphical analysis when the same null hypothesis is accepted. In the last case the result is marked by a G. If $H_{n,q} < 0.5$ the row is filled with question marks.

Third, Table VI reports the results of the empirical proof of the relationship (12) obtained by determining the values of $\alpha_{n,q}H_{n,q}$ (equal to one, from a theoretical point of view).

Finally, Figures 7–16 report the (typical) behavior of some Hurst exponent $H_{n,q}$'s estimates *versus* N. In particular, from this analysis, note that:

• There is a starting interval ($N_0 \leq N \leq N^*$) of estimate arrangement, in which $H_{n,q}$ decreases as N increases (probably due to the low power of the rescale range analysis for small samples).

• There is a second interval ($N^* < N \leq T$) in which both the classical Hurst exponent estimate and the modified one obtain a relative minimum/maximum or are constant (in general, corresponding to the true value of the Hurst exponent).

• The underlying memory structure is confirmed by reanalyzing the same time series after a random alteration of their time order, because the reestimated $H_{n,q}$ values tend to 0.5 (i.e., no more long-term correlation) and, so reveal the destruction of a long-term dependence that exists in the unscrambled original time series.

The previous three tables allow one to deduce several things. The graphical analysis indicates evidence of long-term memory for all the daily (i.e., $n = 1$) returns time series (see Table IV). In particular, the results of this analysis are qualitatively the same, assuming both independence ($q = 0$) and dependence, so one can conjecture that the influence of the short-term memory is negligible. Moreover, such results are analogous to the ones found by Peters (1989) for the U.S. stock market. Notice that the graphical approach detects positive dependence [i.e., $H \in (0.5,1)$]

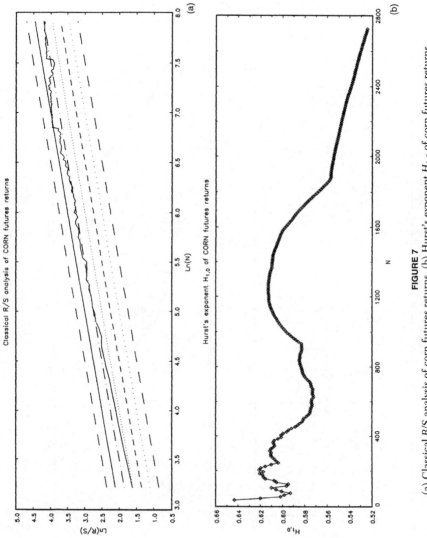

**FIGURE 7**

(a) Classical *R/S* analysis of corn futures returns. (b) Hurst's exponent $H_{1,0}$ of corn futures returns.

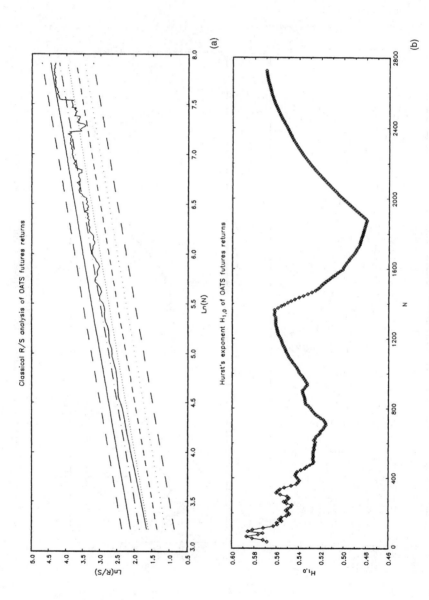

**FIGURE 8**

(a) Classical *R/S* analysis of oats futures returns. (b) Hurst's exponent $H_{1,0}$ of oats futures returns.

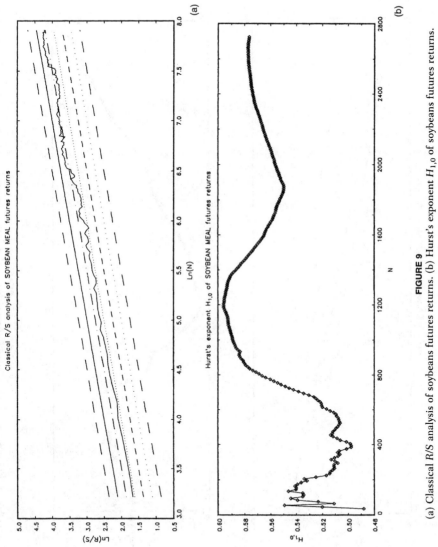

**FIGURE 9**

(a) Classical *R/S* analysis of soybeans futures returns. (b) Hurst's exponent $H_{1,0}$ of soybeans futures returns.

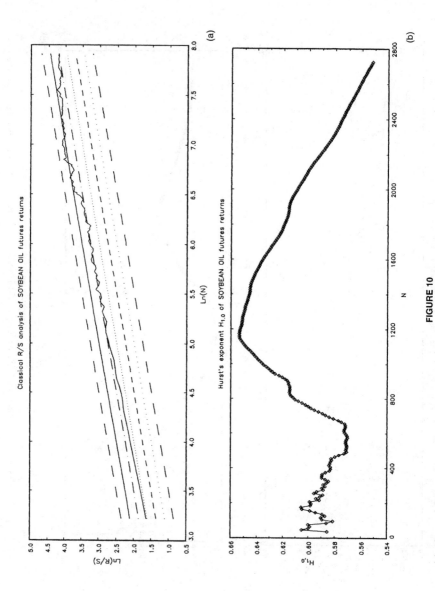

**FIGURE 10**

(a) Classical *R/S* analysis of soybean meal futures returns. (b) Hurst's exponent $H_{1,0}$ of soybean meal futures returns.

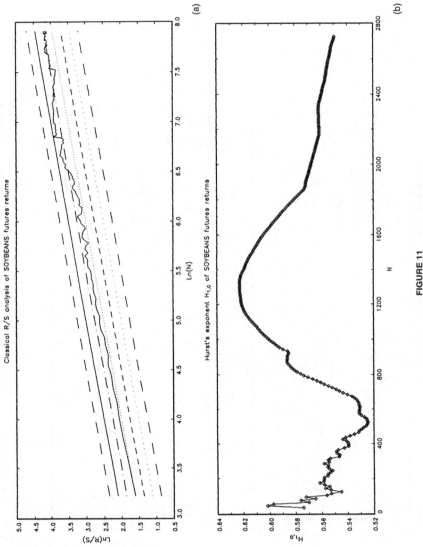

**FIGURE 11**

(a) Classical *R/S* analysis of soybean oil futures returns. (b) Hurst's exponent $H_{1,0}$ of soybean oil futures returns.

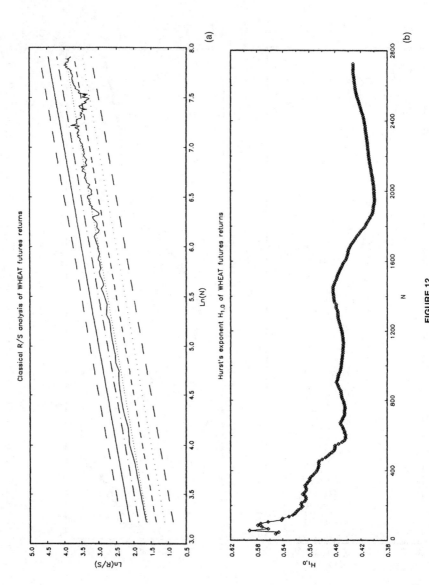

**FIGURE 12**

(a) Classical *R/S* analysis of wheat futures returns. (b) Hurst's exponent $H_{1,0}$ of wheat futures returns.

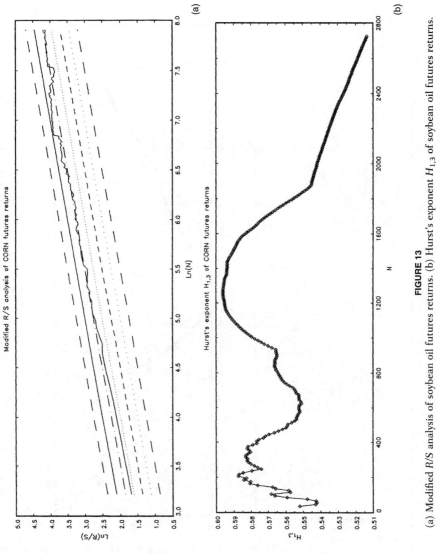

**FIGURE 13**

(a) Modified *R/S* analysis of soybean oil futures returns. (b) Hurst's exponent $H_{1,3}$ of soybean oil futures returns.

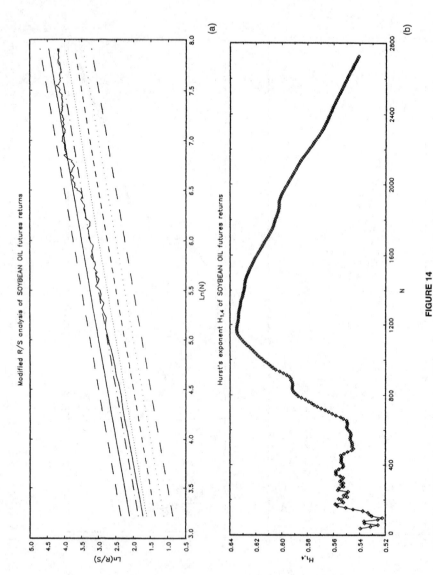

**FIGURE 14**

(a) Modified *R/S* analysis of soybean oil futures returns. (b) Hurst's exponent $H_{1,4}$ of soybean oil futures returns.

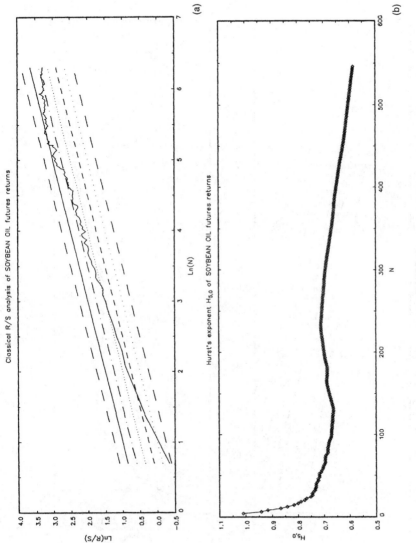

**FIGURE 15**

(a) Classical R/S analysis of soybean oil futures returns. (b) Hurst's exponent $H_{5,0}$ of soybean oil futures returns.

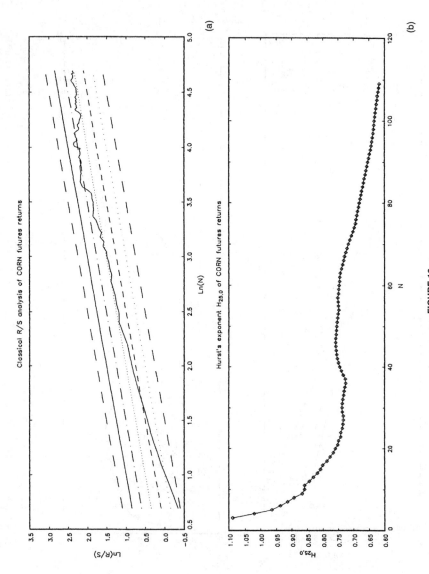

**FIGURE 16**

(a) Classical *R/S* analysis of soybean oil futures returns. (b) Hurst's exponent $H_{25,0}$ of soybean oil futures returns.

for corn, oats, soybeans, soybean meal, and soybean oil and detects negative dependence [i.e., $H \in (0,0.5)$] for wheat. This can be explained in this way. For the positive dependence case, the ability of economic agents to make optimal decisions under uncertainty is easier because buy and hold strategies yield returns in the same direction. However, because of the irregular arrival of new important information to the market, persistent return movements can at times reverse direction suddenly, and decisions are more difficult at turning points. For the negative dependence case, because of to some exogenous structural sociopolitical changes, the arrival of contrasting information to the market can induce the economic agents to frequently change the rule-governed behavior.

The values of the MOP associated to the daily returns time series go from 950 (i.e., about less than 4 years) to 1350 (i.e., about more than 5 years) for the positive dependence case and go from 1800 (i.e., about more than 7 years) to 1950 (i.e., about more than 8 years) for the negative dependence case, assuming both independence ($q = 0$) and dependence. Notice that for time lags greater than MOP, the underlying stochastic processes lose their long-term memory and the corresponding daily returns become long-term independent.

The results of the graphical analysis for both weekly (i.e., $n = 5$) and monthly (i.e., $n = 25$) returns time series (see Table V) are qualitatively the same for both $H_{n,0}$ estimates and MOP values with the exception of wheat.

The results of the statistical analysis when it rejects the null hypothesis of no long-term dependence for the daily, weekly, and monthly returns time series (see Tables IV and V) confirm the results obtained from the graphical analysis for both $H_{n,q}$ estimates and MOP values.

Because $1/H_{n,q} \in [1.25, 1.89]$, with $H_{n,q} \in [0.5, 1]$ (see Tables IV and V), it is verified empirically that the dimension of the underlying process probability distributions are not integer. It is another confirmation of the fractal nature of such processes.

Recall that for FBM the Hurst exponent is also equal to the statistical self-similarity parameter, K; therefore the property of invariability by time-scale change for the analyzed time series is confirmed, proving again the relationship (12) (see Table VI). In particular, this result holds better for daily returns than for weekly or monthly ones.

## CONCLUDING REMARKS

It is not enough to reject randomness and market efficiency hypotheses. To make scientific progress, alternatives to randomness must be specified.

This article offers an answer to the question: if asset returns do not follow random walk what are they? Using daily agricultural futures data, this study finds that returns are fractal.

What does it mean to say that returns are fractal? Returns are fractal if they are characterized by properties such as fine structure, local and global irregularities, self-similarity, and noninteger dimension. Such fractal processes generalize the well-known random walks and martingales of financial economics.

To support this claim that agricultural futures returns are fractal, three pieces of statistical evidence are presented. Tests are conducted that reject the hypothesis that returns are normally distributed. Then, the four parameters of the Pareto–Lévy stable distribution are estimated. This distribution generalizes the special case of the normal distribution. With the use of certain mathematical facts, it is found that the estimates of the four parameters are consistent with the conjecture that the stochastic process generating the returns is fractal.

The second set of tests uses the classical rescaled range analysis by computing the Hurst exponent. The third test is an extension of the second using a recent modification proposed by Lo (1991). With the use of both these tests, evidence is found that returns are fractal.

What are the implications of these findings? Suppose that all financial returns (not only the agricultural futures studied in this article are fractal. This would imply that financial returns behave in ways that are more general than random walks. Put differently, random walks are only a very special case of general fractal processes. Technically, this means that although a fractal process may have a Hurst exponent that ranges theoretically over (0, 1) set, the random walk is only one special case when the Hurst exponent receives the value 0.5. This means that market efficiency is a special theory and not a general theory; it holds sometimes but not always. In other words, the empirical evidence that efficiency holds in some cases and does not hold in others is now consistent with the evidence that returns are fractal. Obviously, much more research is needed to confirm or reject the fractal behavior of returns for nonagricultural futures.

## BIBLIOGRAPHY

Akgiray, V., and Booth, G. (1988): "The Stable Law Model of Stock Returns," *Journal of Business & Economic Statistics,* 6:51–57.

Andrews, D. W. K. (1991): "Heteroscedasticity and Autocorrelation Consistent Covariance Matrix Estimation," *Econometrica,* 59(5):817–858.

Bachelier, L. (1900): "Téorie de la Spéculation," *Annales de l'Ecole Normale Superieure*, 21–86.

Bigman, D., Goldfarb, D., and Schechtman, E. (1983): "Futures Market Efficiency and the Time Content of the Information Sets," *The Journal of Futures Markets*, 3:321–334.

Bird, P. J. W. N. (1985): "Dependency and Efficiency in the London Terminal Markets," *The Journal of Futures Markets*, 5:433–446.

Canarella, G., and Pollard, S. K. (1985): "Efficiency of Commodity Futures: A Vector Autoregression Analysis," *The Journal of Futures Markets*, 5:57–76.

Canestrelli, E., and Nardelli, C. (1991): "Distribuzioni Stabili di Lévy dei Rendimenti del Mercato Azionario Italiano," *Atti del XV Convegno A.M.A.S.E.S.*, Grado, pp. 145–158.

Canestrelli, E., Cipriani, M. C., and Corazza, M. (1993): "Determinazione dei Parametri di una Funzione di Distribuzione Pareto-Lévy Stabile," *Rendiconti del Comitato per gli Studi Economici*, XXX–XXXI:111–134.

Chance, D. M. (1985): "A Semi-Strong Form Test of the Efficiency of Treasury Bond Futures Market," *The Journal of Futures Markets*, 5:385–405.

Cole, C. S., Impson, M., and Reichenstein, W. (1991): "Do Treasury Bill Futures Rates Satisfy Rational Expectation Properties?," *The Journal of Futures Markets*, 11:591–601.

Corazza, M., and Nardelli, C. (1992): "Software Tools to Calculate the Correlation Dimension, the Higher Exponent of Liapunov and the Exponent of Hurst," unpublished.

Corazza, M., and Nardelli, C. (1993a): "Fenomeno della Dipendenza a Lungo Termine nel Mercato Finanziario Italiano," *Atti del XVII Convegno A.M.A.S.E.S.*, Ischia, pp. 359–382.

Corazza, M., and Nardelli, C. (1993b): "Analisi della Struttura Frattale del Mercato Finanziario Italiano," *Rendiconti del Comitato per gli Studi Economici*, XXX–XXXI:171–186.

Cornew, R., Town, D., and Crowson, L. (1984): "Stable Distribution, Futures Prices, and the Measurement of Trading Performance," *The Journal of Futures Markets*, 4:531–557.

Cutland, N. J., Kopp, P. E., and Willinger, W. (1993): "Stock Price Returns and the Joseph Effect: Fractional Version of the Black–Scholes Model," *Mathematics Research Reports*, 297–306.

Decoster, G. P., Labys, W. C., and Mitchell, D. W. (1992): "Evidence of Chaos in Commodity Futures Prices," *The Journal of Futures Markets*, 12:291–305.

Dusak, K. (1973): "Futures Trading and Investor Returns: An Investigation of Commodity Market Risk Premiums," *Journal of Political Economy*, 81:1387–1405.

Elam, E., and Dixon, B. L. (1988): "Examining the Validity of a Test of Futures Market Efficiency," *The Journal of Futures Markets*, 8:365–372.

Falconer, K. (1990): *Fractal Geometry*, New York: Wiley.

Fama, E. F. (1963): "Mandelbrot and the Stable Paretian Hypothesis," *Journal of Business*, 36:420–429.

Fama, E. F. (1965): "Portfolio Analysis in a Stable Paretian Market," *Management Science*, 11:404–419.

Fama, E. F. (1965): "The Behavior of Stock Market Prices," *Journal of Business,* 38:34–105.

Fama, E. F. (1970): "Efficient Capital Markets: Review of Theory and Empirical Work," *Journal of Finance,* 25:383–417.

Fama, E. F. (1991): "Efficient Capital Markets: II," *Journal of Finance,* 46(5):1575–1617.

Fama, E. F., and Roll, R. (1968): "Some Properties of Symmetric Stable Distributions," *Journal of the American Statistical Association,* 63:817–836.

Fama, E. F., and Roll, R. (1971): "Parameter Estimates for Symmetric Stable Distributions," *Journal of the American Statistical Association,* 66:331–338.

Feder, J. (1988): *Fractals,* New York: Plenum Press.

Feller, W. (1971): *An Introduction to Probability Theory and its Applications* (Vols. 1 and 2), New York: Wiley.

Glassman, D. (1987): "The Efficiency of Foreign Exchange Futures Markets in Turbulent and Non-Turbulent Periods," *Journal of Futures Markets,* 7:245–267.

Greene, M. T., and Fielitz, B. D. (1977): "Long-Term Dependence in Common Stock Returns," *Journal of Financial Economics,* 4:339–349.

Gribbin, D. W., Harris, R. W., and Lau, H. S. (1992): "Futures Prices Are Not Stable-Paretian Distributed," *Journal of Futures Markets,* 12:475–487.

Gross, M. (1988): "A Semi-Strong Test of the Efficiency of the Aluminum and Copper Markets at the LME," *The Journal of Futures Markets,* 8:67–77.

Grossman, S. J., and Stiglitz, J. E. (1980): "On the Impossibility of Informationally Efficient Markets," *The American Economic Review,* 70:393–408.

Guimaraes, R. M., Kingsman, B. G., and Taylor, S. J. (1989): *A Reappraisal of the Efficiency of Financial Markets,* Berlin: Springer.

Hall, J., Brorsen, B., and Irwin, S. (1989): "The Distribution of Future Prices: A Test of the Stable Paretian and Mixture of Normals Hypothesis," *Journal of Financial and Quantitative Analysis,* 24:105–116.

Harpaz, G., Krull, S., and Yagil, J. (1990): "The Efficiency of the U.S. Dollar Index Futures Market," *The Journal of Futures Markets,* 10:469–479.

Helms, B. P., and Martell, T. F. (1985): "An Examination of the Distribution of Futures Price Changes," *The Journal of Futures Markets,* 5(2):259–272.

Hsieh, D. A. (1989): "Testing for Nonlinear Dependence in Daily Foreign Exchange Rates," *Journal of Business,* 62:339–368.

Hudson, M., Leuthold, R., and Sarassoro, G. (1987): "Commodity Futures Prices Changes: Recent Evidence for Wheat, Soybeans, and Live Cattle," *The Journal of Futures Markets,* 7:287–301.

Hurst, H. E. (1951): "Long-Term Storage of Reservoirs," *Transactions of the American Society of Civil Engineers,* 116.

Klemkosky, R. C., and Lasser, D. J. (1985): "An Efficiency Analysis of the T-Bond Futures Market," *The Journal of Futures Markets,* 5:607–620.

Koutrouvelis, I. A. (1980): "Regression-Type Estimation of the Parameters of Stable Laws," *Journal of the American Statistical Association,* 75(37):918–928.

Koutrouvelis, I. A. (1981): "An Iterative Procedure for the Estimation of the Parameters of Stable Law," *Communications in Statistics, Simulation and Computation,* B10(1):29–39.

Lévy, P. (1925): *Calcul des Probabilités*, Paris: Gauthier-Villars.

Lo, A. W. (1991): "Long-Term Memory in Stock Market Prices," *Econometrica*, 59(5):1279–1313.

Maberly, E. D. (1985): "Testing Futures Market Efficiency—A Restatement," *The Journal of Futures Markets*, 5:425–432.

MacCulloch, H. J. (1986): "Simple Consistent Estimators of Stable Distribution Parameters," *Communications in Statistics, Simulation and Computation*, 15(4):1109–1136.

MacDonald, S. S., and Hein, S. E. (1993): "An Empirical Evaluation of Treasury Bill Futures Market Efficiency: Evidence From Forecast Efficiency Tests," *The Journal of Futures Markets*, 13:199–211.

Machones, M., Mase, S., Plunkett, S., and Thrash, R. (1994): "Price Prediction Using Nonlinear Techniques," *The Magazine of Artificial Intelligence in Finance*, Fall, 51–56.

Mandelbrot, B. B. (1963): "The Variation of Certain Speculative Prices," *Journal of Business*, 36:394–419.

Mandelbrot, B. B., and Taqqu, M. S. (1979): "Robust R/S Analysis of Long Run Serial Correlation," lecture presented at the International Statistical Institute, 42nd Session, Manila.

Mandelbrot, B. B., and Taylor, H. (1967): "On the Distribution of Stock Price Differences," *Operations Research*, 15:1057–1062.

Mandelbrot, B. B., and van Ness, J. (1968): "Fractional Brownian Motion, Fractional Noises and Applications," *SIAM Review*, 10:422–437.

Mandelbrot, B. B., and Wallis, J. R. (1969): "Robustness of the Rescaled Range R/S in the Measurement of Noncyclic Long Run Statistical Dependence," *Water Resources Research*, 5.

Newey, W., and West, K., (1987): "A Simple Positive Definite, Heteroscedasticity and Autocorrelation Consistent Covariance Matrix," *Econometrica*, 55:703–705.

Osborne, M. F. M. (1959): "Brownian Motion in the Stock Market," *Operations Research*, 7:145–173.

Peters, E. E. (1989): "Fractal Structure in the Capital Markets," *Financial Analyst Journal*, July.

Peters, E. E. (1991a): "A Chaotic Attractor for the S&P 500," *Financial Analyst Journal*, March.

Peters, E. E. (1991b): *Chaos and Order in the Capital Markets*, New York: Wiley.

Peters, E. E. (1994): *Fractal Market Analysis*, New York: Wiley.

Samuelson, P. (1965): "Proof that Properly Anticipated Prices Fluctuate Randomly," *Industrial Management Review*, 6:41–49.

Saunders, E. M., and Mahajan, A. (1988): "An Empirical Examination of Composite Stock Index Futures Pricing," *The Journal of Futures Markets*, 8:210–228.

Sinai, Y. G. (1976): "Self-Similar Probability Distributions," *Theory of Probability and its Applications*, 1:64–80.

So, J. (1987): "The Sub-Gaussian Distribution of Currency Futures: Stable Paretian or Non-stationary?," *Review of Economics and Statistics*, 69:100–107.

Stevenson, R. A., and Bear, R. M. (1970): "Commodity Futures: Trends or Random Walks?," *The Journal of Finance*, 25:65–81.

Tomek, W. (1994): "Dependence in Commodity Prices: A Comment," *The Journal of Futures Markets*, 14:103–109.

Walter, C. (1990): "Lévy-Stable Distributions and Fractal Structure on the Paris Market," *AFIR Intern. Colloq.* (Paris), 3:242–259.

Working, H. (1934): "A Random-Difference Series for Use in the Analysis for Time Series," *Journal of the American Statistical Association*, 29:11–24.

# [11]

# VOLUME AND PRICE
# RELATIONSHIPS:
# HYPOTHESES AND TESTING
# FOR AGRICULTURAL
# FUTURES

## A. G. MALLIARIS
## JORGE L. URRUTIA

## 1. INTRODUCTION

The relationship between trading volume and price variability has been examined extensively. The theoretical motivation of earlier studies such as Ying (1966), Crouch (1970), Clark (1973), Copeland (1976), Epps and Epps (1976), Westerfield (1977), Rogalski (1978), and Upton and Shannon (1979) was the demand and supply model of microeconomic theory. Some authors have investigated the price–volume relationship with the use of data from futures markets; these include Cornell (1981), Tauchen and Pitts (1983), Rutledge (1984), Grammatikos and Saunders (1986), Garcia, Leuthold, and Zapata (1986), and Bhar and Malliaris (1996). Other researchers have studied the determinants of volume with the use of macroeconomic and financial variables other than price vari-

We are thankful for useful comments to David B. Mirza, Bruce D. Phelps, and Stanley Pliska. The article has also benefited from the comments and suggestions of three anonymous referees, Professor Hector Zapata and the Editor, Mark Powers. Earlier versions of the article were presented at the Futures and Options Seminar at the University of Illinois at Chicago, and at the annual meetings of the Financial Management Association, and the Midwest Finance Association. We are grateful to our research assistant Raffaella Cremonesi, and especially to Caglar Alkan for extensive computer work.

■ A. G. Malliaris is the Walter F. Mullady Senior Professor of Business Administration at Loyola University of Chicago.

■ Jorge L. Urrutia is a Professor of Finance at Loyola University of Chicago.

The Journal of Futures Markets, Vol. 18, No. 1, 53–72 (1998)
© 1998 by John Wiley & Sons, Inc.                    CCC 0270-7314/98/010053-20

ability. Key references in this direction of research are Carlton (1983, 1984) and Martell and Wolf (1987). Theoretical models of trading volume have been developed also by Karpoff (1986), Huffman (1987), and Pagano (1989).

Researchers have emphasized the importance of the relationship between price and volume. Karpoff (1987) gives several reasons why the price–volume relationship is crucial in capital markets. He argues that the price–volume relationship can provide insight about the market structure, because information is more available for heavily traded securities than for thinly traded securities. Also, larger volumes make trade more competitive and lower the bid–ask spread. Trading volume also plays an important role in futures markets. Most economic reports published by the futures exchanges and regulatory agencies use volume data to measure the growth or decline of futures contracts. Volume data are also used to measure shifts in the composition of futures markets.

Furthermore, volume is of great significance in technical analysis. Unlike the efficient market hypothesis, which underscores the importance of asset prices and claims that prices fully incorporate all relevant information, technical analysis extends this notion to volume as well. Murphy (1985) and DeMark (1994) emphasize that both volume and price incorporate valuable information. Bullish news causes not only prices to increase, but also trading volume. A technical analyst gives less significance to a price increase with low trading volume than to a similar price increase with substantial volume.

Finally, some authors, such as Peck (1981), study the role of speculation and price volatility. Speculation is closely related to trading volume. Although the study of price volatility can be carried out without reference to volume, as in Streeter and Tomek (1992), most often these two variables are linked together, as in Cornell (1981).

This article contributes to the literature of price–volume relationship and the determinants of trading volume by postulating several hypotheses and testing them with data for agricultural commodity futures contracts. The model developed in this article formalizes the intuitive idea that price and quantity are interrelated. The theoretical model presented in the article differs from the earlier works of Crouch (1970), Rogalski (1978), Martell and Wolf (1987), Karpoff (1986), Huffman (1987), and Pagano (1989) by using stochastic calculus and Itô's processes. The empirical portion of the article differs from previous research in several aspects. Clark (1973), Rutledge (1978), Cornell (1981), Tauchen and Pitts (1983), and Grammatikos and Saunders (1986) concentrate on the investigation of the relationship between volume and price volatility. Martell and Wolf (1987) examine the determinants of trading volume. Garcia et al. (1986) investigate lead–lag relationships between trading volume and price variability. This article conducts tests of long-run relationships, or tests of cointegration, between price and volume, and also applies an error correction model to volume and price. Finally, tests of the determinants of trading volume are also reported. All these tests use an extended data set that covers the time period 1981–1995.

The remainder of the article is organized as follows: Section 2 presents the postulated model and hypotheses; Section 3 describes the methodology; Section 4 presents the data; Section 5 analyzes the empirical results, and Section 6 summarizes and concludes the article.

## 2. MODEL AND HYPOTHESES

Following the previous work of Crouch (1970), Rogalski (1978), Garcia et al. (1986), and Bhar and Malliaris (1996), it is postulated that volume is a function of price and time:

$$V = V(t, P) \tag{1}$$

where $V$ denotes trading volume, $P$ denotes futures price, and $t$ denotes time. The relationship between volume and price can indeed be highly complicated, and it can dynamically change over time. This change over time is expressed by the argument, $t$, in (1). In other words, expression (1) goes beyond the static supply and demand model by emphasizing a dynamic relationship. This is more appropriate for futures markets where the price–quantity relationship changes almost continuously.

Assume that the function, $V$, in (1) is twice continuously differentiable and that $P$ follows an Itô process with drift, $\mu$, and volatility, $\sigma$, written as

$$dP = \mu\, dt + \sigma\, dZ \tag{2}$$

In (2), $Z$ denotes a standardized Weiner process. The appropriateness of (2) to describe asset prices is reviewed extensively in Merton (1982), who offers arguments in support of the use of Itô processes to characterize the behavior of asset prices. Among these arguments, the most compelling one is that Itô processes describe continuous random walks with a drift.

An application of Itô's lemma presented in Malliaris and Brock (1982) yields

$$dV = V_t + V_P \, dP + \frac{1}{2} V_{PP} \, (dP)^2$$

$$= V_t \, dt + V_P \, [\mu \, dt + \sigma \, dZ] + \frac{1}{2} V_{PP} \, \sigma^2 \, dt$$

$$= [V_t + V_P \, \mu + \frac{1}{2} V_{PP} \, \sigma^2] \, dt + V_P \, \sigma \, dZ \qquad (3)$$

where $V_t$, $V_P$, and $V_{PP}$ denote partial derivatives. The relationships described by eqs. (1)–(3) allow one to formulate several hypotheses.

Observe that both $P$ and $V$ in (1)–(3) are random variables with certain distribution functions. If these distribution functions change over time, then $V$ and $P$ are nonstationary. Also, eq. (2) describes futures prices as a diffusion process. Because diffusion processes are continuous-time random walks, eqs. (1)–(3) claim the following: If futures prices follow a random walk, then trading volume also follows a random walk. Tests of randomness and stationarity for both price and volume allow verification of the validity of this first hypothesis.

Secondly, eqs. (1)–(3) suggest that futures price and the corresponding trading volume are interrelated and can affect each other. Cointegration and error correction methodologies are used to test this second hypothesis—that price and volume relate to each other in the long run and in the short run.

If the expectations of (3) are taken into account, the following expression is derived:

$$E \, (dV) = V_t + V_P \, \mu + \frac{1}{2} V_{PP} \, \sigma^2 \qquad (4)$$

Equation (4) suggests that the change in trading volume depends on three determinants: (i) a trend factor, $V_t$; (ii) the drift coefficient of price, $\mu$; and (iii) the volatility of price, $\sigma^2$. This third hypothesis is tested with the following expression:

$$E \, (dV) = \alpha \, t + \beta \, \mu + \gamma \, \sigma^2 \qquad (5)$$

Finally, stochastic calculus techniques allow derivation of the volatility of trading volume from (3) as

$$Var \, (dV) = V_P^2 \, \sigma^2, \qquad (6)$$

which says that the volatility of trading volume is a function of price volatility. This is the fourth hypothesis of this article and is tested with the following relationship:

$$Var\ (dV) = \alpha + \delta\ \sigma^2 \qquad (7)$$

## 3. METHODOLOGY

The four hypotheses are tested with augmented Dickey and Fuller tests of stationarity, tests of cointegration, and the error correction methodology. Brief descriptions of these methods follow.

### 3.1 Tests of Stationarity

The stationarity of price and trading volume is tested with the augmented Dickey and Fuller (ADF) (1979), test:

$$X_t - X_{t-1} = b_0 X_{t-1} + \sum_{i=1}^{T} b_i(X_{t-i} - X_{t-i-1}) + \varepsilon_t \qquad (8)$$

where $X_t$ represents the level or the first difference of the variables. The null hypothesis of nonstationarity is $b_0 = 0$. If the null hypothesis cannot be rejected for the level of the variable but is rejected for the first difference, then the variable is stationary in the first difference and it is said that the variable is integrated of order 1, denoted by I(1).

### 3.2 Tests of Cointegration

If two time series, $X_t$ and $Y_t$, are both nonstationary in levels but stationary in the first difference, it is said that variables, $X_t$ and $Y_t$, are integrated of order 1, denoted as I(1). If two variables, $X_t$ and $Y_t$, are both I(1), their linear combinations, $Z_t = X_t - \alpha Y_t$, are generally also I(1). However, if there is an $\alpha$ such as that $Z_t$ is I(0), then $Z_t$ is integrated of order 0 or stationary in level. If $Z_t$ is I(0), then the linear combination of $X_t$ and $Y_t$ is stationary and it is said that the two variables are cointegrated. Cointegration represents a long-run equilibrium relationship between two variables.

Engle and Granger (1987) propose several methods to test for cointegration between two time series. This study follows the approach of first running the cointegration regression:

$$X_t = \alpha_0 Y_t + \varepsilon_t \tag{9}$$

and then running the ADF regression

$$\varepsilon_t - \varepsilon_{t-1} = b_0 \varepsilon_{t-1} + \sum_{i=1}^{T} b_i(\varepsilon_{t-i} - \varepsilon_{t-i-1}) + \mu_t \tag{10}$$

on the residuals of (9). The null hypothesis of no cointegration is $\mathbf{H}_0$: $b_0$ = 0. If the null hypothesis is rejected, then the variables, $X_t$ and $Y_t$, are cointegrated and there is some long-term relationship between them.

In addition to the cointegration methodology described in (9) and (10) the maximum likelihood method is used to estimate the cointegrating relationship between variables developed by Johansen (1988). The Johansen methodology assumes that $X_t$ in (11) is an unrestricted vector autoregressive (VAR) process of $N$ variables:

$$X_t = \Pi_1 X_{t-1} + \Lambda + \Pi_k X_{t-k} + \varepsilon_t \tag{11}$$

where each II is an $N \times N$ matrix of parameters. The system in (11) can be expressed in the error correction form (ECM) as

$$\Delta X_t = \Gamma_1 \Delta X_{t-1} + \Gamma_2 \Delta X_{t-2} + \Lambda$$

$$+ \Gamma_{k-1} X_{t-k+1} + \Gamma_k \Delta X_{t-k} + \varepsilon_t \tag{12}$$

where

$$\Gamma_i = -I + \Pi_1 + \Pi_2 + \Lambda - \Pi_i, \qquad i = 1,2,\Lambda k$$

If $X_t$ is a vector of I(1) variables, then the left-hand side and the first ($k$ − 1) elements on the right-hand side of (12) are I(0) and the $k$th term is a linear combination of I(1) variables. Johansen shows by use of a canonical correlations method how to estimate all the distinct combinations of levels of $X$ that produce high correlations with the stationary elements of (12). These combinations are the cointegrating vectors. Johansen (1991) also shows how to test which of these distinct cointegrating vectors are statistically significant and derives critical values for this test.

### 3.3 Granger Causality and Error Correction Model (ECM)[1]

A time series, $Y_t$, causes another time series, $X_t$, if the current value of $X$ can be predicted better by using past values of $Y$ than by not doing so,

[1]The authors are grateful to Professor Hector Zapata for his guidance and instruction in this section.

considering also other relevant information, including past values of X. Specifically, Y is causing X if some coefficient, $a_i$, is not zero in the following equation:

$$X_t - X_{t-1} = c_0 + \sum_{i=1}^{T} a_i(Y_{t-i} - Y_{t-i-1})$$

$$+ \sum_{j=1}^{T} b_j(X_{t-j} - X_{t-j-1}) + \varepsilon_t \tag{13}$$

Similarly, X is causing Y if some coefficient, $\alpha_i$, is not zero in eq. (14):

$$Y_t - Y_{t-1} = \gamma_0 + \sum_{i=1}^{T} \alpha_i(X_{t-i} - X_{t-i-1})$$

$$+ \sum_{j=1}^{T} \beta_j(Y_{t-j} - Y_{t-j-1}) + \mu_t \tag{14}$$

If both events occur, there is a feedback. T is the number of lags for the variable, selected with the use of the Akaike criterion.[2]

By integrating the concepts of cointegration and causality in the Granger sense, it is possible to develop a model that allows for the testing of the presence of both a short-term and a long-term relationship between the variables, $X_t$ and $Y_t$. This model is known as the error correcting model (ECM) proposed by Engle and Granger (1987) and discussed in numerous papers. Key recent references include Zapata and Rambaldi (in press) and Giannini and Mosconi (1992). In particular, Zapata and Rambaldi (in press) provide Monte Carlo evidence for tests based on maximum-likelihood estimation of ECM. They confirm that in large samples all tests perform well in terms of size and power. Because sample size of this study has 3,649 observations, there are no small sample problems.

In (15), the ECM model investigates the potential long-run and short-run impact of the variable, $Y_t$, on the variable, $X_t$:

$$X_t - X_{t-1} = a_1\hat{Z}_{t-1} + \sum_{i=1}^{T} c_i(Y_{t-i} - Y_{t-i-1})$$

$$+ \sum_{j=1}^{T} d_j(X_{t-j} + X_{t-j-1}) + \varepsilon_t \tag{15}$$

[2]The Akaike criterion suggested the use of three lags for the variables used.

The ECM model represented by eq. (15) decomposes the dynamic adjustments of the dependent variable, $X_t$, to changes in the independent variable, $Y_t$, into two components: first, a long-run component given by the cointegration term, $a_1 \hat{Z}_{t-1}$, also known as the error correction term, and second, a short-term component given by the first summation term on the right-hand side of eq. (15). Observe the difference between eq. (13) and (15), namely, the cointegration term, $a_1 \hat{Z}_{t-1}$, is added in eq. (15). Recall from the discussion preceding (9) that $\hat{Z}_t = X_t - \alpha_0 Y_t$.

Similarly, the long-run and short-run impact of $X_t$ on $Y_t$ can be captured by the following ECM model:

$$Y_t - Y_{t-1} = \beta_1 \hat{Z}_{t-1} + \sum_{i=1}^{T} \phi_i(X_{t-i} - X_{t-i-1})$$

$$+ \sum_{j=1}^{T} \theta_j(Y_{i-j} + Y_{t-j-1}) + \varepsilon_t \qquad (16)$$

From eqs. (15) and (16) one may deduce that the variables, $X_t$ and $Y_t$, exhibit long-run movements when at least one of the coefficients, $a_t$ or $\beta_1$, is different from zero. If $a_1$ is statistically different from zero but $\beta_1$ is not, then the implication is that $X_t$ follows and adjusts to $Y_t$ in the long run. The opposite occurs when $\beta_1$ is statistically different from zero but $a_1$ is not. If both coefficients, $a_1$ and $\beta_1$, are statistically different from zero, a feedback relationship exists, implying that variables, $X_t$ and $Y_t$, adjust to one another over the long run.

The coefficients, $c_i$'s and $\phi_i$'s, in eqs. (15) and (16), respectively, represent the short-term relationships between the variables, $X_t$ and $Y_t$. If the $c_i$'s are not all zero in a statistical sense but all $\phi_i$'s are, then $Y_t$ is leading or causing $X_t$ in the short run. The reverse case occurs when the $\phi_i$'s are not all zero in a statistical sense but all $c_i$'s are. If both events occur, then there is a feedback relationship and the variables, $X_t$ and $Y_t$, affect each other in the short run.

### 3.4 Tests of the Determinants of Trading Volume

Expressions (4) and (5) are implemented by running the following regressions:

$$\Delta V_t = \alpha_0 + \alpha_1 t + \beta(\Delta P_t) + \gamma |\Delta P_t| \qquad (17)$$

where

$\Delta V_t = V_t - V_{t-1}$, change in trading volume

$t$ = time trend

$\Delta P_t = P_t - P_{t-1}$, change in price

$|\Delta P_t|$ = absolute change in price as a measure of price volatility

The following regression is used to empirically test eqs. (6) and (7):

$$|\Delta V_t| = \alpha + \delta |\Delta P_t| \qquad (18)$$

where

$|\Delta V_t|$ = absolute change in volume as a measure of trading volume's volatility.

$|\Delta P_t|$ = absolute change in price as a measure of price volatility

## 4. DATA

The data correspond to daily settlement prices and trading volume for six agricultural futures contracts: corn, wheat, oats, soybean, soybean meal, and soybean oil, provided by Knight-Ridder Financial. The data sample covers the time period from January 2, 1981 through September, 29, 1995. There are a total of 3649 observations for prices and volumes for each of the six agricultural futures. The prices are for the nearby contract, and the trading volume corresponds to the nearby plus the more distant contracts. At the expiration of a given futures contracts, the price reported refers to the new nearby contract.[3]

## 5. ANALYSIS OF EMPIRICAL RESULTS

The first empirical issue investigated in this article is the time-series properties of price and volume of trade. Tables I and II present the augmented Dickey and Fuller tests of stationarity. The number of lags used in the test of stationarity cointegration, and error correction are determined by using the Akaike information criterion.[4] The null of nonstationarity cannot be rejected for the levels of price and trading volume, but it is strongly

---

[3]A referee raised the question of possibly abnormal returns between the price of the expiring contract and the price of the new nearest by contract. Such returns could bias the results due to jumps. To address this issue, all tests are run twice: once with data containing a possible jump at expiration and once by smoothing such jumps with the use of the last three observations from the expiring contract and the first three observations from the new contract and averaging these six to reduce the jump. The difference in the results between these two sets of data are fortunately insignificant.

[4]Recall remarks in Footnote 2.

**TABLE I**

Augmented Dickey-Fuller Tests of Stationarity for Prices

| Commodity | Price Level | | Price First Difference | |
|---|---|---|---|---|
| | $b_0$, t stat | $R^2$, F stat | $b_1$, t stat | $R^2$, F stat |
| Corn | −0.0002 | 0.021474 | −0.890166 | 0.428502 |
| | (−1.0308) | (26.63458) | (−30.12368) | (909.7432) |
| Wheat | −0.000198 | 0.011331 | −0.892157 | 0.452767 |
| | (−0.968202) | 13.90953 | (−28.92019) | (1003.882) |
| Oats | −0.000331 | 0.026696 | −0.813420 | 0.421430 |
| | (−1.101373) | (33.28851) | (−28.38429) | (883.7920) |
| Soybean | −0.000210 | 0.002314 | −0.996215 | 0.484499 |
| | (−0.887785) | (2.814699) | (−30.53370) | 1140.365 |
| Soybean meals | −0.000216 | 0.004851 | −0.973412 | 0.475030 |
| | (−0.872463) | (5.916781) | (−30.34343) | (1097.909) |
| Soybean oil | −0.000126 | 0.012044 | −0.918213 | 0.451168 |
| | (−0.478395) | 14.79532 | (−29.37228) | (997.4227) |

*Notes:* The model is

$$\Delta X_t = b_0 X_{t-1} + \sum_{i=1}^{T} b \, \Delta_t X_{t-i} + \varepsilon_t.$$

The null hypothesis is $\mathbf{H_0}$: $b_0 = 0$ ($X_t$ is not stationary). The MacKinnon critical values for rejection of the null hypothesis are 1% critical value = −2.57, 5% critical value = −1.94, 10% critical value = −1.62. The *t* statistics and the *F* statistics are given in parentheses.

**TABLE II**

Augmented Dickey-Fuller Tests of Stationarity for Volume

| Commodity | Volume Level | | Volume First Difference | |
|---|---|---|---|---|
| | $b_0$, t stat | $R^2$, F stat | $b_1$, t stat | $R^2$, F stat |
| Corn | −0.000132 | 0.216407 | −2.273773 | 0.714922 |
| | (−0.323009) | (335.1810) | (−45.00779) | (3042.816) |
| Wheat | −0.000260 | 0.216504 | −2.428902 | 0.722048 |
| | (−0.470215) | (335.3734) | (−48.66764) | (3151.925) |
| Oats | −0.000835 | 0.215610 | −2.249846 | 0.715478 |
| | (−0.818090) | (333.6086) | (−44.61281) | (3051.124) |
| Soybean | −0.000175 | 0.260330 | −2.434077 | 0.741507 |
| | (−0.432610) | (427.1560) | (−46.33018) | (3480.548) |
| Soybean meals | −0.000284 | 0.215100 | −2.351476 | 0.715977 |
| | (−0.509007) | (332.6033) | (−47.04102) | (3058.621) |
| Soybean oil | −0.000251 | 0.212574 | −2.291039 | 0.715331 |
| | (−0.459208) | (327.6424) | (−45.82745) | (3048.929) |

*Notes:* The model is

$$\Delta X_t = b_0 X_{t-1} + \sum_{i=1}^{T} b \, \Delta_t X_{t-i} + \varepsilon_t.$$

The null hypothesis is $\mathbf{H_0}$: $b_0 = 0$ ($X_t$ is not stationary). The MacKinnon critical values for rejection of the null hypothesis are 1% critical value = −2.57, 5% critical value = −1.94, 10% critical value = −1.62. The *t* statistics and the *F* statistics are given in parentheses.

**TABLE III**

Engle and Granger Test of Cointegration of Price and Volume

| Commodity | Dependent Variable (X) | Independent Variable (Y) | $b_0$, t stat |
|---|---|---|---|
| Corn | Price | Volume | -0.022970 (-4.901632) |
| | Volume | Price | -0.207838 (-13.96623) |
| Wheat | Price | Volume | -0.032884 (-5.898205) |
| | Volume | Price | -0.273314 (-16.15283) |
| Oats | Price | Volume | -0.005926 (-3.268762) |
| | Volume | Price | -0.161456 (-12.22476) |
| Soybean | Price | Volume | -0.067062 (-7.769626) |
| | Volume | Price | -0.280663 (-15.89687) |
| Soybean meal | Price | Volume | -0.022256 (-4.737286) |
| | Volume | Price | -0.309020 (-17.22669) |
| Soybean oil | Price | Volume | -0.020450 (-4.495214) |
| | Volume | Price | -0.289937 (-16.74409) |

*Notes:* The model is

$$X_t = a_0 + a_1 Y_{t-1} + \varepsilon_t$$

$$\Delta \varepsilon_t = b_0 \varepsilon_{t-1} + \sum_{t=1}^{T} \Delta \varepsilon_{t-i} + \mu_t$$

The null hypothesis is **H₀**: $b_0 = 0$ ($X_t$ is not stationary). The MacKinnon critical values for rejection of the null hypothesis are 1% critical value = -2.57, 5% critical value = -1.94, 10% critical value = -1.62.

rejected for the first differences of the variables. It is concluded that price and volume of trade follow nonstationary random processes and are integrated of order one, I(1), which is a condition for testing for cointegration.

The tests of cointegration presented in Tables III and IV indicate the existence of long-term relationships between price and trading volume for the six agricultural commodity futures contracts. Observe from Table III that the relationship is stronger from price to volume, suggesting that trading volume tends to follow and adjust to price over the long run. These results are also confirmed with the use of the Johansen (1988, 1991)

**TABLE IV**

Johansen Test of Cointegration of Price and Volume

| | | | *Likelihood-Ratio test* | | | |
|---|---|---|---|---|---|---|
| | *Corn* | *Wheat* | *Oats* | *Soybeans* | *Soybean Meal* | *Soybean Oil* |
| $r = 0$ | 13.82613* | 29.49035** | 25.13110** | 17.91067** | 19.74685** | 13.17534* |
| $r \leq 1$ | 0.251170 | 0.432751 | 0.676079 | 0.284707 | 0.362984 | 0.103778 |

*Cointegrating Vector Corresponding to the Largest Eigenvalue*

| | *Corn* | *Wheat* | *Oats* | *Soybeans* | *Soybean Meal* | *Soybean Oil* |
|---|---|---|---|---|---|---|
| Price | −0.000360 | −0.000369 | −0.000436 | −0.000197 | −0.000571 | −0.003797 |
| Volume | 0.007502 | 0.011649 | 0.008203 | 0.010073 | 0.010861 | 0.008962 |

*Notes:* The 1% and 5% critical values for the Johansen test are 16.31 and 12.53 for $r = 0$ and 6.51 and 3.84 for $r \leq 1$, respectively, where $r$ represents the number of cointegrating vectors. A value of the likelihood-ratio test statistic less than the corresponding 5% critical value implies that the corresponding hypothesis regarding $r$ cannot be rejected. If $r = 0$ cannot be rejected the price and volume series are not cointegrated. If the price and volume series are cointegrated, then using the coefficients in the lower panel, a linear combination can be created which will be stationary.
*Null hypothesis rejected at the 5% confidence level.
**Null hypothesis rejected at the 1% confidence level.

methodology presented in Table IV. The likelihood-ratio test rejects the null hypothesis of no cointegration between price and volume for all six of the agricultural commodities. Thus, both cointegration methodologies offer strong evidence in support of the hypothesis that price and volume are interrelated.

Having established the existence of cointegration between price and volume for all six of the agricultural commodities, it is natural to test for causality. Observe that if there is cointegration between two variables, for sure there is causality in at least one direction. This implies information about instantaneous causality, in contrast to cointegration, which captures the long-run relationship. The idea is highlighted in Giannini and Mosconi (1992).[5]

The error-correction methodology allows the simultaneous study of the long-term and short-term impacts of one variable upon the other. Table V confirms that for all six contracts, a strong long-term relationship exists, both from price to volume and from volume to price. Strong long-term relationship means statistically significant in terms of both the $t$ and $F$ statistics. The $t$ statistic identifies the significance of each coefficient

[5]An anonymous referee printed out the logical relationship between cointegration and causality.

**TABLE V**

Error-Correction Model (FCM) for Testing for Long-Term and Short-Term Relationship for Price and Volume of Agricultural Futures Contracts

| Dependent Variable | Independent Variable | $a_1, \beta_1$ (t stat) | $c_1, \phi_1$ (t stat) | $c_2, \phi_2$ (t stat) | $c_3, \phi_3$ (t stat) | $H_0$: No Relationship* F stat Probability | | |
| --- | --- | --- | --- | --- | --- | --- | --- | --- |
| | | | | | | No LT Impact | No ST Impact | No LT or ST Impact |
| **Corn** | | | | | | | | |
| Price | Volume | -0.003544 (-3.1947) | -0.355585 (-2.0996) | 0.301002 (1.67314) | 0.081684 (0.48425) | 10.04098 (0.001544) | 4.175649 (0.00583) | 5.466020 (0.00022) |
| Volume | Price | -0.004371 (-1.9566) | 7.03E-05 (0.04386) | 0.003132 (1.93465) | 0.003132 (1.95626) | 3.828360 (0.050469) | 2.992141 (0.02974) | 3.317081 (0.01012) |
| **Wheat** | | | | | | | | |
| Price | Volume | -0.005998 (-3.7838) | -0.023995 (-0.1232) | 0.259590 (1.26386) | 0.101044 (0.52654) | 14.31724 (0.000157) | 0.720722 (0.53951) | 4.338591 (0.001677) |
| Volume | Price | -0.016703 (-3.9304) | 0.000964 (0.68592) | 0.002813 (1.99197) | 0.002092 (1.48737) | 15.44748 (0.000086) | 2.519165 (0.05627) | 6.135502 (0.000064) |
| **Oats** | | | | | | | | |
| Price | Volume | -0.003876 (-3.0144) | -0.119789 (-1.2957) | 0.019810 (0.20248) | 0.028703 (0.31518) | 9.086771 (0.002592) | 0.852794 (0.46493) | 2.702998 (0.028919) |
| Volume | Price | -0.017363 (-4.0187) | -0.005668 (-1.9134) | 0.003842 (1.28042) | 0.004212 (1.41967) | 16.14965 (0.00006) | 2.353265 (0.07020) | 5.992997 (0.000084) |
| **Soybeans** | | | | | | | | |
| Price | Volume | -0.006625 (-3.7615) | -0.542397 (-1.0867) | 0.585619 (1.07938) | 0.791203 (1.60232) | 14.14859 (0.000172) | 2.109241 (0.09698) | 5.027534 (0.000486) |
| Volume | Price | -0.006004 (-2.0264) | 0.000919 (1.69036) | 0.001901 (3.49267) | 0.001030 (1.89013) | 4.106199 (0.042799) | 6.424873 (0.00025) | 6.21101 (0.000056) |
| **Soybean meal** | | | | | | | | |
| Price | Volume | -0.005343 (-3.4003) | -0.091127 (-0.6555) | 0.377531 (2.56817) | 0.210950 (1.53121) | 11.56196 (0.000680) | 3.573351 (0.01342) | 5.742636 (0.000132) |
| Volume | Price | -0.009943 (-2.8275) | 0.001770 (0.90888) | 0.001228 (0.63063) | 0.000861 (0.44276) | 7.994982 (0.004716) | 0.496905 (0.68444) | 2.494907 (0.040958) |

**TABLE V (Continued)**

Error-Correction Model (FCM) for Testing for Long-Term and Short-Term Relationship for Price and Volume of Agricultural Futures Contracts

| Dependent Variable | Independent Variable | $a_1, \beta_1$ (t stat) | $c_1, \phi_1$ (t stat) | $c_2, \phi_2$ (t stat) | $c_3, \phi_3$ (t stat) | $H_0$: No Relationship* F stat Probability | | |
|---|---|---|---|---|---|---|---|---|
| | | | | | | No LT Impact | No ST Impact | No LT or ST Impact |
| Soybean oil | Volume | -0.003877 (-2.8314) | 0.010730 (0.57792) | 0.031233 (1.57920) | 0.014418 (0.78050) | 8.016719 (0.004660) | 0.841103 (0.47123) | 2.859816 (0.022186) |
| Price | | | | | | | | |
| | | | | | | 5.163859 (0.023120) | 0.354977 (0.78555) | 1.639376 (0.161457) |
| Volume | Price | -0.006460 (-2.2724) | 0.007828 (0.53685) | 0.002989 (0.20393) | 0.012188 (0.83524) | | | |

*Notes:* The model is

$$Y_t - Y_{t-1} = \beta_1 \hat{Z}_{t-1} + \sum_{j=1}^{T} \theta_j(Y_{t-j} + Y_{t-j-1}) + \epsilon_t \; ; \; X_t - X_{t-1} = a_1 \hat{Z}_{t-1} + \sum_{j=1}^{T} c(Y_{t-j} - Y_{t-j-1}) + \sum_{j=1}^{T} d(X_{t-j} + X_{t-j-1}) + \epsilon_t$$

The null hypotheses are
No long-run relationship from volume to price: $\mathbf{H}_0$: $a_t = 0$
No long-run relationship from price to volume: $\mathbf{H}_0$: $\beta_t = 0$
No short-run relationship from volume to price: $\mathbf{H}_0$: $c_t = 0$
No short-run relationship from price to volume: $\mathbf{H}_0$: $\phi_t = 0$

*The null hypotheses are tested with a Wald test. Since the sample is very large, the critical values of an $F$ distribution are used. The corresponding probabilities for the F statistics are reported in the table below the $F$ value.

**TABLE VI**

Determinants of Trading Volume

| Commodity | $\alpha_0$, t stat | $\alpha_1$, t stat | $\beta$, t stat | $\gamma$, t stat | $R^2$, F stat |
|---|---|---|---|---|---|
| Corn | −0.071519* | 5.09E-06 | −0.000779 | 0.028986* | 0.037966 |
| | (−5.747092) | (0.977801) | (−0.442677) | (11.90414) | (47.93624) |
| Wheat | −0.135956* | −1.70E-06 | −0.001106 | 0.042548* | 0.087619 |
| | (−9.099619) | (−0.172827) | (−0.730850) | (18.61862) | (116.6483) |
| Oats | −0.102397* | 7.86E-06 | −0.003675 | 0.043561* | 0.026137 |
| | (−4.633792) | (0.846691) | (−1.125881) | (9.759891) | (32.59998) |
| Soybeans | −0.068124* | 8.01E-06 | −0.000613 | 0.009182* | 0.034222 |
| | (−5.374561) | (1.500056) | (−0.981719) | (11.14503) | (43.04184) |
| Soybean meal | −0.069666* | 6.16E-06 | −0.001114 | 0.032646* | 0.035350 |
| | (−5.225460) | (1.085940) | (−0.517445) | (11.51866) | (44.51247) |
| Soybean oil | −0.080254* | 5.97E-06 | −0.016591 | 0.279555* | 0.042921 |
| | (−6.089857) | (1.081941) | (−1.039628) | (12.73598) | (54.47215) |

*Notes:* The model is

$$\Delta V_t = \alpha_0 + \alpha_t t + \beta(\Delta P_t) + \gamma|\Delta P_t| + \varepsilon_t$$

where
$\Delta V_t$ = change in futures trading volume
$t$ = time trend
$\Delta P_t$ = change in price
$|\Delta P_t|$ = absolute change in price (price volatility)
The $t$ statistics and $F$ statistics are given in parentheses.
*Significant at the 5% confidence level.

of the independent variables in the ECM, and the $F$ statistic refers to the Wald test for causality. As described in Lutkepohl (1981, Chapter 3). This study test whether any subset of variables have zero coefficients and might thus lead to rejection of the causality.

Table V also illustrates the existence of short-term impact between price and volume for corn, soybeans, and soybean meal, but weak impact (statistically insignificant) for wheat, oats, and soybean oil. This short-term relationship is particularly strong in both directions (from price to volume and volume to price) for corn, soybean, and soybean meal. In general, the direction of causality is stronger from price to trading volume, suggesting for all six of the agricultural commodities that price tends to lead trading volume in the short run.

The third testable hypothesis postulates that changes in trading volume over time depends on three factors: time trend, price, and volatility of price, as indicated by eqs. (4) and (5). Table VI shows that only the volatility of price has a statistically significant impact on trading volume. Finally, Table VII presents the results of the fourth testable hypothesis suggested in eqs. (6) and (7) that is, the volatility of trading volume as a

TABLE VII

Volatility of Trading Volume as a Function of Price Volatility

| Commodity | $\alpha$, t stat | $\delta$, t stat | $R^2$, F stat |
|---|---|---|---|
| Corn | 0.229860* | 0.015294* | 0.027023 |
|  | (48.48618) | (10.06300) | (101.2639) |
| Wheat | 0.299558* | 0.006986* | 0.006001 |
|  | (46.48788) | (4.691702) | (22.01207) |
| Oats | 0.424524* | 0.016529* | 0.009038 |
|  | (49.56369) | (5.766557) | (33.25318) |
| Soybeans | 0.237279* | 0.003917* | 0.014522 |
|  | (49.39436) | (7.329965) | (53.72839) |
| Soybean meal | 0.254984* | 0.014905* | 0.018209 |
|  | (50.88843) | (8.223298) | (67.62262) |
| Soybean oil | 0.259160* | 0.075420* | 0.007901 |
|  | (51.02458) | (5.388397) | (29.03482) |

*Notes:* The model is

$$|\Delta V_t| = \alpha + \delta |\Delta P_t| + \varepsilon_t$$

where
$|\Delta V_t|$ = Absolute change in futures trading volume (volume's volatility)
$|\Delta P_t|$ = Absolute change in price (price volatility)
The *t* statistics and F statistics are given in parentheses.
*Significant at the 5% confidence level.

function of price volatility. Table VII shows that price volatility significantly impacts volume's volatility.

## 6. SUMMARY AND CONCLUSIONS

This article investigates several hypotheses about the time series properties of price and trading volume, the short-term and long-term relationships between price and trading volume, and the determinants of trading volume. The data correspond to daily settlement prices and trading volume covering the time period, January 1981–September 1995, for six agricultural commodity futures contracts: corn, wheat, oats, soybeans, soybean meal, and soybean oil.

It is found that the time series of price and trading volume are nonstationary in levels but stationary in the first differences; that is, they are integrated of order 1, I(1). Because the two variables are cointegrated, there is causality in the Granger sense between price and volume of trade at least in one direction. Thus, price and trading volume are interrelated in the long run and in the short run. Cointegration, the direction of causality, and the error correction methodology suggest that trading volume tends to adjust to price in the long run and that price tends to lead trading volume in the short run. The results also indicate that price volatility is a determinant of both trading volume and volatility of trading volume.

The theoretical contribution of the article can be summarized as follows: The article develops a dynamic model relating price and volume. The model allows both price and volume to be random variables with arbitrary probability distributions that can change over time. The model postulates that price follows a continuous-time random walk with a trend known as an Itô's process. The model uses stochastic calculus to derive the result that trading volume also follows a stochastic equation of the Itô type. If volume follows an Itô process, one can compute its first two moments. The model is completed by estimating the expected volume and its volatility. The model suggests that volume is impacted by price and price volatility, and that volume's volatility is proportional to price volatility. The empirical results confirm most of the postulated hypotheses: (i) price and trading volume follow random walks and they are integrated of order 1; (ii) price and trading volume are cointegrated in the long run; (iii) the third hypothesis is confirmed only for price variability; that is, trading volume is a function of price variability; (iv) volatility of trading volume is a function of price variability.

The article finds that price and volume are cointegrated, and that this long-run relationship is stronger from price to volume. Also, this article reports bidirectional causality between price and volume and establishes the clear importance of a long-run relationship, rather than short run, between price and volume from the error correction methodology. The finding that price variability is a determinant of volume confirms previous results of Cornell (1981), Garcia et al (1986), and others. In addition, a new result is found that price variability has an impact on volume's variability.

The long-run and short-run relationships between price and volume implied by the tests of cointegration and error correction highlight the relevance of volume and offer support to technical analysis. Recall that unlike the efficient market hypothesis, which ignores trading volume, technical analysis has long emphasized the significance of volume. These results also suggest that academicians should consider the role of technical analysis in future research.

The results reported in this article have implications for speculators and hedgers. In effect, Rutledge (1979) indicates that changes in daily trading volume are a measure of variations in speculation because speculative transactions comprise most of daily trading volume. The bidirectional causality reported in this article suggests that speculators should pay attention not only to price changes, but also to changes in volume. On the other hand, the long-run underlying relationship between price and volume found in this article should be of more interest to hedgers, who hold their position in the futures markets much longer than speculators.

For example, consider a representative hedger who follows the standard methodology of computing a hedge ratio with the use of the Ederington (1979) approach. Suppose that volume is low and not very responsive to price volatility. This suggests that the market is rather illiquid, with a large bid–ask spread leading to higher volatility and affecting the size of the hedge ratio. Knowing that price volatility causes a similar change in volume has informational value. The hedger can count on volume responsiveness due to price changes. In other words, liquidity is present when price and volume are interrelated. Furthermore, such liquidity could, more often than not, reduce further price volatility and possibly decrease potential losses from ineffective hedges. Obviously, this topic requires further analysis.

## BIBLIOGRAPHY

Bhar, R., and Malliaris, A. G., (1996): "Volume and Volatility in Currency Futures Markets," Working Paper, Loyola University Chicago.

Carlton, D. (1983): "Futures Trading, Market Interrelationships, and Industry Structure," *American Journal of Agricultural Economics*, 65:380–387.

Carlton, D. (1984): "Futures Markets: Their Purpose, Their History, Their Growth, Their Successes and Failures," *Journal of Futures Markets*, 4:237–271.

Clark, P. (1973): "A Subordinated Stochastic Process Model with Finite Variance for Speculative Prices," *Econometrica*, 41:135–155.

Copeland, T. (1976): "A Model of Asset Trading Under the Assumption of Sequential Information Arrival," *Journal of Finance*, 31:1149–1168.

Cornell, B. (1981): "The Relationship between Volume and Price Variability in Futures Markets," *Journal of Futures Markets*, 1:303–316.

Crouch, R. (1970): "A Nonlinear Test of the Random-Walk Hypothesis," *American Economic Review*, 60:199–202.

DeMark, T. R. (1994): *The New Science of Technical Analysis*, New York: John Wiley & Sons, Inc.

Dickey, D. A., and Fuller, W. A. (1979): "Distribution of the Estimators for Autoregressive Time Series with a Unit Root," *Journal of the American Statistical Association*, 74:427–431.

Ederington, L. (1979): "The Hedging Performance of the New Futures Markets," *Journal of Finance*, 34:157–170.

Engle, R. F., and Granger, C. W. J. (1987): "Cointegration and Error Correction Representation, Estimation and Testing," *Econometrica*, 55:251–276.

Epps, T., and Epps, M. (1976): "The Stochastic Dependence of Security Price Changes and Transaction Volumes: Implications for the Mixture-of-Distributions Hypothesis," *Econometrica*, 44:305–321.

Garcia, P., Leuthold, R., and Zapata, H. (1986): "Lead–Lag Relationships between Trading Volume and Price Variability: New Evidence," *Journal of Futures Markets*, 6: 1–10.

Giannini, C., and Mosconi, R. (1992): "Non-Causality in Cointegrated Systems: Representation, Estimation and Testing," *Oxford Bulletin of Economics and Statistics*, 54: 399–417.

Grammatikos, T., and Saunders, A. (1986): "Futures Price Variability: A Test of Maturity and Volume Effects," *Journal of Business*, 59:319–330.

Granger, C. W. J. (1969): "Investigating Causal Relations by Econometric Models and Cross-Spectral Models," *Econometrica*, 37:428–438.

Huffman, G. W. (1987): "A Dynamic Equilibrium Model of Asset Prices and Transaction Volume," *Journal of Political Economy*, 95:138–159.

Johansen, S. (1988): "Statistical Analysis of Cointegration Vectors," *Journal of Economic Dynamics and Control*, 12:231–254.

Johansen, S. (1991): "Estimation and Hypothesis Testing of Cointegration Vectors in Gaussian Vector Autoregressive Models," *Econometrica*, 59:1551–1580.

Karpoff, J. M. (1986): "A Theory of Trading Volume," *The Journal of Finance*, 41:1069–1082.

Karpoff, J. M. (1987): "The Relationship between Price Changes and Trading Volume: A Survey," *Journal of Financial and Quantitative Analysis*, 22:109–126.

Lutkepohl, H. (1981): *Introduction to Multiple Time Series Analysis*, New York: Springer Verlag.

Malliaris A., and Brock, W. (1982): *Stochastic Methods in Economics and Finance*, Amsterdam: North Holland Publishing Company.

Martell, T., and Wolf, A. (1987): "Determinants of Trading Volume in Futures Markets," *Journal of Futures Markets*, 7:233–244.

Merton, R. C. (1982): "On the Mathematics and Economics Assumption of Continuous-Time Models," in W. F. Sharpe and C. M. Cootner (Eds.) *Financial Economics: Essays in Honor of Paul Cootner*, Englewood Cliffs, NJ: Prentice Hall, pp. 19–51.

Murphy, J. J. (1985): *Technical Analysis of the Futures Market*, New York Institute of Finance, Englewood Cliffs: Prentice Hall.

Pagano, M. (1989): "Trading Volume and Asset Liquidity," *The Quarterly Journal of Economics*, 104: 255–274.

Peck, A. (1981): "Measures and Price Effects of Changes in Speculation on the Wheat, Corn, and Soybean Futures Markets," *Research on Speculation*, Chicago Board of Trade, pp. 138–149.

Rogalski, R. (1978): "The Dependence of Prices and Volume," *Review of Economics and Statistics*, 60:268–274.

Rutledge, D. J. S. (1978/1984): "Trading Volume and Price Variability: New Evidence on the Price Effects of Speculation," in A. E. Peck (Ed.), *Selected Writings on Futures Markets*, 4, Chicago Board of Trade, vol. 4, pp. 237–251.

Streeter, D. H., and Tomek, W. G. (1992): "Variability in Soybean Futures Prices: An Integrated Framework," *The Journal of Futures Markets,* 12:705–728.

Tauchen, G., and Pitts, M. (1983): "The Price Variability–Volume Relationship on Speculative Markets," *Econometrica,* 51:485–505.

Upton, D. E., and Shannon, D. S. (1979): "The Stable Paretian Distribution, Subordinated Stochastic Processes, and Asymptotic Lognormality: An Empirical Investigation," *Journal of Finance* 34:1031–1039.

Westerfield, R. (1977): "The Distribution of Common Stock Price Changes: An Application of Transactions Time and Subordinate Stochastic Models," *Journal of Financial and Quantitative Analysis,* 12:743–765.

Ying, C. (1966): "Stock Market Prices and Volume of Sales," *Econometrica,* 34:676–685.

Zapata, O. H., and Rambaldi, A. N. (in press): "Monte Carlo Evidence on Cointegration and Causation," *Oxford Bulletin of Economics and Statistics.*

# [12]

# Financial Modelling: From Stochastics to Chaotics and Back to Stochastics[1]

A. G. MALLIARIS[2] and JEROME L. STEIN[3]

[2] Department of Economics, Loyola University Chicago, Chicago, Illinois 60611, USA.

[3] Department of Economics, Brown University, Providence, Rhode Island 02912, USA.

**Abstract.** In this paper we argue that the stochastic paradigm of asset prices has prevented us from understanding market behavior because most of the variance of the variables of economic interest is often attributed to random shocks. One implication of the tests of the Efficient Market Hypothesis is that most of the variation in prices is due to our ignorance of the underlying structure. As an alternative to the stochastic methodology we propose an economic interpretation of the most famous chaotic map called the Lorenz system. We briefly describe the major characteristic of this chaotic system and we also use financial data for its empirical testing.

**Keywords.** Stochastics, Chaos, Lorenz System, Econometric System, Estimation.

## 1. Introduction

The early observation by Holbrook Working (1934), that certain sensitive commodity price differences tended to be largely random, eventually directed researchers to seek theories for such a statistical phenomenon. Paul Samuelson (1965) developed the Efficient Market Hypothesis (EMH) to rationalize the random walk behavior, whereby the current price p(t) fully reflects all relevant information. Since the flow of information between now and the next period cannot be anticipated, price changes in an efficient market are serially uncorrelated.

Neither the EMH nor the numerous statistical studies about random walk investigate the analytical properties or characteristics of the information set beyond the assumption of the existence of a probability space $(\Omega, F, P)$. The flow of real world information is then modelling as a process of random sampling, at certain time

---

[1] We are thankful to Henry Wen-herng King, Dimitrios Bouroudzoglou and Raffaella Cremonesi for extensive computations. An earlier version of this paper was presented at the EUROPEAN WORKING GROUP ON FINANCIAL MODELLING, June 1-3, 1995 at the University of Bergamo, ITALY. We are very grateful to Professor Marida Bertocchi for the invitation to participate and to two anonymous referees for constructive criticisms.

intervals, from such an arbitrary space. Furthermore, because sampling is random, the EMH claims that price changes are also random. In other words the statistical notion of a random sample from an information set during a given time interval is connected by the EMH to the economic notion of unpredictable price changes.

In section 2 we argue that the stochastic paradigm of asset prices has prevented us from understanding market behavior to such an extent that most of the variance of the variables of economic interest are attributed to random shocks, that is, the error term. This is just a euphemism for ignorance. The implication of the tests of the EMH is that most of the variation in prices is due to our ignorance of the underlying structure. To contrast the stochastic approach to modelling financial markets with the alternative of chaotic modelling, we offer in section 3 an economic interpretation of the Lorenz system. This is the best known three-dimensional chaotic system  whose time trajectories look like random when they are actually fully deterministic and converge to a strange attractor. Some important properties of this chaotic system are presented in section 4. In section 5 we use financial data to estimate econometrically the various parameters of the Lorenz system. Our conclusion are summarized in the last section.

## 2. Stochastic Modelling

During the past twenty years, the EMH has been refined analytically, mathematically and statistically. The concept of information was made precise. The notion of random walk was generalized to martingales and Itô processes; and numerous sophisticated statistical tests were employed to test the theory. Moreover, a very large literature developed concerning the statistical distribution  of the changes in spot or futures prices: are they normal, or are they leptokurtic and if leptokurtic, how fat are the tails? The theoretical foundations underlying these studies are not always clear. It was not surprising to find that along with numerous studies confirming market efficiency, there were many rejecting it, and that there is no agreement concerning the statistical distri- bution functions of price changes.  Nevertheless, the most convenient and widely acceptable paradigm postulates that returns are normally distributed which means that asset prices follow lognormal distributions.  Both modern portfolio theory and the Black-Scholes methodology of pricing derivative assets are founded on such a paradigm.

The randomness of asset price changes hypothesized by the EMH naturally leads to questions about the behavior of the variance of such changes. If price changes are induced by changes in information, can shocks in fundamental factors affecting the economy explain the observed price volatility? Or, is the variance of price changes due to other factors? This topic is exposited in Shiller (1989), known as volatility tests and efficient markets. This literature documents that prices are too volatile and al- though this evidence does not imply rejection of the EMH, it raises the crucial question: what factors other than fundamental shocks could explain such evidence of high volatility. Among several such factors, speculation has received special attention.

The topic of speculation and price volatility has been studied at both the theoretical and the empirical level. In an efficient market, since price changes are unpredictable, speculation should not be profitable. Milton Friedman (1953) argued that profitable speculation reduces the price variance. This insight has generated many empirical papers which examined the profitability of speculation. However, it was shown in Hart and Kreps (1986), that his conclusion only follows under special conditions, and that plausible models can be developed explaining excess volatility by the speculative behavior of noise traders.

There are additional reasons why the stochastic approach should be reevaluated. First, when asset price researchers postulate that tomorrow's expected price is equal to today's actual price, they readily acknowledge that these models are not suitable for prediction or theoretical explanation. Put differently, the influence of the postulated random shock dominates the importance of the independent variables; and because such a shock is necessarily theoretically unpredictable, so is the value of the dependent variable.

Secondly, stochastic models typically discourage active economic policy or regulation designed to improve market performance. This is a consequence of the unpredictability of future shocks. Randomness does not render itself to a clear diagnosis of market behavior or understanding of the relation between changes in the fundamentals and economic performance.

## 3. Chaotic Dynamics

This state of events has led researchers to investigate a key question: Is there a nonlinear deterministic methodology, as an alternative to the stochastic approach of the EMH, which generates a time series sequence of price changes that appear random when in fact such a sequence is nonrandom ?

Numerous expository articles such as Brock (1988), Baumol and Benhabib (1989), and Boldrin and Woodford (1990) have appeared that use various single variable chaotic maps as a metaphor to illustrate the intellectual possibilities of the deterministic approach.

We wish to go beyond these illustrations and explain the behavior of volatility in a nonlinear dynamical system that establishes a relationship of such asset volatility to speculation and to Bayesian learning processes followed by the traders.  In other words, we show in this section how nonlinear dynamics, as an alternative to linear stochastic models, can clarify the relation between price variability and speculation, and also explain why the empirical studies of the time series properties of asset prices are ambiguous and inconclusive.

Consider three key variables: price volatility, speculation and errors made by traders.  We propose a model of three differential equations that relate these three

4

variables. This model is known in the dynamical systems literature as the Lorenz equations. This system is perhaps the most famous chaotic map in the mathematical literature of dynamical systems and has been studied extensively for its remarkable properties. See for example Sparrow (1982).

Let x denote excess volatility of a given financial variable. For example x may denote the excess volatility of the futures price of corn. Volatility is given the standard definition of the annualized standard deviation of returns. Note that we wish to model excess volatility defined as the volatility of the price of an asset less the volatility of fundamentals. In the example of the volatility of the futures price of corn we substract the volatility of corn inventories which accounts for a measure of the volatility of fundamentals.

Malliaris and Stein (1995) develop a detailed economic model to derive

$$(3.1) \qquad dx/dt = s(-x + y)$$

which says that changes in the excess volatility of an asset depend on two factors: first, the level of excess volatility and also the volatility of Bayesian errors by traders, denoted by y.

Equation (3.2) describes the dynamics of the Bayesian error. The Bayesian error depends upon the noisiness of the system and the average costs of sampling by the market participants. The latter depends upon the types of people attracted to the market. Moreover, given the noisiness of the system, the volatility of the Bayesian error converges as time increases. Equation (3.2) is one specification of this process.

$$(3.2) \qquad dy/dt = x(r - z) - y$$

Equation (3.2) above involves a parameter r and three financial variables: x, y and z. Recall that x denotes excess volatility of the price of a financial asset while y denotes the volatility of the average Bayesian error. This error is measured as the difference between the subjective estimate of the price today and the objective price at the expiration of the futures price. The third variable z is a measure of excess speculation.

Holbrook Working (1949) and Ann Peck (1985) have developed a measure of excess speculation which they refer to as the z index. It measures the amount of speculation in excess of what is necessary to accommodate the hedgers. This index can be expressed as

$$z = 1 + Ss/Hs, \qquad \text{if } Hs > Hl; \text{ or}$$
$$z = 1 + Sl/Hl, \qquad \text{if } Hs < Hl,$$

where Ss=short speculation, Hs=short hedging, Sl=long speculation and Hl=long hedging. For example if z=1, then speculation is minimal. Insofar as a rise in z is due to the entrance of more small traders, the price variance will rise. If the rise in z is due to the entrance of more large commercial and non-commercial traders, price variance will decline.

Equation (3.2) states that, given excess volatility x and the amount of excess speculation z, the variance of the Bayesian error will converge. If x and z are zero, $dy/dt = -y$, i.e. the Bayesian error converges to zero.

The variance of the Bayesian error is driven by a term related to the noisiness of the system and an amount of speculation, of the form $x(r - z)$. The noisiness of the system increases price variance in thin markets, if there is a small amount of speculation $(r > z)$, but as speculation increases $(z > r)$ then the variance of the Bayesian error decreases. The logic of the term $x(r-z)$ is that in thin markets, where there is little speculation $(r > z)$, slight changes in hedging pressure produce large changes in the futures price. Moreover, when there is a low level of speculation the information set of the speculators is small: the speculators in total have taken small samples from the information set. When there is a lot of speculation $(z > r)$, then there is a considerable number of speculators who operate in a Bayesian manner, and take large samples from the information set, as described in Stein, (1992), so that the variance of the sample mean around the population mean (concerning the fundamentals) is low and the market on average is better informed.

Equation (3.3) states again that speculation tends to be stabilizing. Given the noisiness of the system and the Bayesian error, the amount of speculation converges to xy/b. The logic here is that speculation is induced by profits to speculators and the noisiness of the system. The profits of speculators converge, given xy, and are driven to zero when $xy = 0$.

$$(3.3) \quad dz/dt = -bz + xy$$

This is an extremely rich system in its implications for the time series of price changes and amounts of excess speculation. There are three crucial parameters (b,s,r), where r is the most important. Parameter b reflects the speed of convergence of excess speculation to zero. Hence b reflects how speculation affects profits or losses which in turn induce entry or exit of non-commercials into speculative markets. Parameter s reflects the speed of convergence of the volatility to a constant, if the Bayesian errors are given.

Parameter r (which is $d(dy/dt)/dx$ when $y=0$) reflects the critical amount of excess speculation such that speculation is stabilizing. As the noisiness of the system increases, the variance of the Bayesian error will change depending upon the composition of the induced excess speculation, z. If $z < r$, the market is thin, the speculators are dominated by noise traders, and the variance of the Bayesian error rises. But if $z > r$, then there is a broad market of speculators who are dominated by rational traders. Then more noise induces more rational speculators who take samples from the information set and

6

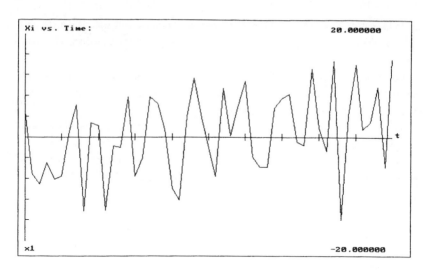

Figure 1

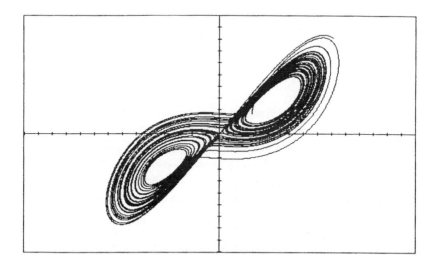

Figure 2

accelerate the process of price discovery. Denote r as the critical amount of speculation.

## 4. Analysis of the Lorenz System

The dynamics of the system depend upon the critical amount of speculation (r) relative to the speeds of convergence (b,s). Almost anything is possible in this system, depending upon the specification of the parameters: asymptotic stability or strange attractors as a special case of chaotic dynamics . A strange attractor is a closed, simply connected region, containing the origin (equilibrium point), such that the vector field is directed everywhere inwards on the boundary. Chaotic dynamics are produced when:

(i) $r > r^*$ and (ii) $s > 1 + b$, where (iii) $r^* = s(s+b+3)/(s-b-1)$.

Thus we may say that chaotic dynamics are   produced when
(iv) $r > r^* > 0$.

There is an economic interpretation of condition (iv), based upon (i)-(iii). First, notice that speculation is stabilizing when it exceeds r, in equation (3.2). Broad markets with a lot of speculation reduce the variance of the Bayesian error, as seen in equation (3.2).    Second, notice the amount of speculation is stable because of the first term in (3.3). There is a critical value of r. If the actual value of parameter r exceeds $r^*$, then condition (i) for chaos is satisfied. If $z > r > r^*$, that is speculation z exceeds r which (is stabilizing in (3.2)) exceeds $r^*$, condition (i) is satisfied.

Third: parameter b in (3.3) reflects the speed of convergence of speculation to zero; and parameter s in (3.1) reflects the speed of convergence of the variance of price changes. Condition (ii) for chaos is that the speed of convergence of speculation to zero should not be too large: it must be less than s-1. For example, column (a) is a set of parameters which yield a strange attractor; and columns (b) and (c) produce asymptotic stability.

| parameters | strange attractor | asymptotic stability | |
|---|---|---|---|
| | (a) | (b) | (c) |
| b | 1 | 1 | 4 |
| s | 5 | 5 | 5 |
| r | 15 | 14 | 15 |

There are important economic implications of this analysis, for the questions and issues raised in the introduction. First, if the economic model were as described by (3.1)-(3.3), then the pattern of the variables would change qualitatively as a result of "slight" changes in parameter values. Compare column (a) with the other two columns.

Second, when the parameters satisfy condition (iv) above, the variables do not follow random walks, but are constrained by the strange attractor. This is a pleasing result to the economist who does not like the random walk conclusion that the variable could end up anywhere. Within the strange attractor, the behavior of the variables seem random.

Third, the behavior of the variables within the strange attractor are qualitatively dependent upon the initial conditions. Each set of initial conditions will generate a different trajectory within the strange attractor. Therefore, without perfect knowledge of the system, it is impossible to predict the movement of the variables except to say that it lies within the strange attractor SA*. Instead of the old concept of equilibrium as a point, we may have a different concept: the equilibrium as a set SA*. The solution stays within the set SA*, but its behavior in that set is unpredictable without perfect knowledge of initial conditions; and its behavior with the equilibrium SA* seems almost indistinguishable from random.

As an illustration of the above discussion consider the Figure 1 depicting the first 100 simulated observations of the x variable of our model. An inspection of this graph may lead an efficient market hypothesis advocate to proclaim that random walk holds. However, this graph is generated by our system of deterministic differential equations.

Examine Figure 2. It clearly demonstrates the existence of a strange attractor for x. Obviously, this illustration is not a mathematical proof since the phase diagram is based on only 5000 observations. Nevertheless, there seems to be a clear pattern which also holds for the other two variables.

## 5. Testing the Chaotic System: Back to Stochastics

Recall that we propose that price volatility, price errors and speculation are dynamically interrelated in the system (3.1)-(3.3).

In our estimation we approximate the system above by

$$(5.1) \qquad x_t - (1-s)x_{t-1} - s y_{t-1}$$

$$(5.2) \qquad y_t - x_{t-1}(r - z_{t-1})$$

$$(5.3) \qquad z_t - (1-b)z_{t-1} + x_{t-1} y_{t-1} \ .$$

Before we discuss econometric estimation we need to describe our data and the definition of the three variables. We have weekly (Friday) settlement futures prices, open interest, and volume of trading contracts mid 1990 to mid 1991 (around 52 observations for each variable) for the three most important agricultural contracts traded at the Chicago Board of Trade: soybeans, corn and wheat.

We define volatility as the annualized standard deviation of actual prices during the

**Table 5.1**

| Values of coefficients from system estimation: |
| :---: |
| $x_t = [1- c(1)] \, x_{t-1} + c(1) \, y_{t-1}$ |
| $y_t = x_{t-1} \, [c(2) - z_{t-1}]$ |
| $z_t = [1- c(3)] \, z_{t-1} + x_{t-1} \, y_{t-1}$ |

| Commodity | Period | c(1) | c(2) | c(3) |
| :---: | :---: | :---: | :---: | :---: |
| Corn | Jul.-Dec. 1990 | 0.0470 (1.6219)* | -5.0957 (-21.9658) | -358.7827 (-2.5248) |
| Corn | Jan.-May 1991 | -0.0182 (-0.7405) | -5.2891 (-14.9401) | -20.0286 (-2.4418) |
| Corn | Mid'90-Mid'91 | 0.0253 (1.2582) | -5.1519 (-26.6335) | -204.1049 (-2.6126) |
| Soybeans | Jul.-Dec. 1990 | 0.0096 (0.3487) | -2.1558 (-8.8256) | -351.1682 (-0.8964) |
| Soybeans | Jan.-May 1991 | -0.0048 (-0.1498) | 2.6764 (-12.6192) | -78.3869 (-3.1661) |
| Soybeans | Mid'90-Mid'91 | 0.0053 (0.2536) | -2.3642 (-14.0872) | -207.2729 (-1.2827) |
| Wheat | Jul.-Dec. 1990 | 0.0769 (2.7245) | -298.3307 (-3.5635) | -13.0968 (-11.3333) |
| Wheat | Jan.-May 1991 | 0.0012 (0.0411) | -5.6681 (-3.5442) | 1.9839 (0.7788) |
| Wheat | Mid'90-Mid'91 | 0.0589 (2.7715) | -235.8173 (-4.1789) | -12.4531 (-14.2118) |

*NOTE: t-statistics are in parentheses.

# Table 5.2

| Wald Coefficient Tests | | | | |
|---|---|---|---|---|
| Model 1: $$x_t = [1 - c(1)] \, x_{t-1} + c(1) \, y_{t-1}$$ $$y_t = x_{t-1} \, [c(2) - z_{t-1}]$$ $$z_t = [1 - c(3)] \, z_{t-1} + x_{t-1} \, y_{t-1}$$ | | | | |
| Parameter Restriction Null Hypotheses | Commodity | Period | $\chi^2$ | Probability |
| Restriction 1 $C(1)=0$ | Corn | Mid 90 - Mid 91 | 5.0422 | 0.0803 |
|  | Soybeans | Mid 90 - Mid 91 | 0.0643 | 0.7997 |
|  | Wheat | Mid 90 - Mid 91 | 7.6817 | 0.0055 |
| Restriction 2 $C(1)=0$ $C(2)=0$ | Corn | Mid 90 - Mid 91 | 709.5517 | 0.0000 |
|  | Soybeans | Mid 90 - Mid 91 | 213.1050 | 0.0000 |
|  | Wheat | Mid 90 - Mid 91 | 26.7233 | 0.0000 |
| Restriction 3 $C(1)=0$ $C(2)=1$ | Corn | Mid 90 - Mid 91 | 1011.527 | 0.0000 |
|  | Soybeans | Mid 90 - Mid 91 | 432.7341 | 0.0000 |
|  | Wheat | Mid 90 - Mid 91 | 26.8786 | 0.0000 |
| Restriction 4 $C(1)=0$ $C(2)=0$ $C(3)=0$ | Corn | Mid 90 - Mid 91 | 862.2086 | 0.0000 |
|  | Soybeans | Mid 90 - Mid 91 | 230.2828 | 0.0000 |
|  | Wheat | Mid 90 - Mid 91 | 250.9293 | 0.0000 |
| Chaotic Hypotheses | Corn | Mid 90 - Mid 91 | 87962.36 | 0.0000 |
| Restriction 1 $C(1)=-5$ $C(2)=15$ $C(3)=-1$ | Soybeans | Mid 90 - Mid 91 | 58169.94 | 0.0000 |
|  | Wheat | Mid 90 - Mid 91 | 57297.17 | 0.0000 |
| Restriction 2 $C(1)=-5$ $C(2)=14$ $C(3)=-1$ | Corn | Mid 90 - Mid 91 | 86543.85 | 0.0000 |
|  | Soybeans | Mid 90 - Mid 91 | 57738.92 | 0.0000 |
|  | Wheat | Mid 90 - Mid 91 | 57296.38 | 0.0000 |
| Restriction 3 $C(1)=-5$ $C(2)=15$ $C(3)=-4$ | Corn | Mid 90 - Mid 91 | 87951.31 | 0.0000 |
|  | Soybeans | Mid 90 - Mid 91 | 58170.07 | 0.0000 |
|  | Wheat | Mid 90 - Mid 91 | 57177.25 | 0.0000 |

past ten weeks (i.e. we use a sample of 10 weekly data to compute a historical standard deviation which is then annualized). The errors are annualized differences between the current futures price today and the futures at the expiration of the contract. When both the futures price of the nearby contract and the cash price converge to become equal, the traders' errors are zero. Finally, we compute the degree of speculation as 1-[open interest/volume]. This definition could be improved if we had daily data about large hedging and speculative positions.

The results are presented in Table 5.1. We use seemingly unrelated regression system estimation method. Because our system is nonlinear, the residuals are recalculated and the residual covariance matrix is updated. Estimation of (5.1)-(5.3) is performed on

$$(5.4) \qquad x_t = [1 - c(1)] \, x_{t-1} + c(1) \, y_{t-1} + \varepsilon_1$$

$$(5.5) \qquad y_t = x_{t-1} \, [c(2) - z_{t-1}] + \varepsilon_2$$

$$(5.6) \qquad z_t = [1 - c(3)] \, z_{t-1} + x_{t-1} \, y_{t-1} + \varepsilon_3$$

and is repeated until convergence is achieved. This technique is asymptotically full information maximum likelihood.

The system in (5.4)-(5.6) is estimated three times for each of the three commodities: corn, soybeans and wheat. First, it is estimated for the second half of 1990, then for the first half of 1991 and finally for the entire sample period. With minor exceptions, the coefficients appear stable, but diagnostics indicate that the model is poorly specified. The appropriateness of our model can be judged by the set of graphs in Figures 3, 4 and 5, where model and actual values are presented for volatility as the dependent variable.

The null hypothesis for a "strange attractor" would be conditions (i)-(iii) above. The random walk hypothesis requires that $c(1)=0$. To have a strange attractor coefficient $r=c(2)$ must exceed unity. A week test is whether coefficient $c(1)=0$, and $c(2)$, which estimates $r$, is significantly greater than unity. These are necessary conditions.

The results presented in Table 5.1 reject the "strange attractor". In all cases coefficient $c(2)$ which estimates $r$ is negative and hence does not exceed unity. In the cases of corn and soybeans, coefficient $c(1)$ is not significantly different from 0. Thus, it is compatible with the random walk, and not the strange attractor hypothesis. The case of wheat generally rejects random walk, $c(1)>0$, but also rejects the strange attractor case.

Table 5.2 presents the results of Wald tests based upon Table 5.1. We are most concerned with price volatility, variable x. The sample period that we focus upon in the text is the longest period mid 1990 to mid 1991. Restriction $c(1)=0$ and $c(2)=0$

12

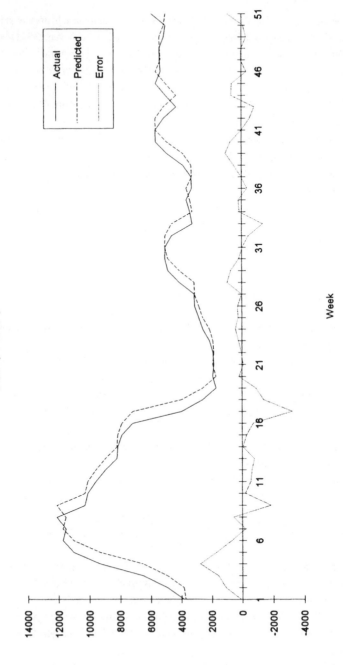

Figure 3: Actual and Predicted Price Volatility in Corn Futures Contracts, using coefficients from Table 5.1 (weekly data July 1990–June 1991)

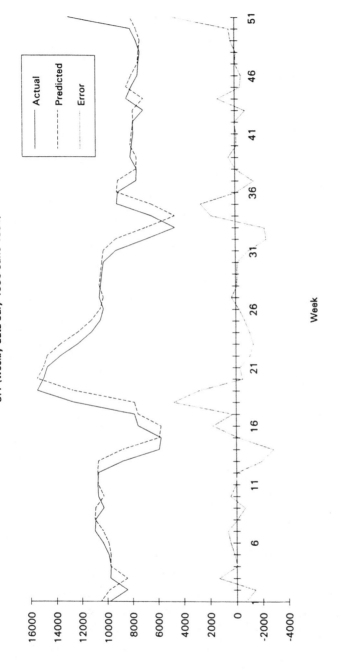

Figure 4: Actual and Predicted Price Volatility in Soybeans Futures Contracts, using coefficients from Table 5.1 (weekly data July 1990–June 1991)

14

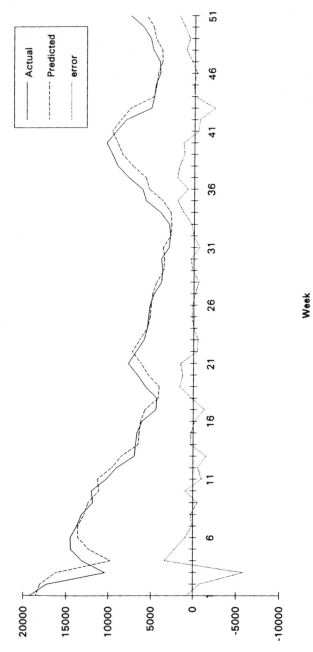

Figure 5: Actual and Predicted Price Volatility in Wheat Futures Contracts, using coefficients from Table 5.1 (weekly data July 1990–June 1991)

would mean that the variance in time t just depends upon its lagged value. However, this restriction is rejected. This means current price variability is not equal to its past value plus an error term, and that past Bayesian error y(t-1) does influence price variability.

Our results suggest that although the theoretical model that we developed is capable of generating a chaotic time series as a special case, the fitted model yields parameter values which support in seven out of nine cases the random walk and in the remaining two cases our deterministic model gives better results than the random walk.

## 6. Conclusions

In this paper we offer a rapid evaluation of the efficient market hypothesis as a theory which claims that the random arrival of relevant information is fully reflected in asset prices. Because information is random so are also prices.

Brock, Hsieh and LeBaron (1991) offer an extensive evaluation of the EMH and empirical evidence that asset prices are not always purely random. Often asset prices appear to be random but once rigorously tested by various techniques of chaotic dynamics are found not to be random. Our goal in this paper is to hypothesize that three important economic variables are related in a particular way described by the chaotic system known as the Lorenz equations.

The three variables we consider are excess asset price volatility, volatility of errors and degree of speculation. The financial formulation that we offer of the Lorenz equations extends the random walk paradigm by replacing errors terms by nonerror variables. Thus the Lorenz equations transform the random walk paradigm into a fully determinist system. This system exhibits a rich variety of trajectories depending on the values of its parameters.

The econometric system estimation of our hypothesized Lorenz model however does not yield coefficient values that would allow us to claim chaotic dynamics. The rejection of the Lorenz system by the data, in most but not all cases, does not mean that researchers should not continue developing models of chaotic dynamics. However, one must realize that despite the numerous shortcomings of the stochastic approach, it remains at the present time, the dominant methodology.

## REFERENCES

Baumol, William and J. Benhabib (1989), Chaos: Significance, Mechanism and Economic Applications. *Journal of Economic Perspectives*: 3, 77-105.

Boldrin, M. and M. Woodford (1990), Equilibrium Models Displaying Endogenous Fluctuations and Chaos. *Journal of Monetary Economics*: 25, 189-222.

Brock, William A., David A. Hsieh and Blake Le Baron (1991), *Nonlinear Dynamics, Chaos and Instability: Statistical Theory and Economic Evidence.* Cambridge, Massachusetts. MIT Press

Brock, William A. (1988), Nonlinearity and Complex Dynamics in Economics and Finance, in *The Economy as an Evolving Complex System*, SFI Studies in the Sciences of Complexity. Addison-Wesley Publishing Company.

Friedman, Milton (1953), The Case for Flexible Exchange Rates, in *Essays in Positive Economics*, University of Chicago Press.

Hart, O. and D. Kreps (1986), Price Destabilizing Speculation. *Journal of Political Economy*: 94, 927-52.

Malliaris A.G. and J.L. Stein (1995), "Micro Analytics of Price Volatility", Working Paper, Department of Economics, Loyola University of Chicago, Chicago, Illinois.

Peck, Anne (1985), The Economic Role of Traditional Commodity Futures Markets in Anne E. Peck (ed.) *Futures Markets: Their Economic Role*. Washington, DC., American Enterprise Institute.

Samuelson, P. (1965), Proof that Properly Anticipated Prices Fluctuate Randomly, *Industrial Management Review*: 6, 41-49.

Shiller, R, (1989), *Market Volatility*, The MIT Press, Cambridge, MA.

Sparrow, C. (1982), *The Lorenz Equations: Bifurcations, Chaos and Strange Attractors*. New York. Springer-Verlag.

Stein, Jerome (1992), Cobwebs, Rational Expectations and Futures Markets. *Review of Economics and Statistics*: 74, 127-34.

Working, Holbrook (1934), A Random-Difference Series for Use in the Analysis of Time Series. *Journal of the American Statistical Association*: 29.

------------------(1949), Investigation of Economic Expectations. *American Economic Review*: 39.

# PART IV

# FINANCIAL FUTURES

# [13]

# Tests of Random Walk of Hedge Ratios and Measures of Hedging Effectiveness for Stock Indexes and Foreign Currencies

A. G. Malliaris

Jorge Urrutia

## INTRODUCTION

Hedging theory in futures markets is developed in Working (1953, 1962), Johnson (1960), Stein (1961), and more recently, Rutledge (1972), Ederington (1979), and Franckle (1980). According to the portfolio theory approach to hedging, the hedge ratio and the measure of hedging effectiveness correspond to the regression coefficient, $B$, and the coefficient of determination, $R^2$, obtained from regressing the spot price changes on futures price changes. The coefficients $B$ and $R^2$ are extensively examined.[1] However, previous studies of hedging performance of futures markets are subject to criticism because they are based on the assumption that the regression coefficient, which corresponds to the hedge ratio, is stable over the whole sample period. Indeed, Grammatikos and Saunders (1983), find that the hedge ratios for five major foreign currency futures are unstable over time. This article further explores the nonstationarity of the hedge ratio and the measure of the hedging effectiveness.

We are grateful to J. Clay Singleton for his useful comments. The article has greatly benefitted from the constructive suggestions of two anonymous referees of The Journal of Futures Markets. We also wish to thank Charles Corrado, George Kaufman, and David Mirza of Loyola University of Chicago for their helpful discussions and encouragement. Finally, we are grateful to Wichai Saenghirunwattana for computational assistance. All remaining errors are ours.

[1]Hedge ratios and measures of hedging effectiveness are estimated for GNMA futures by Ederington (1979), Hill, Liro, and Schneeweis (1983); for foreign currency futures by Hill and Schneeweis (1982), Grammatikos and Saunders (1983) and Grammatikos (1986); for T-bond futures by Hill and Schneeweis (1984); for CD futures by Overdalh and Starleaf (1986); for T-bill futures by Ederington (1979), Franckle (1980), and Howard and D'Antonio (1984); and for stock market index futures by Figlewski (1984, 1985), and Junkus and Lee (1985).

---

*A. G. Malliaris is the Walter F. Mullady, Sr. Professor of Economics at Loyola University of Chicago.*

*Jorge Urrutia is an Assistant Professor of Finance at Loyola University of Chicago.*

The Journal of Futures Markets, Vol. 11, No. 1, 55–68 (1991)

© 1991 by John Wiley & Sons, Inc.          CCC 0270-7314/91/010055-14$04.00

The random walk hypothesis is tested with two models. One is based on the traditional methodology of Dickey and Fuller (1979, 1981) and the other follows the approach of Lo and MacKinlay (1988), known as the variance-ratio test. The empirical results confirm the random walk hypothesis for two stock index futures: Standard and Poor's 500 and New York Stock Exchange; and for four foreign currency futures: British Pound, German Mark, Japanese Yen, and Swiss Franc. The findings imply that hedgers cannot consistently place optimal hedges and that dynamic hedging techniques must be considered.

## HYPOTHESIS OF RANDOM WALK

The main purpose of the article is to detect patterns in the instability of the coefficients $B$ and $R$-squared, postulating that they vary randomly over time. Specifically, it is claimed that the hedge ratio and the measure of hedging effectiveness follow a random walk process.

The concept of a random walk is much more precise in financial analysis than the notion of instability. Authors such as Grammatikos and Saunders (1983) use the term "unstable hedge ratios" to mean that these ratios are not constant over time. In mathematical economic analysis the notion of instability is given a more precise meaning. Numerous definitions, theorems and applications of stability and instability are presented in Brock and Malliaris (1989). Intuitively, one can say that the sequence of hedge ratios $B_0, B_1, B_2, B_3, \ldots$ is unstable if the absolute deviations of these hedge ratios from the equilibrium hedge ratio become large after a certain time period. Clearly, it is difficult to test this notion of instability for at least two reasons: First, one needs a very long sequence and secondly, a precise meaning of "equilibrium hedge ratio" needs to be established.

Attention is devoted here to the nonconstant behavior of hedge ratios and coefficients of hedging effectiveness in terms of random walk, a notion familiar to financial analysts. Random walk may eventually lead to instability but that instability need not necessarily imply random walk. One reason for studying the random walk behavior is the methodological clarification it provides of the time series behavior of the hedge ratio and coefficient of hedging effectiveness.

There are additional reasons for interest in random walk. First, in an efficient market, changes of spot prices over time are random and reflect the arrival of new information. In other words, price changes on any particular day are uncorrelated with past historical price changes. Empirical research in futures markets suggests that futures price changes also follow a random walk, reflecting efficiency in futures markets as well.[2] The hedge ratio is the ratio of dollar amounts invested in a spot asset and a futures contract. It is reasonable to assume that the behavior of this ratio reflects the behavior of these prices. Therefore, given that prices follow a random walk process, one can also expect the hedge ratio to vary randomly over time.

Second, the random walk behavior of the hedge ratio may be explained by the theories of speculation and the effects of such speculation on price changes on both cash and futures markets. There are, in general, two theories about the effects of speculation on price variability. One theory claims that speculation increases price variability because speculators tend to buy as prices are rising and tend to sell as

---

[2]Empirical evidence of the random walk hypothesis for security prices is reported, among others, by Fama (1965), and Fama and Blume (1966); and, for futures markets by Fama (1976), Cornell (1977), and others.

prices are falling, generating a bandwagon effect which contributes to larger swings in price volatility. The opposing theory argues that speculation reduces price variability and has been defended by Milton Friedman (1953) who argues that only unprofitable speculation can have a destabilizing effect on prices. These theories are reviewed extensively by Tirole (1989). Simply put, this article assumes that the stability or instability of speculation, with similar or dissimilar intensity in cash and futures markets, may cause hedge ratios and coefficients of hedging effectiveness to follow random walks.

Third, the random walk behavior of the hedge ratio may be caused by differences in the microstructure of cash and futures markets. In this article, spot prices are determined in dealership markets with futures prices formulated in open outcry auction markets. There is an increasing literature that emphasizes the role of different trading mechanisms with special emphasis given to the role of "noise" and "feedback" traders on price formulation and the time series properties of such prices. A representative article in this literature is Cutler, Poterba, and Summers (1990). It seems reasonable to postulate that such differences in the microstructure of cash and futures markets and dissimilarities in trading mechanisms and types of traders may cause hedge ratios to vary over time.

## DATA

The data correspond to weekly spot prices and futures prices for the nearby contracts (0–3 months) for the following instruments: (i) Stock Indexes: Standard and Poor's 500 Index, and New York Stock Exchange Index; (ii) Foreign Currencies: British Pound, German Mark, Japanese Yen, and Swiss Franc.

The time periods under study extend from March 4, 1980 through December 27, 1988 for the foreign currency instruments and, from January 1, 1984 through December 27, 1988 for the stock index instruments. The futures prices are Tuesday closing prices (Monday or Wednesday closing prices are used when a Tuesday closing price is missing) obtained from the Wall Street Journal.

## METHODOLOGY AND EMPIRICAL RESULTS

First, hedge ratios and measures of hedging effectiveness are generated by means of a moving window regression procedure. Second, the hypothesis that the hedge ratio and the measure of hedging effectiveness follow a random walk process is tested by means of two models. The models are based on the Dickey and Fuller methodology and the variance-ratio approach of Lo and MacKinlay.

### Moving Window Regression Procedure

Estimates of the hedge ratio and the measure of hedging effectiveness are obtained by running OLS regressions of the change of the spot price on the change of the corresponding futures price; that is:

$$S_t - S_{t-k} = A + B(F_t - F_{t-k}) + \epsilon_t \tag{1}$$

where:

$S_t, S_{t-k}$ = spot prices at time $t$ and $t - k$, respectively.
$F_t, F_{t-k}$ = futures prices at time $t$ and $t - k$, respectively.
$k$ = the length of hedging horizon measured in weeks.

In Eq. (1), the regression coefficient, $B$, and the coefficient of determination, $R^2$, correspond to the hedge ratio and the measure of hedging effectiveness, respectively. Since the behavior of the hedge ratio, over time, is of interest, it is assumed that for each contract the hedging horizon, $k$, is two-weeks.[3] The regressions are run using changes in cash and futures prices.[4]

$B$'s and $R^2$'s are generated using an overlapping or moving window regression procedure[5] in two steps. First, the hedge ratios and measures of hedging effectiveness are initially estimated for a one-year period: March 1980–February 1981, for foreign currencies, and January 1984–December 1984 for stock indexes. They are, subsequently, reestimated every quarter by adding a new quarter of spot and futures data and deleting the initial quarter's data and keeping a one-year estimation period. In this way, by regressing the change of the spot price on the change of the futures price, (for a two-week hedging horizon) moving $B$'s and $R^2$'s are estimated for each quarter.[6]

## RANDOM WALK TESTS

The data used in testing for random walk correspond to the hedge ratios and measures of hedging effectiveness obtained from the moving window regressions.

### Dickey and Fuller Tests of Random Walk

To test for random walk using the Dickey and Fuller methodology the following regressions are run:

$$\text{Full: } Y_t = b_0 + b_1 Y_{t-1} + b_2 T + \epsilon_t$$
$$\text{Reduced: } Y_t - Y_{t-1} = b_2 T + \epsilon_t \qquad (2)$$

where:

$Y_t, Y_{t-1}$ = hedge ratio or measure of hedging effectiveness.
$T$ = time trend.
$\epsilon_t$ = residual term at time $t$.

The null hypothesis that the hedge ratio and the measure of hedging effectiveness follow random walks, corresponds to $H_0$: $(b_0, b_1) = (0, 1)$ and is tested with an $F$-test based on a distribution suggested by Dickey and Fuller (1981). The results, presented in Table I for the hedge ratios and in Table II for the measures of hedging effectiveness, show that one cannot reject the null hypothesis at the 1% or 5% levels of significance. That is, the results of the Dickey and Fuller tests presented in

---

[3]The two-week hedging horizon is the most commonly found assumption in the futures hedging literature. See, i.e., Grammatikos and Saunders (1983).

[4]Price changes are used, among others, by Ederington (1979), Franckle (1980), Dale (1981), and Grammatikos and Saunders (1983). Other researchers, such as McCabe and Franckle (1983), Hammer (1988), use percentage changes or natural logarithm of prices. Some tests using percentage price changes were conducted (not reported here) which do not change the results.

[5]The same procedure is used by Grammatikos and Saunders (1983).

[6]The hedge ratios and measures of hedging effectiveness obtained from this procedure exhibit major deviations from the average long-term $B$'s and $R^2$'s. The average long-term hedge ratios and measure of hedging effectiveness are estimated by running the OLS regression (1) for the full time periods. These results indicate that the hedge ratio and the measure of hedging effectiveness are unstable over time, which confirms earlier results found in the literature. The average long-term $B$'s and $R^2$'s and the $B$'s and $R^2$'s estimated from the moving window regression procedure are not reported here for the sake of space but they are available from the authors upon request.

these two tables indicate that the hedge ratios and the measures of hedging effectiveness follow random walk processes.

### Variance Ratio Tests of Random Walk

The regression models postulated in Eq. (2) assume that the disturbances $\epsilon_t$ are independent and identically distributed gaussian random variables. However, there is mounting evidence that financial time series posses time-varying volatilities and deviate from normality. Lo and MacKinlay (1988) have developed a test-statistic for random walk which is sensitive to correlated price changes but which is otherwise robust with respect to many forms of heteroskedasticity and nonnormality of the random disturbances. This new test of random walk is known as the variance-ratio test. This article adopts the Lo and MacKinlay approach to reinforce the results of the Dickey and Fuller test and to provide further empirical evidence that the hedge ratios and the measures of hedging effectiveness are governed by a random walk behavior.

The intuition behind the variance ratio test is the following: If the natural logarithm of a time series denoted $Y_t$, is a pure random walk of the form

$$Y_t = \mu + Y_{t-1} + \epsilon_t$$

then, the variance of its $k$-differences grows linearly with the difference $k$. For example, the variance of monthly sampled series must be four times as large as the variance of a weekly sampled series. That is, if the series follows a random walk, it must be the case that the variance of the $k$-differences is $k$ times the variance of the first-difference:

$$VAR(Y_t - Y_{t-k}) = kVAR(Y_t - Y_{t-1}).$$

Therefore, under the random walk hypothesis, the ratio of $(1/k)$ times the variance of the $k$-differences over the variance of the first-differences is expected to be equal to one. In other words, a test of random walk is equivalent to testing the null hypothesis:

$$H_0 : (1/k)VAR(Y_t - Y_{t-k})/VAR(Y_t - Y_{t-1}) = 1.$$

The results of the variance ratio tests shown in Table III and IV indicate that one cannot reject the null hypothesis. In fact, the variance ratios are not statistically different from one at the 5% level of significance. Thus, the results of the variance ratio tests reinforce those reported by the Dickey and Fuller methodology and indicate the robustness of the random walk hypothesis for the hedge ratios and the measures of hedging effectiveness.

A slightly different interpretation of the variance ratio test is given by Cochrane (1988) who argues that a series can be decomposed into fluctuations that are partly temporary and partly permanent. The random walk carries the permanent component of a change and the stationary series carries the temporary part of a change. In this case, the $(1/k)VAR(Y_t - Y_{t-k})$ should settle down to the variance of the shock of the random walk or permanent component. Therefore, the variance ratio corresponds to an estimate of the measure of the random component of the series. Following Cochrane's argument, the large variance ratios reported in Table III and IV seem to indicate that hedge ratios and measures of hedging effectiveness contain a large permanent or random walk component and a small temporary component.

**Table I**

**TEST OF RANDOM WALK OF THE HEDGE RATIO**

Model: Full: $Y_t = b_0 + b_1 Y_{t-1} + b_2 T + \epsilon_t$   Reduced: $Y_t - Y_{t-1} = b_2 T + \epsilon_t$

$$H_0: (b_0, b_1) = (0, 1) \qquad F = \frac{(SSE_R - SSE_F)/2}{SSE_F/(n-3)}$$

| Futures Contract | Model | Coefficients of Independent Variables (t values and std. errors in parenthesis) | | | $R^2$ (adj.) (F) (pr.) | SSE | F | F critical[c] 5%, 1% |
|---|---|---|---|---|---|---|---|---|
| | | $b_0$ | $b_1$ | $b_2$ | | | | |
| British Pound | Full | 0.34421 (3.561) (0.0966) | 0.62142 (5.262) (0.11809) | 0.00064 (0.402) (0.00159) | 0.5586 (19.98) (0.0001) | 0.13089 | 6.665[b] | 5.18 |
| | Reduced | | | 0.00022 (0.289) (0.00075) | 0.0028 (0.084) (0.774) | 0.19320 | | 7.18 |
| German Mark | Full | 0.26772 (2.40) (0.11137) | 0.71606 (5.64) (0.12688) | 0.00028 (0.320) (0.00088) | 0.6398 (27.642) (0.0001) | 0.03328 | 3.664[a] | 5.18 |
| | Reduced | | | 0.0000004 (0.001) (0.00035) | 0.0001 (0.00) (0.9991) | 0.04199 | | 7.18 |
| Japanese Yen | Full | 0.14813 (1.50) (0.09888) | 0.81930 (7.62) (0.10757) | 0.00064 (0.33) (0.00191) | 0.6556 (29.55) (0.0001) | 0.25216 | 1.425[a] | 5.18 |

| Market | Model | | | | | $R^2$ | F | F-critical |
|---|---|---|---|---|---|---|---|---|
|  | Reduced |  |  | 0.000056 (0.063) (0.00090) | 0.0001 (0.004) (0.9505) | 0.27782 |  | 7.18 |
| Swiss Franc | Full | 0.24742 (2.22) (0.11124) | 0.70227 (5.28) (0.13291) | 0.001592 (1.50) (0.00106) | 0.6887 (34.19) (0.0001) | 0.04604 | 2.512[a] | 5.18 |
|  | Reduced |  |  | 0.000105 (0.263) (0.000398) | 0.0023 (0.069) (0.7946) | 0.05430 |  | 5.18 |
| S&P 500 | Full | 0.271952 (1.80) (0.15142) | 0.64774 (3.67) (0.17650) | 0.002106 (0.90) (0.002353) | 0.3832 (7.21) (0.0050) | 0.076685 | 2.269[a] | 5.18 |
|  | Reduced |  |  | 0.000434 (0.39) (0.001125) | 0.0074 (0.15) (0.7035) | 0.096020 |  | 7.18 |
| NYSE | Full | 0.229945 (1.74) (0.13204) | 0.671400 (3.98) (0.16857) | 0.004161 (1.05) (0.003976) | 0.5377 (12.63) (0.0004) | 0.178330 | 1.920[a] | 5.18 |
|  | Reduced |  |  | 0.000174 (0.103) (0.001689) | 0.0005 (0.011) (0.92) | 0.216376 |  | 7.18 |

[a] The null hypothesis cannot be rejected at the 5% confidence level.
[b] The null hypothesis cannot be rejected at the 1% confidence level.
[c] F-critical obtained from Table IV of Dickey and Fuller (1981).

## Table II
### TEST OF RANDOM WALK OF THE MEASURE OF HEDGING EFFECTIVENESS

Model: Full: $Y_t = b_0 + b_1 Y_{t-1} + b_2 T + \epsilon_t$   Reduced: $Y_t - Y_{t-1} = b_2 T + \epsilon_t$

$H_0: (b_0, b_1) = (0,1)$   $F = \dfrac{(SSE_R - SSE_F)/2}{SSE_F/(n-3)}$

| Futures Contract | Model | Coefficients of Independent Variables (t values and std. errors in parenthesis) | | | $R^2$ (adj.) (F) (pr.) | SSE | F | F critical[c] 5%, 1% |
|---|---|---|---|---|---|---|---|---|
| | | $b_0$ | $b_1$ | $b_2$ | | | | |
| British Pound | Full | 0.36964 (3.55) (0.10406) | 0.60958 (4.90) (0.12441) | -0.00087 (-0.52) (0.00169) | 0.4435 (12.95) (0.0001) | 0.17095 | 6.716[b] | 5.18 |
| | Reduced | | | -0.00019 (-0.226) (0.00086) | 0.0017 (0.051) (0.8225) | 0.25296 | | 7.18 |
| German Mark | Full | 0.26518 (2.85) (0.09322) | 0.73544 (6.98) (0.10541) | -0.00110 (-1.65) (0.00067) | 0.6164 (25.10) (0.0001) | 0.02589 | 7.122[b] | 5.18 |
| | Reduced | | | -0.00024 (-0.719) (0.00034) | 0.0170 (0.518) (0.4774) | 0.03906 | | 7.18 |
| Japanese Yen | Full | 0.24210 (2.24) (0.10796) | 0.72008 (5.83) (0.12344) | 0.00119 (1.75) (0.00068) | 0.7739 (47.93) (0.0001) | 0.01707 | 2.583[a] | 5.18 |

|  |  |  |  |  |  |  |  |  |
|---|---|---|---|---|---|---|---|---|
|  | Reduced |  |  | 0.00005 (0.208) (0.00024) | 0.0014 (0.043) (0.8364) | 0.2022 |  | 7.18 |
| Swiss Franc | Full | 0.33621 (2.64) (0.12756) | 0.61320 (4.03) (0.152028) | 0.001204 (1.15) (0.00047) | 0.5827 (21.95) (0.0001) | 0.04135 | 3.680[a] | 5.18 |
|  | Reduced |  |  | 0.000048 (0.123) (0.000390) | 0.0005 (0.015) (0.9031) | 0.05222 |  | 7.18 |
| S&P 500 | Full | 0.362901 (2.58) (0.140466) | 0.447433 (2.24) (0.19939) | 0.007037 (2.31) (0.003046) | 0.5504 (13.24) (0.0003) | 0.081003 | 3.958[a] | 5.18 |
|  | Reduced |  |  | 0.00850 (0.69) (0.00124) | 0.023 (0.47) (0.50) | 0.116630 |  | 7.18 |
| NYSE | Full | 0.250761 (1.80) (0.139585) | 0.635419 (3.45) (0.184028) | 0.003848 (1.53) (0.002521) | 0.4813 (10.28) (0.0011) | 0.77059 | 2.134[a] | 5.18 |
|  | Reduced |  |  | 0.000848 (0.76) (0.001121) | 0.028 (0.57) (0.4580) | 0.095328 |  | 7.18 |

[a]The null hypothesis cannot be rejected at the 5% confidence level.
[b]The null hypothesis cannot be rejected at the 1% confidence level.
[c]F-critical obtained from Table IV of Dickey and Fuller (1981).

Table III

VARIANCE RATIO TEST OF RANDOM WALK HYPOTHESIS OF THE HEDGE RATIO*

| Foreign Currency | | 1 | 2 | 3 | 4 | 5 | 6 | 7 | 8 |
|---|---|---|---|---|---|---|---|---|---|
| | | | | | *k* (quarters) | | | | |
| British Pound | $\sigma_k^2$ | 0.009440 | 0.006844 | 0.008301 | 0.007653 | 0.007367 | 0.006999 | 0.006442 | 0.006033 |
| | $\sigma_k^2/\sigma_1^2$ | 1.0000 | 0.7250 | 0.8793 | 0.8107 | 0.7804 | 0.7414 | 0.6842 | 0.6391 |
| | $Z_k$ | | −1.506 | −0.443 | −0.554 | −0.549 | −0.573 | −0.638 | −0.668 |
| German Mark | $\sigma_k^2$ | 0.001558 | 0.001944 | 0.001823 | 0.001694 | 0.001535 | 0.001365 | 0.001281 | 0.001125 |
| | $\sigma_k^2/\sigma_1^2$ | 1.0000 | 1.2478 | 1.1701 | 1.0873 | 0.9852 | 0.8761 | 0.8222 | 0.7221 |
| | $Z_k$ | | 1.357 | 0.625 | 0.256 | −0.037 | −0.275 | −0.357 | −0.515 |
| Japanese Yen | $\sigma_k^2$ | 0.021903 | 0.020844 | 0.025015 | 0.030200 | 0.029728 | 0.031345 | 0.031014 | 0.030229 |
| | $\sigma_k^2/\sigma_1^2$ | 1.0000 | 0.9517 | 1.1421 | 1.3788 | 1.3573 | 1.4311 | 1.4160 | 1.3801 |
| | $Z_k$ | | −0.265 | 0.522 | 1.109 | 0.893 | 0.955 | 0.836 | 0.704 |
| Swiss Franc | $\sigma_k^2$ | 0.002235 | 0.002663 | 0.003149 | 0.003344 | 0.003012 | 0.002568 | 0.002201 | 0.001942 |
| | $\sigma_k^2/\sigma_1^2$ | 1.0000 | 1.1915 | 1.4089 | 1.4962 | 1.3477 | 1.1490 | 0.9848 | 0.8689 |
| | $Z_k$ | | 1.049 | 1.502 | 1.453 | 0.869 | 0.330 | −0.031 | −0.243 |
| S&P 500 | $\sigma_k^2$ | 0.007440 | 0.006796 | 0.006847 | 0.007722 | 0.006765 | 0.006025 | 0.005098 | 0.004458 |
| | $\sigma_k^2/\sigma_1^2$ | 1.0000 | 0.9134 | 0.9203 | 1.0379 | 0.9093 | 0.8098 | 0.6852 | 0.5992 |
| | $Z_k$ | | −0.387 | −0.239 | 0.091 | −0.185 | −0.344 | −0.516 | −0.606 |
| NYSE | $\sigma_k^2$ | 0.014981 | 0.016598 | 0.017452 | 0.018396 | 0.015934 | 0.013222 | 0.011540 | 0.011628 |
| | $\sigma_k^2/\sigma_1^2$ | 1.0000 | 1.1079 | 1.1649 | 1.2280 | 1.0636 | 0.8826 | 0.7703 | 0.7762 |
| | $Z_k$ | | 0.483 | 0.495 | 0.545 | 1.298 | −0.212 | −0.377 | −0.338 |

*$\sigma_k^2$ corresponds to $1/k$ times the variance of the $k$-differences, that is, $\sigma_k^2 = (1/k) \, \mathrm{VAR}\,(Y_t - Y_{t-k})$; $\sigma_k^2/\sigma_1^2$ is the variance ratio, and $Z_k$ is the normal $Z$-statistics with $Z_{crit} = 1.96$ for a two-tailed test at the 5 percent of significance level.

Table IV
VARIANCE RATIO TEST OF RANDOM WALK HYPOTHESIS OF THE MEASURE OF HEDGING EFFECTIVENESS*

| Foreign Currency | | $k$ (quarters) | | | | | | | |
|---|---|---|---|---|---|---|---|---|---|
| | | 1 | 2 | 3 | 4 | 5 | 6 | 7 | 8 |
| British Pound | $\sigma_k^2$ | 0.013937 | 0.011529 | 0.011872 | 0.013629 | 0.012063 | 0.010886 | 0.010201 | 0.009716 |
| | $\sigma_k^2/\sigma_1^2$ | 1.0000 | 0.8272 | 0.8518 | 0.9779 | 0.8655 | 0.7811 | 0.7319 | 0.6971 |
| | $Z_k$ | | −0.962 | −0.554 | −0.066 | −0.342 | −0.493 | −0.548 | −0.570 |
| German Mark | $\sigma_k^2$ | 0.001673 | 0.002183 | 0.002444 | 0.002228 | 0.001928 | 0.001861 | 0.001855 | 0.001931 |
| | $\sigma_k^2/\sigma_1^2$ | 1.0000 | 1.3048 | 1.4608 | 1.3317 | 1.1524 | 1.1124 | 1.1088 | 1.1542 |
| | $Z_k$ | | 1.697 | 1.721 | 0.987 | 0.387 | 0.253 | 0.222 | 0.290 |
| Japanese Yen | $\sigma_k^2$ | 0.000816 | 0.001048 | 0.001276 | 0.001373 | 0.001365 | 0.001213 | 0.001051 | 0.000868 |
| | $\sigma_k^2/\sigma_1^2$ | 1.0000 | 1.2843 | 1.5637 | 1.6826 | 1.6728 | 1.4865 | 1.2880 | 1.0637 |
| | $Z_k$ | | 1.583 | 2.105 | 2.031 | 1.710 | 1.096 | 0.588 | 0.120 |
| Swiss Franc | $\sigma_k^2$ | 0.002417 | 0.001358 | 0.001682 | 0.001587 | 0.001336 | 0.001528 | 0.001453 | 0.001551 |
| | $\sigma_k^2/\sigma_1^2$ | 1.0000 | 0.5619 | 0.6959 | 0.6566 | 0.5528 | 0.6322 | 0.6012 | 0.6417 |
| | $Z_k$ | | −2.439 | −1.136 | −1.022 | −1.136 | −0.8280 | −0.815 | −0.674 |
| S&P 500 | $\sigma_k^2$ | 0.009756 | 0.005874 | 0.005990 | 0.006180 | 0.005572 | 0.005345 | 0.005652 | 0.006282 |
| | $\sigma_k^2/\sigma_1^2$ | 1.0000 | 0.6021 | 0.6140 | 0.6335 | 0.5711 | 0.5479 | 0.5793 | 0.6439 |
| | $Z_k$ | | −1.823 | −1.187 | −0.898 | −0.897 | −0.838 | −0.707 | −0.552 |
| NYSE | $\sigma_k^2$ | 0.008596 | 0.010899 | 0.012479 | 0.012484 | 0.010790 | 0.009658 | 0.008448 | 0.00784 |
| | $\sigma_k^2/\sigma_1^2$ | 1.0000 | 1.2679 | 1.4517 | 1.4523 | 1.2552 | 1.1235 | 0.9828 | 0.9160 |
| | $Z_k$ | | 1.2277 | 1.389 | 1.108 | 0.534 | 0.229 | −0.029 | −0.130 |

*$\sigma_k^2$ corresponds to $1/k$ times the variance of the $k$-differences, that is, $\sigma_k^2 = (1/k) \, VAR \, (Y_t - Y_{t-k})$; $\sigma_k^2/\sigma_1^2$ is the variance ratio, and $Z_k$ is the normal Z-statistics with $Z_{crit} = 1.96$ for a two-tailed test at the 5 percent of significance level.

## DISCUSSION OF RESULTS

The empirical tests confirm the hypothesis that the hedge ratios and the measures of hedging effectiveness follow a random walk. One way of interpreting these results is to think in terms of market efficiency. In this sense, the findings reinforce previous research confirming market efficiency in both spot and futures markets. The major implication of this random walk hypothesis is that hedgers cannot consistently place perfect hedges and need to continuously readjust their hedges. This can be done by using appropriate computational methods that take into account the variable nature of the hedge ratio and the measure of hedging effectiveness. A few of these methods are briefly summarized below.

Cechetti, Cumby, and Figlewski (1986) apply the Autoregressive Conditional Heteroskedasticity (ARCH) method to hedging in futures markets. Their approach maximizes the expected logarithmic utility of an investor and gives estimates of optimal hedges. Another methodology which measures hedging effectiveness and which avoids many of the estimation problems caused by nonstationarity in expected returns, is developed in McCabe and Solberg (forthcoming). This technique is based on conditional probability distributions, and the results reported by the authors indicate that varying assumptions about conditional expectations can greatly alter the effectiveness measures. Anderson and Danthine (1982) propose a multi-period model of hedging which allows for the futures position to be revised within the cash market holding period. Finally, Herbst, Kare, and Coples (1989) estimate optimal hedge ratios by using the ARIMA methodology of Box and Jenkins. Their approach successfully solves the problem of autoregressive disturbances.

The findings of this research imply that the already complex relationships among hedge ratios, measures of hedging effectiveness, volume of trade and open interest require further empirical research. Individual investors, institutional investors, and corporations seeking to reduce or eliminate risk are aware that the hedging process is complicated. It is possible that dynamic hedging is more costly than traditional hedging because the continuous readjustment of the hedge might increase transaction costs. However, the opposite effect is also possible. Herbst, Kare, and Coples (1989) report that their hedge ratios are lower than those rendered by the traditional OLS regression technique which implies a reduction in the required margin deposit and in commissions incurred by hedgers.

# Bibliography

Anderson, Ronald W., and Danthine, Jean-Pierre. (1982): "The Time Pattern of Hedging and the Volatility of Futures Prices," *Review of Economic Studies,* 50:249–265.

Brock, W. A., and Malliaris, A. G. (1989): *Differential Equations, Stability and Chaos in Dynamic Economics,* North Holland Publishing Company, Amsterdam and New York.

Cechetti, Stephen, Cumby, Robert, and Figlewski, Stephen. (1986): "Estimation of the Optimal Futures Hedge," WP Series Graduate School of Business, New York University.

Cochrane, John H. (1988): "How Big Is the Random Walk in GNP?," *Journal of Political Economy,* 96:833–920.

Cornell, B. (1977): "Spot Rates, Forward Rates and Exchanges Market Efficiency," *Journal of Financial Economics,* 5:55–65.

Cutler, D., Poterba, J., and Summers, L. (1990): "Speculative Dynamics and the Role of Feedback Traders," *American Economic Review: Papers and Proceedings,* 80:63–68.

Dale, C. (1981): "The Hedging Effectiveness of Currency Futures Markets," *The Journal of Futures Markets,* 1:77–88.

Dickey, D. A., and Fuller, W. A. (1979): "Distribution of the Estimators of the Autoregressive Time Series With A Unit Root," *Journal of the American Statistical Association,* 74:427–431.

Dickey, D. A., and Fuller, W. A. (1981): "Likelihood Ratio Statistics for Autoregressive Time Series With A Unit Root," *Econometrica,* 49:1057–1072.

Ederington, L. H. (1979): "The Hedging Performance of the New Futures Markets," *Journal of Finance,* 34:157–170.

Fama, E. (1976): "Forward Rates as Predictors of Futures Spot Rates," *Journal of Financial Economics,* 3:361–377.

Fama, E. (1965): "The Behavior of Stock Market Prices," *Journal of Business,* 38:38–105.

Fama, E., and Blume, M. (1966): "Filter Rules and Stock-Market Trading," *Journal of Business,* 39:226–241.

Figlewski, Stephen. (1985): "Hedging With Stock Index Futures: Theory and Application In a New Market," *The Journal of Futures Markets,* 5:183–199.

Figlewski, Stephen. (1984): "Hedging Performance and Basis Risk in Stock Index Futures," *The Journal of Finance,* 39:657–669.

Franckle, Charles T. (1980): "The Hedging Performance of the New Futures Markets: Comments," *The Journal of Finance,* 35:1273–1279.

Friedman, M. (1953): "Essays in Positive Economics," Chicago: University of Chicago Press.

Grammatikos, Theoharry. (1986): "Intervalling Effects, and the Hedging Performance of Foreign Currency Futures," *Journal of Financial Research,* 5:95–104.

Grammatikos, T., and Saunders, Anthony. (1983): "Stability and the Hedging Performance of Foreign Currency Futures," *Journal of Futures Markets,* 3:295–305.

Hammer, Jerry A. (1988): "Hedging and Risk Aversion in the Foreign Currency Market," *Journal of Futures Markets,* 8:657–686.

Herbst, A. F., Kare, D. D., and Coples, S. C. (1989): "Hedging Effectiveness and Minimum Risk Hedge Ratios in the Presence of Autocorrelation: Foreign Currency Futures," *The Journal of Futures Markets,* 9:185–197.

Hill, Joanne, and Schneeweis, Thomas. (1982): "The Hedging Effectiveness of Foreign Currency Futures," *Journal of Financial Research,* 5:95–104.

Hill, Joanne, and Schneeweis, Thomas. (1984): "Reducing Volatility with Financial Futures," *Financial Analysts Journal,* 40:34–40.

Hill, Joanne, Liro, Joseph, and Schneeweis, Thomas. (1983): "Hedging Performance of GNMA Futures Under Rising and Falling Interest Rates," *Journal of Futures Markets,* 3:403–413.

Howard, Charles T., and D'Antonio, Louis J. (1984): "A Risk-Return Measure of Hedging Effectiveness," *Journal of Financial and Quantitative Analysis,* 19:101–112.

Johnson, L. (1960): "The Theory of Hedging and Speculation in Commodity Futures," *Review of Economic Studies,* 27:139–151.

Junkus, Joan C., and Lee, Cheng F. (1985): "Use of Three Stock Index Futures in Hedging Decisions," *Journal of Futures Markets,* 5:201–222.

Lo, A., and MacKinlay, A. C. (1988): "Stock Market Prices Do Not Follow Random Walks: Evidence From A Simple Specification Test," *Review of Financial Studies,* 1:41–66.

McCabe, George M., and Solberg, Donald P. (1988): "Hedging in the Treasury Bill Futures Markets When the Hedged Instrument and the Deliverable Instrument Are Not Matched," Working paper University of Nebraska, forthcoming in *Journal of Financial Management.*

McCabe, George M., and Franckle, Charles T. (1983): "The Effectiveness of Rolling the Hedge Forward in the Treasury Bill Futures Market," *Journal of Financial Management,* 12:21–29.

Overdahl, James A., and Starleaf, Dennis R. (1986): "The Hedging Performance of the CD Futures Markets," *Journal of Futures Markets,* 6:71–81.

Rutledge, D. J. S. (1972): "Hedgers' Demand for Futures Contracts: A Theoretical Framework With Applications to the United States Soy-Bean Complex," *Food Research Institute Studies,* 11:237–256.

Stein, J. L. (1961): "The Simultaneous Determination of Spot and Futures Prices," *American Economic Review,* 51:1012–1025.

Tirole, Jean. (1989): "Theories of Speculation," in Bhattacharya S. and G. M. Constantinides, Ed, *Financial Markets and Incomplete Information,* Rowman and Littlefield Publishers, Inc., Totowa, N. J.

Working, H. (1953): "Futures Trading and Hedging," *American Economic Review,* 43: 314–343.

Working, H. (1962): "New Concepts Concerning Futures Markets and Prices," *American Economic Review,* 52:431–459.

# [14]

# The Impact of the Lengths of Estimation Periods and Hedging Horizons on the Effectiveness of a Hedge: Evidence from Foreign Currency Futures

A. G. Malliaris
Jorge L. Urrutia

## INTRODUCTION

Johnson (1960), Stein (1961), and more recently, Ederington (1979), McEnally and Rice (1979), Franckle (1980), and Hill and Schneeweis (1982) apply the principles of portfolio theory to show that the optimal or minimum-risk hedge ratio of a futures contract is given by the ratio of the covariance between the changes in the spot and futures prices and the variance of the changes in the futures prices. The hedger's objective is to minimize the variance of price changes:

$$\text{Min Var}(\Delta H_t) = \text{Var}(\Delta S_t) + N_f^2 \text{Var}(\Delta F_t) + 2N_f \text{Cov}(\Delta S_t, \Delta F_t) \qquad (1)$$

s.t.

$$\Delta H_t = E(\Delta S_t) + N_f E(\Delta F_t)$$

where: $\Delta S_t$, $\Delta F_t$ = price changes during period $t$ of the spot currency and the futures contract, respectively; and $\Delta H_t$ = target change in value (or target profit from the hedged portfolio) during period $t$ of a portfolio composed of one unit of the spot currency and $N_f$ units of the futures contract.

We are thankful to the Columbia Futures Center for supplying us with some data used in this study and to Wichai Saenghirunwattana for computational assistance. Two anonymous referees and Mark Powers of this *Journal* provided us with excellent comments which helped us greatly in improving our paper. Any errors are our responsibility.

---

*A. G. Malliaris is the Walter F. Mullady Professor of Economics at Loyola University of Chicago.*

*Jorge L. Urrutia is an Assistant Professor of Finance at Loyola University of Chicago.*

The Journal of Futures Markets, Vol. 11, No. 3, 271–289 (1991)
© 1991 by John Wiley & Sons, Inc.                    CCC 0270-7314/91/030271-19$04.00

The minimum-risk hedge ratio is determined by setting the derivative of the hedged portfolio variance with respect to $N_f$ equal to zero and solving for $N_f^*$:

$$N_f^* = -\frac{\text{Cov}(\Delta S_t, \Delta F_t)}{\text{Var}(\Delta F_t)} \tag{2}$$

The optimal or minimum-risk hedge ratio is equivalent to the negative of the slope coefficient of a regression of spot price changes on futures price changes. That is, $N_f^*$ can be estimated by running an OLS regression with $\Delta S$ as the dependent variable and $\Delta F$ as the independent variable:

$$\Delta S_t = a + b\Delta F_t + \varepsilon_t \tag{3}$$

where $b = N_f^* = $ beta or optimal hedge ratio.

The above regression gives the optimal or correct hedge ratio for a particular dataset. The effectiveness of the minimum-variance hedge can be determined by examining the percentage of risk reduced by the hedge. The measure of hedging effectiveness is defined as the ratio of the variance of the unhedged position, $\text{Var}(U)$, minus the variance of the hedged position, $\text{Var}(H)$, over the variance of the unhedged position:

$$E_f = \frac{\text{Var}(U) - \text{Var}(H)}{\text{Var}(U)} = 1 - \frac{\text{Var}(H)}{\text{Var}(U)}, \tag{4}$$

where $E_f$ denotes the measure of hedging effectiveness. Ederington (1979) shows also that $E_f$ is equal to $R^2$, the coefficient of determination of the OLS regression of eq. (3). That is,

$$E_f = R^2 = \frac{N_f^2 \, \text{Var}(\Delta F_t)}{\text{Var}(\Delta S_t)} \tag{5}$$

Given that $R^2$ is the square of the correlation coefficient, the higher the correlation between spot and futures price changes, the more effective the futures contract is as a hedging instrument, provided the $R^2$ is correctly interpreted as suggested by Lindahl (1989).

Minimum-risk hedge ratios and measures of hedging effectiveness are estimated for GNMA futures by Ederington (1979), Hill, Liro, and Schneeweis (1983), and Hill and Schneeweis (1984); for foreign currency futures by Hill and Schneeweis (1981, 1984), Grammatikos and Saunders (1983), and Grammatikos (1986); for CD futures by Overdahl and Starleaf (1986); for T-bill futures, by Ederington (1979), Franckle (1980), and Howard and D'Antonio (1984); and for stock market index futures by Figlewski (1984, 1985) and Junkus and Lee (1985).

The major conclusions of these studies are: (1) futures contracts perform well as hedging vehicles, (2) optimal hedge ratios are less than one, and (3) hedge ratios and measures of hedging effectiveness change with the length of the hedging horizon. Grammatikos and Saunders (1983) criticize previous studies of hedging performance of futures markets that use regression analysis. They examine the question of hedge ratio stability (which is an implicit assumption of the OLS regression) for five major foreign currency futures and find that hedge ratios are unstable over time. Instability of hedge ratios and measures of hedging effectiveness is reported also by Malliaris and Urrutia (1991).[1]

This article further explores the consequences of changes in the hedge ratio and measure of hedging effectiveness. The analysis concentrates on determining the impact on the effectiveness of the hedge by the length of the estimation period (i.e., the number of observations in the sample used in estimating betas and $R^2$'s by running OLS regressions) and the length of the hedging horizon (i.e., the length of the period the hedge is in effect). The data cover the period from March 4, 1980 to December 27, 1988, and correspond to spot exchange rates and nearby settlement futures prices for five foreign currencies: British pound, Japanese yen, Canadian dollar, German mark, and Swiss franc.

## MOTIVATION OF THE RESEARCH

The motivation of this study is two-fold. First, the effect of changes in the length of the estimation period on the effectiveness of the hedge is examined. It is postulated that if hedge ratios are constant over time, then a longer estimation period should give a better estimate of the futures beta and improve the effectiveness of the hedge. If, on the other hand, hedge ratios are changing over time, then using data from long ago may lead to a poorer estimate of the futures beta and worsen the effectiveness of the hedge. In other words, if betas are unstable, the use of shorter estimation periods is advisable because they should give better hedges. Shorter estimation periods also save time and money because smaller data samples are easier to collect and analyze.

Second, the length of the hedging horizon is examined to see if it impacts on the effectiveness of the hedge. It is postulated that, if shorter hedges are more effective than longer ones, then hedgers are better off hedging their cash position for shorter periods of time, recomputing their hedge ratios, and rolling the hedges over rather than keeping the hedge for longer periods of time. If the opposite is true, then longer hedging horizons are advisable.

There are no theoretical guidelines in addressing both problems, that is, the impact of the length of the estimation period and the length of the hedging horizon on the effectiveness of a hedge. The modern portfolio theory approach to futures hedging derives the optimal hedge as the beta of a specific regression but offers no clues as to the length of the estimation period nor the appropriate length of the hedging horizon. Obviously, foreign exchange hedgers consider both issues of great practical significance.

The hedging issues addressed in this study are irrelevant for foreign currencies if one considers forward contracts instead of futures contracts. For example, if a firm has a 30-day yen liability, it can buy Yen forward and it is perfectly hedged. The emphasis here is on the futures markets because, in many cases of both real and theoretical interest, use of futures is unavoidable.

---

[1]The notion of hedge ratio instability is not given a rigorous definition in the futures literature. It is used to indicate that the hedge ratio does not remain constant over time. Malliaris and Urrutia (1991) confirm earlier results by other authors that hedge ratios for several foreign currencies change over time and go further to investigate the time series characteristics of these changing hedge ratios. For a rigorous mathematical definition of the notion of instability as used in economic analysis see Brock and Malliaris (1989).

## DATA

The data correspond to weekly spot exchange rates and settlement futures prices for the nearby contract (0–3 months) for five foreign currencies traded in the International Monetary Market of the Chicago Mercantile Exchange: British pound, German mark, Canadian dollar, Japanese yen, and Swiss franc. Spot exchange rates, and nearby settlement futures contract prices are from the Center for Futures Markets of Columbia University and from the *Wall Street Journal* for the time period March 4, 1980 to December 27, 1988. Weekly Monday settlement prices are used to minimize the possible influence of the release of U.S. Treasury bills auction results. Usually, the U.S. Treasury releases the results of its weekly short-term T-bill auction after currency futures markets close on Monday. Therefore, Monday foreign currency settlement prices are not affected by short-term interest rates determined in this auction.[2]

## METHODOLOGICAL REMARKS

Ederington's technique of estimating optimal minimum risk hedge ratios using ordinary least squares (OLS) regression yields unbiased estimates only when the data satisfy (among other standard assumptions) the assumptions of homoscedasticity (constant variance) and no-autocorrelation (uncorrelated error terms). Franckle (1980) and Hill and Schneeweis (1982) point out that time series data on spot and futures rates for foreign currencies show significant serial correlation. Autocorrelation of residuals yields unbiased but inefficient estimates of hedge ratios (the regression coefficients are no longer minimum variance). The true standard errors are underestimated and, therefore, the significance tests using $t$ and $F$ distributions are no longer strictly applicable. In addition, the presence of autocorrelation causes overestimation of the $R^2$ statistic. Other authors, such as Herbst, Kare, and Caples (1989) report heteroscedasticity problems in time series data of foreign currency futures. If the assumption of equal error variances is violated, the estimates obtained by OLS procedures are no longer minimum variance (even though they are still unbiased and consistent).

Preliminary regressions performed on the data reveal the presence of heteroscedasticity and autocorrelation. The first problem is corrected by taking the natural logarithm of the data. The problem of autocorrelation among residuals is corrected using an autoregression (AR) model. The SAS procedure AUTOREG is used.[3]

## EX POST HEDGING RESULTS

Hedge ratios and measures of hedging effectiveness are estimated by running OLS regressions of the form of eq. (3) for two different lengths of the estimation periods

[2]The selection of a specific day of the week is not of great significance.

[3]Herbst, Kare, and Caples (1989) show that their Box–Jenkins ARIMA procedure is superior to an autoregression in correcting for autocorrelation in the residuals. They also indicate that their ARIMA procedure yields optimal hedge ratios that are lower than those obtained by using OLS regressions. These authors also point out that the autoregressive models proved to offer no improvement because the error terms showed infinite memory. In this study, with different data sets, two lags are sufficient to adjust for most of the presence of autocorrelation. In addition, the major concern is not the absolute magnitude of the hedge ratio but the relative impact of changes in the lengths of the estimation period and the hedging horizon on the effectiveness of the hedge. With this objective in mind, the use of the procedure AUTOREG for correcting for autocorrelation in the regression residuals allows meaningful comparisons among hedge ratios and measures of hedging effectiveness computed from different estimation periods and for different hedging horizons.

and two different lengths of the hedging horizons. The lengths of the hedging horizons are one week (weekly hedge) and four weeks (monthly hedge). For both the weekly and monthly hedging horizon the lengths of the estimation periods are 26 and 104 weeks (half a year and two years).[4] To generate a distribution of betas and

### A: One-Week Ex Post Hedging Horizon

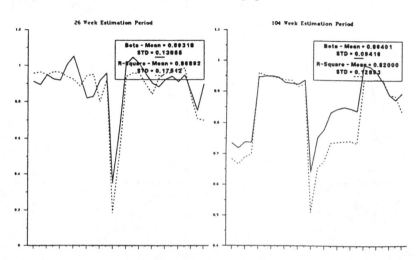

### B: Four-Week Ex Post Hedging Horizon

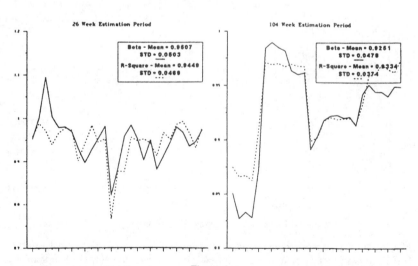

**Figure 1**
Hedge Ratios and Measures of Hedging Effectiveness for British Pound.

[4]Two additional intermediate estimation periods of 52 and 78 weeks were considered but are not included here due to space constraints.

## A: One-Week Ex Post Hedging Horizon

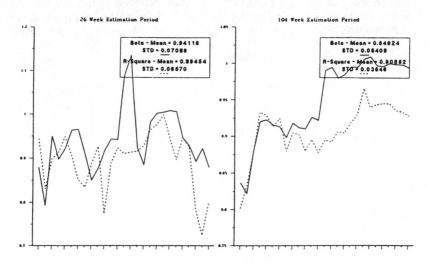

## B: Four-Week Ex Post Hedging Horizon

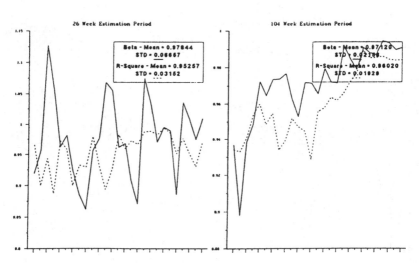

**Figure 2**
Hedge Ratios and Measures of Hedging Effectiveness for German Mark.

$R^2$'s, an overlapping or moving window procedure is used, consisting of deleting the first 12 weeks (a quarter), and adding a new quarter's data, keeping the length of the estimation period constant.

The moving hedge ratios and measures of hedging effectiveness are shown graphically in Figures 1–5 for weekly and monthly hedging horizons. The data in the figures confirm findings reported by authors such as Grammatikos and Saun-

**A: One-Week Ex Post Hedging Horizon**

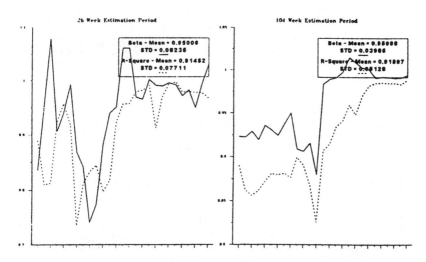

**B: Four-Week Ex Post Hedging Horizon**

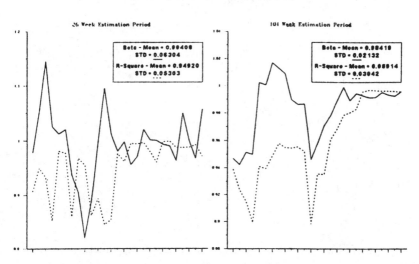

**Figure 3**
Hedge Ratios and Measures of Hedging Effectiveness for Japanese Yen.

ders (1983) and Malliaris and Urrutia (1991) about the instability of betas and $R^2$'s over time. The mean betas and $R^2$'s and their corresponding standard deviations are shown also in the figures. The average hedge ratios are less than one but they are not significantly different from one in a statistical sense. These findings agree with Grammatikos (1986) but not with Hill and Schnceweis (1982) who find betas to be significantly less than one. The average $R^2$'s are large, indicating that foreign

**A: One-Week Ex Post Hedging Horizon**

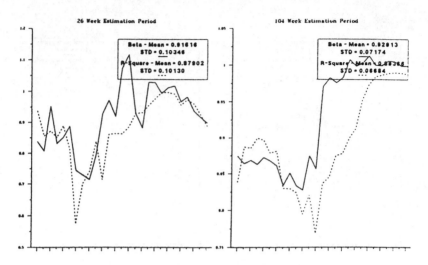

**B: Four-Week Ex Post Hedging Horizon**

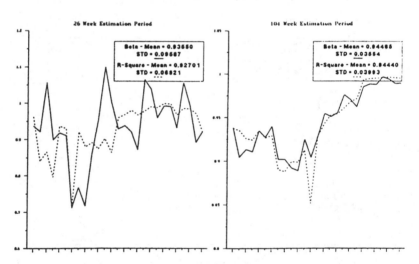

**Figure 4**
Hedge Ratios and Measures of Hedging Effectiveness for Swiss Franc.

currency futures are good hedging instruments. Also, the results confirm findings by Dale (1981) who reports that foreign currency futures, as hedging instruments, are as effective as the more traditional agricultural commodities futures.

The results for weekly hedging horizons in Figures 1–5 show, on average, the $R^2$'s for the Japanese yen, German mark, and Swiss franc tend to slightly increase with the length of the estimation period. The opposite is observed for the British pound and the Canadian dollar. A similar pattern is observed for the monthly hedging

## A: One-Week Ex Post Hedging Horizon

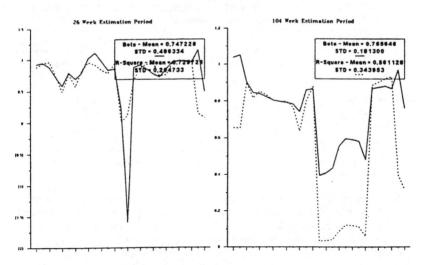

## B: Four-Week Ex Post Hedging Horizon

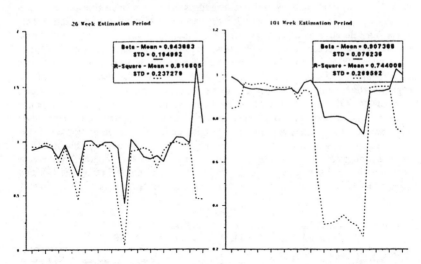

**Figure 5**
Hedge Ratios and Measures of Hedging Effectiveness for Canadian Dollar.

horizons. The betas for the weekly and monthly hedging horizons follow similar patterns to $R^2$ because of their relationship in eq. (5). From Figures 1–5, one can conclude that, for *ex post* hedges, the length of the estimation period does not appear to have an important impact in betas and $R^2$'s. In effect, the $t$-statistics of the difference of mean $R^2$'s presented in Table I indicate that for *ex post* hedging, except for the Canadian dollar (weekly hedge), the length of the estimation period does not have a statistically significant impact in the effectiveness of weekly or

**Table I**
*t*-STATISTICS FOR THE DIFFERENCE OF MEAN $R^2$'s FOR *EX POST* HEDGES
OBTAINED FROM 26-WEEK AND 104-WEEK ESTIMATION PERIODS

| $H_0: R^2_{104\,weeks} - R^2_{26\,weeks}$ | | $H_A: R^2_{104\,weeks} > R^2_{26\,weeks}$ |
|---|---|---|
| **Futures Contract** | **Weekly Hedging Horizon** | **Monthly Hedging Horizon** |
| British pound | 1.19 | 1.01 |
| German mark | 0.99 | 1.09 |
| Japanese yen | 0.26 | 0.86 |
| Swiss franc | 0.65 | 1.15 |
| Canadian dollar | 1.97 | 1.07 |

*Note:* The null hypothesis, $H_0$, cannot be rejected except for the Canadian dollar (Weekly Hedging Horizon) at the 5% confidence level.

monthly hedges. Thus, the effectiveness of the *ex post* hedge seems not to be affected by the length of the estimation period. These results provide some empirical evidence in support of the hypothesis that hedge ratios are unstable over time (if hedge ratios are stable over time, longer estimation periods would yield consistently higher $R^2$'s).

Figures 1–5 also suggest that, for *ex post* hedges, the $R^2$'s are larger for monthly hedges than for weekly hedges. Table II shows the *t*-statistics for the difference of mean $R^2$'s for *ex post* monthly and weekly hedges. The hypothesis that the effectiveness of *ex post* hedging improves with the length of the hedging horizon is confirmed for all currencies, except for the Canadian dollar (26-week estimation period). These results agree with those reported by other authors. Hill and Schneeweis (1982), in studying several foreign currency futures, covering the time period March, 1974 through December, 1978, find that the effectiveness of the hedge improves with the length of the hedging horizon. Ederington (1979) also finds that for GNMA, T-bills, wheat, and corn futures, the hedging effectiveness increases with the length of the hedging horizon. Since this research covers a more recent period, the findings about *ex post* hedges can be considered an update of previous studies and a confirmation of their major conclusion, namely that the measure of hedging effectiveness improves with the length of the hedging horizon.

To summarize, for *ex post* hedging, the evidence presented in Figures 1–5 and Tables I and II indicates that the length of the hedging horizon is a critical invest-

**Table II**
*t*-STATISTICS FOR THE DIFFERENCE OF MEAN $R^2$'s
FOR *EX POST* MONTHLY AND WEEKLY HEDGES

| $H_0: R^2_{monthly\,hedge} - R^2_{weekly\,hedge}$ | | $H_A: R^2_{monthly\,hedge} > R^2_{weekly\,hedge}$ |
|---|---|---|
| **Futures Contract** | **26-Week Estimation Period** | **104-Week Estimation Period** |
| British pound | 2.22 | 4.47 |
| German mark | 4.21 | 7.01 |
| Japanese yen | 1.96 | 3.57 |
| Swiss franc | 2.07 | 3.45 |
| Canadian dollar | 1.22 | 2.21 |

*Note:* The null hypothesis, $H_0$, is rejected in favor of the alternative, $H_A$, for all currencies except for the Canadian dollar (26-week estimation period) at the 5% confidence level.

ment decision, while the length of the estimation period is a statistical issue of less importance.

## EX ANTE HEDGING RESULTS

Past data is used now to generate hedge ratios by running the standard OLS regression, and then these betas are used to hedge a cash position on an *ex ante* basis. The purpose of these tests is to provide new empirical evidence about the hypothesis of the instability of hedge ratios over time and the impact of the length of the hedging horizon on the effectiveness of the hedge. Furthermore, the *ex post* hedging effectiveness measured in statistical terms by the magnitude of $R^2$ is contrasted with the economic consequence of a hedge which is evaluated in terms of returns.

The argument is as follows: In a regression-based strategy, hedgers must estimate the optimal hedge ratio using past data and then employ the estimated ratio to form the hedge. If the true hedge ratio is constant over time, then use of the longest possible estimation period should provide the best estimate of the hedge ratio and the most effective hedge. If, on the contrary, betas change over time, then using data from long ago may lead to a poor estimate of the futures beta and worsen the hedge. In this case, it would be better to use a shorter estimation period. Therefore, the hedging effectiveness of betas computed over various lengths of estimation periods is compared by computing the returns of a long hedge.

The following long hedging strategy is employed.[5] The hedge consists of buying futures contracts and closing out the position by selling the futures contracts when the spot market transaction occurs. Risk is reduced to the extent that the gain from the futures position offsets the loss in the spot position. In a perfect hedge, the gain (loss) in the futures position, completely offsets the loss (gain) in the spot. That is, in a perfect hedge, the return from a hedging strategy is on average equal to zero. Therefore, the more effective the hedge is, the closer to zero the return is on the hedged portfolio. Denote by $R_H$ the return on the hedged portfolio; $R_H$ is computed as follows:

$$R_H = [(F_{t+i} - F_t)H_R - (S_{t+i} - S_t)] \times 100 \qquad (6)$$

where

$F_{t+i}, F_t$ = futures contract prices at time $t$ and $t + i$ for $i = 1,4$ (weekly and monthly hedging horizons); and $S_{t+i}, S_t$ = spot foreign currency rates at time $t$ and $t + i$ for $i = 1,4$.

The hedge ratios are estimated by running regressions of the form of eq. (3). The lengths of the hedging horizons are one week and four weeks. As in the *ex post* case, an overlapping or moving window procedure is used to generate a distribution of betas.

The distribution of returns on the hedged position obtained from the hedge ratios generated by means of the moving window procedure are shown in Figures 6–10 for weekly and monthly hedging horizons. In general, the mean returns for weekly and monthly hedges, with the exception of the British pound, decrease slightly when the length of the estimation period is increased from 26 weeks to 104 weeks. The figures show that the length of the estimation period does not seem to have an important impact in the effectiveness of the hedge. In effect, the *t*-statistics reported in Table III indicate that, for the *ex ante* hedges, the length of the estimation period does not have a statistically significant impact in the effectiveness of

---

[5]The numerical results would be analogous if a short hedge is used instead of a long one.

**A: One-Week Ex Ante Hedging Horizon**

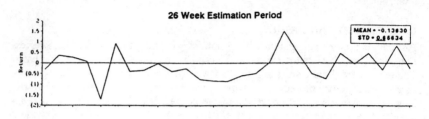

**26 Week Estimation Period**

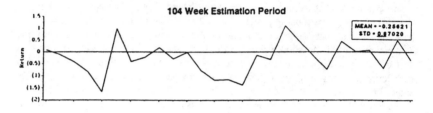

**104 Week Estimation Period**

**B: Four-Week Ex Ante Hedging Horizon**

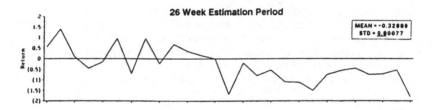

**26 Week Estimation Period**

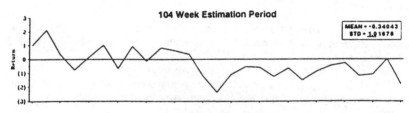

**104 Week Estimation Period**

**Figure 6**
Return Graph of British Pound.

weekly or monthly hedges. This is essentially the same conclusion reached for the *ex post* analysis presented in the previous section. Recall the hypothesis that if hedge ratios are constant over time, one should expect longer estimation periods to provide more effective hedges than shorter ones. Therefore, the results for the *ex ante* hedges provide some empirical evidence in favor of the hypothesis that mean hedge ratios are unstable over time.

The comparison of the hedging effectiveness of the *ex ante* weekly and monthly hedges shows that the hedged portfolio mean returns for the four-week holding

### A: One-Week Ex Ante Hedging Horizon

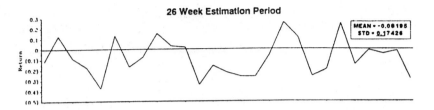

**26 Week Estimation Period**

MEAN = -0.08195
STD = 0.17426

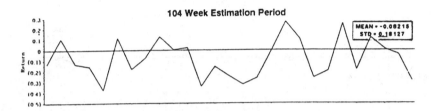

**104 Week Estimation Period**

MEAN = -0.08215
STD = 0.18127

### B: Four-Week Ex Ante Hedging Horizon

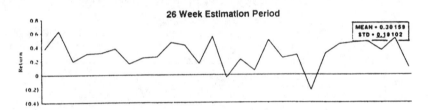

**26 Week Estimation Period**

MEAN = 0.30159
STD = 0.18102

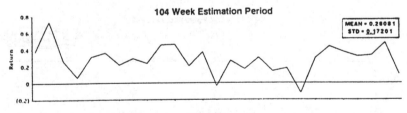

**104 Week Estimation Period**

MEAN = 0.29081
STD = 0.17201

**Figure 7**
Return Graph of German Mark.

horizon are larger than those of the one-week holding period. In fact, the mean returns for the monthly holding period are two (for the British pound) to six (for the Canadian dollar) times the mean returns of the weekly holding period. That is, the effectiveness of the *ex ante* hedges appears to improve when the length of the hedging horizon is shortened from four weeks to one week. Recall that a perfect hedge is defined as one yielding a return of zero. Table IV reports the *t*-statistics for the difference of mean returns for the hedged portfolios for *ex ante* weekly and monthly

**A: One-Week Ex Ante Hedging Horizon**

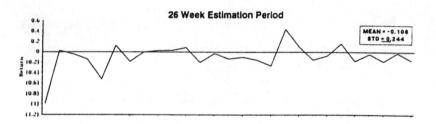

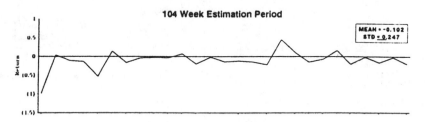

**B: Four-Week Ex Ante Hedging Horizon**

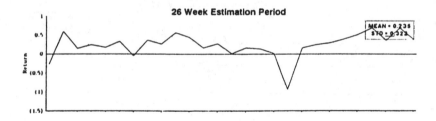

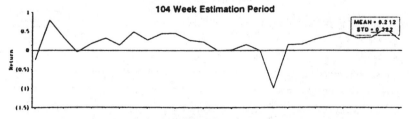

**Figure 8**
Return Graph of Japanese Yen.

hedges. The hypothesis that, the effectiveness of an *ex ante* hedge is higher for shorter (weekly) hedges than for longer (monthly) hedges is confirmed for all currencies, except the British pound. These results are the opposite of those obtained in section 5 and those reported by other authors for the *ex post* hedges. Observe the results in Table II that suggest that the effectiveness of the hedge improves with the length of the hedging horizon.

A: One-Week Ex Ante Hedging Horizon

26 Week Estimation Period

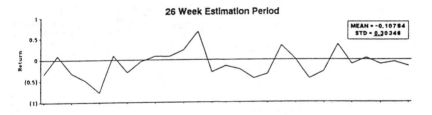

104 Week Estimation Period

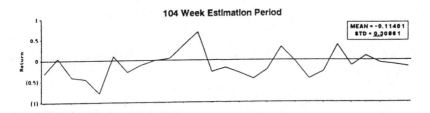

B: Four-Week Ex Ante Hedging Horizon

26 Week Estimation Period

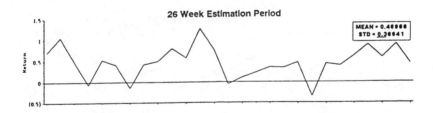

104 Week Estimation Period

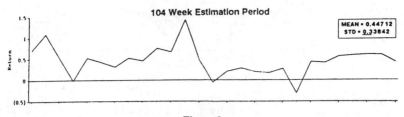

**Figure 9**
Return Graph of Swiss Franc.

Upon reflection, it is not hard to offer an explanation of these seemingly contradictory results. Observe that the *ex post* methodology judges the effectiveness of the hedge by the $R^2$ while the *ex ante* methodology uses portfolio returns. Financial theory suggests that arbitrage forces changes in spot currency and changes in nearby futures currency prices to be correlated. Therefore, as the sample size increases, a larger portion of the variability in the spot price changes is explained by the futures

**A: One-Week Ex Ante Hedging Horizon**

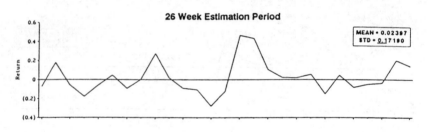

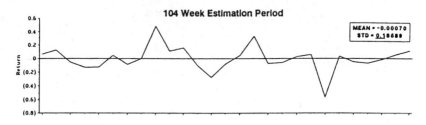

**B: Four-Week Ex Ante Hedging Horizon**

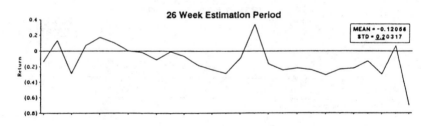

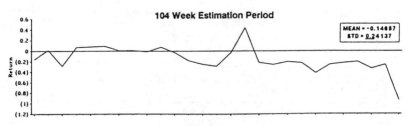

**Figure 10**
Return Graph of Canadian Dollar.

price changes. In other words, the economic relationship between $\Delta S_t$ and $\Delta F_t$ and the statistical methodology of OLS can explain the *ex post* results which plainly demonstrate a good fit which becomes better as the sample size increases. However, a good fit does not result necessarily in good forecasting. The *ex ante* methodology

### Table III
### t-STATISTICS FOR THE DIFFERENCE OF MEAN HEDGED PORTFOLIO
### RETURNS ($\bar{R}$) FOR *EX ANTE* HEDGES OBTAINED
### FROM 26-WEEK AND 104-WEEK ESTIMATION PERIODS

| $H_0: \bar{R}_{104\,weeks} - \bar{R}_{26\,weeks}$ | | $H_A: \bar{R}_{104\,weeks} < \bar{R}_{26\,weeks}$ |
|---|---|---|
| Futures Contract | Weekly Hedging Horizon | Monthly Hedging Horizon |
| British pound | 0.40 | 0.23 |
| German mark | 0.004 | 0.43 |
| Japanese yen | 0.08 | 0.27 |
| Swiss franc | 0.08 | 0.24 |
| Canadian dollar | 0.44 | 0.40 |

*Note:* The null hypothesis, $H_0$, cannot be rejected for all currencies, at 5% confidence level.

### Table IV
### t-STATISTICS FOR THE DIFFERENCE OF MEAN HEDGED PORTFOLIO RETURNS
### ($\bar{R}$) FOR *EX ANTE* MONTHLY AND WEEKLY HEDGES

| $H_0: \bar{R}_{monthly\,hedge} - \bar{R}_{weekly\,hedge}$ | | $H_A: \bar{R}_{monthly\,hedge} > \bar{R}_{weekly\,hedge}$ |
|---|---|---|
| Futures Contract | 26-Week Estimation Period | 104-Week Estimation Period |
| British pound | 0.95 | 0.36 |
| German mark | 7.71 | 7.55 |
| Japanese yen | 4.24 | 4.02 |
| Swiss franc | 6.31 | 6.37 |
| Canadian dollar | 2.66 | 2.37 |

*Note:* The null hypothesis, $H_0$, is rejected in favor of the alternative, $H_A$, for all currencies except the British pound, at the 5% confidence level.

judges the effectiveness of the hedge by returns. The shorter the hedging horizons, the smaller the probability of large deviations from zero and, therefore, the better the hedge. Note that *ex ante* hedges are judged best when the hedger's expected return is zero. Obviously, the *ex ante* methodology appears more relevant in economic applications, with an emphasis on returns rather than good fitting based on past data.

It is important to note that the effectiveness of the *ex ante* and the *ex post* methodologies are not comparable. Grant and Eaker (1989) propose a variance reduction measure to compare complex hedging strategies. This study is not interested in a direct comparison of *ex post* and *ex ante* hedging. The purpose of this study is to illustrate that using $R^2$, as proposed by the portfolio approach to hedging as an indicator of hedging effectiveness, is not always accurate. $R^2$ becomes an accurate indicator of hedging effectiveness if the hedge ratios are reasonably stable over time. Otherwise, with variable hedge ratios shorter hedging horizons are more desirable because they reduce the financial exposure to economic uncertainty and keep expected hedged portfolio returns close to zero.

In summary, the evidence presented in Figures 6–10 and the statistical testing exhibited in Tables III and IV confirm once again that the length of the estimation period remains a less critical decision, even if judged on an *ex ante* basis. Also, it is confirmed that the hedging horizon continues to be the most important decision.

However, contrary to *ex post* hedging, which supports a longer hedging horizon, the *ex ante* hedging analysis supports a shorter hedging horizon.

## SUMMARY AND CONCLUSIONS

This article presents empirical evidence of the effect of the lengths of estimation periods and the hedging horizons on the hedging effectiveness for five foreign currency futures contracts: British pound, Japanese yen, Canadian dollar, German mark, and Swiss franc. The data is weekly spot exchange rates and futures prices for the time period March 4, 1980 to December 27, 1988. By means of a moving window procedure, OLS regression betas and $R^2$'s are generated for estimation periods of two lengths, 26 and 104 weeks, and for two hedging horizons, one week and four weeks. The effectiveness of the five foreign currency futures contracts as hedging devices is evaluated: first, in an *ex post* basis, by using the betas and the coefficients of determination of the OLS regressions; second, in an *ex ante* basis, by computing the returns of hedged portfolios of futures and cash positions constructed with hedge ratios estimated by OLS regressions.

The following conclusions confirm and update results previously reported by other authors:

1. *Ex post* hedge ratios are less than one and show instability over time. However, it is found that, on the average, betas are not significantly different from one, which contradicts results previously reported by some researchers.
2. Measures of hedging effectiveness are large, indicating that foreign currency futures contracts are good hedging devices.
3. For *ex post* hedges, it is found that longer hedges (one-month hedging horizons) are more effective than shorter hedges (one-week hedging horizons).

The following results are new and original findings:

4. The length of the estimation period, used for computing the betas and $R^2$'s by means of OLS regressions, does not appear to have an impact on the effectiveness of the hedge both on an *ex post* hedging (evaluated in terms of $R^2$) and on an *ex ante* hedging (evaluated in terms of returns). This result provides some empirical evidence in favor of the hypothesis that hedge ratios are unstable over time.
5. For *ex ante* hedges, it is found that shorter hedges (weekly hedging horizons) are more effective than longer hedges (monthly hedging horizons). This finding is the opposite of the one obtained for the *ex post* hedges, but not necessarily contradictory, since the *ex post* and *ex ante* methodologies utilize different criteria.

The last two results raise two important questions: First, does a similar behavior occur in other futures markets? Second, do these results depend on the sampling period, 1980–1988, or are they more general? Obviously, there is room for further research on this topic.

## Bibliography

Brock, W. A., and Malliaris, A. G. (1989): *Differential Equations, Stability, and Chaos in Dynamic Economics,* Amsterdam and New York: North Holland Publishing Co.

Dale, C. (1981): "The Hedging Effectiveness of Currency Futures Markets," *Journal of Futures Markets,* 1:77–88.

Ederington, L. H. (1979): "The Hedging Performance of the New Futures Markets," *Journal of Finance,* 34:157–170.

Figlewski, S. (1984): "Hedging Performance and Basis Risk in Stock Index Futures," *Journal of Finance*, 39:657–669.

Figlewski, S. (1985): "Hedging With Stock Index Futures: Theory and Application In A New Market," *Journal of Futures Markets*, 5:183–199.

Franckle, C.T. (1980): "The Hedging Performance of the New Futures Markets: Comments," *Journal of Finance*, 35:1273–1279.

Grammatikos, T. (1986): "Intervalling Effects and the Hedging Performance of Foreign Currency Futures," *Financial Review*, 21:21–36.

Grammatikos, T., and Saunders, A. (1983): "Stability and The Hedging Performance of Foreign Currency Futures," *Journal of Futures Markets*, 3:295–305.

Grant, D., and Eaker, M. (1989): "Complex Hedges: How Well Do They Work?," *Journal of Futures Markets*, 9:15–27.

Herbst, A. F., Kare, D. D., and Caples, S. C. (1989): "Hedging Effectiveness and Minimum Hedge Ratios in The Presences of Autocorrelation: Foreign Currency Futures," *Journal of Futures Markets*, 9:185–197.

Hill, J., and Schneeweis, T. (1981): "A Note on the Hedging Effectiveness of Foreign Currency Futures," *Journal of Futures Markets*, 1:659–664.

Hill, J., and Schneeweis, T. (1982): "The Hedging Effectiveness of Foreign Currency Futures," *Journal of Financial Research*, 5:95–104.

Hill, J., Liro, J., and Schneeweis, T. (1983): "Hedging Performance of GNMA Futures Under Rising and Falling Interest Rates," *Journal of Futures Markets*, 3:403–413.

Hill, J., and Schneeweis, T. (1984): "Reducing Volatility with Financial Futures," *Financial Analysts Journal*, 30:34–40.

Howard, C.T., and D'Antonio, L. J. (1984): "A Risk-Return Measure of Hedging Effectiveness," *Journal of Financial and Quantitative Analysis*, 19:101–112.

Johnson, L. (1960): "The Theory of Hedging and Speculation in Commodity Futures," *Review of Economic Studies*, 27:139–151.

Junkus, J.C., and Lee, C. F. (1985): "Use of Three Stock Index Futures in Hedging Decisions," *Journal of Futures Markets*, 5:201–222.

Lindahl, M. (1989): "Measuring Hedging Effectiveness With $R^2$: A Note," *Journal of Futures Markets*, 9:469–475.

Malliaris, A. G., and Urrutia, J. (1991): "Tests of Random Walk of Hedge Ratios and Measures of Hedging Effectiveness for Stock Indexes and Foreign Currencies," *Journal of Futures Markets*, 11: 55–68.

McEnally, R.W., and Rice, M. L. (1979): "Hedging Possibilities in the Flotation of Debt Securities," *Financial Management*, 10:12–18.

Overdahl, J. A., and Starleaf, D. R. (1986): "The Hedging Performance of the CD Futures Markets," *Journal of Futures Markets*, 6:71–81.

Stein, J. L. (1961): "The Simultaneous Determination of Spot and Futures Prices," *The American Economic Review*, 51:1012–1025.

# TIME SERIES PROPERTIES OF FOREIGN CURRENCY HEDGE RATIOS

A. G. Malliaris
Professor of Economics
Loyola University of Chicago
Chicago, Illinois 60611

Jorge Urrutia
Department of Finance
Loyola University of Chicago
Chicago, Illinois 60611

## Abstract

The hedge ratio and the measure of hedging effectiveness are important statistics for the hedging decisions of futures market participants. In fact, misinformation about the values of hedge ratios and measures of hedging effectiveness may result in costly suboptimal investment and hedging strategies. In this article we test the hypothesis that hedge ratios and measures of hedging effectiveness follow a random walk process. The empirical tests for five foreign currency futures contracts are based on the Lo and MacKinlay variance-ratio test. In general, our results provide support for the random walk hypothesis. Our findings suggest a rethinking of the traditional methods of hedging. In effect, under efficient markets, the random walk behavior of hedge ratios implies that hedgers cannot consistently place perfect hedges and, therefore, continuous dynamic hedging must be considered.

## I. INTRODUCTION

The traditional or classical hedging theory emphasizes the risk avoidance role of futures markets. It consists of taking a futures market position equal in magnitude but of opposite sign to the cash position. However, price changes in the futures contract do not generally match perfectly with price changes in the spot market. Thus, the traditional one-to-one hedging strategy does not entirely eliminate the risk of price changes in the spot market.

Working (1953, 1962) challenged the view of hedgers as pure risk minimizers and emphasized expected profit maximization. He made explicit the speculative aspect of hedging. Working centered his hedge strategy on the concept of basis and argued that price changes in the futures and cash positions would not be offset perfectly, so return could be improved through selective hedging.

Johnson (1960) and Stein (1961) integrated the risk avoidance of the traditional theory with Working's expected profit maximization. They argued that investors buy or sell futures for the same risk-return reasons that they buy any other securities. The portfolio approach to hedging of Johnson and Stein was extended later by Ederington (1979) and Franckle (1980).

## Properties of Foreign Currency Hedge Ratio                    543

The Johnson optimal or minimum variance hedge ratio is given by:

$$H^* = \frac{X_F^*}{X_S^*} = - \frac{COV(\Delta S, \Delta F)}{VAR(\Delta F)} \qquad (1.1)$$

where:

$H^*$ = optimal hedge ratio
$X_F^*$ = dollar amount invested in futures contracts
$X_S^*$ = dollar amount invested in spot commodity
$COV(\Delta S, \Delta F)$ = covariance of spot with futures price changes
$VAR(\Delta F)$ = variance of futures price changes.

Johnson also derived the following measure of hedging effectiveness:

$$E = 1 - \frac{VAR(H)}{VAR(U)} \qquad (1.2)$$

where:

$E$ = measure of hedging effectiveness
$VAR(H)$ = variance of hedged portfolio
$VAR(U)$ = variance of unhedged spot portfolio.

Hedge ratios and measures of hedging effectiveness have been estimated for GNMA futures by Ederington (1979), Hill, Liro and Schneeweis (1983) and Hill and Schneeweis (1984); for T-bond futures by Hill and Schneeweis (1984); for foreign currency futures by Hill and Schneeweis (1982, 1984), Grammatikos and Saunders (1983), Grammatikos (1986) and Malliaris and Urrutia (1991); for CD futures by Overdahl and Starleaf (1986); for T-bill futures by Ederington (1979), Franckle (1980), and Howard and D'Antonio (1984, 1986); for stock market index futures by Figlewski (1984, 1985), and Junkus and Lee (1985).

The major conclusions of these research studies are that: (i) Futures contracts perform well as hedging vehicles (hedged positions proved to be significantly less risky than unhedged positions); (ii) optimal hedge ratios are less than one; (iii) hedge ratios and measures of hedging effectiveness change with the investment horizon of the hedge, and the time to maturity of the futures contract (in general, longer hedges result in higher hedge ratios and measures of hedging effectiveness than shorter hedges). These results are supported both by economic intuition and reality. First, the excellent performance of currency futures is evidenced by their large volume. Second, the fact that optimal hedge ratios are less than one means that futures price changes are more volatile than spot price changes which in turn means that it is sufficient for the future position to be less than the cash position. Third, the fact that hedge ratios change over time implies that the hedging position must be continuously monitored.

Grammatikos and Saunders (1983) criticize previous studies of hedging performance of futures markets that use regression analysis. Basically, one major problem with using the simple OLS regression model over a long period of time is the assumption that the regression coefficient, that corresponds to the hedge ratio, is stable over the whole sample period. By using three econometric approaches these authors examine the question of hedge ratio stability for five major foreign currency futures and find that hedge ratios are unstable over time. The first approach uses a moving or overlapping regression procedure. The second apporach examines whether significant shifts have taken place in the values of the hedge ratios over various subperiods. Finally, the third approach uses a random coefficient model to determine whether hedge ratios changed over time. Unstable slope regression coefficients could significantly bias the estimation of the optimal hedge ratio and measure of hedging effectiveness. Furthermore, such instability could diminish the effectiveness of arbitrage strategies and the hedging role of portfolio insurance. Brennan and Schwartz (1988) develop a theoretical analysis for optimal arbitrage strategies under basis variability.

In this paper we are interested in exploring the time series properties of the hedge ratio and measure of hedging effectiveness using very recent statistical techniques. We examine first their variability over time for several currency futures contracts, and then we concentrate in studying the behavior over time in both variables. Specifically, we postulate that the hedge ratio and the measure of hedging effectiveness

**Properties of Foreign Currency Hedge Ratio** 545

follow a random walk process. We test our random walk hypothesis with the variance ratio test of Lo and MacKinlay (1988). The variance ratio test is both newer and as Lo and MacKinlay (1989) explain, it has more power than the traditional tests of random walk such as the Dickey and Fuller and the Box-Pierce Q tests, which have trouble picking up stationarity components in low frequency data. Furthermore, the variance ratio test is supplemented by a Monte Carlo simulation. These methods differentiate our paper from Malliaris and Urrutia (1991), that tests for random walk by using Dickey and Fuller (1979, 1981) approach. Our empirical results generally provide support for the random walk hypothesis for five foreign currencies: German Mark, Canadian Dollar, Swiss Franc, British Pound, and Japanese Yen. In general, these findings imply that hedgers cannot consistently place optimal hedges even in the very short run, and that dynamic hedging techniques must be considered.

## II. DATA

The data corresponds to spot and futures prices for the nearby contract (0-3 months) for the following foreign currencies: British Pound, German Mark, Japanese Yen, Canadian Dollar and Swiss Franc.

The time period under study extends from April 1, 1980 through December 27, 1988. The prices are Monday settlement prices (Tuesday settlement prices were taken when the Monday settlement price was missing) obtained from the *Wall Street Journal*. We assume that for each contract the hedging horizon is one week. Using a much shorter horizon, say one day, would increase substantially the hedging costs. On the other hand, using 2-week or longer horizons would increase the risks associated with the hedge due to the random behavior of the hedge ratio.

## III. METHODOLOGY

We examine the question of stability of the hedge ratio and the measure of hedging effectiveness by first generating a sequence of the two parameters, using a moving window regression procedure. Then, we use the variance-ratio approach of Lo and MacKinlay to test the hypothesis that the hedge ratio and the measure of hedging effectiveness follow random walk processes.

More specifically, data sets of hedge ratios and measures of hedging effectiveness are generated by means of an overlapping or moving window regression procedure[1]. The hedge ratios and measures of hedging effectiveness are initially estimated for a 24-week period and then reestimated every 6 weeks by adding new spot and futures data and deleting the first 6-week data, always keeping a 24-week estimation period. By regressing the percentage change of the spot price on the percentage change of the futures price (for a one-week hedging horizon) moving hedge ratios and measures of hedging effectiveness are estimated for every six weeks[2,3]. The series of moving hedge ratios and measures of hedging effectiveness are shown graphically in Figures 1-5. For comparison purposes the average long-term values are also plotted in the figures[4]. We can see that the moving hedge ratios and measures of hedging effectiveness exhibit major deviations from their long-run counterparts. That is, the results of the moving window regressions allow us to conclude that the hedge ratios and the measures of hedging effectiveness, for the five foreign currencies under analysis, are not stable over time. Our findings confirm earlier results found in the futures markets literature.

## IV. RANDOM WALK HYPOTHESIS

Next we proceed to further explore the time series properties of the sequence of hedge ratios and measures of hedging effectiveness. Actually, the main purpose of this paper is to detect patterns in the stability of these two parameters. We postulate that the hedge ratio and measure of hedging effectiveness vary randomly over time. Specifically, we claim that each follows a random walk process.

There are several reasons for our hypothesis of random walk. First, various studies, such as Cornell (1977), have established that foreign currency markets are efficient in the standard notion that they fully reflect all relevant publicly available information. In an efficient market, changes of spot prices over time are random and reflect the arrival of new information. In other words, price changes on any particular day are uncorrelated with past historical price changes. Empirical research in futures markets suggests that futures price changes also follow a random walk, reflecting efficiency in futures markets as well[5], since random walk is equivalent to the weak form of the efficient market hypothesis in the sense that there is no way investors can forecast the direction of future prices and develop winning trading strategies based on current prices. The hedge ratio is the ratio of dollar amounts invested in a spot asset and a futures contract. It is reasonable to assume that the behavior of this ratio reflects the behavior of these prices. Therefore, given that prices follow a random walk process, we can also expect the hedge ratio to vary randomly over time.

Second, the random walk behavior of the hedge ratio may be explained by the theories of speculation and the effects of such speculation on price

## Properties of Foreign Currency Hedge Ratio                                     547

changes on both cash and futures markets. There are, in general, two theories about the effects of speculation on price variability. One theory claims that speculation increases price variability because speculators tend to buy as prices are rising and tend to sell as prices are falling, generating a bandwagon effect which contributes to larger swings in price volatility. This idea is developed in models of feedback noise traders such as Porteba and Summers (1986). The opposing theory claims that speculation reduces price variability and has been defended by Milton Friedman (1953) who argued that only unprofitable speculation can have a destabilizing effect on prices. These theories are reviewed extensively by Tirole (1989) and we do not wish to exposit them here in further detail. Simply put, our argument is this:  the stability or instability of speculation, with similar or dissimilar intensity in cash and futures markets, may cause hedge ratios and coefficients of hedging effectiveness to follow random walks.

Third, the random walk behavior of the hedge ratio may be caused by differences in the microstructure of cash and futures markets. In our case, spot prices are determined in dealership markets with futures prices being formulated in open outcry auction markets. There is an increasing literature that emphasizes the role of different trading mechanisms with special emphasis given to the role of "noise" and "feedback" traders on price formation and the time series properties of such prices. A representative paper in this literature is Cutler, Poterba and Summers (1990). It is reasonable to postulate that such differences in the microstructure of cash and futures markets and dissimilarities in trading mechanisms and types of traders may cause hedge ratios to vary over time.

Finally, Brennan and Schwartz (1988) acknowledge the importance of noise in financial markets and develop optimal arbitrage methods under basis variability. Their analysis can be used to support our hypothesis that due to noise in financial markets modelled by an Itô process, hedge ratios may also be noisy and therefore exhibit a random walk behavior[6].

As a result of the above explanations of the random walk hypothesis, out tests below are joint tests of the four explanations we offer.

### V. VARIANCE-RATIO TESTS

Lo and MacKinlay (1988) have developed a test of random walk that is robust with respect to heteroscedasticity and non-normal disturbances. It is known as the variance-ratio test. Indeed, Lo and MacKinlay (1989) show that the variance ratio statistic compares favorably to the Dickey and Fuller procedures in tests of random walk behavior[7]. In this paper we employ the variance-ratio test in order to further investigate the random walk nature of the hedge ratio and the measure of hedging effectiveness.

The intuition behind the variance-ratio test is the following:  If the natural logarithm of a time series denoted $Y_t$, is a pure random walk of the form:

$$Y_t = u + Y_{t-1} + \epsilon_t \qquad (5.1)$$

then, the variance of its k-differences grows linearly with the difference k. For example, the variance of annually sampled series must be four times as large as the variance of a quarterly sampled series. Thus, if the series follows a random walk, it must be the case that the variance of the k-differences is k times the variance of the first difference:

$$VAR(Y_t - Y_{t-k}) = k \cdot VAR(Y_t - Y_{t-1}) \qquad (5.2)$$

In this paper, we follow the procedures used by Poterba and Summers (1988) and we postulate that, under the random walk hypothesis, the ratio of (1/k) times the variance of the k-differences over (1/2) times the variance of the two-differences, to be equal to one. In other words, our test of random walk is equivalent to testing the following null hypothesis[8].

$$H_0 : \frac{(\frac{1}{k}) VAR(Y_t - Y_{t-k})}{(\frac{1}{2}) VAR(Y_t - Y_{t-2})} = 1 . \qquad (5.3)$$

In order to simplify the notation, define the following:

## Properties of Foreign Currency Hedge Ratio 549

$$VAR(k) = VAR(Y_t - Y_{t-k}) \qquad (5.4)$$

$$VAR(2) = VAR(Y_t - Y_{t-2}) \qquad (5.5)$$

$$VAR(k,2) = \frac{(\frac{1}{k})VAR(Y_t - Y_{t-k})}{(\frac{1}{2})VAR(Y_t - Y_{t-2})} = (\frac{2}{k})(\frac{VAR(k)}{VAR(2)}) \qquad (5.6)$$

Therefore, our null hypothesis of random walk becomes:

$$H_0 = VAR(k,2) = 1 \qquad (5.7)$$

There are two problems associated with the use of the variance-ratio statistic. First, its distribution does not have a known functional form; and second, the distribution varies with the sample size and measurement interval. Therefore, it is necessary to prepare tables of critical values from Monte Carlo experiments[9]. Table 1 reports the critical values of mean-adjusted variance-ratio statistics VAR(k,2)/E[VAR(k,2)] and the mean values used to adjust these critical values. The distribution presented in Table 1 is tabulated for a sample size of 70[10]. The measurement intervals range from k = 1 through k = 16.

The results of the variance-ratio tests are presented in Table 2 for the hedge ratio and in Table 3 for the measure of hedging effectiveness. They generally suggest that the variances increase less than proportionally with time. In fact, most variance ratios are less than unity. Following Poterba and Summers (1988), our results indicate that both the hedge ratio and the measure of hedging effectiveness exhibit negative serial correlation. Indeed, the results reported in Tables 2 and 3 provide some evidence of a mean reversion process for the hedge ratios and measures of hedging effectiveness. However, several of the adjusted variance ratios are large. Therefore, we conclude that the statistical evidence does not consistently allow rejection of the random walk hypothesis and acceptance of a mean-reversion process.

Cochrane (1988) gives a different interpretation of the variance-ratio test. He argues that one can model a series whose fluctuations are partly temporary and partly permanent. The random walk carries the permanent component of a change and the stationary series carries the temporary part of a change. Cochrane uses the variance ratio to measure the permanent or random walk component of the series. According to Cochrane's argument the variance ratios shown in Tables 2 and 3 indicate that the hedge ratios and measures of hedging effectiveness for the five foreign currencies contain a significant permanent or random walk component.

## VI. DISCUSSION OF EMPIRICAL FINDINGS

The empirical results presented in the previous sections have partially confirmed the hypothesis that the hedge ratio and the measure of hedging effectiveness for a selected number of foreign currency futures follow a random walk. The findings reinforce previous research confirming random walk in both spot and futures markets and also confirm the explanations offered in section 4 about theories of speculation, differences in microstructure and the importance of noise in financial markets. The findings can also be seen as evidence of weak form of market efficiency since investors cannot develop trading strategies based on current prices that will allow them to beat the market.

The major implication of our random walk hypothesis is that hedgers cannot consistently place perfect hedges and need to continuously readjust their hedges. This can be done by using appropriate computational methods that take into account the variable nature of the hedge ratio and the measure of hedging effectiveness. A few of these methods are briefly summarized below.

Cecchetti, Cumby and Figlewski (1988) apply the Autoregressive Conditional Heteroskedasticity (ARCH) method to hedging in futures markets. Their approach maximizes the expected logarithmic utility of an investor and gives estimates of optimal hedges. Another methodology which measures hedging effectiveness and which avoids many of the estimation problems caused by nonstationarity in expected returns, is developed in McCabe and Solberg (1988). This technique is based on conditional probability distributions, and the results reported by the authors indicate that varying assumptions about conditional expectations can greatly alter the effectiveness measures. Anderson and Danthine (1982) have proposed a multiperiod model of hedging which allows for the futures position to be revised within the cash market holding period. Finally, Herbst, Kare and Caples (1989) estimate optimal hedge ratios by using the ARIMA methodology of Box and Jenkins. Their approach successfully solves the problem of autoregressive disturbances.

These findings imply that the already complex relationships among hedge ratios, measures of hedging effectiveness, volume of trade and open

# Properties of Foreign Currency Hedge Ratio                    551

interest require further empirical research. Individual investors, institutional investors, and corporations seeking to reduce or eliminate risk are aware that the hedging process is complicated. Presumably, dynamic hedging could be more costly that traditional hedging because the continuous readjustment of the hedge would increase the transaction costs. However, the opposite effect is also possible. In effect, Herbst, Kare and Caples (1989) report that their hedge ratios are lower than those rendered by the traditional OLS regression technique. This implies a reduction in the required margin deposit and in commissions incurred by hedgers.

## VII. SUMMARY AND CONCLUSIONS

The paper attempts to detect patterns in the variability of the hedge ratio and the measure of hedging effectiveness. Specifically, we postulate that these two parameters follow a random walk process. The data used in the empirical tests correspond to weekly spot and futures prices for the nearby contracts for five foreign currency futures: British Pound, German Mark, Japanese Yen, Canadian Dollar and Swiss Franc.

Empirical tests based on a moving window regression procedure confirm that the hedge ratios and the measures of hedging effectiveness for the five futures contracts under study are not stable over time. Unstable hedge ratios may create significant bias in the estimation of the hedge ratio and, therefore, in the measure of the hedging effectiveness. Misspecification of the optimal hedge ratio may result in suboptimal hedging decisions with costly consequences for market participants.

The main purpose of the paper is to test the hypothesis of random walk by means of the Lo and MacKinlay variance-ratio approach. In general, our empirical results partially confirm the random walk hypothesis. These findings suggest a rethinking of the traditional methods of hedging. Actually, under efficient markets, the random walk behavior of hedge ratios implies that hedgers could not consistently place perfect hedges and, therefore, dynamic hedging must be considered. In this respect, we encourage the exploration of computational methods that take into account the time-varying nature of hedge ratios and measures of the hedging effectiveness. These methods have already been proposed in previous studies of futures markets hedging.

## ENDNOTES

This paper was presented at the *International Conference on Investment and Hedging in Commodity Markets: Financial Theory and Strategies*, June 20-23, 1990 Gardone, Italy. We are thankful to the organizers of the Conference Professors Giorgio Szegö, Giovanni Zambruno, Silvana Stefani and Marida Bertocchi for the invitation to participate. The paper was also presented at the *Financial*

*Management Association* meeting, in Chicago, October 1991 and the *North American Economics and Finance Association* meeting in New Orleans, January 1992. We also wish to thank Charles Corrado for providing the Monte Carlo simulation computer program. Finally, we are grateful to Wichai Saenghirunwattana for computational assistance and two anonymous referees of the *International Journal of Finance* for their constructive comments. All remaining errors are ours.

[1] The same regression procedure was used by Grammatikos and Saunders (1983) to examine the variability of the hedge ratio and measure of hedging effectiveness for selected foreign currency futures for the time period January 1974–June 1980.

[2] Since our data samples are small, we have chosen 24-week estimation periods, six-week moving windows, and one-week hedging intervals, in order to generate enough observations for the random walk tests. Our moving window regression procedure allows us to generate 69 hedge ratios and measures of hedging effectiveness. We have also used one-year estimation period, 12-week moving windows, and 2-week hedging interval and reestimated it every quarter. This procedure generated fewer hedge ratios and measures of hedging effectiveness but the empirical findings were very similar.

[3] We have computed estimates of the hedge ratio and the measure of hedging effectiveness by running OLS regressions of the percentage change of the spot price on the percentage change of the corresponding futures price. Had we formulated the problem in terms of absolute price changes, it would have been hard to tell whether it is truly randomness or simply non-stationarity.

[4] The average or long-term hedge ratios and measures of hedging effectiveness are estimated by running OLS regressions of the percentage change of the spot price on the percentage change of the appropriate futures price for the full time periods under study.

[5] Empirical evidence of the random walk and the efficient market hypothesis for security prices has been reported, among others, by Fama (1965), and Fama and Blume (1966); and, for futures markets by Fama (1976), Cornell (1977), and others.

[6] The hedge ratio stability problem is isomorphic to the question of beta instability. In this respect, there is a whole body of finance literature devoted to the study of beta instability. In this paper, we do not review the issues and methodologies associated with beta randomness. To the interested reader we suggest to look at Fabozzi and Francis (1978).

[7] Lo and MacKinlay (1988) and Poterba and Summers (1988) have used the variance-ratio test to partially reject the random walk behavior in stock markets.

[8] Our moving window procedure allows us to generate hedge ratios and measures of hedging effectiveness every six weeks. Therefore, the two-difference variances are equivalent to the variances of quarterly sampled series.

[9] We are very grateful to our colleague Charles Corrado for providing the Fortran program necessary to generate the Monte Carlo simulations.

[10] Recall that our data set goes from April 1, 1980 through December 27, 1988. Our moving window procedure generates 68 hedge ratios and measures of hedging effectiveness. Since the distribution of the variance-ratio statistic varies with the sample size, it was necessary to prepare a table of critical values from a sample size of 70 to approximate our data.

Properties of Foreign Currency Hedge Ratio 553

## REFERENCES

1. Anderson, Ronald and Jean-Pierre Danthine (1982), "The Time Pattern of Hedging and the Volatility of Futures Prices", *Review of Economic Studies*, 50: 249-265.
2. Brennan, M.J. and E.S. Schwartz (1988), "Optimal Arbitrage Strategies Under Basis Variability", *Studies in Banking and Finance*, 5: 167-180.
3. Cecchetti, Stephen, Robert Cumby and Stephen Figlewski (1988), "Estimation of the Optimal Futures Hedge", *Review of Economics and Statistics*, 70: 623-630.
4. Cochrane, John H. (1988), "How Big Is the Random Walk in GNP?", *Journal of Political Economy*, 96: 833-920.
5. Cornell, B. (1977), "Spot Rates, Forward Rates and Exchange Market Efficiency", *Journal of Financial Economics*, 5: 55-65.
6. Cuttler, D., J. Poterba and L. Summers (1990), "Speculative Dynamics and the Role of Feedback Traders", *American Economic Review: Papers and Proceedings*, 80: 63-68.
7. Dickey, D. A. and W. A. Fuller (1979), "Distribution of the Estimators of the Autoregressive Time Series With A Unit Root", *Journal of the American Statistical Association*, 74: 427-431.
8. Dickey, D. A. and W. A. Fuller (1981), "Likelihood Ratio Statistics for Autoregressive Time Series With A Unit Root", *Econometrica*, 49: 1057-1072.
9. Ederington, L.H. (1979), "The Hedging Performance of the New Futures Markets", *Journal of Finance*, 34: 157-170.
10. Fabozzi, Frank J. and Jack Clark Francis (1978), "Beta As a Random Coefficient", *Journal of Financial and Quantitative Analysis*, 1: 101-116.
11. Fama, E. (1976), "Forward Rates as Predictors of Futures Spot Rates," *Journal of Financial Economics*, 3: 361-377.
12. Fama, E. (1965), "The Behavior of Stock Market Prices", *Journal of Business*, 38: 38-105.
13. Fama, E. and M. Blume (1966), "Filter Rules and Stock-Market Trading", *Journal of Business*, 39: 226-241.
14. Figlewski, Stephen (1985), "Hedging With Stock Index Futures: Theory and Application In A New Market", *The Journal of Futures Markets*, 5: 183-199.
15. Figlewski, Stephen (1984), "Hedging Performance and Basis Risk in Stock Index Futures", *Journal of Finance*, 39: 657-669.
16. Franckle, Charles T. (1980), "The Hedging Performance of the New Futures Markets: Comments", *Journal of Finance*, 35: 1273-1279.

17. Friedman, M. (1953), *Essays in Positive Economics*, University of Chicago Press, Chicago.

18. Fuller, W.A. (1976), *Introduction to Statistical Time Series*, John Wiley and Sons, Inc., New York.

19. Grammatikos, Theoharry (1986), "Intervailling Effects and the Hedging Performance of Foreign Currency Futures", *Journal of Financial Research*, 5: 95-104.

20. Grammatikos, T. and Anthony Saunders (1983), "Stability and The Hedging Performance of Foreign Currency Futures", *Journal of Futures Markets*, 3: 295-305.

21. Herbst, A.F., D.D. Kares and S.C. Caples (1989), "Hedging Effectiveness and Minimum Risk Hedge Ratios in the Presence of Autocorrelation: Foreign Currency Futures", *The Journal of Futures Markets*, 9: 185-197.

22. Hill, Joanne and Thomas Schneeweis (1982), "The Hedging Effectiveness of Foreign Currency Futures", *Journal of Financial Research*, 5: 95-104.

23. Hill, Joanne and Thomas Schneeweis (1984), "Reducing Volatility with Financial Futures", *Financial Analysts Journal*, 40: 34-40.

24. Hill, Joanne, Joseph Liro and Thomas Schneeweis (1983), "Hedging Performance of GNMA Futures Under Rising and Falling Interest Rates", *Journal of Futures Markets*, 3: 403-413.

25. Howard, Charles T. and Louis J. D'Antonio (1984), "A Risk-Return Measure of Hedging Effectiveness", *Journal of Financial and Quantitative Analysis*, 19: 101-112.

26. Johnson L. (1960), "The Theory of Hedging and Speculation in Commodity Futures", *Review of Economic Studies*, 27: 139-151.

27. Junkus, Joan C. and Cheng F. Lee (1985), "Use of Three Index Futures in Hedging Decisions", *Journal of Futures Markets*, 5: 201-222.

28. Lo, A. and A.C. MacKinlay (1988), "Stock Market Prices Do Not Follow Random Walks: Evidence From a Simple Specification Test", *Review of Financial Studies*, 1: 41-66.

29. Lo, A. and A.C. MacKinlay (1989), "The Size and Power of the Variance Ratio Test in Finite Samples: A Monte Carlo Investigation", *Journal of Econometrics*, 40: 203-238.

30. Malliaris, A. G., and J. Urrutia (1991), "Tests of Random Walk of Hedge Ratios and Measures of Hedging Effectiveness for Stock Indexes and Foreign Currencies", *Journal of Futures Markets*, 11, 55-68.

31. McCabe, George and Donald Solberg (1988), "Hedging in the Treasury Bill Futures Markets When the Hedged Instrument and the Deliverable Instrument Are Not Matched", WP University of Nebraska.

32. Messe, R. and K. Singleton (1982), "On Unit Roots and the Empirical

**Properties of Foreign Currency Hedge Ratio** 555

Modeling of Exchange Rates", *Journal of Finance*, 37: 1029-1035.

33. Overdahl, James A. and Dennis R. Starleaf (1986), "The Hedging Performance of the CD Futures Markets", *Journal of Futures Markets*, 6: 71-81.

34. Poterba, James and Lawrence Summers (1988), "The Persistence of Volatility and Stock Market Fluctuations", *American Economic Review*, 76: 1142-1151.

35. Poterba, James and Lawrence Summers (1988), "Mean Reversion in Stock Prices: Evidence and Implications", *Journal of Financial Economics*, 22: 27-59.

36. Stein, J.L. (1961), "The Simultaneous Determination of Spot and Futures Prices", *American Economic Review*, 51: 1012-1025.

37. Tirole, Jean (1989), "Theories of Speculation" in Bhattacharya S. and G.M. Constantinides, editors, *Financial Markets and Incomplete Information*, Rowman & Littlefield Publishers, Totowa, New Jersey.

38. Working, H. (1953), "Futures Trading and Hedging", *American Economic Review*, 43: 314-343.

39. Working, H. (1962), "New Concepts Concerning Futures Markets and Prices", *American Economic Review*, 52: 431-459.

## TABLE 1
### Distribution of the Variance-Ratio Statistic
#### Sample size n = 70

Critical values of the variance-ratio statistic based on a sample size of $n = 70$, obtained from 1,000 independent Monte Carlo experiments under the null hypothesis of serial independence. The variance-ratio statistic is defined as

$$VAR(k,2) = [var(k)/var(2)]*(2/k)$$

where $var(k)$ and $var(2)$ denote the variance of k-differences and two-differences, respectively. Each variance-ratio is corrected for small sample bias by dividing by the mean value of Monte Carlo experiments, denoted by $E[VAR(k,2)]$.

| | | Probability of a smaller value | | | | | | | |
|---|---|---|---|---|---|---|---|---|---|
| k | E[VAR(k,2)] | .05 | .10 | .20 | .30 | .70 | .80 | .90 | .95 |
| 1 | 1.0573 | 0.8097 | 0.8517 | 0.9065 | 0.9495 | 1.1259 | 1.2079 | 1.3005 | 1.3769 |
| 3 | 0.9643 | 0.7571 | 0.8030 | 0.8564 | 0.8954 | 1.0293 | 1.0732 | 1.1285 | 1.1700 |
| 4 | 0.9285 | 0.6221 | 0.6743 | 0.7488 | 0.8124 | 1.0314 | 1.0926 | 1.1773 | 1.2605 |
| 6 | 0.8971 | 0.4799 | 0.5371 | 0.6325 | 0.7101 | 1.0361 | 1.1467 | 1.3055 | 1.4300 |
| 8 | 0.8175 | 0.3239 | 0.3857 | 0.4865 | 0.5870 | 0.9719 | 1.0971 | 1.3069 | 1.4987 |
| 12 | 0.7240 | 0.2200 | 0.2811 | 0.3706 | 0.4486 | 0.8599 | 1.0368 | 1.2847 | 1.5624 |
| 16 | 0.6303 | 0.1766 | 0.2187 | 0.2770 | 0.3445 | 0.7493 | 0.9107 | 1.2248 | 1.4564 |

## Properties of Foreign Currency Hedge Ratio 557

**TABLE 2**

**Variance Ratio Test of the Random Walk Hypothesis for the Hedge Ratio**

Variance ratio for the hedge ratio for five major foreign currencies and two major stock market indexes. The variance ratio statistic is defined as

$$VAR(k,2) = [var(k)/var(2)]*(2/k)$$

where var(k) denotes the variance of log-level of the k-differences. Each variance ratio is corrected for small sample bias by dividing by the mean value of Monte Carlo experiments, denoted by E[VAR(k,2)].

| Futures | | | | | | | | |
|---|---|---|---|---|---|---|---|---|
| Contract | 1 | 3 | 4 | 6 | 8 | 12 | 16 | |
| | | | | k | | | | |
| Japanese Yen | 1.4498 | 0.9538 | 1.1126 | 0.9531 | 0.8273 | 0.8184 | 0.6126 | |
| British Pound | 1.5919 | 0.8602 | 0.9141 | 0.4724 | 0.2941 | 0.2309 | 0.2187 | |
| Swiss Franc | 1.6016 | 1.0894 | 0.8259 | 0.6043 | 0.5129 | 0.5034 | 0.3816 | |
| German Mark | 0.8897 | 0.7856 | 0.6717 | 0.5234 | 0.4035 | 0.2327 | 0.2402 | |
| Canadian Dollar | 1.1989 | 0.9041 | 0.8270 | 0.6020 | 0.5180 | 0.4088 | 0.2838 | |

## TABLE 3
### Variance Ratio Test of the Random Walk Hypothesis
### for the Measure of Hedging Effectiveness

Variance ratio for the measure of hedging effectiveness for five major foreign currencies and two major stock market indexes. The variance ratio statistic is defined as

$$VAR(k,2) = [var(k)/var(2)]*(2/k)$$

where var(k) denotes the variance of log-level of the k-differences. Each variance ratio is corrected for small sample bias by dividing by the mean value of Monte Carlo experiments, denoted by E[VAR(k,2)].

| Futures | | | | | | | |
| Contract | 1 | 3 | 4 | 6 | 8 | 12 | 16 |
|---|---|---|---|---|---|---|---|
| Japanese Yen | 1.1503 | 0.9958 | 0.9811 | 0.7211 | 0.3949 | 0.4218 | 0.3141 |
| British Pound | 1.6751 | 0.8423 | 0.8458 | 0.4317 | 0.3154 | 0.2335 | 0.2170 |
| Swiss Franc | 1.4390 | 0.8293 | 0.7998 | 0.5666 | 0.5501 | 0.4629 | 0.4847 |
| German Mark | 1.6572 | 0.7499 | 0.6502 | 0.4438 | 0.3271 | 0.2451 | 0.1849 |
| Canadian Dollar | 1.4245 | 0.7625 | 0.7954 | 0.5249 | 0.4373 | 0.3255 | 0.2295 |

(k)

**Properties of Foreign Currency Hedge Ratio** 559

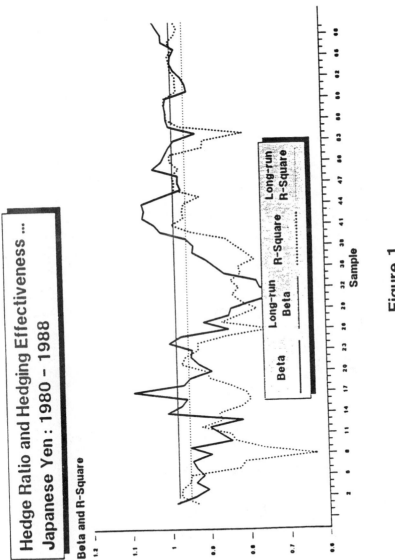

Figure 1

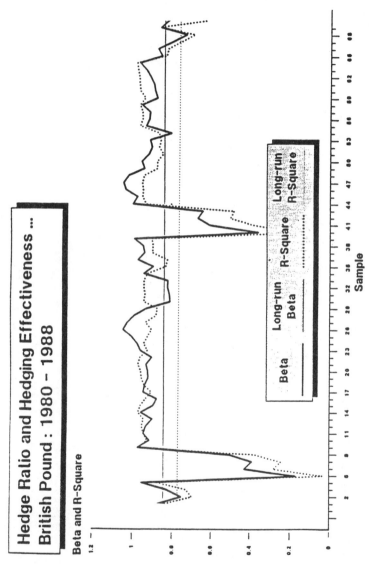

**Figure 2**

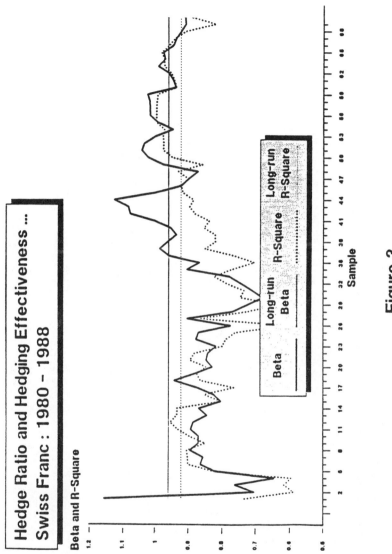

Figure 3

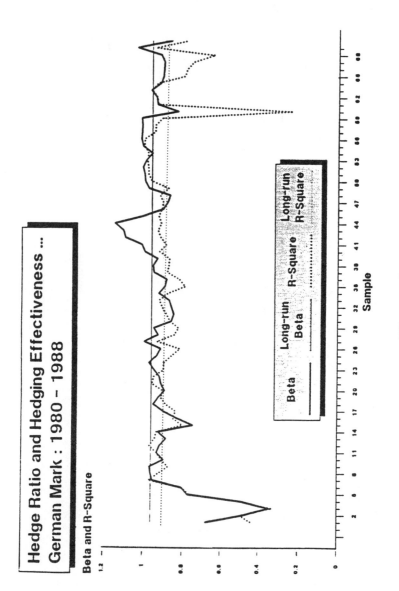

Figure 4

**Properties of Foreign Currency Hedge Ratio**                                    563

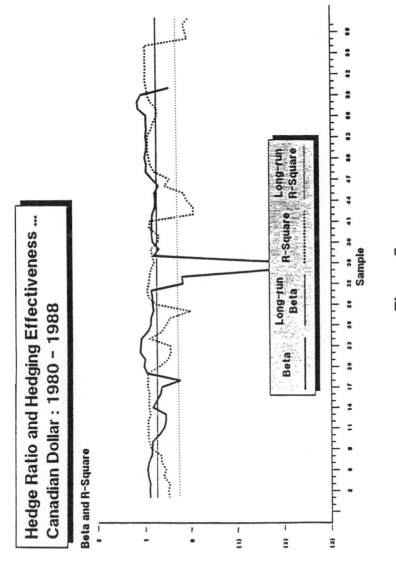

Figure 5

# [16]

# EQUITY AND OIL MARKETS UNDER EXTERNAL SHOCKS

*Jorge Urrutia and A.G. Malliaris*

The chapter investigates two hypotheses: first, that the impact of the Persian Gulf Crisis was stronger on the oil market than in the equity market; and, second, that there was an increase in the causal relationship between stock and oil prices during the crisis. Event-study and Granger causality tests confirm both hypotheses. The acceptance of the first hypothesis is consistent with the nature of the conflict which primarily affected the oil market due to the embargo of Iraqi oil. Also, the high degree of diversification of the S&P 500 index lessened the impact of higher oil prices. The confirmation of the second hypothesis agrees with efficient markets in the sense that equity and oil markets reacted quickly and simultaneously to the event.

## INTRODUCTION

Global events, such as the market crash of October 1987 and the Persian Gulf Crisis of August 1990, have affected the financial markets around the world. The impact of the market crash on national equity markets has been extensively documented (Roll 1988, Malliaris and Urrutia 1992). However, the Persian Gulf War, even though an important crisis highly publicized by the media, has only been a minor topic of academic research (Malliaris and Urrutia 1994).

It is known that the invasion of Kuwait and the successive events had a negative effect on equity prices and a positive effect on oil prices. The purpose of this chapter is to empirically investigate two hypotheses: first, an event-study methodology is used to investigate the hypothesis that the impact of the Gulf Crisis was stronger on the oil market than in the equity markets; and second, Granger causality tests are employed to investigate the hypothesis of a substantial increase in the causal relationship between stock and oil prices during the Persian Gulf Crisis. The rationale for our first hypothesis is twofold: first, the Gulf Crisis was mainly an oil conflict, and second, the equity indexes contain stocks of companies that benefited from the war, while others were adversely affected. Our second hypothesis is motivated by the efficient market hypothesis. That is, if financial and

JORGE URRUTIA AND A.G. MALLIARIS

commodity markets are efficient, then both equity and oil prices change daily responding quickly to fundamental political and war news from the Middle East. This simultaneous reaction to the event increased the short-term linkages between the two markets.

## DATA

Daily closing prices for the time period 1 October 1989 through 31 January 1991 are collected from the *Wall Street Journal* for the following instruments: S&P 500 spot, S&P 500 nearby futures, Arab lite oil spot, and crude oil (sweet light) nearby futures.

Daily returns for the spot instruments and daily percentage changes for the futures contracts are computed as $R_t = 100(\ln(P_t/P_{t-1}))$ where $P_t$ and $P_{t-1}$ are daily prices for days $t$ and $t-1$, respectively. The data are divided into an "Estimation Period," from 1 October 1989 to 31 May 1990 (observations $t = -206$ to $t = -44$), and an "Event Period," from 1 June 1990 to 31 January 1991 (observations $t = -43$ to $t = +119$). Thus, both the estimation period and the event period contain 163 trading days. The event day, $t = 0$, corresponds to 2 August 1990, the day of the Iraqi invasion of Kuwait. Other important dates on the sample are 16 January 1991, the beginning of the war between the International Coalition and Iraq ($t = +112$), and January 24, 1991 the start of the ground attack (t = +118).

## METHODOLOGY

This chapter uses event-study and Granger causality methodologies. A brief description of both methods follows.

### Event study methodology

The mean-adjusted return method is used to compute abnormal returns. In this method, the security's excess return is equal to the difference between the observed return during the event period and the average return of the security during the estimation period. Given the nature of the data used in this chapter the mean-adjusted return is the appropriate methodology since it does not require the use of the "market" portfolio (Masulis 1980; Brown and Warner 1980, 1985).

Let $R_{i,t}$ designate the observed return for security $i$ at day $t$. Define $AR_{i,t}$ as the excess or abnormal return for security $i$ at day $t$ of the event period given by:

$$AR_{i,t} = R_{i,t} - \overline{R}_i \tag{1}$$

where $\overline{R}_i$ is the simple average of security $i$'s daily returns in the $(-206, -44)$ estimation period, computed as

EQUITY AND OIL MARKETS UNDER EXTERNAL SHOCKS

$$\bar{R}_i = \frac{1}{163} \sum_{t=-206}^{-44} R_{i,t}.$$  (2)

The daily abnormal returns for security $i$ are standardized using

$$SAR_{i,t} = \frac{AR_{i,t}}{S_i}$$  (3)

where $SAR_{i,t}$ denotes standardized abnormal return for security $i$ at day $t$, and $S_i$ is standard deviation of returns for security $i$, during the estimation period, computed as:

$$S_i = \sqrt{\frac{1}{162} \sum_{i=-206}^{-44} (AR_{i,t} - \overline{AR})^2}.$$  (4)

where $\overline{AR}$ is the mean abnormal returns.

The $SAR_{i,t}$'s can be accumulated over selected multi-day intervals of the event period as follows:

$$CAR_{t_1,t_2} = \sum_{t=t_1}^{t_2} SAR_{i,t}$$  (5)

where $CAR_{t_1,t_2}$ denotes standardized cumulative abnormal returns for security $i$ during the $(t_1, t_2)$ interval of the event period.

The null hypotheses to be tested are that the abnormal return for security $i$ at day $t$ of the event period, $AR_{i,t}$, and the cumulative abnormal return for security $i$ during the $(t_1, t_2)$ interval of the event period, $CAR_{t_1,t_2}$, are equal to zero. The z-statistic for $AR_{i,t}$ is the $SAR_{i,t}$ given by formula (3). The z-statistic for $CAR_{t_1,t_2}$ is calculated as (Patell 1976, Dodd and Warner 1983):

$$z_{t_1,t_2} = \frac{CAR_{t_1,t_2}}{\sqrt{t_2 - t_1 + 1}}.$$  (6)

### Granger causality tests

The lead-lag tests used in this chapter are based on the Granger tests of causality. A description of several testable forms of Granger causality can be found in Pierce and Haugh (1977), Guilkey and Salemi (1982), and Geweke, *et al.* (1983). The following version of the Granger causal model is used:

$$\ln Y_t = \alpha_o + \sum_{i=1}^{m} \alpha_i \ln X_{t-i} + \sum_{j=1}^{m} \beta_j \ln Y_{t-j} + \varepsilon_t$$  (7)

JORGE URRUTIA AND A.G. MALLIARIS

$$\ln X_t = a_o + \sum_{i=1}^{m} a_i \ln Y_{t-i} + \sum_{j=1}^{m} b_j \ln X_{t-j} + \mu_t. \qquad (8)$$

The definition of causality given above implies that $X$ is causing (leading) $Y$ provided some $\alpha_i$ is not zero in equation (7). Similarly, $Y$ is causing (leading) $X$ if some $a_i$ is not zero in equation (8). If both of these events occur, there is feedback. The statistic is calculated by estimating the above expressions in both unconstrained (full model) and constrained (reduced model) forms, and may be written as:

$$F_1 = \frac{(SSE_r - SSE_f)/m}{SSE_f/(T - 2m - 1)} \qquad (9)$$

where $SSE_r$, $SSE_f$ denote the residual sum squares of the reduced and full models, respectively; $T$ is the total number of observations and $m$ is the number of lags.

### Test of cointegration

Engle and Granger (1987) show that if two nonstationary variables are cointegrated the Granger causality tests of the forms of equations (7) and (8) are misspecified. Therefore, before testing for causality it is necessary to test for cointegration. This paper uses the Augmented Dickey and Fuller (1981), ADF test of cointegration consisting of running first the cointegration regression

$$\ln X_t = a_0 + a_1 \ln Y_t + \varepsilon_t, \qquad (10)$$

and then running the ADF regression on the residuals of (10):

$$\varepsilon_t - \varepsilon_{t-1} = b_0 - b_1 \varepsilon_{t-1} + \sum_{i=1}^{m} b_i(\varepsilon_{t-i} - \varepsilon_{t-i-1}) + \mu_t. \qquad (11)$$

The null hypothesis of no cointegration is $H_0: b_1 = 0$ in equation (11). If the null is rejected, variables $X_t$ and $Y_t$ are cointegrated and the Granger regressions (7) and (8) are misspecified and must be corrected with an error correction term, which corresponds to the lagged residuals $\varepsilon_{t-1}$ of regression (10).

## ANALYSIS OF THE EMPIRICAL RESULTS

This section presents and discusses the results from the event-study and causality tests.

### Event-study results

The behavior of spot and futures prices is examined for an event period containing 163 trading days. Thus, the event period extends from day $-43$

106

EQUITY AND OIL MARKETS UNDER EXTERNAL SHOCKS

to day +119 relative to the initiation of the Persian Gulf Crisis. The day $t = 0$ corresponds to 2 August 1990: the day Iraq invaded Kuwait.

The standardized cumulative abnormal returns are presented in Table 8.1. As expected the CARs are negative for equity and positive for oil. However, the CARs are negative but insignificant for the spot and futures S&P 500. On the other hand, the spot and futures oil exhibit statistically significant positive CARs from one day after the invasion of Kuwait to one day after the initiation of the war (from $t = +1$ to $t = +113$). Therefore, the cumulative abnormal returns confirm our first hypothesis that the Persian Gulf Crisis had a more significant impact on the oil market than in the stock

*Table 8.1* Standardized cumulative abnormal returns (CAR) for the S&P 500 index and oil spot and futures from 43 days before to 119 days after the invasion of Kuwait (day '0' = 2 August 1990)

| | S&P 500 | | | | Oil | | | |
|---|---|---|---|---|---|---|---|---|
| | Spot | | Futures | | Spot | | Futures | |
| Event day | CAR | z-score | CAR | z-score | CAR | z-score | CAR | z-score |
| −40 | 1.121 | 0.560 | 0.921 | 0.461 | −4.085 | −2.042* | −3.827 | −1.914 |
| −30 | −0.706 | −0.189 | −0.065 | −0.017 | −4.248 | −1.135 | −6.632 | −1.772 |
| −20 | −0.508 | −0.104 | −0.117 | −0.024 | −1.878 | −0.383 | −2.824 | −0.576 |
| −10 | 0.174 | 0.030 | 0.395 | 0.068 | 6.007 | 1.030 | 2.367 | 0.406 |
| −5 | −1.371 | −0.220 | −1.220 | −0.195 | 9.193 | 1.472 | 7.102 | 1.137 |
| −4 | −1.632 | −0.258 | −1.526 | −0.241 | 9.249 | 1.462 | 6.989 | 1.105 |
| −3 | −2.165 | −0.338 | −2.117 | −0.331 | 10.141 | 1.584 | 6.389 | 0.998 |
| −2 | −1.738 | −0.268 | −1.553 | −0.240 | 9.782 | 1.509 | 6.836 | 1.055 |
| −1 | 0.228 | 0.035 | −1.493 | −0.228 | 10.803 | 1.647 | 8.021 | 1.223 |
| 0 | −1.774 | −0.267 | −1.747 | −0.263 | 12.727 | 1.919 | 10.031 | 1.512 |
| 1 | −2.639 | −0.393 | −2.509 | −0.374 | 18.073 | 2.694* | 13.518 | 2.015* |
| 2 | −4.067 | −0.600 | −4.075 | −0.601 | 22.333 | 3.293* | 16.399 | 2.418* |
| 3 | −6.365 | −0.928 | −6.786 | −0.990 | 27.566 | 4.021* | 23.096 | 3.369* |
| 4 | −6.291 | −0.908 | −6.174 | −0.891 | 27.997 | 4.041* | 23.581 | 3.404* |
| 5 | −5.529 | −0.790 | −5.667 | −0.810 | 27.867 | 3.981* | 19.359 | 2.766* |
| 10 | −5.230 | −0.712 | −5.272 | −0.717 | 29.893 | 4.068* | 20.458 | 2.784* |
| 20 | −8.934 | −1.117 | −9.419 | −1.177 | 29.551 | 3.694* | 19.771 | 2.471* |
| 40 | −14.761 | −1.611 | −14.752 | −1.610 | 51.733 | 5.645* | 41.159 | 4.491* |
| 60 | −12.825 | −1.258 | −12.896 | −1.265 | 43.184 | 4.235* | 34.757 | 3.408* |
| 90 | −9.182 | −0.793 | −9.349 | −0.808 | 34.425 | 2.974* | 23.285 | 2.011* |
| 110 | −12.379 | −0.998 | −12.422 | −1.001 | 33.059 | 2.664* | 25.230 | 2.033* |
| 111 | −13.044 | −1.048 | −12.900 | −1.036 | 26.234 | 2.107* | 31.172 | 2.504* |
| 112 | −12.764 | −1.022 | −12.889 | −1.032 | 39.133 | 3.133* | 30.059 | 2.407* |
| 113 | −12.204 | −0.974 | −12.002 | −0.958 | 40.259 | 3.213* | 33.146 | 2.645* |
| 114 | −9.495 | −0.755 | −8.820 | −0.702 | 21.969 | 1.748 | 13.514 | 1.075 |
| 115 | −8.551 | −0.678 | −8.405 | −0.667 | 17.510 | 1.389 | 8.255 | 0.655 |
| 116 | −8.828 | −0.698 | −8.632 | −0.682 | 17.837 | 1.410 | 13.257 | 1.048 |

* Significant at the 5 percent level or better.

JORGE URRUTIA AND A.G. MALLIARIS

market. Intuitively, this is because the primary impact of the Iraqi invasion of Kuwait was on oil prices, due to the oil embargo imposed by the allies to Iraq. While the Iraqi invasion was initially interpreted as a local conflict between two Arab oil producing countries, the strong reaction of the US to the Iraqi aggression, along with the UN condemnation and the Iraqi oil embargo, rapidly gave this crisis a global dimension with a significant increase in oil prices. On the other hand, the US equity market experienced a lesser negative impact probably because the S&P 500 index contains only a small number of companies with oil reserves, the stocks of which appreciated because of anticipated higher profits from higher world oil prices. Also, the overall negative impact of an increase in the price of oil in such a broad index is lesser because of the effect of portfolio diversification.

Plots of the CARs are presented in Figures 8.1 to 8.4. As expected, the graphs show the opposite reactions of the equity and oil markets to the Persian Gulf Crisis. Visual inspections of the graphs also suggest that spot and futures returns were highly correlated during the event. This implies

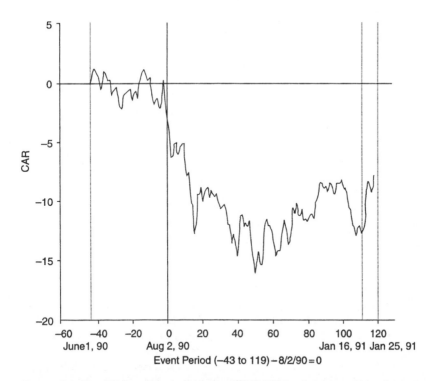

*Figure 8.1* Cumulative abnormal returns (S&P 500 spot), mean adjusted returns method

108

EQUITY AND OIL MARKETS UNDER EXTERNAL SHOCKS

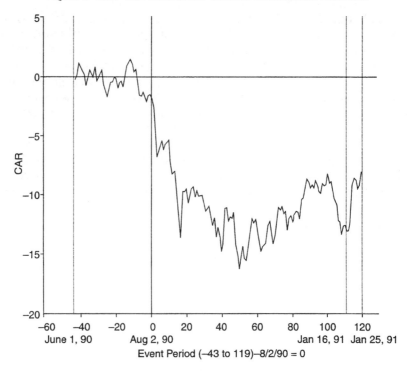

*Figure 8.2* Cumulative abnormal returns (S&P 500 futures), mean adjusted returns method

that the price fluctuations were due to news from the Persian Gulf and not the effect of extra trading activities in the futures exchanges. Thus, it does not seem that futures markets contributed to increase price volatility during the Gulf Crisis.

In order to further explore the differential impact of the Persian Gulf Crisis on the oil and markets, mean differences of CARs are computed. In the days immediately following the invasion of Kuwait – that is, in the (+1,+3) and (+1,+5) intervals – the mean differences of CARs between the spot S&P 500 and oil are $-19.43$ ($z = -7.93$), and $-18.90$ ($z = -5.98$), respectively. For the interval immediate before the start of the war (+111, +112) and the periods immediate after the start of the war (+113, +114) and (+113, +116), the mean differences of CARs are $-6.46$ ($z = -3.23$), 20.43 ($z = 10.22$) and 25.23 ($z = 8.92$) respectively. Similar results (not reported here) are obtained for the futures contracts. All these differences of means are significant at the 5 percent level or better, and reinforce our finding that the Persian Gulf Crisis had a bigger impact on the oil market than on the stock market.

109

JORGE URRUTIA AND A.G. MALLIARIS

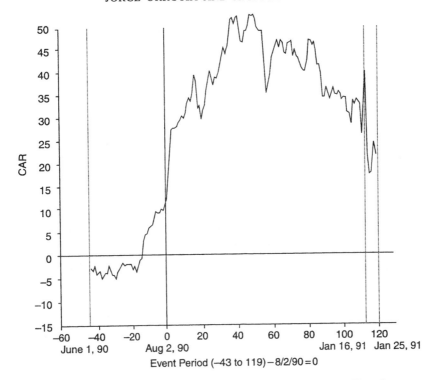

*Figure 8.3* Cumulative abnormal returns (oil spot prices), mean adjusted returns
method

## Causality test results

In order to better capture and contrast the impact of the Gulf Crisis on the
relationship between equity and oil markets, the data have been divided in
two sets: the pre-Gulf Crisis period, from 1 October 1989 to 31 May 1990;
and the Gulf Crisis period from 1 June 1990 to 31 January 1991.

Prior to the implementation of the causality tests we test the time-series
for integration and cointegration. The ADF tests of stationarity for the price
levels are presented in Table 8.2. The null hypothesis of nonstationarity
cannot be rejected for any of the cases; thus, prices are unit roots. The ADF
tests of stationarity for returns or percentage price changes, shown in Table
8.3, indicate that the null of nonstationarity is rejected in all cases. Therefore, prices of S&P 500 and oil, spot and futures, are integrated of order
one, I(1), and it is necessary to test for cointegration.

Panel A of Table 8.4 shows that cointegration for the pre-Gulf Crisis
period is partially rejected. On the other hand, Panel B indicates that all
prices are cointegrated during the Gulf Crisis period. Giving that the results
of the tests of cointegration are mixed we proceed as follows: when the

EQUITY AND OIL MARKETS UNDER EXTERNAL SHOCKS

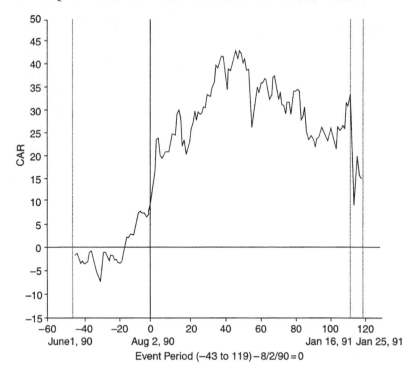

*Figure 8.4* Cumulative abnormal returns (oil futures prices), mean adjusted returns
method

prices are not cointegrated, the causality tests are conducted by running regressions (7) and (8). When cointegration is present the error correcting terms are incorporated in the regressions.

The results of the Granger causality tests are presented in Table 8.5. Panel A indicates that no lead-lag relationship is detected for the pre-Gulf Crisis period. On the other hand, Panel B shows a dramatic increase in causality during the period of the Persian Gulf Crisis. In effect, strong contemporaneous causality and feedback are found during the period of the conflict. These results confirm our second hypothesis that equity and oil markets are efficient and stock and oil prices changed quickly responding to fundamental news coming from the Gulf. The efficient price reaction increased the linkages of these markets during the crisis. Our result is consistent with those reported by other studies about equity prices behavior during global shocks. In this respect, Malliaris and Urrutia (1992) show that during the October 1987 Stock Market Crash contemporaneous causality increased among national equity markets.

111

JORGE URRUTIA AND A.G. MALLIARIS

*Table 8.2* Augmented Dickey–Fuller tests of stationarity for S&P 500 index and oil spot and futures prices

| Contract | $b_0$ | $b_1$ | $b_2$ | $b_3$ | $b_4$ | $R^2$ |
|---|---|---|---|---|---|---|
| | PANEL A: pre-Gulf Crisis Period: 1 Oct 1989 to 31 May 1990 | | | | | |
| S&P 500 spot | 0.504 | −0.086 | −0.215 | −0.025 | −0.047 | 0.099 |
| | (2.08)* | (−2.08)* | (−2.57)* | (−0.30) | (−0.59) | (4.25)* |
| S&P 500 futures | 0.522 | −0.089 | −0.197 | −0.051 | 0.057 | 0.096 |
| | (2.30)* | (2.30)* | (−2.38)* | (−0.49) | (0.71) | (4.09)* |
| Oil spot | −0.003 | 0.001 | −0.105 | −0.001 | 0.010 | 0.011 |
| | (−0.05) | (0.01) | (−1.26) | (−0.02) | (0.12) | (0.42) |
| Oil futures | 0.045 | −0.015 | 0.006 | −0.056 | −0.158 | 0.035 |
| | (0.65) | (−0.67) | (0.08) | (−0.69) | (−1.95) | (1.39) |
| | PANEL B: Gulf Crisis Period: 1 June 1990 to 31 Jan 1991 | | | | | |
| S&P 500 spot | 0.161 | −0.028 | 0.163 | −0.090 | −0.071 | 0.060 |
| | (1.78) | (−1.79) | (2.03)* | (−1.11) | (−0.89) | (2.44)* |
| S&P 500 futures | 0.157 | −0.027 | 0.091 | −0.113 | −0.106 | 0.055 |
| | (1.69) | (−1.69) | (1.14) | (−1.41) | (−1.33) | (2.22) |
| Oil spot | 0.067 | −0.020 | 0.132 | −0.236 | 0.028 | 0.081 |
| | (1.60) | (−1.55) | (1.65) | (−2.98)* | (0.34) | (3.35)* |
| Oil futures | 0.089 | −0.026 | 0.026 | −0.114 | −0.192 | 0.072 |
| | (1.58) | (−1.55) | (−0.34) | (−1.44) | (−2.37)* | (2.95)* |

*Notes*: The model is

$$\ln P_t - \ln P_{t-1} = b_0 + b_1 \ln P_{t-1} + b_2(\ln P_{t-1} - \ln P_{t-2}) + b_3(\ln P_{t-2} - \ln P_{t-3}) + b_4(\ln P_{t-3} - \ln P_{t-4}) + \varepsilon_t$$

The null hypothesis is $b_1 = 0$ (prices are non-stationary). The $t$-critical at the 5 percent level is −2.88 (from Dickey and Fuller 1981).
An asterisk * indicates that the individual regression coefficient is different from zero at the 5 percent of confidence level.

## SUMMARY AND CONCLUSIONS

The chapter has investigated two hypotheses: first, that the impact of the Persian Gulf Crisis was stronger on the oil market than on the equity market; and second, that there was an increase in the causal relationship between stock and oil prices during the Persian Gulf Crisis. We have used data for the spot and futures S&P 500 index and the Arab oil from October 1989 to January 1991. The empirical results have confirmed our hypotheses. In effect, we have found that the impact of the Gulf Crisis was stronger on the oil market than on the equity market. This is consistent with the nature of the conflict, which primarily affected the oil market due to the embargo imposed to Iraqi oil. Also, the lesser impact on the S&P 500 is explained by the high degree of diversification of the index, which includes several stocks that benefited from high oil prices. The Gulf Crisis also produced a dramatic increase in causality between the equity and oil markets. This is consistent with the notion of efficient markets in the sense that both markets reacted quickly and simultaneously to the fundamental

112

EQUITY AND OIL MARKETS UNDER EXTERNAL SHOCKS

*Table 8.3* Augmented Dickey–Fuller tests of stationarity for S&P 500 index and oil spot and futures returns

| Contract | $b_0$ | $b_1$ | $b_2$ | $b_3$ | $b_4$ | $R^2$ |
|---|---|---|---|---|---|---|
| | PANEL A: pre-Gulf Crisis Period: 1 Oct 1989 to 31 May 1990 | | | | | |
| S&P 500 spot | 0.012 | −1.524 | 0.246 | 0.166 | 0.065 | 0.633 |
| | (0.11) | $(-7.60)^a$ | (1.46) | (1.29) | (0.81) | (66.30)* |
| S&P 500 futures | 0.003 | −1.442 | 0.187 | 0.088 | 0.088 | 0.625 |
| | (0.03) | $(-7.34)^a$ | (1.12) | (0.69) | (1.10) | (64.09)* |
| Oil spot | −0.163 | −1.142 | −0.043 | 0.047 | 0.063 | 0.55 |
| | (−0.89) | $(-6.67)^a$ | (0.29) | (0.40) | (0.76) | (47.40)* |
| Oil futures | −0.103 | −1.227 | 0.225 | 0.161 | −0.007 | 0.508 |
| | (−0.63) | $(-7.10)^a$ | (1.58) | (1.41) | (−0.09) | (39.77)* |
| | PANEL B: Gulf Crisis Period: 1 June 1990 to 31 Jan 1991 | | | | | |
| S&P 500 spot | −0.055 | 0.998 | 0.157 | 0.061 | −0.023 | 0.434 |
| | (−0.58) | $(-6.48)^a$ | $(1.21)^a$ | (0.57) | (−0.28) | (29.36)* |
| S&P 500 futures | −0.056 | −1.046 | 0.140 | 0.030 | −0.092 | 0.475 |
| | (−0.56) | $(-6.35)^a$ | (1.03) | (0.27) | (−1.14) | (34.54)* |
| Oil spot | 0.247 | −1.110 | 0.239 | −0.008 | 0.019 | 0.481 |
| | (0.50) | $(-6.74)^a$ | (1.71) | (−0.07) | (0.23) | (35.37)* |
| Oil futures | 0.197 | −1.202 | 0.235 | 0.121 | −0.081 | 0.513 |
| | (0.43) | $(-6.86)^a$ | (1.65) | (1.05) | (−0.97) | (40.25)* |

*Notes*: The model is

$$R_t - R_{t-1} = b_0 + b_1 R_{t-1} + b_2(R_{t-1} - R_{t-2}) + b_3(R_{t-2} - R_{t-3}) + b_4(R_{t-3} - R_{t-4}) + \varepsilon_t$$

where

$$R_t = 100\ln(P_t/P_{t-1})$$

The null hypothesis is $b_1 = 0$ (returns or percentage of price changes are non-stationary). The $t$-critical at the 5 percent level is −2.88 (from Dickey and Fuller 1981).
An "a" indicates rejection of the null at the 5 percent of confidence level.
An asterisk * indicates that the individual regression coefficient is different from zero at the 5 percent of confidence level.

political and war news coming out of the Middle East. Our results agree with the reported increase in causality among financial markets during global events, such as the market crash of October 1989.

Table 8.4 Tests of cointegration between the S&P 500 index and oil spot and futures prices

| Dependent variable | Independent variable | $b_0$ | $b_1$ | $b_2$ | $b_3$ | $b_4$ | $R^2$ |
|---|---|---|---|---|---|---|---|
| | | PANEL A: pre-Gulf Crisis Period: 1 Oct 1989 to 31 May 1990 | | | | | |
| S&P 500 spot | Oil spot | 0.0002 | 0.1644 | -0.3223 | -0.1462 | -0.1341 | 0.169 |
| | | (0.17) | (4.31)*a | (-4.20)* | (-1.84) | (-1.75) | (7.86)* |
| Oil spot | S&P 500 spot | -0.0020 | 0.0544 | -0.1067 | -0.0592 | -0.0355 | 0.053 |
| | | (-1.09) | (2.79)* | (-1.32) | (-0.72) | (-0.43) | (2.15) |
| S&P 500 futures | Oil futures | 0.0001 | 0.1538 | -0.2990 | -0.1786 | -0.0470 | 0.148 |
| | | (0.06) | (3.99)*a | (-3.84)* | (-2.26)* | (-0.60) | (6.73)* |
| Oil futures | S&P 500 futures | -0.0011 | 0.0703 | -0.0535 | -0.1744 | -0.1463 | 0.083 |
| | | (-0.64) | (2.85)* | (-0.67) | (-2.23)* | (-1.85) | (3.49)* |
| | | PANEL B: Gulf Crisis Period: 1 June 1990 to 31 Jan 1991 | | | | | |
| S&P 500 spot | Oil spot | -0.0003 | 0.1829 | -0.1580 | -0.3067 | -0.0769 | 0.174 |
| | | (-0.38) | (4.49)*a | (-1.98)* | (-4.10)* | (-0.99) | (8.07)* |
| Oil spot | S&P 500 spot | -0.0018 | 0.1775 | -0.1714 | -0.3264 | -0.0722 | 0.186 |
| | | (-0.36) | (4.50)*a | (-2.15)* | (-4.39)* | (-0.93) | (8.75)* |
| S&P 500 futures | Oil futures | -0.0003 | 0.2598 | -0.2797 | -0.3088 | -0.2261 | 0.247 |
| | | (-0.41) | (5.83)*a | (-3.67)* | (-4.28)* | (-3.05)* | (12.54)* |
| Oil futures | S&P 500 futures | -0.0014 | 0.2661 | -0.2899 | -0.3135 | -0.2379 | 0.257 |
| | | (-0.39) | (5.98)*a | (-3.82)* | (-4.37)* | (-3.22)* | (13.25)* |

*Notes*: The model used to test for cointegration is the following:

$$\ln P_t = a_0 + a_1 \ln P_{2t} + \varepsilon_t \tag{1}$$

$$\varepsilon_t - \varepsilon_{t-1} = b_0 + b_1 \varepsilon_{t-1} + b_2(\varepsilon_{t-1} - \varepsilon_{t-2}) + b_3(\varepsilon_{t-2} - \varepsilon_{t-3}) + b_4(\varepsilon_{t-3} - \varepsilon_{t-4}) + \mu_t \tag{2}$$

The coefficients in the table are from equation (2).
The null hypothesis is $H_0$: $b_1 = 0$ (no-cointegration).
The $t$-critical at the 5 percent level in 3.17 (from Engle and Granger 1987).
An "a" indicates rejection of the null hypothesis of no-cointegration at the 5 percent of significance level.
An asterisk * indicates that the individual regression coefficient is different from zero at the 5 percent level.

Table 8.5 Causality tests between S&P 500 index and oil spot and futures prices

| Dependent variable | Independent variable | $b_0, \beta_0$ | $b_1, \beta_1$ | $b_2, \beta_2$ | $b_3, \beta_3$ | $H_0: \sum_{i=0}^{3} b_i = 0$ / $H_0: \sum_{i=0}^{3} \beta_i = 0$ |
|---|---|---|---|---|---|---|
| PANEL A: Pre-Gulf Crisis Period: 1 Oct 1989 to 31 May 1990 | | | | | | |
| S&P 500 spot | Oil spot | −0.9487 (−0.98) | −1.6401 (−0.74) | −1.0082 (−0.73) | −0.1379 (0.14) | 1.318 |
| Oil spot | S&P 500 spot | −0.0063 (−0.94) | 0.0164 (2.04)* | −0.0058 (−0.71) | −0.0026 (−0.38) | 1.468 |
| S&P 500 futures | Oil futures | −0.2243 (−0.27) | −1.3758 (−0.43) | −1.5435 (−1.31) | −0.7819 (0.92) | 0.589 |
| Oil futures | S&P 500 futures | −0.0023 (−0.29) | 0.0084 (0.88) | −0.0141 (−1.48) | 0.0092 (1.18) | 0.888 |
| PANEL B: Gulf Crisis Period: 1 June 1990 to 31 Jan 1991 | | | | | | |
| S&P 500 spot | Oil spot | −1.1213 (−5.99)* | 1.5224 (4.97)* | −0.4767 (−1.73) | −0.1837 (0.90) | 10.258[a] |
| Oil spot | S&P 500 spot | −0.1721 (−5.79)* | 0.0646 (1.18) | 0.0211 (0.47) | 0.0764 (2.35)* | 15.581[a] |
| S&P 500 futures | Oil futures | −1.3620 (−8.33)* | 1.7759 (5.33)* | −0.2790 (−1.10) | 0.1661 (0.83) | 19.310[a] |
| Oil futures | S&P 500 futures | −0.2321 (−8.33)* | 0.1490 (2.51)* | 0.0355 (0.78) | 0.0308 (0.92) | 20.87[a] |

*Notes:* The causality models are:

$$\ln X_t = a_0 + a_1 \ln X_{t-1} + a_2 \ln X_{t-2} + a_3 \ln X_{t-3} + b_0 \ln Y_t + b_1 \ln Y_{t-1} + b_2 \ln Y_{t-2} + b_3 \ln Y_{t-3} + C_0 \varepsilon_t + C_0 \varepsilon_{t-1} + \phi_t \ (Y \rightarrow X)$$

$$\ln Y_t = \alpha_0 + \alpha_1 \ln Y_{t-1} + \alpha_2 \ln Y_{t-2} + \alpha_3 \ln Y_{t-3} + \beta_0 \ln X_t + \beta_1 \ln X_{t-1} + \beta_2 \ln X_{t-2} + \beta_3 \ln X_{t-3} + \delta \varepsilon_{t-1} + \varepsilon_t \ (X \rightarrow Y)$$

The null hypotheses are

$$H_0: \sum_{i=0}^{3} b_i = 0, \ \sum_{i=0}^{3} \beta_i = 0$$

An "a" indicates the null hypothesis is rejected at the 1 percent of confidence level.
The $F_{\text{critical}}$ are $F_{152, 4} = 2.37$ at 5 percent; 3.32 at 1 percent
    $F_{153, 3} = 2.60$ at 5 percent; 3.78 at 1 percent
An asterisk * indicates that the individual regression coefficient is different from zero at the 5 percent confidence level.

JORGE URRUTIA AND A.G. MALLIARIS

# REFERENCES

Brown, S.J. and J.B. Warner (1980) "Measuring Security Price Performance," *Journal of Financial Economics*, 8: 205–58.

Brown, S.J. and J.B. Warner (1985) "Using Daily Stock Returns: The Case of Event Studies," *Journal of Financial Economics*, 14: 3–32.

Dickey, D. and W. Fuller (1981) "Likelihood Ratio Statistics for Autoregressive Time Series with a Unit Root," *Econometrica*, 49: 1057–72.

Dodd, P. and J.B. Warner (1983) "On Corporate Governance: A Study of Proxy Contests," *Journal of Financial Economics*, 11: 401–38.

Engle, R.F., and C.W.J. Granger (1987) "Cointegration and Error Correction: Representation, Estimation, and Testing," *Econometrica*, 55: 251– 76.

Geweke, J., R. Meese and W. Dent (1983) "Comparing Alternative Tests of Causality in Temporal Systems," *Journal of Econometrics*, 21: 161–94.

Guilkey, D.K., and M.K. Salemi (1982) "Small Sample Properties of Three Tests for Granger Causal Ordering in a Bivariate Stochastic System," *The Review of Economics and Statistics*, 64: 668–80.

Malliaris, A.G. and J.L. Urrutia (1992) "The International Crash of October 1987: Causality Tests," *Journal of Financial and Quantitative Analysis*, 27: 353–64.

Malliaris, A.G. and J.L. Urrutia (1994) "The Impact of the Persian Gulf Crisis on National Equity Markets," *Advances in International Banking and Finance*, 1: 43–65.

Masulis, R.W. (1980) "The Effect of Capital Structure Change on Security Prices: A Study of Exchange Offers," *Journal of Financial Economics*, 8: 139–78.

Patell, J.M. (1976) "Corporate Forecasts of Earnings per Share and Stock Price Behavior: Empirical Tests," *Journal of Accounting Research*, 14: 246–76.

Pierce, D.A., and L.D. Haugh (1977) "Causality in Temporal Systems: Characterizations and a Survey," *Journal of Econometrics*, 5: 265–93.

Roll, R. (1988) "The International Crash of October 1987," *The Financial Analyst Journal*, 44: 19–35.

# [17]

Review of Quantitative Finance and Accounting, 10 (1998): 285–302
© 1998 Kluwer Academic Publishers, Boston. Manufactured in The Netherlands.

# Volume and Volatility in Foreign Currency Futures Markets

RAMAPRASAD BHAR
*Faculty of Business, School of Finance and Economics, University of Technology, Sydney, PO Box 123, Broadway NSW 2007, Australia*

A. G. MALLIARIS
*Walter F. Mullady, Sr. Professor of Business Administration, Department of Economics, Loyola University of Chicago, 820 N. Michigan Avenue, Chicago, Illinois 60611*

**Abstract.** In this paper we propose and test several hypotheses concerning time series properties of trading volume, price, short and long-term relationships between price and volume and the determinants of trading volume in foreign currency futures. The nearby contracts for British Pound, Canadian Dollar, Japanese Yen, German Mark and Swiss Franc are analyzed in three frequencies i.e. daily, weekly and monthly.

We find supportive evidence for all the five currencies that the price volatility is a determinant of the trading volume changes. Furthermore, the volatility of the price process is a determinant of the unexpected component of the changes in trading volume. Also, there is a significant relationship between the volatility of price and the volatility of trading volume changes for three of the five currencies in the daily frequency and for one currency in the monthly frequency.

**Key words:** Volume, volatility, currency

## 1. Introduction

Most economic reports published by the futures exchanges and regulatory agencies use volume data to measure the growth or decline of the futures contracts. Also, as exchanges research for the possible introduction of a new type of futures contract, the potential futures volume of trade in such a contract receives primary attention as a proxy for the contract's liquidity. Furthermore, volume data are used to measure shifts in the composition of futures markets, as can be illustrated by the phenomenal growth in the contract volume of financial futures compared to agricultural futures.

In addition to exchanges and regulatory agencies being interested in the behavior of the volume of trading, traders themselves pay attention to trading volume. Low volume, usually implies that the market is illiquid and the bid/ask spread will tend to be large, resulting in high price volatility. Such a market will discourage hedgers, but may benefit speculators. On the other hand, high trading volume contributes to high liquidity and the bid/ask spread will tend to be small, resulting in low price variability. Hedgers prefer low day to day volatility while speculators usually do not because low volatility reduces speculators' profits.

The importance of volume of trade in futures markets leads one to ask the question: What are the economic determinants of this variable? It is the purpose of this paper to develop a model of the determinants of trading volume and to test it empirically for several foreign currency futures contracts using daily data.

## 2. Overview of the literature

Several earlier studies have empirically examined the contemporaneous relation between volume traded and security price variability. Ying (1966), Crouch (1970), Clark (1973), Copeland (1976), Westerfied (1977), Epps and Epps (1976), Rogalski (1978), and Upton and Shannon (1979) are among the representative studies to find a positive association between volume and price variability. Price variability is defined differently by various authors. Some define it as the squared price change, $(\Delta p)^2$, or as the absolute price change, $|\Delta p|$, while others offer slightly different measures.

One theoretical motivation of these studies is the supply and demand model. From a given initial equilibrium position under certain assumptions, a net increase (decrease) in demand for a stock will cause the stock price to increase (decrease). Therefore one would expect changes in volume transactions to be influenced by price changes. Crouch (1970) and Rogalski (1978) elaborate this theoretical motivation.

A second theoretical motivation is presented in Clark (1973) and in Epps and Epps (1976) who interpret their empirical findings of the dependence between transactions volume and the change in the logarithm of security price, from one period to the other, as evidence for Clark's thesis. Clark (1973) proposed an alternative to Mandelbrot's (1963, 1967, 1973) argument that speculative prices follow stable laws. More specifically, Clark (1973) argued that the distribution of speculative prices is normal when conditioned on its variance, with such price variance being curvilinearly related to trading volume.

Finally, the third theoretical explanation is proposed by Copeland (1976), who develops a sequential arrival of information model which, under certain assumptions, implies a positive correlation between trading volume and price variability.

These earlier studies were followed by Cornell (1981), Tauchen and Pitts (1983), Rutledge (1984), Grammatikos and Saunders (1986), Garcia, Leuthold and Zapata (1986) and others. These authors investigate the price variability and volume relationship using data and institutional characteristics from futures markets. In particular, Cornell (1981) proposes that the volume of trading is related to price uncertainty where uncertainty introduces two motives for futures trading: the desire to transfer risk and the assessment of differential information.

It can be argued that increases in price uncertainty contribute to increases in trading volume due to both increases in hedging positions and activities based on differential beliefs. Cornell actually goes further, using Grossman's (1981) framework, to derive an expression relating volume of futures trading to price variability. Defining price variability as the variance of daily log price relatives, that is, $\text{Var}[\ln P_{t+1} - \ln P_t]$, a significant, positive and contemporaneous correlation was found between the changes in average daily volume and changes in the standard deviation of daily log price relatives for 14 of the 18 commodities in his sample.

Tauchen and Pitts (1983) extend the price variability and trading volume theory by first, deriving a joint probability distribution of the intra-day price change and trading volume and, second, by showing how this distribution changes as the number of traders change. They encourage researchers to include preliminary tests for trend in the volume of trading before price variance and volume regressions are performed.

Grammatikos and Saunders (1986) contribute to the price variability and volume literature by proposing various price variance estimators. Both classical and Garman-Klass estimators of price volatility were employed and a strong, positive and contemporaneous correlation was confirmed between these estimators and trading volume.

Garcia, Leuthold and Zapata (1986) perform statistical tests of lead-lag relationships between trading volume and futures prices. In a sample of 120 four-month trading periods for several agricultural futures contracts during 1979 and early 1980s, they find that simultaneity exists between volume and price variability in 86.1% of the cases when price variability is defined as adjusted range. The percent of simultaneity drops to only 10.9 when price variability is defined as percent change in daily closing prices.

Finally, some studies such as Carlton (1983, 1984), Malliaris and Urrutia (1991, 1995) and Martell and Wolf (1987) empirically examine determinants of volume, other than price variability. Carlton (1984) emphasizes inflation, while Martell and Wolf (1987) and Malliaris and Urrutia (1991) consider several factors, such as, rate of unemployment, industrial production, inflation, market performance, interest rates and other macroeconomic variables. Furthermore, Malliaris and Urrutia (1995) analyze interrelationships between volume and prices for several agricultural futures contracts.

## 3. An evaluation of the current literature

Despite its diversity, the theoretical interpretations and empirical results of the current literature briefly surveyed in section 2 and more extensively in Karpoff (1987) are reasonably straightforward. Theoretically, the behavior of volume is related to price uncertainty and empirically there is evidence that supports this hypothesis.

It could be argued that price behavior has received a disproportionate degree of attention and that on pure theoretical grounds such price behavior cannot be independent of volume dynamics. Ross (1989) in a review of intertemporal asset pricing argues that there is no extensive research on volume behavior simply because we have no comprehensive theories. Ross (1989) concludes that "it seems clear that the only way to explain the volume of trade is with a model that is at one and the same time appealingly rational and yet permits divergent and changing opinions in a fashion that is other than ad hoc". Similarly, Karpoff (1987, p. 123) concludes his survey remarking that the development of a theoretical model is needed that incorporates rational heterogeneous agents so that "the joint distribution of price and volume could emerge in such a model as a result of idiosyncratic shocks that impinge on individual traders, and aggregate shocks that affect all market agents."

Some authors have developed theoretical models of trading volume. Huffman (1987) develops a dynamic general equilibrium asset pricing model with a logarithmic utility function in which both prices and transaction volume are endogenously determined. In Huffman's model, asset prices, rates of return and transaction volume are all affected by the existing distribution of capital holdings among the heterogeneous agents.

Karpoff (1986) develops a model of trading volume based on heterogeneous investors who periodically and idiosyncratically revise their demand prices. The model describes two ways informational events affect trading volume. One way is consistent with the hypothesis that investor disagreement leads to increased trading. The second way suggests that volume can increase even if investors interpret the information identically, provided they also have divergent prior expectations.

Finally, Pagano (1989) studies the relationship between trading volume and market liquidity. The notion of market liquidity can be measured along two dimensions: the riskiness of the final value of an asset and the availability of a market that can readily absorb the sale without adverse price changes. Pagano (1989) builds on the second dimension to examine how thin markets can absorb large orders only at the cost of adverse price changes and examines how trading volume and absorptive capacity of the market tend to feed positively on each other.

Despite these major studies and several more reviewed by Karpoff (1987), our understanding of the behavior of trading volume in asset markets and in futures markets in particular remains limited. Our goal in this paper is to develop and test a simple stochastic version of a dynamic supply and demand model in continuous time that identifies some determinants of trading volume. As indicated in the introductory section and elaborated in the review of the literature, trading volume is an important economic variable which is influenced by several economic variables. The model presented below explicitly describes some of these determinants of volume.

## 4. Model and hypotheses

Guided by the review of the literature, we now present a model of the determinants of trading volume. Recall that from the earlier models of Crouch (1970) and Rogalski (1978) to more recent ones, such as Garcia, Leuthold and Zapata (1986) and Malliaris and Urrutia (1998), these models are variants of the standard supply and demand framework where quantity is a function of price. Following this fundamental relationship we write that volume is a function of price and time:

$$V = V(t, P) \tag{4.1}$$

where $V$ denotes trading volume, $P$ denotes futures price and $t$ denotes time. The relationship between an equilibrium futures price and an equilibrium volume of trading, as in (4.1), can indeed be highly complicated, and furthermore it can dynamically change over time. This change over time is expressed by the argument $t$ in (4.1).

To allow for full generality in our model we do not specify an explicit relationship in (4.1). Both fundamental and technical factors could influence the dynamic relationship in (4.1). For example, suppose that one observes rising prices with fairly stable volume of trading. A fundamental analyst may interpret this to mean a highly inelastic supply function with shifts in demand while a technical analyst may conclude that the stable volume does not confirm the observed upward trend. Numerous other examples can be given such as increasing prices with increasing volume or decreasing prices with increasing volume. Our model in (4.1) is so general that both fundamental and technical analysts can accept it.

Assume that the function $V$ in (4.1) is twice continuously differentiable and that $P$ follows an Itô process with drift $\mu$ and volatility $\sigma$, written as:

$$dP = \mu dt + \sigma dZ \tag{4.2}$$

In (4.2), $Z$ denotes a standardized Weiner process. The appropriateness of (4.2) to describe asset prices has been reviewed extensively in Merton (1982) who offers numerous arguments in support of the use of Itô processes to characterize the behavior of an asset price. Among these arguments, the most compelling one is that Itô processes describe continuous random walks with a drift and therefore confirm the market efficiency hypothesis. Although Merton (1982) offers numerous theoretical reasons in favor of the use of (4.2), the actual distribution of prices is ultimately an empirical issue and the current evidence as to whether asset returns are normally distributed or not is mixed. See for example Upton and Shannon (1979).

By postulating that price differences, $dP$, follow (4.2) or more generally that price returns, $dP/P$, are as (4.2) we do not commit ourself to random walks or market efficiency. Rather, we write a general relation as in (4.1) and invite the actual data to reveal the relevance of (4.2) and (4.3), below. An application of Itô's lemma presented in Malliaris and Brock (1982) yields where $V_t$, $V_P$ and $V_{PP}$ denote partial derivatives.

$$
\begin{aligned}
dV &= V_t + V_P dP + \frac{1}{2} V_{PP}(dP)^2 \\
&= V_t dt + V_P[\mu dt + \sigma dZ] + \frac{1}{2} V_{PP}\sigma^2 dt \\
&= \left[V_t + V_P\mu + \frac{1}{2} V_{PP}\sigma^2\right]dt + V_P\sigma dZ
\end{aligned}
\tag{4.3}
$$

The model described by equations (4.1) to (4.3) allows us to formulate several hypotheses.

Firstly, note that both $P$ and $V$ in (4.1) are random variables with certain distribution functions. If these distribution functions do not change over time, we say that $V$ and $P$ are stationary. First we perform the appropriate test to check the stationarity of price and volume. Specifically equation (4.2) describes futures prices as a diffusion process. Since diffusion processes are continuous time random walks, our model (4.1)–(4.3) claims the following: if futures prices follow a random walk, then volume of trading also follows a random walk. Test of randomness and stationarity for both prices and volumes allow us to verify the validity of this hypothesis.

One may wonder what is the meaning and significance of this implication of our model. To give such a meaning recall that claiming that prices are random means that they cannot systematically be predicted. This statistical property of asset prices has been supported by the efficient market hypothesis. What our model establishes is that through the relationship of supply and demand in (4.1) market efficiency with its unpredictability of prices translates into the unpredictability of trading volume. To repeat our earlier remark, we do not claim that prices always follow random walks but rather argue that if this is the case then it must necessarily follow that trading volume also inherits this statistical property. One could argue that the unpredictability of prices as a statistical phenomenon is supported by the theory of market efficiency which claims that prices are random because they incorporate and reflect the random arrival of relevant information. What would be the theoretical justification of the random behavior of trading volume? We agree with De-Bondt and Thaler (1995) who argue that the standard financial paradigm has paid only peripheral attention to trading volume and thus does not offer any specific explanations. However, outside academic finance, technical analysis has long emphasized the informational significance of volume. For example, Murphy (1985) explains that most technicians in futures markets follow a three-dimensional approach to market analysis by tracking the movement of price, volume and open interest. Such tracking of price, volume and open interest offers support to (4.3) which translates the random shock $dZ$ of prices, caused by the arrival of new information into a shock in volume. Note however that the shock in volume as described by (4.3) is more complex than that of prices.

Secondly, the implication of (4.1) is that futures prices and the corresponding volume of trading are interrelated and can affect each other. As noted, (4.1) is quite general and this functional relationship is investigated by testing for a statistical lead lag relationship between volume and price. A priori, we cannot expect that the price and volume relationship in (4.1) can always be detected by the existing statistical methodologies. However the model in (4.1) clearly relates price and volume in the spirit of the supply and demand paradigm and we propose to follow an appropriate methodology to study possible relationships between price and volume.

Thirdly, by taking expectations of (4.3) we conclude the following:

$$E(dV) = V_t + V_P\mu + \frac{1}{2}V_{PP}\sigma^2 \tag{4.4}$$

This expression suggests that the average change in volume over a sample period depends on three determinants: (i) a trend factor $V_t$; (ii) the drift coefficient of prices $\mu$; and, (iii) the volatility of futures prices $\sigma^2$. From (4.4) we can write the following testable relationship:

$$E(dV) = \alpha t + \beta\mu + \gamma\sigma^2 \tag{4.5}$$

This expression allows us to empirically confirm or reject these three determinants of volume. Again, one may ask about the meaning of (4.5). This implication of our model is supported by a large literature on the relationship between volume and price variability. The numerous references given earlier such as Cornell (1981), Epps and Epps (1976), Garcia, Leuthold and Zapata (1986), Tauchen and Pitts (1983) and others both argue theoretically and confirm in certain cases empirically the positive relationship between price variability and volume. One simple way to explain this is to observe that volatile markets attract traders and increase volume. Put differently (4.5) says that volatile markets are more liquid than markets with low volatility. This liquidity effect exists much stronger on a day-to-day basis. Obviously, price and volume volatilities on a week-to-week or month-to-month basis are affected by economic fundamentals. The impact of exogenous shocks on both volume and price volatility on a monthly frequency is studied in Malliaris and Urrutia (1991).

Beyond all this, (4.5) supports some of the ideas of technical analysis. Murphy (1985) states that price trends are confirmed by increasing volume and (4.5) specifies this by relating the price trend coefficients, $\mu$, to volume increases $dV$. Thus (4.5) is supported theoretically by both fundamental and technical analysis.

Fourthly, inspection of (4.3) and (4.4) shows that actual changes in trading volume can be considered as composed of an expected part, $E(dV)$, and an unexpected part, $U(dV)$. It is interesting to note that due to the functional relationship in (4.1) and the assumption of the price process given by (4.2), both components of volume changes are influenced by the price volatility. This observation leads to another testable hypothesis,

$$U(dV) = \theta_1 + \theta_2 \sigma \tag{4.6}$$

Bessembinder and Seguin (1993) examine the effect of decomposing the volume in the expected and the unexpected components. To achieve this they model the volume time series using an autoregressive (Box-Jenkins) process of arbitrary length (10). Here we obtain the unexpected component of volume changes as a result of application of Ito's lemma (equation (4.3)). It should be noticed that an econometric test for the equation (4.6) relies upon the variable being generated as part of an earlier regression. We, however, avoid the generated regressor problem (Pagan (1984)) since we are using $U(dV)$ as a regressand and this does not lead to the biases in standard errors. Our rationale in this context is same as that offered by Bessembinder and Seguin (1993, footnote 7, page 30).

Finally, stochastic calculus techniques allow us to derive the volatility of trading volume from (4.3) as:

$$Var(dV) = V_p^2 \sigma^2 \tag{4.7}$$

which says that the volatility of trading volume is a function of the futures price volatility. This is another new result that has not been proposed nor has being empirically investigated before. Thus, our final test consists of exploring various functional forms of

$$Var(dV) = F(\sigma^2) \tag{4.8}$$

where $\sigma^2$ denotes the variance of futures price. Volume of contracts traded has played a key role in several recent papers attempting to explain GARCH effect found in many security return series. For example, Lamoureux and Lastrapes (1990) explain GARCH in individual stock return based upon a theory that the returns are generated from a mixture of distributions where the rate of information arrival is the stochastic mixing variable. Since the rate of information arrival is unobservable, volume has been used as a proxy variable. Furthermore, Bauer and Nieuwland (1995) show that the volume of trade has explanatory power over and above its use as a proxy for information arrival. It is in this context better understanding of the time series properties of volume is important. The framework developed in this paper hypothesizes the link between the price volatility and the volatility of volume changes which can be tested empirically.

We conclude this section by describing our contribution. Motivated by a large literature which searches to explain price-volume relationships, we offer equation (4.1) to express functional relationship between price and volume. This equation is supported by the supply and demand model of price theory and is tested using the Granger causality methodology.

Unless we choose a specific process to describe price behavior our model in (4.1) remains unspecified. In (4.2) we write that prices follow a continuous random walk. The advantage of (4.2) consists of the use of stochastic calculus which allows us to derive the hypothesis that volume follows a continuous random walk whenever prices follow a similar process. This is a new result that has not been proposed in the existing literature. Furthermore, our model offers two additional results: volume is related to price volatility and volume volatility is related to price volatility. Some authors have tested the relationship of price volatility and volume, often without a formal model. Thus, our model offers four testable hypothesis and integrates various theoretical and empirical studies.

## 5. Data

We use daily settlement prices for the nearby futures contract for five foreign currencies traded at the Chicago Mercantile Exchange. The five currencies studied are the British Pound, the Canadian Dollar, the Japanese Yen, the German Mark and the Swiss Franc. Daily data used cover the period May 1972 to November 1994. All tests are done in three frequencies, i.e. daily, weekly and monthly. Weekly data are created using every Wednesday figures and monthly data are created using figures for the first trading day of the month. Volume refers to daily total volume for all traded contracts.

## 6. Methodology

In this section we describe briefly the methods used to test the hypotheses.

## 6.1. Tests of stationarity

The augmented Dickey-Fuller test is based on the following regression for a time series $y_t$:

$$\Delta y_t = \alpha_0 + \alpha_1 y_{t-1} + \alpha_2 t + \sum_{j=1}^{P} \gamma_j \Delta y_{t-j} + \varepsilon_t \tag{6.1}$$

where $\varepsilon_t$ is a Gaussian white noise. The lag order $p$ is set as the highest significant lag order from either the autocorrelation function or the partial autocorrelation function of the $\Delta y_t$ series. The null hypothesis is $\alpha_1 = \alpha_2 = 0$.

Phillips-Perron test requires first calculation of the test statistics from the above equation with p=0 and then apply the transformation suggested by Perron (1988).

## 6.2. Granger causality tests

A time series $x_t$ fails to Granger cause another time series $y_t$ if in a regression of $y_t$ on lagged $y$'s and lagged $x$'s, the coefficients of the latter are zero. We use the following regression:

$$y_t = \sum_{i=1}^{k} \alpha_i y_{t-i} + \sum_{j=1}^{k} \beta_j x_{t-j} + \varepsilon_t. \tag{6.2}$$

If $\beta_j = 0$ ($j = 1,2, \dots k$), then $x_t$ fails to cause $y_t$. The usual $F$-test is applied to test the hypothesis. The lag length in the regression is chosen somewhat arbitrarily.

There is, however, some controversy in the literature about the word "causality". Many argue that what we are essentially testing is whether certain variable precedes another variable.

## 6.3. Tests of the determinants of trading volume

We implement the equations (4.4) and (4.5) by running the following regressions:

$$\Delta V_t = \alpha_0 + \alpha_1 t + \beta \Delta P_t + \gamma \sigma_{P_t}^2 + e_t \tag{6.3}$$

where,

$$\Delta V_t = (V_t - V_{t-1}),$$

$$\Delta P_t = (P_t - P_{t-1}), \text{ and}$$

$\sigma_{P_t}^2$ is the point estimate of the variance of the price process obtained by the method discussed in Bhar (1994).

The residual in (6.5) is unexpected component $\Delta V_t^U$ and the first three terms give $\Delta V_t^E$, the expected component. Thus the hypothesis of the equation (4.6) is implemented with the help of the following regression:

$$\Delta V_t^U = \theta_0 + \theta_1 \sigma_{P_t}. \tag{6.4}$$

Finally, we empirically test (4.8) with the following regression,

$$\sigma_{V_t}^2 = \alpha + \delta \sigma_{P_t}^2 \tag{6.5}$$

where $\sigma_{V_t}^2$ is obtained similar to $\sigma_{P_t}^2$.

## 7. Analysis of empirical results

Before we present the empirical results it is informative to check some of the relationships in the data set graphically. Figure 1 plots the time series of the price and volume data for the entire period covering May 1972 through to November 1994 for Japanese yen using monthly observations. Although co-movement in the volatility (estimation discussed later)

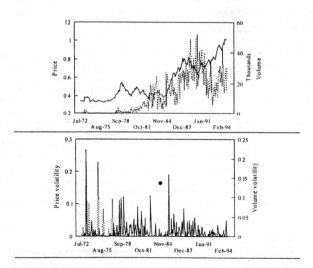

The solid lines represent price data and the dashed lines represent volume data. A possible structural change is noticeable in the upper panel around November 1984. Also, comovement in the volatility series is detected in the lower panel. Further tests are carried out to confirm these observations.

*Figure 1.* PRICE AND VOLUME: JAPANESE YEN MONTHLY DATA (MAY 1972–NOVEMBER 1994)

*Table 1.* TEST FOR STRUCTURAL BREAK (MAY 1972–NOVEMBER 1994)

|      | DAILY | WEEKLY | MONTHLY |
|------|-------|--------|---------|
| GBP  | 0.071 | 0.148  | 0.192   |
| CAD  | 0.577 | 0.831  | 0.801   |
| DEM  | 0.016 | 0.017  | 0.049   |
| JPY  | 0.028 | 0.007  | 0.036   |
| CHF  | 0.027 | 0.043  | 0.060   |

Structural break is examined using Chow test with the help of a regression where the price is regressed against its lagged value and a constant. The null hypothesis is that the two sets of coefficients across the break point are equal and has a $F$-distribution. The entries in the table are $p$-values for the computed $F$-statistic. A value less than 0.05 implies that the null hypothesis can be rejected at 0.05 level. As suggested by the Figure 1, the break point is assumed to be around November 1984.
The results support the existence of a structural break for DEM, JPY and CHF.

series is noticeable, a major shift in price series appears to have occurred around November 1984. It is, therefore, important to test for any structural break in the data for all the currencies before any other tests are carried out. Table 1 presents the results for testing structural break using Chow test with the help of a regression where the price is regressed against lagged price and a constant. In all three frequencies i.e. daily, weekly and monthly and at 0.05 level of significance the series for DEM, JPY and CHF have undergone a structural break around November 1984. There is not, however, enough evidence for this in the other two currencies. For the sake of consistency all further tests are carried out using the sample spanning December 1984 to November 1994 for all the five currencies.

We first investigate the time series properties of the five currency futures contracts. Table 2 shows the results of the stationarity tests. It appears that in terms of Augmented

*Table 2.* TESTS OF STATIONARITY IN MONTHLY DATA (DECEMBER 1984–NOVEMBER 1994)

| Series | Price Level | | Price First Differenced | | Volume Level | | Volume First Differenced | |
|--------|------|------|------|------|------|------|------|------|
|        | ADF  | PP   | ADF  | PP   | ADF  | PP   | ADF  | PP   |
| GBP | −2.55 | −2.31 | −4.59* | −10.15* | −3.22* | −8.36* | −5.45* | −19.19* |
| CAD | −0.82 | −0.53 | −2.85 | −11.26* | −2.70 | −8.68* | −4.60* | −19.53* |
| DEM | −2.18 | −2.18 | −2.69 | −11.06* | −2.19 | −8.20* | −6.33* | −19.47* |
| JPY | −2.81 | −2.02 | −2.02 | −11.07* | −3.59* | −7.38* | −6.38* | −23.29* |
| CHF | −2.24 | −2.26 | −2.22 | −10.46* | −2.94 | −9.94* | −5.00* | −22.29* |

ADF: Augmented Dickey-Fuller test statistic with the number of lag terms chosen to ensure errors are uncorrelated. The number of lags needed varied between 60 and 75 for daily data, 15 to 35 for weekly data and 0 to 16 for monthly data. This is decided by the highest significant autocorrelation function or the partial autocorrelation function of the differenced series.
PP: Phillips-Perron test statistic using Newey and West (1987) method of constructing estimate of error variance. Truncation lag parameter = 1 used.
The underlying data generating process is assumed to have a drift component and log transformation is used in the tests. Although not presented, the results assuming no drift component are not much different.
Critical value at 10% significance level: −3.13 for both the tests, and * indicates rejection of the null hypothesis that the series is $I(1)$.

Dickey-Fuller (ADF) tests all the daily data series are $I(1)$ in the level for price and only three series are $I(1)$ for the volume series. But Phillips-Perron tests reject the hypotheses of $I(1)$ for any of the volume data in the level. Similarly, the Phillips-Perron test reject the hypotheses of $I(1)$ for all the first differenced price series. suggest that the volume series are not $I(1)$ in the level. We, therefore, conclude that the price series are $I(1)$ in the level and $I(0)$ in the first differences whereas the level volume series are stationary. The result for the weekly and monthly series (not presented in the table) are similar.

It has been reported in the literature that the prices of different currencies in the same market are cointegrated i.e. maintain a long-term relationship. Our objective here, on the other hand, has been to examine long term relationship between the currency price and the volume of contracts traded for that currency. Since we find that volume series are stationary we do not pursue this investigation further and conclude that the price and volume are not cointegrated.

We next investigate the short-term interrelationship between price and volume using Granger causality test and these results are given in Table 3. At 0.05 level significance the result indicate that lagged GBP price changes are determinant of volume changes in the weekly data. This is supportive of our volume price relationship given by (4.1). We do not find evidence of such interrelationship in any other frequencies (not reported in the table).

Our next testable hypothesis is that changes in trading volume over time depend on three factors, namely i) a trend factor, ii) the drift component of the price process, and iii) the volatility of the price process. These results are shown in the Table 4. The actual test equation implemented is also shown in that table. The proxy for the volatility of the price process in obtained as a point estimate as described in Bhar (1994). The method is based upon a non-parametric technique developed by Chesney, Elliott, Madan and Yang (1993)

*Table 3.* TESTS OF GRANGER CAUSALITY IN PRICE & VOLUME WEEKLY DATA (DECEMBER 1984–NOVEMBER 1994)

| Price | GBP | CAD | DEM | JPY | CHF |
|---|---|---|---|---|---|
| $R$-Square | 0.027 | 0.019 | 0.027 | 0.026 | 0.023 |
| DW | 2.001 | 1.997 | 2.001 | 1.999 | 2.003 |
| FBEX | 1.037 | 1.371 | 1.121 | 0.589 | 0.670 |
| $p$-values | 0.252 | 0.224 | 0.348 | 0.739 | 0.672 |

| Volume | GBP | CAD | DEM | JPY | CHF |
|---|---|---|---|---|---|
| $R$-Square | 0.351 | 0.337 | 0.288 | 0.289 | 0.288 |
| DW | 2.036 | 2.022 | 2.030 | 2.012 | 2.002 |
| FBEX | 2.339 | 1.060 | 0.562 | 0.869 | 1.137 |
| $p$-values | 0.031 | 0.383 | 0.761 | 0.497 | 0.339 |

The panels show the relevant statistics from Granger causality test using a Vector Auto Regression (VAR) representation of the first differenced series. The upper panel is for Price as the dependent variable and the lower panel is for Volume as dependent variable. The VAR lag length of 6 is used for weekly data.

DW means Durbin-Watson statistic for serial correlations in the residual, and FBEX is the $F$-test for block exogeneity and the number in parentheses are corresponding $p$-values. For the upper panel if the $p$-value for FBEX test is greater than 0.05 then the coefficients of the lagged Volume are collectively zeros at 0.05 level. Similarly for the lower panel this corresponds to the lagged Price.

*Table 4.* DETERMINANTS OF TRADING VOLUME DAILY DATA (DECEMBER 1984–NOVEMBER 1994)

| | GBP | CAD | DEM | JPY | CHF |
|---|---|---|---|---|---|
| $\alpha_0$ | −0.0185 | −0.0195 | −0.0281* | −0.0317 | −0.0365 |
| | (0.308) | (0.395) | (0.045) | (0.230) | (0.045) |
| $\alpha_1$ | −0.76E-5 | −0.73E-5 | −0.66E-5 | −0.23E-5 | −0.48E-5 |
| | (0.237) | (0.287) | (0.272) | (0.762) | (0.394) |
| $\beta$ | −1.3467 | −0.8364 | 1.5702 | 2.4399 | 1.0929 |
| | (0.378) | (0.826) | (0.266) | (0.211) | (0.348) |
| $\gamma$ | 2.8159* | 18.7422* | 3.2687* | 2.7783* | 2.6353* |
| | (0.000) | (0.000) | (0.000) | (0.000) | (0.000) |
| DW | 2.617 | 2.569 | 2.612 | 2.552 | 2.622 |
| R-Sq. | 0.065 | 0.053 | 0.087 | 0.095 | 0.089 |

The model used is:

$$\Delta V_t = \alpha_0 + \alpha_1 t + \beta \Delta P_t + \gamma \sigma^2_{P_t}$$

where $\sigma^2_{P_t}$ is the point estimate of the variance of the price process obtained by using the method described in Bhar (1994).

The coefficients obtained from ordinary least square estimation are as given in the table with corresponding *p*-values in the parentheses below the coefficients. For example, a *p*-value greater than 0.05 means that the null hypothesis of the corresponding coefficient equals zero can not be rejected at 0.05 level.

An * indicates that the coefficient is statistically different from zero.

which assumes a scalar diffusion process for the price and discretizes it using Milstein's scheme. This results in an estimator for the diffusion coefficient and Chesney et al also show how to minimize the variance of this estimator. We find that the volatility component is statistically significant for all the currencies and the Table 4 display this for the daily data. For weekly data the result is similar, but for monthly data only DEM and JPY prices show such significant relationship. The results for weekly and monthly data are not shown in Table 4. Interestingly, the changes in the volume of contracts traded for CAD are much more strongly influenced by the price volatility than for any of the other four currencies examined. There are, of course, other methods by which the estimate of price volatility can be obtained. For example, it is well documented that the currency futures return series exhibit a GARCH effect. Nelson (1990) shows that a GARCH process can be approximated by a diffusion process as the time intervals between observations goes to zero. We have also tested another specification where the price volatility is given by the absolute value of the price changes. The general nature of the result just described does not change from the alternative specification of the price volatility.

We then implement the testable form of the hypothesis described by the equation (4.6) in the Table 5. Based upon the specification given by the equations (4.1) and (4.2) we expect that the unexpected component of volatility change is influenced by the price volatility. This is supported by the results in the Table 5. Bessembinder and Seguin (1993), however, find that the unexpected change in volume affect asymmetrically the price volatility. Here we find the other side of the equation in price and volume relationship although we do not observe this with weekly or monthly data.

*Table 5.* UNEXPECTED TRADING VOLUME & PRICE VOLATILITY DAILY DATA (DECEMBER 1984–NOVEMBER 1994)

|         | GBP      | CAD      | DEM      | JPY      | CHF      |
|---------|----------|----------|----------|----------|----------|
| $\theta_0$ | −0.0528* | −0.0619* | −0.0357* | −0.0445* | −0.0373* |
|         | (0.000)  | (0.000)  | (0.009)  | (0.011)  | (0.004)  |
| $\theta_1$ | 0.6418*  | 1.9628*  | 0.4187*  | 0.5645*  | 0.3746*  |
|         | (0.000)  | (0.000)  | (0.000)  | (0.000)  | (0.000)  |
| DW      | 2.67     | 2.67     | 2.71     | 2.82     | 2.78     |
| R-Sq.   | 0.005    | 0.006    | 0.002    | 0.003    | 0.003    |

The model used is:

$$\Delta V_t^U = \theta_0 + \theta_1 \sigma_{P_t}$$

where $\sigma_{P_t}^2$ is the point estimate of the variance of the price process obtained by using the method described in Bhar (1994). $\Delta V_t^U$ is the unexpected component of the trading volume and is the difference between the actual change in trading volume less the expected part given by the model estimated in Table 3. It is, therefore, the residual of the regression described in Table 3.

The coefficients obtained from ordinary least square estimation are as given in the table with corresponding p-values in the parentheses below the coefficients. For example, a p-value greater than 0.05 means that the null hypothesis of the corresponding coefficient equals zero can not be rejected at 0.05 level. An * indicates that the coefficient is statistically different from zero.

Finally, we document another important relationship not reported elsewhere. We test the hypothesis of functional relationship between the volatility of trading volume changes and the volatility of price. The Tables 6 to 8 in this respect present the results for daily, weekly and monthly data respectively. We find evidence of support for the relationship (6.7) in three out of five currencies using daily data and only with one currency using monthly data. These results tend to confirm that with high frequency data price volatility is an important determinant of volume volatility. Similar results are also reported for agricultural futures by Malliaris and Urrutia (1995). While explaining the GARCH effect stock

*Table 6.* VOLATILITY OF TRADING VOLUME AS A FUNCTION OF PRICE VOLATILITY DAILY DATA (DECEMBER 1984–NOVEMBER 1994)

|         | GBP      | CAD      | DEM      | JPY      | CHF      |
|---------|----------|----------|----------|----------|----------|
| $\alpha$ | 0.0376*  | 0.0948*  | 0.0265*  | 0.0094   | −0.0324  |
|         | (0.000)  | (0.001)  | (0.001)  | (0.653)  | (0.019)  |
| $\delta$ | −0.0738  | −3.0226  | 0.6838*  | 8.1545*  | 3.8992*  |
|         | (0.530)  | (0.533)  | (0.002)  | (0.000)  | (0.000)  |
| DW      | 1.951    | 1.996    | 1.986    | 1.977    | 1.982    |
| R-Sq.   | 0.001    | 0.001    | 0.002    | 0.051    | 0.030    |

The model used is:

$$\sigma_{V_t}^2 = \alpha + \delta \sigma_{P_t}^2$$

where $\sigma_{P_t}^2$, $\sigma_{V_t}^2$ are the point estimates of the variances of the price process and the volume process, respectively, obtained by using the method described in Bhar (1994).

The coefficients obtained from ordinary least square estimation are as given in the table with corresponding p-values in the parentheses below the coefficients. For example, a p-value greater than 0.05 means that the null hypothesis of the corresponding coefficient equals zero can not be rejected at 0.05 level. An * indicates that the coefficient is statistically different from zero.

*Table 7.* VOLATILITY OF TRADING VOLUME AS A FUNCTION OF PRICE VOLATILITY WEEKLY DATA (DECEMBER 1984–NOVEMBER 1994)

|        | GBP      | CAD      | DEM      | JPY      | CHF      |
|--------|----------|----------|----------|----------|----------|
| $\alpha$ | 0.0085*  | 0.0074*  | 0.0038*  | 0.0386*  | 0.0051*  |
|        | (0.000)  | (0.000)  | (0.000)  | (0.032)  | (0.000)  |
| $\delta$ | −0.0314  | −0.2026  | 0.0314   | −0.4668  | −0.9302  |
|        | (0.430)  | (0.545)  | (0.134)  | (0.531)  | (0.772)  |
| DW     | 1.771    | 1.997    | 1.714    | 1.985    | 1.882    |
| $R$-Sq. | 0.005   | 0.003    | 0.002    | 0.004    | 0.001    |

The model used is:

$$\sigma_{V_t}^2 = \alpha + \delta\sigma_{P_t}^2$$

where $\sigma_{P_t}^2$, $\sigma_{V_t}^2$ are the point estimates of the variances of the price process and the volume process, respectively, obtained by using the method described in Bhar (1994).

The coefficients obtained from ordinary least square estimation are as given in the table with corresponding $p$-values in the parentheses below the coefficients. For example, a $p$-value greater than 0.05 means that the null hypothesis of the corresponding coefficient equals zero can not be rejected at 0.05 level. An * indicates that the coefficient is different from zero.

returns Bauer and Nieuwland (1995) suggest that the volume of trade represents a measure of diversity of interpretation of information among the participants. In our approach, however, if price already reflects this diversity of interpretation of information then price volatility must affect trading volume volatility.

*Table 8.* VOLATILITY OF TRADING VOLUME AS A FUNCTION OF PRICE VOLATILITY MONTHLY DATA (DECEMBER 1984–NOVEMBER 1994)

|        | GBP      | CAD      | DEM      | JPY      | CHF      |
|--------|----------|----------|----------|----------|----------|
| $\alpha$ | 0.0015*  | 0.0027   | 0.0038*  | 0.0013   | 0.0018*  |
|        | (0.000)  | (0.053)  | (0.018)  | (0.321)  | (0.010)  |
| $\delta$ | 0.0155  | 0.2221   | −0.0307  | 0.1691*  | −0.0029  |
|        | (0.296)  | (0.435)  | (0.580)  | (0.000)  | (0.076)  |
| DW     | 1.891    | 1.916    | 1.911    | 1.616    | 1.835    |
| $R$-Sq. | 0.004   | 0.002    | 0.001    | 0.066    | 0.001    |

The model used is:

$$\sigma_{V_t}^2 = \alpha + \delta\sigma_{P_t}^2$$

where $\sigma_{P_t}^2$, $\sigma_{V_t}^2$ are the point estimates of the variances of the price process and the volume process, respectively, obtained by using the method described in Bhar (1994).

The coefficients obtained from ordinary least square estimation are as given in the table with corresponding $p$-values in the parentheses below the coefficients. For example, a $p$-value greater than 0.05 means that the null hypothesis of the corresponding coefficient equals zero can not be rejected at 0.05 level. An * indicates that the coefficient is statistically different from zero.

## 8. Summary and conclusions

We propose and test several hypotheses in this paper concerning time series properties of trading volume, price, short and long-term relationships between price and volume and the determinants of trading volume in foreign currency futures. The data covering the period May 1972 to November 1994, relating to the nearby currency futures for British Pound, Canadian Dollar, Japanese Yen, German Mark and Swiss Franc, are analyzed in three frequencies i.e. daily, weekly and monthly. Of these, the German Mark, Japanese Yen and the Swiss Franc are found contain structural break around November 1984.

We find that the price series are non-stationary in the levels for all the three currencies but the volume series are stationary. Only in case of British Pound we find that the volume change Granger causes price change. We also find evidence in all the five currencies that the price volatility is a determinant of the trading volume changes. Furthermore, the price volatility is a determinant of the unexpected volume changes. Also, there is a significant relationship between the volatility of price and the volatility of trading volume changes for three of the five currencies in the daily frequency and for only one currency in the monthly frequency.

## References

Bauer, R. and F. Nieuwland, "A multiplicative model for volume and volatility." *Applied Mathematical Finance* 2, 135–154, (1995).

Bessembinder H. and P.J. Seguin, "Price Volatility, Trading Volume, and Market Depth: Evidence from Futures Markets." *Journal of Financial and Quantitative Analysis* 28, 21–39, (1993).

Bhar, R., "Testing for Long-term Memory in Yen/Dollar Exchange Rate." *Financial Engineering and the Japanese Market* 1(2), 101–109, (1994).

Carlton, D., "Futures Trading, Market Interrelationships, and Industry Structure." *American Journal of Agricultural Economics* 65, 380–387, (1983).

Carlton, D., "Futures Markets: Their Purpose, Their History, Their Growth, Their Successes and Failures." *Journal of Futures Markets* 4, 237–271, (1984).

Chesney, M., R.J. Elliott, D. Madan, and H. Yang, "Diffusion Coefficient Estimation And Asset Pricing When Risk Premia And Sensitivities Are Time Varying." *Mathematical Finance* 3, 85–99, (1993).

Clark, P., "A Subordinated Stochastic Process Model With Finite Variance for Speculative Prices." *Econometrica* 41, 135–155, (1973).

Copeland, T., "A Model of Asset Trading Under the Assumption of Sequential Information Arrival." *Journal of Finance* 31, 1149–1168, (1976).

Cornell, B., "The Relationship Between Volume and Price Variability in Futures Markets." *Journal of Futures Markets* 1, 303–316, (1981).

Crouch, R., "A Nonlinear Test of the Random-Walk Hypothesis." *American Economic Review* 60, 199–202, (1970).

DeBondt W. and R. Thaler, "Financial Decision-Making in Markets and Firms: A Behavioral Perspective." In R. Jarrow and others, editors, *Handbook of Finance*, North Holland Publishing Company, New York, 1995.

Dickey, D.A. and W.A. Fuller, "Distribution of the Estimators for Autoregressive Time Series with a Unit Root." *Journal of the American Statistical Association* 74, 427–431, (1979).

Engle, R.F. and C.W.J. Granger, "Cointegration and Error Correction: Representation, Estimation and Testing." *Econometrica* 55, 251–276, (1987).

Epps, T. and M. Epps, "The Stochastic Dependence of Security Price Changes and Transaction Volumes: Implications for the Mixture-of-Distributions Hypothesis." *Econometrica* 44, 305–321, (1976).

Garcia, P., R. Leuthold, and H. Zapata, "Lead-Lag Relationships Between Trading Volume and Price Variability: New Evidence." *Journal of Futures Markets* 6, 1–10, (1986).

Grammatikos, T. and A. Saunders, "Futures Price Variability: A Test of Maturity and Volume Effects." *Journal of Business* 59, 319–330, (1986).

Granger, C.W.J., "Investigating Causal Relations by Econometric Models and Cross-Spectral Models." *Econometrica* 37, 428–438, (1969).

Grossman, S., "An Introduction to the Theory of Rational Expectations Under Asymmetric Information." *Review of Economic Studies* 48, 541–559, (1981).

Huffman, G.W., "A Dynamic Equilibrium Model of Asset Prices and Transaction Volume." *Journal of Political Economy* 95, 138–159, (1987).

Johansen, S., "Statistical Analysis of Cointegration Vectors." *Journal of Economic Dynamics and Control* 12, 231–254, (1988).

Karpoff, J.M., "A Theory of Trading Volume." *The Journal of Finance* 41, 1069–1082, (1986).

Karpoff, J.M., "The Relationship Between Price Changes and Trading Volume: A Survey." *Journal of Financial and Quantitative Analysis* 22, 109–126, (1987).

Lamoureux, C.G. and W.D. Lastrapes, "Heteroskedasticity in stock return data." *The Journal of Finance* 1, 221–229, (1990).

Lo, A. and A.C. MacKinlay, "Stock Market Prices Do Not Follow Random Walks: Evidence From a Simple Specification Test." *The Review of Financial Studies* 1, 41–66, (1988).

Malliaris A. and W. Brock, *Stochastic Methods in Economics and Finance.* Amsterdam, North Holland Publishing company, 1982.

Malliaris A. and J. Urrutia, "Economic Determinants of Trading Volume in Futures Markets." *Economics Letters* 35, 301–305, (1991).

Malliaris, A.G. and J. Urrutia, "Volume and Price Relationships: Hypotheses and Testing for Agricultural Futures Markets." *The Journal of Futures Markets* 18, 53–72, (1998).

Mandelbrot, B., "The Variation of Certain Speculative Prices." *Journal of Business* 36, 394–419, (1963).

Mandelbrot, B., "The Variation of Some Other Speculative Prices." *Journal of Business* 40, 393–413, (1967).

Mandelbrot, B., "Comments on: A Subordinated Stochastic Process Model With Finite Variance for Speculative Prices'." *Econometrica* 41, 157–159, (1973).

Martell, T. and A. Wolf, "Determinants of Trading Volume in Futures Markets." *Journal of Futures Markets* 7, 233–244, (1987).

Merton, R.C., "On the Mathematics and Economics Assumptions of Continuous-Time Models." In W.F.Sharpe and C.M. Cootner, editors, *Finacial Economics: Essay in Honour of Paul Cootner*, Prentice Hall, 19–51, 1982.

Murphy, J.J., *Technical Analysis of the Futures Market*, New York Institute of Finance, Prentice Hall, 1985.

Nelson, D.B., "ARCH Models As Diffusion Approximations." *Journal of Econometrics* 45, 7–38, (1990).

Newey, W. and K. West, "A Simple, Positive Semi-definite, Heteroskedasticity and Autocorrelation Consistent Covariance Matrix." *Econometrica*, 55, 703–708, (1987).

Pagan, A., "Econometric Issues in the Analysis of Regressions with Generated Regressors." *International Economic Review* 25, 221–247, (1984).

Pagano, M., "Trading Volume and Asset Liquidity." *The Quarterly Journal of Economics* 104, 255–274, (1989).

Perron, P., "Trends and Random Walks in Macroeconomic Time Series." *Journal of Economic Dynamics and Control* 12, 297–312, (1988).

Poterba, J.M. and L.H. Summers, "Mean-reversion in Stock Prices: Evidence and Implications." *Journal of Financial Economics* 22, 27–59, (1988).

Rogalski, R., "The Dependence of Prices and Volume." *Review of Economics and Statistics* 60, 268–274, (1978).

Ross, S.A., "Intertemporal Asset Pricing." In G. Constantinides and S. Bhattacharya, editors, *Theory of Valuation*, Rowman and Littlefield, Totowa, New Jersey, 1989.

Rutledge, D.J.S., "Trading Volume and Price Variability: New Evidence on the Price Effects of Speculation." In A.E. Peck, editor, *Selected Writings On Futures Markets* 4, Chicago Board of Trade, 237–251, (1984).

Tauchen, G. and M. Pitts, "The Price Variability-Volume Relationship on Speculative Markets." *Econometrica* 51, 485–505, (1983).

Upton, D.E. and D.S. Shannon, "The Stable Paretian Distribution, Subordinated Stochastic Processes, and Asymptotic Lognormality: An Empirical Investigation," *Journal of Finance* 34, 1031–1039, (1979).

Westerfield, R., "The Distribution of Common Stock Price Changes: An Application of Transactions Time and Subordinate Stochastic Models." *Journal of Financial and Quantitative Analysis* 12, 743–765, (1977).

Ying, C., "Stock Market Prices and Volume of Sales." *Econometrica* 34, 676–685, (1966).

# PART V

# CONCLUSIONS

# [18]

---

# Directions for future research

---

> Keep the gold and keep the silver,
> but give us wisdom.
>
> (Arabian proverb)

There is very little disagreement that financial markets are currently more competitive than two decades ago. Several factors have been influential in the increased confidence of market economies in general, and financial markets in particular. Among these factors are: the end of the Cold War, the triumph of the free market ideology, the restructuring of US corporations, numerous technological advances, the rapid and inexpensive transmission of information, governmental deregulation, low inflation and interest rates, world trade growth and global financial integration.

As markets for financial assets have expanded, derivative markets have also grown, often at a much faster rate because of their special characteristics of low margin requirements, daily resettlement practices and their favourable risk and return profiles.

Futures markets play a significant role among derivative markets and the rapid growth in the trading volume of futures contracts is evidence of the attractiveness of these markets. Research economists and financial scholars have understandably been attracted to do research in this area.

The previous chapters offered a sample of this research activity. Nevertheless, several important questions remain unsettled and will require the future attention of financial scholars. A few of these questions will be formulated in the next sections. The selection of the topics presented below is influenced by the contents of this book. Emphasis is given to broader issues.

## Futures markets efficiency

Holbrook Working (1934) was one of the first economists to study the behaviour of asset prices. By the behaviour of futures or any asset pricing we mean the dynamic, period by period, change in the price level of an asset, such as the closing price of a stock or the settlement price of a futures contract. This literature on the random walk behaviour of asset prices eventually led to the formulation of a theory known as 'market efficiency'.

The theory of market efficiency is currently the most widely accepted paradigm that describes how prices behave in financial markets. It hypothesizes that asset prices fully reflect all available information. Information is valuable and therefore not wasted. As soon as new information becomes available, market participants quickly evaluate it and take action, thus causing asset prices to change and mirror immediately the newly released information. Despite the existence of several puzzling and conflicting results, particularly in futures markets, the theory of efficient markets remains a central pillar of modern financial economics.

*333*

Paul Samuelson (1965) developed the efficient market hypothesis to rationalize the random walk behaviour, whereby the current price $p(t)$ fully reflects all relevant information. Since the flow of such information between now and the next period cannot be anticipated, asset price changes are serially uncorrelated. In other words, the randomness in price changes originates in the random flow of unanticipated information.

During the past thirty years, the theory of market efficiency has been refined analytically, mathematically and statistically. The concept of information has been made more precise. The notion of the random walk was generalized to martingales and Itô processes. Numerous sophisticated statistical tests were employed to test the theory. Moreover, a very large literature was developed concerning the statistical distribution of the changes in spot or futures prices: are they log-normal? Or are they leptokurtic? And if leptokurtic, how fat are the tails?

The actual distribution of spot or futures price changes or returns is an issue of great importance to financial economists. An efficient market requires that such returns are normally distributed.

The theoretical assumptions underlying these studies are not always clear. Grossman and Stiglitz (1980) have addressed several important analytical issues of the theory of efficient markets. They argued that the notion of market efficiency is inconsistent with the reality of costly information gathering and arbitrage. They developed a simple model with a constant absolute risk-aversion utility function and showed that costless information is both necessary and sufficient for prices to reflect fully all available information. Efficient markets theorists realize that costless information is a sufficient condition for market efficiency. However, they are not always clear that it is also a necessary condition.

It was not surprising to find that along with numerous empirical studies confirming market efficiency, there are numerous studies rejecting it, and that there is no agreement concerning the statistical distribution functions of price changes. Nevertheless, the most convenient and widely accepted paradigm postulates that returns are normally distributed, meaning that asset prices follow log-normal distributions. Both modern portfolio theory and the Black–Scholes methodology of pricing derivative assets are based on such a paradigm.

Although market efficiency remains the central theory of financial economics, numerous studies exist that have questioned its twin foundations: random walk or martingale process and log-normal distribution of asset prices. Notice, however, that it is not enough to reject randomness or log-normality. In order to make scientific progress we must specify alternatives to randomness and log-normality.

To motivate the eventual formulation of potential research topics we briefly review next the existing literature on randomness and log-normality. They are both extensive, particularly the one on randomness. We concentrate on a few key references rather than offering an exhaustive survey, particularly because these ideas are generally well known. Chapters 3, 5, 6, 7, 8, 9 and 10 in this book address similar issues of market efficiency.

The three fundamental literature reviews are Fama (1970, 1991) and LeRoy (1989). These apply to asset prices in general rather than to futures prices specifically. Among the numerous papers that studied the appropriateness of the random walk or the martingale model in futures markets, we mention selectively the following: the Treasury-Bill and Treasury-Bond futures markets were investigated by Chance (1985), Klemkosky and Lasser (1985), Cole, Impson and Reichenstein (1991), MacDonald and Hein (1993) and Lin (1996).

The agricultural commodities markets were studied by Bigman, Goldfarb and Schechtman (1983), Canarella and Pollard (1985), Maberly (1985), Bird (1985), Elam and Dixon (1988), Johnson, Zulauf, Irwin and Gerlow (1991), and Aulton, Ennew and Rayner (1997). The metal futures market was researched by Gross (1988) and Chowdhury (1991).

Finally, the foreign currency futures and stock index futures were examined by Glassman (1987), Saunders and Mahajan (1988), Harpaz, Krull and Yagil (1990), Lai and Lai (1991), Chung (1991) and Antoniou and Holmes (1996). Obviously, many more futures markets exist and their efficiency has been researched in a large literature that covers significantly many more studies than the ones mentioned here.

Evaluating the above papers, one observes that many writers hold positive opinions on market efficiency. For example, Chance (1985) believes that the Treasury bond futures market correctly anticipates the information contained in the announcement of the rate of change of the Consumer Price Index. MacDonald and Hein (1993) comment that the Treasury-bill futures market may not be as inefficient as once presumed in terms of weak form efficiency, though it does not provide optimal forecasts. Lin (1996) further explains the puzzle of inefficiencies in the Treasury-bill futures markets. Maberly (1985) demonstrates that in the grains, the inference that the market is inefficient for more distant futures contracts is due to the bias that results from using ordinary least squares to estimate parameters in models with censored data. Elam and Dixon (1988) attack the inefficient grain market argument by conducting several Monte-Carlo experiments to find out that very often the F-test tends wrongly to reject the true model.

Canarella and Pollard's (1985) research suggests that the efficient market hypothesis cannot be rejected for corn, wheat, soybeans and soybean oil. Gross (1988) claims that the hypothesis of efficient copper and aluminium markets cannot be rejected on the evidence of his semi-strong efficiency tests. Saunders and Mahajan (1988), Chung and Antoniou and Holmes show that the pricing of various index futures both in the US and Great Britain is efficient.

However, numerous other authors provide negative evidence on market efficiency. Bird (1985) discovers that for coffee and sugar the efficient market hypothesis is not empirically supported and for cocoa there is evidence of inefficiency, but it is of limited economic significance. Harpaz, Krull and Yagil (1990) perform tests for the efficiency of the USDX futures contracts during the period 1985–88 which result in their rejection of the null hypothesis that the USDX futures market is efficient during that period. By using methods of cointegration applied to the five major forward currency markets, Lai and Lai (1991) report evidence not favourable to the joint hypotheses of market efficiency and no-risk premium. The empirical results presented in Chowdhury's (1991) research indicate the rejection of efficient market hypothesis for four nonferrous metals – copper, lead, tin and zinc – traded on the London Metal Exchange.

Finally, several authors, neither totally support nor reject the efficient market hypothesis but reach different answers under different situations. Bigman, Goldfarb and Schechtman (1983) conclude that although the market can be generally characterized as efficient for the futures contracts on wheat, soybeans and corn, six weeks or less before delivery, their tests reject the efficiency hypothesis for longer-term futures contracts. Johnson, Zulauf, Irwin and Gerlow (1991) use a combination of profit margin trading rules to test the market efficiency of the soybean complex. Their findings suggest that while nearby soybean complex futures price spreads are efficient according to Fama's criterion, distant soybean complex futures price spreads are not efficient. The results of Klemkosky and Lasser (1985) on Treasury-bond market efficiency do not agree totally with the conclusions drawn from earlier studies. Glassman (1987) reports evidence of multi-market and joint multi-market inefficiency in foreign currency futures markets during some of the thirty-eight contract periods studied. Much of the inefficiency appeared to be short term in duration (one week or less). Cole, Impson and Reichenstein (1991) conclude that the Treasury bill futures rates provide rational one- and two-quarters-ahead forecasts of future spot rates, which are the forecast horizons that seem to be of most interest to the public. However, they believe the rationality of four-quarters-ahead futures forecasts should be rejected. Aulton, Ennew and Rayner (1997) find that some agricultural futures markets in Britain are efficient while others are not.

The various empirical studies that have rejected the theory of market efficiency have encouraged financial economists to seek alternative explanations for the time series behaviour of asset returns. This literature is known as the chaotic dynamics approach to asset returns. Several studies such as Frank and Stengos (1989), Hsieh (1991), Blank (1991), DeCoster, Labys and Mitchell (1992), Yang and Brorsen (1993), Streips (1995) and Wei and Leuthold (1998) have offered evidence that futures prices appear to follow low-dimensional chaotic dynamics.

Addressing next the issue of the distribution of futures returns, observe once again that the bulk of research concentrates on stock returns. After the seminal papers by Osborne (1959), Fama (1965), Mandelbrot (1963), Fama and Roll (1968 and 1971) and Mandelbrot and Taylor (1967), numerous other papers have followed. These are carefully reviewed in Akgiray and Booth (1988). Although most papers reject the normal distribution of asset returns in favour of the stable Lèvy-Paretian, studies exist that further reject the stable Lèvy-Paretian distribution, but not in favour of normality.

Earlier, Stevenson and Bear (1970) and Dusak (1973) offered evidence in support of the stable Lèvy-Paretian distribution, while more recently Helms and Martell (1985), using data for all commodities traded on the Chicago Board of Trade, conclude that returns on futures prices, although they are not normally distributed, are closer to normal than to any other member of the family of Pareto distributions. Contrary to their results, Cornew, Town and Crowson (1984) claim that the stable Lèvy-Paretian distribution offers a better fit for futures returns of several contracts than the normal distribution. Similarly, So (1987) confirms that currency futures and spot returns are stable Lèvy-Paretian while Hall, Brorsen and Irwin (1989) and Hudson, Leuthold and Sarassono (1987) claim that futures returns are not stable Lèvy-Paretian. Finally Gribbin, Harris and Lau (1992) use a newly developed statistical methodology to conclude that futures prices are not stable Lèvy-Paretian distributed. For further details, see also Chapters 3, 7 and 10 in this book.

The above rapid and eclectic review of several issues related to the theory of market efficiency leads to the basic conclusion reported by Andrew W. Lo that 'the efficient market hypothesis is disarmingly simple to state, has far reaching consequences for academic pursuits and business practice and yet is surprisingly resilient to empirical proof or refutation. Even after three decades of research and literally thousands of articles, economists have not yet reached a consensus about whether markets – particularly financial markets – are efficient or not.' See Lo (1997, p.239).

Nevertheless, financial researchers may revisit market efficiency in asset and derivative markets by: (a) developing better theoretical formulations; (b) testing empirically the theory of futures market efficiency with recent and more powerful statistical tools and new data sets; (c) exploring the consequences of electronic trading in contrast to the traditional open outcry auction system; (d) investigating the distributional properties of both asset prices and asset returns; and (e) studying the appropriateness of non-stochastic methodologies, such as chaotic and nonlinear dynamics.

## Hedging

Futures markets are widely used for hedging by both producers and users of commodities. For example, consider an oil-producing firm that anticipates declines in the price of its output. By entering a short position in the oil futures market, the firm is safeguarded against further price declines of its output.

Likewise, if a stock mutual fund manager fears a market correction and does not wish to liquidate part or all of his/her portfolio, selling an appropriate amount of a stock indexed futures contract may offer the protection needed.

For several decades, the accepted hedging strategy for commodities was to assume that the basis, ie the difference between the cash and futures price, remains constant and to take a futures position opposite to the one in the cash market. This idea is carefully presented in Chapter 3. However, it is well known that the basis does not remain constant. Indeed, the basis gradually decreases to zero as the futures contract approaches its expiration date.

Ederington (1979) offers a hedging theory when the basis is not constant. Numerous authors have similarly developed hedging strategies for financial futures instruments. Chapters 13, 14 and 15 review some of the implications of these new theories of hedging. These chapters address the question: suppose that a given position in a commodity or financial instrument needs to be hedged with a futures position. What is the best way to do it? Or, how can this be done optimally?

The ratio of the futures position divided by the cash position is called the hedge ratio. Traditionally, under the assumption of a constant basis, the hedge ratio is 1. Researchers may wish to revisit these questions: what is the magnitude of the hedge ratio when the basis is not constant? What criteria are appropriate in defining an 'optimal' hedge ratio? How can we develop a generalized notion of a hedge ratio when the cash and futures positions involve dissimilar products or financial instruments? How do we compute an optimal hedge ratio? How do hedge ratios behave over time? Finally, if positions are hedged to reduce risk, how do we judge the performance of hedging activities? More generally, how do we monitor the risk of any position? For an overview of issues related to value at risk, see Duffie and Pan (1997).

## Speculation

The simplest form of speculation occurs when a trader buys (short sells) a futures contract and holds it for later resale (repurchase) motivated by the anticipation of a price increase (decrease). In other words, speculation is a trading activity driven by rational price forecasting. This is often described as the knowledgeable forecasting hypothesis. Working (1953, 1962) has elaborated this idea by arguing that speculation is premised upon anticipations of price changes.

Alfred Marshall, according to Dardi and Gallegati (1992), proposed the idea that speculators forecast not future price movements but other people's forecasts of future events. Keynes (1930) argues that firms which produce or own a commodity and therefore face the risk of a price drop try to induce other traders (called speculators) to absorb their net short selling by paying a risk premium. Thus, Keynes suggests another definition of speculation by introducing the notion of insurance. More specifically, Keynes argues that speculators are often the futures traders who are willing to share some of the producers' risk for a risk premium. Some authors call Keynes's proposition normal backwardation while others refer to it as 'the risk-transfer hypothesis'.

Hirshleifer (1977) contrasts the Keynesian view that speculation is caused by differences in risk-aversion with the hypothesis of Working which states that speculation is caused by differences in information. Hirshleifer develops a detailed theoretical model and shows that speculative trading occurs only by traders whose opinions regarding the futures states of the world diverge from the representative beliefs in the market.

Related to speculation, economists have studied the issue of market stability and welfare economics. For example, some authors, such as Kaldor (1939), hypothesize that, under certain conditions, speculators destabilize markets. Others, such as Friedman (1953), have supported exactly the opposite view: that destabilizing speculation is not possible. If speculators destabilize markets, then they contribute to welfare reduction. Jerome Stein's book (1986) and papers by Jeremy Stein (1987), Froot, Scharfstein and Stein (1992), Guesnerie and Rochet (1993) and Madrigal (1996) are useful references.

Financial economists and futures markets researchers may revisit these fundamental questions about speculation by developing more sophisticated theoretical models of speculative behaviour, by addressing issues related to the microstructure of futures markets and by doing empirical work to test the various hypotheses about speculation. Chapters 2 and 12 offer additional discussions on speculation and Brock and Malliaris (1989) give an exhaustive exposition of stability methods.

## Volatility

Volatility has always played an important role in the development of futures markets. Volatile cash markets such as foreign currencies, equity indexes, government bonds, energy and agricultural products have generated the need for risk management and thus supported futures trading. In contrast, markets with low volatility, such as milk, steel or rental apartments, have not attracted futures trading.

Volatility studies have proceeded along two key questions: (a) what is the behaviour of asset price volatility? and (b), do futures markets increase or decrease price volatility in cash markets? The first question has generated an enormous amount of research and is reviewed in LeRoy (1989) and Shiller (1989). The second question is more relevant to futures markets and is discussed in Chapter 2.

Consider a cash market for a certain asset and suppose that one can measure the price volatility during a certain period. Suppose next that a futures market is developed successfully for this market and after a certain period we have an additional measure of the asset's volatility in the cash market. Will the estimate of the asset's volatility after the introduction of the futures market be higher or lower compared to the volatility prior to the existence of the futures market? There are two hypotheses. The first hypothesis claims that the introduction of a futures market can, under certain conditions, increase volatility. This can happen if the futures market attracts unskilled speculators. The argument is similar to the one about destabilizing speculation proposed by Kaldor (1939). The second hypothesis proposes that trading in futures improves market efficiency by enhancing the processing of information. There are numerous studies supporting both hypotheses and there is currently little interest in further studies along these lines.

A more fruitful line of research is the search for determinants of price volatility as well as the implications of such volatility. Chapter 12 and Malliaris and Stein (1999) offer some suggestions about factors determining futures volatility. Chapters 11 and 17 show that volatility impacts on the volume of futures trading. Two questions: what are the determinants of volatility? and also, what are the implications of such volatility? are important and need to be explored further.

When asset volatility increases significantly beyond certain historically reasonable levels, one may associate this volatility with the phenomenon of a bubble or a crash. Both the existence of asset bubbles and the occurrence of asset price crashes are areas of current research interest. For example, the October 1987 stock market crash has been researched extensively. In particular, the interplay between the New York cash stock market and the Chicago stock futures and stock options markets has been investigated as a potential factor of the crash. Yet, economists have been unable to suggest either a satisfactory theoretical explanation or conclusive empirical evidence of the causes of the crash. Crashes and asset price bubbles are research topics closely related to the microstructure of cash and futures markets and are currently topics of great research interest.

**Macro markets**
Futures markets exist for firms and individuals to manage their individual risks. During the past several decades, these markets have performed admirably well. Actually, since the early 1970s, futures markets have expanded to include the trading of financial futures, such as foreign currency, bonds and stock indices quite successfully. A question naturally arises: what other risks exist and how can markets be created to share such risks?

A little reflection identifies risks such as natural disasters, medical emergencies, technological accidents, terrorist activities, war casualties, political revolutions, social unrest, health epidemics and others that expose individuals and societies to great risks. For some of these risks, private and government insurance may be obtainable, but what if nothing is available? Furthermore, what if major economic disasters occur, such as asset deflation or inflation, recession or depression, waves of massive unemployment, government default and others? Do we allow the standards of living, both of the individual and of society, to be determined by random events?

In a fascinating monograph, Shiller (1993) addresses these issues in detail and offers both theoretical solutions and practical suggestions for the development of new futures contracts. Much new and exciting research is expected to be generated by the topic of creating institutions for managing society's largest economic risks. Actually, global economic and financial integration raises the even more difficult topic of creating international institutions for managing the world's major economic risks.

In conclusion, the five areas of current and potential research activity presented above illustrate that futures markets is an important and expanding branch of financial economics. It is hoped that this book will encourage adventuresome researchers to enter the field of futures markets.

## References

Akgiray, V. and G. Booth (1988), 'The stable law model of stock returns', *Journal of Business & Economic Statistics*, **6**, 51–7.

Antoniou, A. and P. Holmes (1996), 'Futures markets efficiency, the unbiasedness hypothesis and variance-bounds tests: the case of the FTSE-100 futures contract', *Bulletin of Economic Research*, **48**, 115–28.

Aulton, A.J., C.T. Ennew and A.J. Rayner (1997), 'Efficiency test of futures markets for UK agricultural commodities', *Journal of Agricultural Economics*, **48**, 408–24.

Bigman, D., D. Goldfarb and E. Schechtman (1983), 'Futures market efficiency and the time content of the information sets', *The Journal of Futures Markets*, **3**, 321–34.

Bird, P. (1985), 'Dependency and efficiency in the London terminal markets', *The Journal of Futures Markets*, **5**, 433–46.

Blank, S.C. (1991), 'Chaos in futures markets: a nonlinear dynamical analysis', *The Journal of Futures Markets*, **11**, 711–28.

Brock, W.A. and A.G. Malliaris (1989), *Differential Equations, Stability and Chaos in Dynamic Economics*, Amsterdam: North-Holland.

Canarella, G. and S.K. Pollard (1985), 'Efficiency of commodity futures: a vector autoregression analysis', *The Journal of Futures Markets*, **5**, 57–76.

Chance, D.M. (1985), 'A semi-strong form test of the efficiency of treasury bond futures markets', *The Journal of Futures Markets*, **5**, 385–405.

Chowdhury, A.R. (1991), 'Futures market efficiency: evidence from cointegration tests', *The Journal of Futures Markets*, **11**, 577–89.

Chung, Y. Peter (1991), 'A transaction data test of stock index futures market efficiency and index arbitrage profitability', *The Journal of Finance*, **46**, 1791–809.

Cole, C.S., M. Impson and W. Reichenstein (1991), 'Do treasury bill futures rates satisfy rational expectation properties?', *The Journal of Futures Markets*, **11**, 591–601.

Cornew, R., D. Town and L. Crowson (1984), 'Stable distribution, futures prices, and the measurement of trading performance', *The Journal of Futures Markets*, **4**, 531–57.

Dardi, M. and M. Gallegati (1992), 'Alfred Marshall on speculation', *History of Political Economy*, **24**, 571–94.

DeCoster, G.P., W.C. Labys and D.W. Mitchell (1992), 'Evidence of chaos in commodity futures prices', *The Journal of Futures Markets*, **12**, 291–305.

Duffie, D. and J. Pan (1997), 'An overview of value at risk', *Journal of Derivatives*, **3**, 7–49.

Dusak, K. (1973), 'Futures trading and investor returns: an investigation of commodity market risk premiums', *Journal of Political Economy*, **81**, 1387–405.

Ederington, L. (1979), 'The hedging performance of the new futures markets', *The Journal of Finance*, **11**, 711–28.

Elam, E. and B.L. Dixon (1988), 'Examining the validity of a test of futures market efficiency', *The Journal of Futures Markets*, **8**, 365–72.

Fama, E.F. (1965), 'The behavior of stock market prices', *Journal of Business*, **38**, 34–105.

Fama, E.F. (1970), 'Efficient capital markets: review of theory and empirical work', *The Journal of Finance*, **25**, 383–417.

Fama, E.F. (1991), 'Efficient capital markets: II', *The Journal of Finance*, **70**, 1575–617.

Fama, E.F. and R. Roll (1968), 'Some properties of symmetric stable distributions', *Journal of the American Statistical Association*, **63**, 817–36.

Fama, E.F. and R. Roll (1971), 'Parameter estimates for symmetric stable distributions', *Journal of the American Statistical Association*, **66**, 331–8.

Frank, M. and T. Stengos (1989), 'Measuring the strangeness of gold and silver rates of return', *Review of Economic Studies*, **56**, 553–67.

Friedman, M. (1953), 'The Case for Flexible Exchange Rates', in *Essays in Positive Economics*, Chicago: The University of Chicago Press.

Froot, K., D.S. Scharftstein and J.C. Stein (1992), 'Herd on the street: informational inefficiencies in a market with short-term speculation', *The Journal of Finance*, **47**, 1461–84.

Glassman, D. (1987), 'The efficiency of foreign exchange futures markets in turbulent and non-turbulent periods', *The Journal of Futures Markets*, **7**, 245–67.

Gribbin, D.W., R.W. Harris and H.S. Lau (1992), 'Futures prices are not stable-Paretian distributed', *The Journal of Futures Markets*, **12**, 475–87.

Gross, M. (1988), 'A semi-strong test of the efficiency of the aluminum and copper markets at the LME', *The Journal of Futures Markets*, **8**, 67–77.

Grossman, S.J. and J.E. Stiglitz (1980), 'On the impossibility of informationally efficient markets', *American Economic Review*, **70**, 393–408.

Guesnerie, R. and Jean-Charles Rochet (1993), '(De)stabilizing speculation in futures markets: an alternative view point', *European Economic Review*, **37**, 1043–63.

Hall, J., B. Brorsen and S. Irwin (1989), 'The distribution of future prices: a test of the stable Paretian and mixture of normals hypothesis', *Journal of Financial and Quantitative Analysis*, **24**, 105–16.

Harpaz, G., S. Krull and J. Yagil (1990), 'The efficiency of the U.S. dollar index futures market', *The Journal of Futures Markets*, **10**, 469–79.

Helms, B.P. and T.F. Martell (1985), 'An examination of the distribution of futures price changes', *The Journal of Futures Markets*, **5**, 259–72.

Hirshleifer, J. (1977), 'The theory of speculation under alternative regimes of markets', *The Journal of Finance*, **32**, 975–99.

Hsieh, D.A. (1991), 'Chaos and nonlinear dynamics: application to financial markets', *The Journal of Finance*, **46**, 1839–77.

Hudson, M., R. Leuthold and G. Sarassoro (1987), 'Commodity futures prices changes: recent evidence for wheat, soybeans, and live cattle', *The Journal of Futures Markets*, **7**, 287–301.

Johnson, R.L., C.R. Zulauf, S.H. Irwin and M.E. Gerlow (1991), 'The soybean complex spread: an examination of market efficiency from the viewpoint of a production process', *The Journal of Futures Markets*, **11**, 25–37.

Kaldor, N. (1939), 'Speculation and economic stability', *Review of Economic Studies*, **7**, 1–27.

Keynes, J.M. (1930), *A Treatise on Money. Volume II: The Applied Theory on Money*, London: Macmillan.

Klemkosky, R.C. and D.J. Lasser (1985), 'An efficiency analysis of the T-bond futures market', *The Journal of Futures Markets*, **5**, 607–20.

Lai, K.S. and M. Lai (1991), 'A cointegration test for market efficiency', *The Journal of Futures Markets*, **11**, 567–75.

LeRoy, S. (1989), 'Efficient capital markets and martingales', *Journal of Economic Literature*, **27**, 1583–621.

Lin, J.W. (1996), 'Arbitrage risk and market efficiency: the case of treasury bill futures', *Review of Quantitative Finance and Accounting*, **7**, 187–203.

Lo, A.W. (1997), 'Fat tails, long memory, and the stock market since the 1960s', *Economic Notes*, **2**, 213–46.

Maberly, E.D. (1985), 'Testing futures market efficiency – a restatement', *The Journal of Futures Markets*, **5**, 425–32.

MacDonald, S.S. and S.E. Hein (1993), 'An empirical evaluation of treasury bill futures market efficiency: evidence from forecast efficiency tests', *The Journal of Futures Markets*, **13**, 199–211.

Madrigal, V. (1996), 'Non-fundamental speculation', *The Journal of Finance*, **51**, 553–78.

Malliaris, A.G. and J.L. Stein (1999), 'Methodological issues in asset pricing: random walks or chaotic dynamics', *Journal of Banking and Finance*, **23**.

Mandelbrot, B.B. (1963), 'The variation of certain speculative prices', *Journal of Business*, **36**, 394–419.

Mandelbrot, B.B. and H. Taylor (1967), 'On the distribution of stock price differences', *Operations Research*, **15**, 1057–62.

Osborne, M.F.M. (1959), 'Brownian motion in the stock market', *Operations Research*, **7**, 145–73.

Samuelson, P. (1965), 'Proof that properly anticipated prices fluctuate randomly', *Industrial Management Review*, **6**, 41–9.

Saunders, E.M. and A. Mahajan (1988), 'An empirical examination of composite stock index futures pricing', *The Journal of Futures Markets*, **8**, 210–28.

Shiller, R. (1989), *Market Volatility*, Cambridge, MA: The MIT Press.

Shiller, R. (1993), *Macro Markets*, Oxford: Clarendon Press.

So, J. (1987), 'The sub-Gaussian distribution of currency futures: stable Paretian or non-stationary?', *Review of Economics and Statistics*, **69**, 100–107.

Stein, Jerome L. (1986), *The Economics of Futures Markets*, Oxford: Basil Blackwell.

Stein, Jeremy C. (1987), 'Informational externalities and welfare-reducing speculation', *Journal of Political Economy*, **95**, 1123–45.

Stevenson, R.A. and R.M. Bear (1970), 'Commodity futures: trends or random walks?', *The Journal of Finance*, **25**, 65–81.

Streips, M.A. (1995), 'The problem of the persistent hog price cycle: a chaotic solution', *American Journal of Agricultural Economics*, **77**, 1397–403.

Wei, A. and R.M. Leuthold (1998), 'Long agricultural futures prices: ARCH, long memory, or chaos processes?', OFOR Paper Number 98-03, Department of Agricultural and Consumer Economics, The University of Illinois at Champaign-Urbana.

Working, H. (1934), 'A random-difference series for use in the analysis for time series', *Journal of the American Statistical Association*, **29**, 11–24.

Working, H. (1953), 'Futures trading and hedging', *American Economic Review*, **43**, 314–43.

Working, H. (1962), 'New concepts concerning futures markets and prices', *American Economic Review*, **52**, 431–59.

Yang, S.R. and B.W. Brorsen (1993), 'Nonlinear dynamics of daily futures prices: conditional heteroscedasticity or chaos?', *The Journal of Futures Markets*, **13**, 175–91.

# Name index